The Spirits' Book

(New English Edition)
Enlarged Print

Other Works by Allan Kardec

The Medium's Book
The Gospel According to Spiritism
Heaven and Hell
Genesis: Miracles and Predictions According to Spiritism
What is Spiritism?

Spiritualist Philosophy

The Spirits' Book

(New English Edition)
Enlarged Print

Containing
The Principles of the Spiritist Doctrine

On the Immortality of the Soul,
the Nature of Spirits and Their Relationship with Human Beings,
the Moral Laws, the Present Life, the Future Life,
and the Destiny of Mankind

According to the Teachings
Transmitted by Superior Spirits,
with the Assistance of Various Mediums

Collected and Organized
by
Allan Kardec

Luchnos

The Spirits' Book (New English Edition) — Enlarged Print
Translation Series of Classical Spiritist Works: 1

Original Title:	*Le Livre des Esprits*
	(Paris, 1st edition 1857, 2nd edition 1860, 5th edition 1861, 8th edition 1862)
Author:	Allan Kardec
Translation:	E. G. Dutra
	Translated from the 2nd, 5th and 8th French editions
Copy Editing:	Jessi Rita Hoffman
Cover Photo:	Nacho Domínguez Argenta (Unsplash Inc.)

LCCN:	2021931936
ISBN paperback:	978-1-950030-24-8
ISBN hardcover:	978-1-950030-25-5
ISBN eBook:	978-1-950030-26-2
ISBN hardcover:	978-1-950030-27-9 (enlarged print)

Copyright © 2021 by Luchnos Media LLC
30 N Gould St, Ste 2852
Sheridan, WY 82801
http://www.luchnos.com

Manufactured in the United States of America
First Edition: March 2019
Second Edition: February 2021

Contents

Translator's Preface

The Spirits' Book is the foundational work of Spiritism, a school of thought first established in France in the mid-nineteenth century by the French educator Allan Kardec. Currently, Spiritism includes over fifteen million adherents, the eleventh largest spiritual following worldwide, ahead of more historically traditional religions such as Judaism (twelfth) and Jainism (fourteenth). [a]

The first edition of the book was published on April 18, 1857, being received with much interest and requiring a new edition soon after. The second edition was released on March 18, 1860, and incorporated a significant amount of additional material that the author amassed in the intervening years, doubling the size of the book. The second edition established the structure with which readers are familiar today, undergoing only minor modifications made by the author in later editions. The book went through a total of seventeen editions in France alone between its initial release in 1857 and Kardec's death in 1869.

Starting with the second edition, Kardec decided to place the description *Philosophie Spiritualiste* (Spiritualist Philosophy) at the top of the title page of the book. Most readers would not immediately grasp the meaning of such a deceptively simple description, which only provides a faint indication of the extraordinary breadth and depth of topics covered in this seminal work. Despite the relative brevity—considering its large scope—the book represents nothing short of a philosophical treatise. Most important, however, is that, beyond its comprehensive content, the work stands out because of the ideas it conveys, some of which were truly revolutionary at the time. Some of them can, in fact, still be considered revolutionary to this date.

A Book Surprisingly Ahead of its Time

The book came out two years *before* Charles Darwin published the classic *On the Origin of Species*. Remarkably, question #50 of *The Spirits' Book* (question #21 in the first edition) [b] already stated that "the man you call Adam was neither the first nor the only one to populate the Earth," acknowledging that "physical … differences come from … climate, lifestyle, and habits" (question #52 in the second edition, #22 in the first edition), and that "living beings … are … subject to the law of progress." Indeed, Kardec's book went on to state that "the race that populates the Earth today will disappear someday and will be replaced gradually by more perfect beings. Such races will succeed the current one, just as the current one succeeded others that were even more primitive" (question #185 in the second edition, #138 in the first edition).

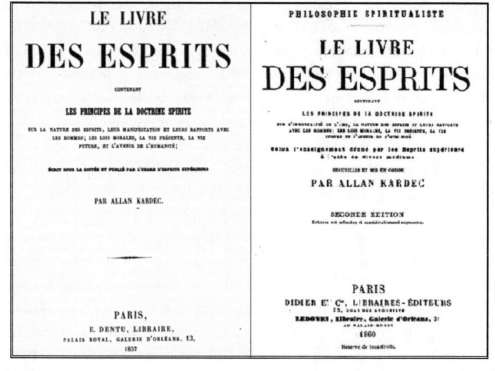

Figure 1: Title pages of the first and second editions of *Le Livre des Esprits*. The first edition of the book was published in Paris in 1857 and included 501 questions. The much augmented second edition was published in 1860, and contained 1019 questions, establishing the structure that readers are familiar with today. (Translator's collection)

By itself, the mention in Kardec's book of the concept of a species' gradual progress (evolution) is extraordinary. But in a radical take, the book proposes that it is not only organic beings that are subject to the evolutionary process. Animals, for instance, "have ... in them a principle independent of matter ... which survives their body" (#597), "a soul ... much less evolved than that of man" (#597) that "follows a law of progress" (#601), demonstrating "the unity of design and progress discernible in all of God's works" and that "everything in nature is connected by links" that man "cannot yet discern" (#604). By knowing that "the intelligent principle is refined, gradually individualized, and prepared for life," however, man must realize that "there is nothing humiliating about this origin." Rather it is a demonstration of "the greatness of God in the marvelous harmony that establishes the solidarity of all things in nature" (#607), through this gradual development that allows the spirit to "enter the human phase" (#609). Thus, even before the debate *creation versus evolution* presented itself, *The Spirits' Book* had already established an elegant framework to reconcile the row: *both the material and the spiritual principles evolve in parallel and interdependently.* "Therefore, everything serves a purpose, everything is linked in nature, from the primitive atom to the archangel, who also began as an atom, in an admirable law of harmony, which [our] limited intellect cannot yet grasp in its entirety" (#540).

In other instances, the book makes surprising predictions of scientific discoveries, such as the existence of matter that does not conform to the classical definition that prevailed in the nineteenth century—any substance that has mass and takes up space—because it is "so ethereal and subtle as to not make any impression upon [our] senses ... yet, it is still matter, even though [we] do not see it as such." (#22). The detection of the electron in 1897 was only the first step in a series of discoveries that proved the limitations of the classical concept of matter. Similarly, in question #29 we read that particles exist which are "imponderable"—in other words, massless, something that science would only confirm well into the twentieth century. Equally surprising is the later confirmation by science that "there is no void" in "any part of universal space" (#36), since fields—electromagnetic, gravitational, or otherwise—fill up space completely.

On a much different topic, four years before the United States would enter a civil war over the issue of slavery—resulting in the loss of over a million people, or three percent of its population back then—*The Spirits' Book* ascertained in question #829 (#419 in the first edition) that "slavery is an abuse of power that will gradually disappear with progress, as will all other abuses." At that time of the writing, slavery was still legal not only in the USA, but also in Russia, China, India, Persia, Brazil, and other countries. It was progressively abolished with time, as predicted by the Spirits.

In its coverage of ethics, many of the book's tenets are radically pioneering. Question #822 establishes that "in order to be fair, human law must sanction the equality of rights between men and women. Any special privilege granted to one and not the other is contrary to justice. The emancipation of women heralds the progress of civilization; their servitude is an indication of barbarity." This was advocated at a time when women's rights were severely lacking in all areas. In the case of voting rights alone, the United States would enact women's suffrage in 1920. France would do it in 1944.

This small sample gives us a glimpse into the wide scope and advanced concepts present in the book. In fact, the word *Spiritisme* did not even exist before *Le Livre des Esprits* was published, which is tantamount to saying that it does not make sense to talk about the Spiritist Doctrine without recourse to Kardec in general, and to *The Spirits' Book* in particular. Kardec's later books may all be seen as the expansion of themes that can be traced back to this foundational work. [c]

The number of translations that have been made is surprising: two translations in Italian, two in Japanese, two in Polish, two in Russian, three in German, three in Spanish, twelve in Portuguese, six in English (including the present one), and three in Esperanto, in addition to one translation each in Arabic, Bulgarian, Czech, Danish, Dutch, Finnish, Hungarian, Norwegian, Persian, Romanian, Swedish, Tagalog, Turkish, and Vietnamese. [d]

In fact, the present English version derived from the preparation of the first Chinese translation. Appendix 1 includes a detailed account of the reasons for this new English edition, as well as many considerations about the translation process.

The publishing of *The Spirits' Book* jumpstarted the dissemination of Spiritist ideas, which attracted the interest of a significant number of people. In France alone, it drew the attention of prominent writers such as Victor Hugo[e], Théophile Gautier (who wrote the novel *Spirite*), Honoré de Balzac (whose novels *Les proscrits*, *La recherche de l'absolu*, and *Peau de chagrin* are filled with Spiritist concepts), and Victorien Sardou (who wrote the play *Spiritisme*). It also attracted the interest of a host of scientists, including the famous astronomer Camille Flammarion (who gave a eulogy at Kardec's funeral) and Nobel Prize winners Charles Richet (medicine), Marie Curie (physics and chemistry) and Pierre Curie (physics). Much to their own astonishment, the Curies' verdict on Spiritist phenomena did not leave room for doubt, as they considered their séance experiences "convincing, a matter of the highest interest," [f] and "impossible to deny." [g]

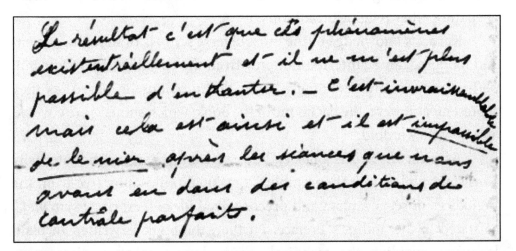

Figure 2: Excerpt from Pierre Curie's letter dated April 14, 1906, to his friend George Gouy, professor at the Faculté des Sciences de Lyon: "The result is that these phenomena really exist, and it is no longer possible for me to doubt it. It is incredible, but that's the way it is, and it is <u>impossible to deny it</u> after the séances we have been to under perfect control conditions." (Image courtesy of the Bibliothèque nationale de France)

A Philosophical Guide for Ordinary People

The overarching plan of *The Spirits' Book* can be understood by comparing its structure with the traditional branches of classical philosophy.

The first chapter of Part 1 covers *God*, *existence*, and *causation*, the objects of *metaphysics*. The remainder of Part 1 and the whole of Part 2 cover *natural philosophy*, discussing both the physical and the spiritual worlds, which are to be understood as the two segments of the manifested universe—the latter, in fact, being the fundamental one, because it "preexists and outlasts everything else" (#85).

Part 3 is a detailed study of *ethics*, adapting the concept of *natural law* to the Mosaic Decalogue in order to analyze the extensive list of subjects covered there. Finally, based on the metaphysical foundations established in Part 1, and from the study of reincarnation in Part 2, and the moral laws in Part 3, a self-consistent *theodicy* emerges smoothly in Part 4, recognizing the sublime character of Christian teachings without alienating other religious traditions.

Kardec's knowledge of the most diverse schools of thought, ancient and modern, can be inferred not only from the comments he wrote but, perhaps even more revealingly, from the *questions* he posed, as they represent, as it were, the backbone of the book: which subjects are covered, and how they unfold.

As such, *The Spirits' Book* embodies a comprehensive and internally consistent philosophical ensemble, "a rational philosophy free from the prejudices of sectarianism and preconceived ideas [*l'esprit de système*]," as stated in the author's Preface. Further, the book is written in plain language, avoiding the technical terminology that often discourages readers, but without ever being superficial. Its completeness and consistency are recognized even by critics. [h]

By using the question-and-answer format, Kardec is able to test assumptions, following the Socratic method of hypothesis elimination, and later confronting these provisional tenets with future information and facts. The compliance with scientific evidence is therefore critical, since "science has been given to [man] for his advancement in all matters" (#19). Furthermore, the question-and-answer structure follows a long and universal tradition that goes back to Plato's *Republic* and Confucius's *Analects*.

The reader familiar with the classic texts of philosophy will readily recognize many of the themes discussed here, even though they are intentionally stripped of technical jargon.

The Spirits' Book opens by questioning the existence of God, testing the Cartesian *ontological argument* (*God as the infinite*), and Spinoza's *pantheism*. [i] Thomistic *quinque viæ* are dealt with greater or lesser emphasis here, focusing unsurprisingly on the *secunda via* (the argument of the first cause).

Part 1 finishes by establishing a type of Cartesian *dualism*, making remarkable predictions, such as the fact that standard elements are, in fact, made of smaller constituents (#30), as well as the existence of non-ponderable matter (i.e., massless particles, #29). This dualism, however, should be regarded as the best working model available, not as a peremptory rebuttal of *monism*, as Kardec writes in his comment to question #28:

> One evident fact impinges on all hypotheses: we see matter which is not intelligent, and we see an intelligent principle that is independent of matter. Their origin and connection are unknown to us. If they have a common origin or necessary points of contact, if intelligence exists independently on its own, or if it is only a property or effect, or even, as some claim, if it is an emanation of the Divinity—all of it is unknown to us.

This is typical of Kardec's pragmatic approach and avoidance of the *esprit de système* mentioned before. Certain longstanding disputes, however, are actually efficiently resolved. For instance, Part 2 of the book examines the various aspects of the process of immersion of spirit in matter—or *reincarnation*—presenting the *problem of knowledge* in a framework that reconciles the epistemological dispute between *idealism* and *empiricism*. Summarizing the implications of the exposition presented there, and in particular of Kardec's "Theoretical Essay of

Sensation in Spirits" in Chapter 6, Herculano Pires notes in his *Introduction to Spiritist Philosophy:* [j]

> Senses are only tools of capture. And these tools belong to the existential condition of incarnate man, of man in the world. Man is made of spirit and body. The body is the diving suit that the spirit dons to plunge into the depths of matter. When one gets out of a diving suit, one's equipment no longer functions. When one leaves the body, one's instrument perishes. In Spiritist philosophy, therefore, the spirit duality of the Aristotelian theory does not exist. Man is essentially a spirit. Therefore, the spirit is man's substance, and the body is man's accident. Perception is a faculty of the spirit, not of the body. It is the diver who sees through the glass window of his diving suit, not the diving suit that sees through its glass.

Part 2 investigates many of the processes involving the spirit, including the characteristics of the soul, the incarnation in human form, the forgetfulness of previous existences, the choice of trials of incarnate beings, dreams, death, the return to the spirit world, spirit life between consecutive incarnations, the influence of spirits on living creatures, spirit hierarchy, and so on.

In this section of the book, the justice of reincarnation is reaffirmed, "as it offers us the means of atoning for our mistakes through new trials" (#171). Spiritism demystifies a number of enduring notions of traditional theological teachings. On the one hand, demons are to be understood as imperfect spirits who will eventually repent and resume their advancement (#131). "Epileptics and insane individuals," on the other hand, who "have often been considered to be possessed" by demons, often "in fact … needed a physician, rather than an exorcist" (#474). This is not to say that spirits do not "have any influence on our thoughts and actions," as "their influence is much greater than [we] would believe, for very frequently it is they who drive [us]" (#459). Indeed, the importance of the interplay between the living and the spirit world is increasingly acknowledged by mental health practitioners nowadays. [k]

Part 3 of *The Spirits' Book* represents a detailed analysis of the ethical implications of Spiritism. A vast array of topics is covered in this section, from abortion to divorce, from wars to the death penalty, from private property to slavery, all with deep implications for the debate on statutory law.

A typical example can be found in question #880, which, in line with many empiricist philosophers, establishes that "the first of all the natural rights of man" is "the right to live," and further, that man has "the right to amass the means of living" (#881) as well as "to defend what he has amassed through his work." These statements could have come straight from John Locke's vindication of private property.

Private property and the viability of socialism were in fact the object of heated debate when the book was first released, and the works of at least a few socialist philosophers were certainly known to Kardec (Karl Marx and Friedrich Engels's *Communist Manifesto* was published in London nine years before the first edition of *The Spirits' Book*). Significantly, question #811 (#409 in the first edition) establishes that "the absolute equality of wealth … is not possible," and when inquired about "those … who believe it to be the remedy for all social ills," the Spirits responded, rather emphatically, that "they are either dogmatic, or greedy and jealous" and that "they do not understand that the equality they dream of would be quickly undone by the very force of things." As a final word of caution, the Spirits instructed: "Fight selfishness, for that is your social cancer. Do not pursue utopias." In view of the many millions who would come to die under the yoke of the various versions of socialism, such stern warning sounds ominously prophetic.

Finally, Part 4, "Hopes and Consolations," investigates the many aspects of the afterlife and salvation, establishing that suffering, either on Earth or in the spiritual world, must necessarily be only temporary, thus resolving the *problem of evil*: "Punishment is the goad that stimulates the soul—by bitterly piercing it—to turn into itself, driving it back to the path of salvation. The goal of punishment is none other than to rehabilitate and liberate. To assume eternal punishment for transient wrongs would be to deny any reason for it to exist" (#1009).

In a glaring exception among religious traditions, the claim does not exist that it is "necessary to believe in Spiritism in order to guarantee our happiness in the next life," because "only … good deeds can guarantee … future happiness" (#982).

The Spirits' Book clearly indicates that the progress of humankind results from the advancement of each individual. "The good shall reign on Earth when good spirits prevail over those who are evil, amid those who come to inhabit the planet" (#1019). In that sense, it would be disingenuous to group Spiritism with political movements that aimed at "social reform," and most certainly not with those with a materialistic bent.

In fact, "Spiritism is the most feared opponent of materialism," (Conclusion, Section II), and—quite unlike the social upheaval that revolutionary doctrines fostered—the Spiritist Doctrine strives to "make people better to each other, less avid for material possessions, and more resigned before the decrees of Providence." Thus, Spiritism ends up "providing a guarantee of order and tranquility." (Conclusion, Section VI).

Indeed, contrary to collectivist ideologies that pretended to "create heaven on Earth," [1] Spiritism establishes that it is the personal improvement separately accomplished by each individual that creates the "dominant character of a nation," allowing justice to be "reflected in its laws" (#521). Collective progress is always a bottom-up process, not the other way around. As "history shows," "many nations" have "relapsed into barbarity" (#786). Civilization represents, therefore, the result of a continuous effort that must be carried out individually, and from generation to generation.

But the overall message of *The Spirits' Book* is clearly optimistic. The Spirits argue that it is unreasonable to believe "that among the billions of worlds that orbit through the immensity of space, only one—one of the smallest of them all, lost in the crowd—had the exclusive privilege of being inhabited" (#236). At the time, this was a revolutionary idea, preceding by over a century this now pervasive notion in popular culture. Although "man on Earth is far from being the first in intelligence, goodness, or perfection" (#55), to the point that the knowledge about other worlds "would disturb" him (#181), Spiritism gives us hope that, through the gradual advancement of each one of us, humanity may eventually take its place among the universal family, for "all worlds are united in solidarity" (#176).

Toward that end, the words of the spirit of Saint Vincent de Paul could not be more befitting: "Love one another: here is the whole law, the divine law through which God governs the worlds. Love is the law of attraction for living … beings, as much as attraction is the law of love for inorganic matter." (#888)

E. G. Dutra
Phoenix, December 22, 2017

●●●

[a] Data obtained from the website Adherents, accessed December 23, 2017, http://www.adherents.com/Religions_By_Adherents.html.

[b] Unless otherwise indicated, question numbers always refer to the second edition. See Appendix 1 for a detailed analysis of the different editions of the book.

[c] The five main books that Kardec published on the Spiritist Doctrine were: Le Livre des Esprits (The Spirits' Book, 1857), Le Livre des Médiums (The Medium's Book, 1861), L'Évangile selon le Spiritisme (The Gospel According to Spiritism, 1864), Le Ciel et L'Enfer (Heaven and Hell, 1865), and La Genèse (Genesis, 1868).

[d] The list of existing translations is probably not exhaustive, and was put together by researching the versions available on commercial websites, and through Spiritist publishers, as well as versions in the online library catalog, accessed June 01, 2018, https://www.worldcat.org/.

[e] John Chambers, Victor Hugo's Conversations with the Spirit World: A Literary Genius's Hidden Life (Rochester, VT: Destiny Books, 1998).

[f] "Lettre de Marie Curie à la comtesse Élisabeth Greffulhe," April 16, 1906, in Karin Blanc and Fröman Nanny, Marie Curie et le Nobel (Paris: Seuil, 2000).

[g] "Lettre de Pierre Curie à Georges Gouy," April 14, 1906. This letter was written only five days before Pierre Curie's untimely death. The six-page letter can be retrieved from the website of the Bibliothèque nacionale de France, accessed June 01, 2018. http://gallica.bnf.fr/ark:/12148/btv1b9080328m/f60.image.r=curie%20georges%20gouy.

[h] Yvonne Castellan, Le Spiritisme, 7e éd. (Paris: Presses Universitaires de France, 1987), Chapitre III, "Allan Kardec et la philosophie spirite."

[i] V. René Descartes, *Meditations on First Philosophy*, Fifth Meditation; and B. Spinoza, *Ethics*, definition VI of Part 1.

[j] J. Herculano Pires, *Introdução à Filosofia Espírita* (São Paulo: Paidéia, 1983), Chapter III, "Teoria Espírita do Conhecimento."

[k] Emma Bragdon, PhD, Editor, *Spiritism and Mental Health* (Philadelphia: Singing Dragon, 2012).

[l] Or the "immanentization of the eschaton," in the words of the German-American philosopher Eric Voegelin, *The New Science of Politics* (Chicago: The University of Chicago Press, 1952), p. 120.

Notice about the Second [French] Edition

In the first edition of this work, we announced that there would be a supplement to it, encompassing all the questions that could not be included in that edition, or that later circumstances and additional studies might beget. However, since those questions refer to and expand topics already discussed, a separate volume with them alone would lack continuity. We preferred to wait for the reprinting of the book in order to combine all of it together, and we also seized this opportunity to arrange the contents in a more methodical order, while at the same time eliminating repetitions. This new edition may be therefore considered a new work, although the principles have undergone no changes, except for a few cases which constitute complements and explanations rather than actual modifications.

The consistency of the principles put forward—despite the diversity of sources from which they were drawn—is an important element for the consolidation of the Spiritist science. Effectively, our correspondence shows that communications that were in every respect identical, if not in form at least in substance, were obtained in different places, and even before the publication of our book, providing confirmation and uniformity. History, for its part, demonstrates that most of its principles have been admitted by the most eminent minds in ancient and modern times, lending these principles additional credence.

Strictly speaking, the instructions on spirit manifestations as well as on mediums comprise an area of study which is in a way distinct from the doctrine's philosophy, meriting a dedicated analysis of its own. This area has developed considerably with the additional experience acquired, leading us to conclude that it is more appropriate to make a separate volume of it, including the answers *obtained to all the questions regarding manifestations and mediums,* as well as numerous observations on *practical Spiritism.* This work will constitute a sequel or supplement to *The Spirits' Book.* [1] [a]

Allan Kardec

[1] At the press. —Auth.

[a] This notice appeared in the second edition of *Le Livre des Esprits* (Paris, March 18, 1860). The original first edition from 1857 totaled five hundred and one questions, whereas the second edition included one thousand and nineteen questions. Kardec's footnote is a reference to *Le Livre des Médiums* (*The Mediums' Book*), which would be published in 1861. —Trans.

Introduction
to the Study of the Spiritist Doctrine

I. Spiritism and spiritualism [a]

New ideas require new words, for the sake of linguistic precision and to avoid the inevitable confusion stemming from use of words with multiple meanings. The words *spiritual*, *spiritualist*, and *spiritualism* all have well-defined meanings. To give them a new one in reference to the doctrine of the Spirits would be to multiply the already numerous causes of ambiguity.

Strictly speaking, spiritualism is the opposite of materialism: he who believes that there is in him anything more than matter is a spiritualist. It does not necessarily follow, however, that he believes in the existence of spirits or in their communication with the visible world. To refer to this latter belief, instead of the words *spiritual* and *spiritualism*, we use the words *spiritist and Spiritism*, which echo their origin and root meaning, and for that very reason have the advantage of being readily intelligible, leaving the word *spiritualism* to its original interpretation. We shall therefore say that the principles of *Spiritism*, or of *the Spiritist Doctrine*, derive from the relationship between the material world and the spirits, or beings of the invisible world. The adherents of Spiritism shall be called *spiritists*.

Specifically, *The Spirits' Book* contains the *Spiritist Doctrine*. In a general sense, it is linked to the spiritualist school, representing one of its branches. For this reason, we have inscribed the words "Spiritualist Philosophy" above the title of this book.

II. Soul, vital principle, and vital fluid

There is another word on which we must also agree, since it is the keystone of every moral system, being the subject of numerous controversies due to the lack of a well-defined meaning—the word *soul*.

The diverging opinions about the nature of the soul arise from the particular sense that each one attaches to this word. A perfect language, in which each idea had its own specific term, would avoid many disputes. With a single word for each thing, everyone would understand each other.

According to some, the soul is the principle of material organic life; it has no existence of its own and ceases to exist upon death: this is the purely materialistic interpretation. In this sense, and by comparison, one may say of a broken instrument—one that no longer produces any sound—that it has no soul. According to this opinion the soul would be an effect, not a cause.

Others believe that the soul is the principle of intelligence, the universal agent of which each being absorbs a portion. According to these, there is only one soul for the entire universe, distributing a spark of itself to the various intelligent beings during their lives. Upon death, each spark returns to the common source, when it then merges back with the whole, just as brooks and rivers go back to the ocean where they initially came from. This opinion differs from the preceding one in that, according to this hypothesis, there is something other than matter within us that remains after death. But it is almost as if nothing actually remained; since one would not possess one's individuality anymore, one would no longer have consciousness of one's self. According to this opinion, the universal soul would be God, and each being would be a portion of God; this represents a version of *pantheism*.

Finally, according to others, the soul is a moral being distinct from and independent of matter, preserving its individuality after death. This conception is indisputably the most prevalent because, under one name or another, the idea of this being that survives the body is to be found as an instinctive belief, independent of education, and among all cultures, whatever their degree of development. This theory, according to which the soul is *a cause and not an effect*, is that of *spiritualists*.

Without discussing the merit of these opinions, and considering only the linguistic aspect of the issue, we shall say that these three uses of the word *soul* entail three distinct ideas, each one demanding a different terminology. The word has thus three meanings, and each one is correct from its own point of view, according to the interpretation given to it. Language itself is to blame for having only one word for three different ideas. In order to avoid any confusion, it would be necessary to limit the meaning of the word *soul* to one of those three ideas; the choice is unimportant, a simple matter of convention, as the key issue is to achieve mutual comprehension. We believe it is most logical to use the word's most common meaning. For that reason, we employ the word *soul* in reference to the *immaterial and individual being that exists within us and survives the body*. Even if this entity did not really exist, representing only a construct of the imagination, a word would still be needed to designate it.

For the lack of a specific term for each of the other two meanings, we shall use *vital principle* to designate the principle of the material and organic life, whatever its source may be, which is common to all living beings, from plants to humans. As life may exist irrespective of the faculty of thought, the vital principle is something distinct from and independent of it. The word *vitality* would not express the same idea. For some, the vital principle is a property of matter, an effect produced whenever matter is found under certain conditions. According to others—and this is the most usual opinion—it is found in a special, universally distributed fluid, of which all beings absorb and assimilate a portion throughout their lives, much as inert bodies absorb light. This would be therefore the *vital fluid*, which, according to the opinion of a few, would be the same thing as the animalized electric energy, also designated as *magnetic fluid*, *nervous fluid*, and so on.

Whatever the case may be, the unquestionable truth which results from observation is as follows: that organic beings possess in themselves an inner force that produces the phenomenon of life, so long as this force exists; that physical life is common to all organic beings and that it is independent of intelligence and thought; that intelligence and thought are faculties inherent to certain organic species; and, finally, that among the organic species endowed with intelligence and thought, there is one that is endowed with a special moral sense, giving it an incontestable superiority over the others: the human species.

We realize that in its multiple meanings the word *soul* does not exclude either materialism or pantheism. Spiritualists themselves can very well understand the word *soul* according to either one of the first two definitions, without rejecting the existence of a distinct immaterial being, to which they would give another name. As it is, the word *soul* does not represent a unique concept: it is a blank that one may fill in as one sees fit, giving rise to interminable disputes.

We could equally avoid any confusion, even if we were to use the word *soul* in any of its three possible interpretations, by simply adding a qualification that could specify the vantage point from which we are considering it, or how we are employing it at the time. It would then be a generic word representing simultaneously the principle of material life, of intelligence, and of moral faculties. Each of these three would be distinguished by a given attribute, as is done with the word *gas*, for example, which we differentiate by appending a word such as *hydrogen*, *oxygen*, or *nitrogen* to it. We could, perhaps more aptly, use the term *vital soul* for the principle of material life, *intellectual soul* for the principle of intelligence, and *spiritual soul* for the principle of our individuality after death.

As can be seen, it is all a matter of words, but a very important one in order to establish a precise comprehension. In this last alternative, the *vital soul* would be common to all organic beings: plants, animals, and men; the *intellectual soul* would be the attribute of animals and men; and the *spiritual soul* would only apply to human beings.

We believe it is necessary to insist on such explanations, as the Spiritist Doctrine is naturally based on the existence within us of an entity independent of matter which survives the death of the body. As the word *soul* shall be frequently employed throughout this work, it was important to establish the meaning we attach to it in order to avoid any misunderstanding.

We now come to the main subject of this preliminary explanation.

III. Spiritism and its detractors

Like any new idea, Spiritism has its followers and its detractors. We will attempt to respond to some of the latter's objections by examining the validity of the arguments upon which such objections are based, without having, however, the pretension of trying to convince everybody, as there are those who believe they have a monopoly on reason. We shall address ourselves to those of good faith, who are without preconceptions or prejudices, and who harbor a sincere desire to arrive at the truth. We shall prove to them that most of their objections to the Spiritist Doctrine derive from an incomplete observation of facts and from a judgment passed too rashly and too hurriedly.

First, let us recall briefly the gradual sequence of phenomena that gave rise to the Spiritist Doctrine.

The first phenomenon to be observed was the movement of various objects, popularly called *table-turning*. This phenomenon appears to have been first observed in America—or, rather, rediscovered in that country, since history shows that it goes back to remote antiquity—occurring in association with other strange incidents, such as unusual noises and raps produced without any known apparent cause. From America, the phenomenon rapidly spread to Europe and to other parts of the world. It was met with much incredulity at first, but the multiplicity of experiences would soon leave no room to question its reality.

If the phenomenon had been limited only to the movement of material objects, it might have been explained by some purely physical cause. We are far from knowing about all the secret agents of nature, or even all the properties of those we do know about. Electricity, for instance, provides man with ever newer possibilities every day, and it appears to be on the verge of casting a radically new light upon science. It would not be at all impossible that, if electricity were modified by certain circumstances or by some unknown agent, it could be the cause of those movements. In a gathering of more people, the increased intensity of the action seemed to support this theory, as we could consider such a group as a type of multi-cell battery, the power of which is proportional to the number of its elements.

The circular movement is not extraordinary; it is frequently found in nature. All the heavenly bodies move in circles. We could have before us nothing more than a small example of the typical movement of the universe. Or perhaps more accurately, an as-yet-unknown agent could be accidentally producing in small objects, under certain conditions, a force analogous to the one that drives the planets.

Movements, however, were not always circular. They were frequently jolting and disorderly. The object would be violently shaken, overturned, carried about in every direction, and, contrary to all the laws of mechanics, lifted from the ground and held up in the air. Still, there was nothing in these events that might not be explained by the action of some invisible physical force. After all, do we not see electricity knock down buildings, uproot trees, and hurl the heaviest objects at the greatest distances, by either attracting or repelling those objects?

Supposing the unusual noises and raps were not due to ordinary wood expansion or some other accidental cause, then they could very well have been produced by the accumulation of some unknown charge. Does electricity not produce the most violent noises?

One can see that up to this point everything might be considered to belong exclusively to the domain of physics and physiology. Even without going beyond this specific territory, the subject at hand would already be worthy of serious study and attention on the part of researchers. Why was that not the case?

It is hard to admit, but that was due to reasons that prove, like many times before, the flippancy of men. First of all, a table—the object used in the earliest experiments—has a mundane, not-at-all-extraordinary, character. What an influence a simple word can have on the most serious matters! The fact that the movement could be imparted to any other object was never considered. Tables were certainly a popular choice because a table is a convenient object, and because people can sit around a table more easily than around any other piece of furniture.

Now, some so-called *superior minds* can be sometimes so childish that one can easily imagine many cultivated men consider it beneath themselves to investigate what was commonly called *the dance of tables*. If the phenomenon observed by Galvani [b] had been, instead, observed by ordinary men and given some ludicrous nickname, it would probably have been ranked with the magic wand. Wouldn't scientists find it rather derogatory to busy themselves with *the dance of frogs*?

A few men, however, humble enough to admit that Nature might not have yet revealed to them the last of her secrets, decided to check out the matter for themselves, out of a sense of duty. But it just so happened that the phenomenon did not always correspond to their expectations, and since it was not consistently produced at will or according to their established empirical method, they came to a negative conclusion.

Despite their verdict, however, many a table continued to turn, so that we may affirm with Galileo, "and yet, it moves!" [c] And we can further add that the events have multiplied to such an extent that nowadays they have garnered a legitimacy of their own, to the point that what is needed now is to find a rational explanation for them.

May anything be inferred about the reality of the phenomenon from the fact that it cannot always be produced in exactly the same way and according to the wishes and demands of the observer? Electrical and chemical phenomena are subject to certain conditions; may we deny the existence of electrical or chemical phenomena if they are not observed because the required conditions are not in place? Therefore, is it at all surprising that the phenomenon of the movement of objects under the influence of this newly discovered action also requires its own set of conditions, and that it no longer takes place when the observer—fixated on his own perspective—attempts to replicate it at his whim, or to subject it to laws pertaining to different fields, without realizing that a new class of phenomena may, or even must, require new laws? Now, in order to understand such laws, it is necessary to study the circumstances under which the phenomena are produced, and such a study must be the result of a sustained, attentive, and often rather long observation.

"But," some people often object, "There is frequently evident trickery." We in turn would like to ask them if they are quite sure that it is trickery, or if they might be calling trickery those things that they were unable to account for, the same way an illiterate peasant might mistake a scientist who conducts his experiments for a skillful magician. And even supposing that fraud does sometimes occur, would that be a reason to deny the phenomenon itself? Must we deny physics simply because there are conjurers who call themselves physicists?

Moreover, it is necessary to consider the character of those supposedly fraudulent people and what interest they might have in deceiving. Could it all be just a prank? A prankster may find his mischief amusing for a while, but before long it becomes as wearisome to the prankster as it is to the victim. Besides, a prank performed all around the world and among the most serious, respected, and knowledgeable people would be something at least as extraordinary as the phenomenon itself.

IV. Intelligent manifestations

If the phenomena under consideration had been limited only to the movement of objects, they would have remained, as we have said, within the domain of the physical sciences. But that is not what happened: they were to set us on the path of events of a strange order. It is unclear on whose initiative, but it was eventually discovered that the movement imparted to the objects was not simply the result of some blind mechanical force, but that there was the intervention of an intelligent agent in the phenomena. Once this door was opened, a whole new field of study emerged, lifting the veil of numerous mysteries. But is there indeed an intelligent power involved? This is the question to be answered initially. If this power does exist, what is it? What is its nature, its origin? Is it above mankind? Such are the other questions that follow from the first.

The initial intelligent manifestations occurred in the form of tables that would go up and then strike the floor with one leg a number of times, thereby replying "yes" or "no" to the question asked, according to an agreed-upon code. So far, however, there was nothing very convincing to skeptics, as one could imagine the "answers" to be purely random.

But later, more sophisticated answers were received through the use of the letters of the alphabet: by striking the floor a number of times corresponding to the order of each letter, the moving object composed words and sentences in response to the questions proposed. The exactness of the answers and their connection with the questions caused astonishment. When asked about its own nature, the mysterious entity who answered in that way, declared that it was a *spirit* or *genie*; it provided a name as well as several facts about itself.

This circumstance is very important to highlight. No one had ever even thought of spirits as a way to explain the phenomenon; instead, it was the phenomenon itself that provided the explanation. In science, hypotheses are frequently formulated as a starting point for a line of reasoning, but that is not what happened in this case.

This means of communication was slow and wearisome. A spirit— and this is also a point worth noting—suggested another way to communicate. One of those invisible beings gave the instruction to attach a pencil to a small basket or other object. When placed over a sheet of paper, the basket was set in motion by the same hidden power that had turned the tables. But instead of a simple regular movement, all by itself the pencil would start writing characters that formed words, and then sentences, and then finally entire essays, filling many pages that dealt with the deepest questions of philosophy, ethics, metaphysics, psychology, and so on—and all that as quickly as if written by hand.

This instruction was given in America, France, and several other countries simultaneously. It was transmitted in the following terms in Paris on June 10, 1853 to one of the most fervent followers of the doctrine, who for many years since 1849 had occupied himself with the evocation of spirits: "Fetch the little basket from the next room; attach a pencil to it and then place it on a sheet of paper and put your fingers on the edge." Then, after a few moments, the basket began to move and the pencil wrote this sentence very legibly: "I expressly forbid you to tell anyone what I have just told you; the next time I write, I shall provide more details."

Since the object to which the pencil was attached was merely an instrument, its nature and form were not important. The most convenient configuration was researched, and it was thus that many people started using a planchette. [d]

The basket or planchette does not move, however, except under the influence of certain people gifted with a special ability in this respect, who we call *mediums*, that is to say, mediators or intermediaries between spirits and men. The conditions that produce this special ability are linked to both physical and moral factors that are still imperfectly identified, as one can find mediums are of all ages, of both sexes, and of all degrees of intellectual development. Moreover, this faculty can be further developed through practice.

V. The development of *psychography*

Later on, it was recognized that the basket and the planchette formed in fact only an appendage to the hand, and that the medium, by holding the pencil directly, could begin writing by an involuntary, almost frenzied impulse. [e] In this way, communications became faster, easier, and more complete. Nowadays, this is the most widespread method, all the more so because the number of people endowed with this ability is quite considerable and increases continually. Finally, experience revealed many other types of mediumship, and it was discovered that communications could also occur through speech, hearing, sight, touch, and even through the direct writing of spirits, that is, without using the medium's hand or the pencil.

Once this fact had been established, there was still one essential point to consider: the role of the medium in the answers and the part the medium might play, mechanically and intellectually. Two critical circumstances, which would not escape the attentive observer, make it possible to settle the question. The first is the way in which the basket moves under the medium's influence, by simply placing the fingers on its edge. A simple inspection will demonstrate the impossibility of guiding the basket in any particular direction. This impossibility becomes especially obvious when two or three people are touching the basket at the same time. It would require a truly phenomenal coordination of movements, in addition to a unity of thought, to enable them to agree on the answer to be given to the question asked.

Another no-less-unique fact adds to the complexity of the problem: the radical change in writing according to the spirit who communicates, as well as the fact that, whenever the same spirit returns, the same style of writing reappears. Thus, the medium would have to change the writing style an indefinite number of ways, and, in addition, be able to remember the style that corresponded to each communicating spirit.

The second circumstance results from the very nature of the responses, which are—in most cases, and particularly when dealing with abstract or scientific questions—obviously beyond the knowledge, and sometimes the intellectual reach, of the medium. Besides, mediums are usually unaware of what is being written through their assistance, or may not even hear or understand the question posed, as it may be asked in a foreign language or even only mentally, and the answer may be given in that same language. Finally, it often happens that the basket may write spontaneously, without a prior question being asked, and about some random and altogether unexpected subject.

In certain cases, the responses feature such wisdom, depth, and pertinence—revealing thoughts that are so elevated, so sublime—that they can only emanate from a superior intelligence imbued with the purest morality. At other times, they are so facetious, so frivolous, and so trite, that reason refuses to believe they could have derived from the same source. Such diversity of content and linguistic register can only be explained by the diversity of the intelligences who manifest themselves. Are such intelligences human or not? That is the question to elucidate, and for which a complete explanation shall be found in this book, as conveyed by the Spirits [f] themselves.

These are therefore the patent phenomena that are produced outside the circle of our habitual observations, phenomena that do not occur mysteriously but in broad daylight. This way everyone can see and verify them, as they are not the privilege of one individual in particular, but phenomena that are replicated by a multitude of people every day and repeatedly. These effects have necessarily a cause, and since they reveal the action of an intelligence and a will, they go beyond the domain of purely physical phenomena.

Many theories have been suggested regarding these phenomena. We shall examine them before long, and will see if they can explain all the facts that take place. Meanwhile, however, let us assume the existence of beings distinct from mankind, as that is the explanation provided by the very intelligences that manifest, and let us see what they have to say to us.

VI. Summary of the Spirits' teachings

As we have said, the beings who communicate have identified themselves as spirits or genies, and at least some of them claim to have been among the human beings who have lived on Earth. They comprise the spirit world, as we constitute, during our earthly life, the corporeal world.

We shall now briefly summarize the main points of the teachings that they have transmitted to us, so as to more easily reply to certain objections:

• God is eternal, immutable, immaterial, unique, all-powerful, and sovereignly just and good.

• He has created the universe, which includes all animate and inanimate, material and immaterial beings.

• The material beings constitute the visible or corporeal world, while the immaterial beings constitute the invisible or spirit world, that is to say, the world of spirits.

• The spirit world is the normal, primitive, and eternal world, preexisting and outlasting all else.

• The corporeal world is only secondary; it could cease to exist—or it might never have existed at all—without changing the essence of the spirit world.

• Spirits temporarily don a perishable material envelope, the destruction of which at death restores them to freedom.

- From among all the different species of corporeal beings, God has chosen the human species for the incarnation of spirits who have reached a certain degree of development. This endows them with a moral and intellectual superiority to all the others.

- The soul is an incarnate spirit, the body representing but its envelope.

- There are three things in man: first, the body or material being, analogous to that of animals, and animated by the same vital principle; second, the soul or immaterial being, the spirit incarnated in the body; and third, the link which unites the soul with the body, an intermediary principle between matter and spirit.

- Man has therefore two natures: by means of his body he participates in the nature of animals, sharing the same instincts; by means of his soul he participates in the nature of spirits.

- The link or *perispirit* that unites the body and the spirit is a type of semi-material envelope. Death destroys only the denser of the two envelopes, namely, the physical body. The spirit keeps the second envelope, the perispirit, which constitutes its ethereal body, invisible to us in its normal state, but which can be occasionally made visible—and even tangible—as happens in the phenomenon of apparitions.

- Therefore, a spirit is not an undefined, abstract entity that can only be conceived of by thought; it is a real, circumscribed being that in certain cases may become perceptible through the senses of *sight*, *hearing*, and *touch*.

- Spirits belong to different orders, and they are not all equal in power, intelligence, knowledge, or morality. Those of the first order are the most highly evolved spirits, distinguishable from the others by their perfection, wisdom, closeness to God, purity of feelings, and their love of the good: they are the angels or pure spirits. The other orders distance themselves from such perfection to varying degrees. The spirits of the lowest orders are inclined to most of our passions, such as hatred, envy, jealousy, pride, and so on, taking pleasure in evil. Among them there are spirits who are neither very good nor very evil, and who are usually more annoying and unruly than exactly mean, with mischief and thoughtlessness seeming to be their common trait: they are the foolish and frivolous spirits.

•   Spirits do not belong to the same order forever. They all advance, going through the different degrees of the spirit hierarchy. This improvement takes place through incarnation, which is imposed on some as an expiation, and on others as a mission. Earthly life is a trial they must undergo many times, until they have reached absolute perfection. It is a kind of filter or purifier from which they emerge, to varying degrees, more advanced.

•   Upon leaving the body, the soul reenters the spirit world from which it came, initiating an interval between incarnations, a period of time which may be more or less extended; once completed, the spirit starts a new material existence.

•   As the spirit must go through many incarnations, it follows that we all have had many existences, and that we will have still others, in which we will be more or less successful, either on Earth or on other worlds.

•   The incarnation of spirits always occurs in the human species. It would be a mistake to believe that the soul or spirit could incarnate in the body of an animal.[1]

•   The successive corporeal existences of a spirit are always progressive and never retrograde, but the speed of progress depends on the efforts that are made to reach perfection.

•   The qualities of the soul are those of the spirit incarnated in us. This way, a good man is the incarnation of a good spirit, while a bad man is that of a spirit of lesser advancement.

•   The soul possesses its individuality before incarnating and preserves it after abandoning the body upon death.

•   Upon its return to the spirit world, the soul reencounters all those whom it had known on Earth, and all of its previous lives are brought

---

[1] Between the doctrine of reincarnation and that of metempsychosis, as held by certain sects, there is a characteristic distinction which is explained later on in the book. —Auth.

back to memory, along with the recollection of all the good and evil that was done.

• The incarnate spirit is under the influence of matter. The man who overcomes this influence by improving and purifying his soul grows closer to the good spirits, with whom he will be ranked one day. However, he who allows himself to be controlled by his base passions, and places all his enjoyment in the satisfaction of his crude appetites, brings himself closer to imperfect spirits, by yielding to the influence of his animal nature.

• Incarnate spirits populate various globes throughout the universe.

• Discarnate spirits do not occupy any fixed and circumscribed region. They are everywhere, in space and next to us, constantly watching and interacting with us. They constitute a whole invisible population that is always active around us.

• Spirits exert a continuous action upon the mental and even upon the physical world. They act upon matter and thought, representing one of the powers of nature, and lie at the source of a myriad of phenomena hitherto poorly or not at all explained, and which cannot find a rational solution except in Spiritism.

• The interactions between spirits and men are constant. Good spirits inspire us to do good, sustaining us in the trials of life and helping us to endure them with courage and acceptance. Evil spirits tempt us to evil: It is a pleasure for them to see us fail, mirroring their own imperfection.

• The communication between spirits and humans can be either concealed or apparent. Concealed communications occur through the good or bad influence they exert unbeknownst to us; it is upon us to use our judgment to recognize their positive or pernicious inspirations. Ostensive communications occur through writing, speech or other physical means, more commonly through mediums who operate as their instruments.

• Spirits manifest either spontaneously or by being evoked. Any spirit can be evoked, whether they have animated obscure mortals or the most illustrious personalities, regardless of when they lived. One can evoke one's relatives, friends, or enemies, and obtain—through written or verbal communications—advice, information about their situation beyond the grave, their thoughts about us, and whatever revelations they are allowed to make.

• Spirits are attracted according to their affinity with the moral attributes of the party that evokes them. Spirits of superior standing enjoy serious meetings, where love of the good and a sincere desire to learn and advance prevail. Their presence repels spirits of lower degree, who, conversely, find unrestricted access and freedom of action over people of frivolous character or who are guided by mere curiosity, and wherever evil instincts may be found. Far from receiving either good advice or useful information from these entities, we should expect nothing but trivialities, lies, mischief, and deceit, as they frequently borrow venerable names in order to mislead us more easily.

• Distinguishing between good and evil spirits is rather straightforward. The language of spirits of a higher order is consistently dignified, noble, imbued with the highest morality, and devoid of any earthly passion. Their advice displays the most genuine wisdom and always aims for our advancement and for the good of mankind. On the other hand, the language of lower spirits is thoughtless, often commonplace and at times even obscene. Although they may sometimes say things that are good and true, more often than not they make false and absurd statements out of mischief or ignorance. They play with people's credulity and amuse themselves at the expense of those who ask them questions, by flattering the latter's vanity and stimulating their desires with false hopes. In short, serious communications, properly speaking, only occur in serious groups, where members are united by an intimate communion of thoughts in the pursuit of the good.

• Like that of the Christ, the moral teaching of spirits of higher orders may be summed up in the Gospel maxim: "Do unto others as you would like them to do unto you"; in other words, do good and not evil. In this principle man finds the universal rule of conduct for even his simplest actions.

- They teach us that selfishness, pride, and sensuality are passions that bring us closer to our animal nature, enslaving us to matter … that the man who, during his earthly stay, frees himself from the yoke of matter through the detachment from worldly futilities and through the love of his neighbor, brings himself closer to his spiritual nature … that each one of us should be useful, according to the abilities and means that God has placed in our hands for our trials … that the strong and powerful should help and protect the weak, for he who abuses his strength and power in order to oppress his fellow beings violates the law of God. Lastly, they teach us that, as nothing can be hidden in the spirit world, the hypocrite will be unmasked and all his wickedness exposed; that the inevitable and constant presence of those whom we have wronged is one of the punishments reserved for us; that our inferior or superior standing as spirits results, respectively, in afflictions or joys that are unknown to us on Earth.

- Nevertheless, they also teach us that there are no unforgivable errors, none that cannot be erased by expiation. Man can find the necessary means to atone for them in the many existences that enable him to advance, according to his will and efforts, along the path of progress toward perfection, which is his final destiny.

This is the summary of the Spiritist Doctrine as it results from the teachings of Spirits of higher order. Let us now look at the objections raised against it.

VII. Argument from authority and Spiritism

For many people, the opposition from the learned world represents, if not a proof, at least a strong unfavorable indication. We are not among those who inveigh against scholars, lest we be accused of a cowardly disloyalty, or perhaps of sour grapes. On the contrary, we hold them in great esteem and would be rather honored to be numbered among them. Their opinion, however, cannot be considered as a final verdict in every circumstance.

When science goes beyond the objective observation of facts and attempts to appraise and explain them, the field opens wide for speculation; each one then advances a theory of his own, trying to make it prevail and defending it relentlessly. Do we not see every day the most contradictory opinions, one after another, be proposed and rejected, sometimes repealed as absurd errors, only to be later proclaimed as indisputable truths? Facts are the sole criterion of reality, the argument that admits of no reply. In the absence of facts, doubt is the choice of the wise man.

On matters that have been fully studied, scholars' opinions are justifiably authoritative, because their knowledge of them is broader and deeper than that of common folk. But when it comes to new principles, to unknown fields, scholars' opinion is only speculative, as they are no more exempt from bias than anybody else. One could perhaps say that scholars are bound to be even more biased than other people, due to their natural tendency to see everything from the vantage point of their specialization: mathematicians only accept proof from algebraic demonstrations, chemists ascribe everything to the interaction of elements, and so on. Those who specialize in a particular field subordinate all their ideas to it. Outside their specialization their reason often falters, as they attempt to measure everything by their own yardstick, a consequence of their human weakness.

We would happily and confidently consult with a chemist about a question of stoichiometry, a physicist about the inner workings of electricity, and an engineer about a power engine. But without jeopardizing the high esteem in which we hold them for their area of expertise, they must allow us not to take their negative opinion about Spiritism into consideration any more than we would accept an architect's judgment on a question about music.

Physical sciences are based on the properties of matter, which one may experiment with and manipulate at one's discretion. Spirit phenomena, on the other hand, depend on the action of intelligences who have their own will, and who continuously show us that they are not subject to our whims. Therefore, the observation of spirit phenomena cannot be carried out in the same way; it requires special conditions and a different approach. Trying to submit these phenomena to the same methods of investigation would be to establish a parallel that does not exist. That is why conventional science is unable to offer a verdict on the subject of Spiritism. It cannot deal with it, and a favorable or unfavorable opinion would carry no weight.

Spiritism results from a personal conviction that scholars may hold as individuals, irrespective of their status as scholars. Submitting this subject to science would be equivalent to asking a group of physicists and astronomers to decide on the existence of the soul. In fact, Spiritism rests entirely on the existence of the soul and its condition after death. It would be highly illogical to imagine that a man must be a great psychologist simply because he is a great mathematician or anatomist.

Suppose an anatomist dissects a human body in search of the soul, but because he does not find it under his scalpel as he would find a nerve, nor sees it expand like a gas, he concludes that the soul does not exist. This is because he positions himself at an exclusively material vantage point. But it does not follow that he is right and everyone else is wrong.

This is why Spiritism does not fall under the jurisdiction of established science. When Spiritist beliefs become known and accepted by the masses—and judging by the speed at which they are spreading, that time is not far off—the same thing will happen with Spiritism as has happened with all other new ideas that encountered opposition: scholars will yield to the force of evidence. They will arrive at it, one by one, by the very force of things. But until then it would be premature to distract them from their area of specialization and force them to focus on something which is foreign to both their responsibility and to their program of research.

Meanwhile, those who take a negative stance without a previous detailed study of the issue, and who ridicule those who do not agree with their opinion, forget that the same has happened with the majority of the great discoveries that have honored mankind. They risk seeing their names added to the list of illustrious deniers of new ideas and being ranked with those of the erudite assembly which in 1752 laughed loudly at Franklin's paper on lightning rods, considering it unworthy of being presented to them, or with those who made France lose its pioneering role in steam-powered navigation by declaring Fulton's design an impracticable dream. Yet, both topics were within their jurisdiction. If those assemblies, which included some of the greatest scholars in the world, had only ridicule and sarcasm for ideas they did not understand, but which a few years later would revolutionize science, customs, and industry, what hope is there that an issue completely foreign to their skill-set should be met with any more receptiveness?

Such mistakes, though detrimental to their honor, in our view do not diminish their authority with respect to other subjects. But is an official diploma necessary for one to have common sense, and are there only fools and simpletons outside academic halls? Let us analyze the ranks of followers of the Spiritist Doctrine to determine if among them there are only uneducated people, and if the vast number of trustworthy individuals who have embraced the doctrine warrants ranking it with folktale and superstition. Their character and knowledge authorize us to conclude that, if people of such capacity uphold it, there must be at least something to it.

We repeat once more that if the phenomena with which we busy ourselves had been restricted to the mechanical movement of objects, the research of their physical cause would fall within the realm of established science. But since they involve manifestations outside the scope of known laws, they are therefore beyond the competence of physical sciences, as they cannot be explained either by numbers or by mechanical action. When a new fact arises that does not fit within the scope of any known science, scientists, in order to study it, must lay their knowledge aside and realize that a new research program lies before them, one that cannot be carried out under the influence of preconceived ideas.

The man who believes his reason to be foolproof is very close to error. Even those whose ideas are among the most false, base them on their reason, and, accordingly, reject everything that seems impossible to them. Those who in the past rejected the admirable discoveries that are the glory of the human mind did so in the name of reason. For what we call reason frequently is only pride in disguise, and he who believes himself infallible pretends to be God's equal.

We therefore address ourselves to those who are reasonable enough to suspend their judgment with regard to what they have not yet seen, and who, judging the future by the past, do not believe that man has reached his zenith, or that Nature has turned over for him the last leaf of her book.

VIII. The need for commitment and seriousness

Let us add that the study of Spiritism, which suddenly opens for us such a novel and grand field of research, can only be successfully carried out by individuals who are serious, persevering, unbiased, and animated by a firm and sincere desire to arrive at the truth. This qualification cannot possibly include those who make *a priori* judgments, casually and without having observed everything, or those who neglect pursuing their research with the necessary steadiness, consistency, and focus. And it should certainly not include those who, to maintain their record of witticism, seek to find something to ridicule in matters that are studied by individuals whose knowledge, character, and convictions should command the respect of anyone with a modicum of good manners. Let those who do not deem these facts worthy of their attention therefore abstain. No one intends to violate their beliefs; for their part, however, they should respect the beliefs of others.

Steadiness is the hallmark of serious study. Should we therefore be surprised at not receiving reasonable responses to questions that, however serious by themselves, are asked at random and point-blank, among a host of ludicrous queries? In order to be fully explained, a complex question requires others that are preliminary or complementary. Whoever wishes to understand a particular science must study it methodically, starting at the very beginning, and follow the chain and development of ideas.

Would it be at all useful for people to pose random questions to a scholar about a science they completely ignore? Could even a well-intentioned scholar provide them with satisfactory answers? Such out-of-context responses would be unavoidably incomplete, and, for that same reason, often unintelligible, or might even seem absurd and inconsistent.

The same applies to the relationship that we establish with spirits. If we desire to learn from them, we must enroll in their course of study; however, just as we do among ourselves, we must select our instructors with care and work diligently.

We have stated that superior spirits only participate in serious meetings, especially those characterized by the perfect unity of thoughts and feelings toward the pursuit of the good. Frivolousness and idle curiosity repel them just as, on Earth, they would repel any reasonable person; such attitudes open the field to throngs of deceitful and frivolous spirits who are always on the lookout for opportunities to mock us and amuse themselves at our expense.

What would happen to any serious question asked in such a gathering? An answer shall be given, but by whom? It would be like being at a party in the company of pleasure-seeking people and posing questions such as, "What is the soul? What is death?" or any other out-of-place inquiry. If we want serious answers, we must be serious in every sense of the word, meeting all the necessary conditions: only then will we obtain worthwhile results. Thus, we must be most diligent and persevering in our studies. Otherwise, spirits of higher standing shall abandon us, as instructors would abandon their negligent students.

IX. Monopolists of reason

The movement of inanimate objects is a proven fact. What is left to be verified is whether or not there is action of an intelligence in this movement, and if so, what the source of this intelligence is.

We are not talking about the manifestations involving the intelligent movement of certain objects, the manifestations involving verbal communications, or communications written directly by a medium's hand. These types of manifestation—evident to those who have studied the subject in depth—may not at first glance seem sufficiently independent of the medium's will, to convince a new observer. So, we will only focus on the writings obtained with the help of a small object, such as a basket or a planchette, with a pencil attached to it. As we said before, the way in which the medium's fingers are placed on the object challenges the notion that even the most consummate skill may play a part in the way letters and words are drawn. But even if we assume that, by some exceptional ability, the medium is able to deceive the most acutely scrutinizing eye, how can one explain the nature of the answers when they go way beyond the scope of the medium's ideas and knowledge?

Let us emphasize that we are not referring here to one-syllable answers, but frequently to many pages written with astonishing speed, spontaneously or on a subject previously chosen. From under the hand of a medium completely unversed in literature, poems emerge of such sublimity and flawless style that would leave nothing to be desired if compared with the work of the best human poets. Adding to the strangeness of these phenomena is that they are being replicated everywhere and that the number of mediums increases rapidly. Are these phenomena real or not? We can only reply to this question: watch and see. The opportunities will not be lacking. Above all, observe often, for a long time, and according to the appropriate conditions.

How do adversaries respond to the evidence? They say, "You are victims of either a fraud or of an illusion." First, we will reply that *fraud* is not likely where there is no profit to be made—charlatans do not work for free. It would be a prank at the most. But by what strange coincidence could pranksters have reached an agreement among themselves all around the world so as to act in the same way, to produce the same effects, and to give answers on the same subjects—and in different languages— that are identical in meaning, if not in words? Why would serious, respectable, and educated people fall prey to such ruses, and for what purpose? How is it that even children may be gifted with the patience and skill required? After all, unless mediums are mere passive instruments, they would need to have skills and knowledge incompatible with their age and social position.

They then add that, if no fraud is involved, perhaps both parties might be victims of an illusion. To be sure, there is no question that the quality of the witnesses does carry a certain weight. It is therefore reasonable to ask whether the Spiritist Doctrine, which today counts millions of adherents, recruits only among the uneducated. The phenomena on which Spiritism is based seem so extraordinary that we can comprehend such doubt; but we cannot admit the pretension of certain skeptics to hold a monopoly on common sense, skeptics who, disrespectful of conventions and of the moral worth of their adversaries, unceremoniously charge with ineptitude all those who do not agree with their opinion. In the eyes of judicious people, the opinions of learned individuals who have observed, studied, and pondered at length a certain question will always be, if not a proof, at least a presumption in favor of their interpretation, as the question grabbed the serious attention of those who have neither an interest in propagating an error nor the time to waste on futilities.

X. Spirits' language and the demonic hypothesis

Among the objections made, some are more credible at first glance, because they are based on observation and are raised by serious individuals.

One such objection refers to the language of certain spirits, which does not seem compatible with the loftiness that one may attribute to supernatural beings. However, if we refer to the summary of the Spirits' teachings presented above, we see that spirits themselves explain that they are not equal in knowledge or moral qualities, and that we should not take at face value everything that spirits say. One must use reason to distinguish the good from the bad. Assuredly, those who infer from this fact that we deal solely with maleficent entities—whose only intention is to deceive—are unfamiliar with the communications that occur in meetings in which spirits of a superior standing manifest, otherwise they would think differently.

It is unfortunate that chance has served them so badly, by showing them only the negative side of the spirit world, as we would not suppose that an affinity of dispositions attracts evil, deceitful, and obscene spirits to them, rather than good ones. We could conclude at most that the strength of their principles may not always be solid enough to shield them from evil, and that as they find a certain pleasure in satisfying their curiosity with respect to these phenomena, imperfect spirits take advantage of that to slip in among them, whereas good spirits stay away.

Judging the question of spirits by these facts would be as illogical as judging the character of an entire population by the words and actions of a gang of a few foolish or disreputable individuals—a group in which neither learned nor reasonable people ever take part. Those who thus judge are in the position of a foreigner who, upon entering a great capital through a crime-infested district, proceeds to judge all the residents of the city by the habits and language of that one neighborhood. In the spirit world, there is also a good and an evil society.

If such individuals were to study what happens amid superior spirits, they would realize that the celestial city does not comprise only the dregs of society. "But," they might ask, "do spirits of higher standing truly come to us?" To which we would reply: "Do not remain on the outskirts. Watch, observe, and judge for yourselves. The facts are there for everyone to see, except for those to whom the words of Jesus apply: 'They have eyes but do not see; they have ears but do not hear.'"

A variation on this opinion consists in seeing in all spirit communications—and all physical phenomena which they give rise to—nothing more than the intervention of some demonic power, a new type of Proteus [g], or shapeshifting entity, that can assume any form in order to better deceive us. We do not believe such thesis to be worthy of serious examination, and therefore will not dwell on it here: it has already been refuted by what we have just said. We would only add that, if such were the case, we would have to agree that the Devil is at times very wise, very reasonable, and, above all, very moral, or else that there are good devils, too.

But how could we believe, indeed, that God would only allow the Spirit of Evil to manifest itself in order to mislead us, without providing us the counsels of good spirits as a counterbalance? If God could not allow good spirits to assist us, He would have limited powers; if God could but did not, that would be incompatible with His goodness. Either supposition would be blasphemous. One must point out that to admit the communication of evil spirits is to admit that spirit manifestations do occur. And as they do occur, it is only with divine permission. Therefore, how can we believe, without impiety, that God would only allow the manifestation of evil spirits to the exclusion of good ones? Such a theory is contrary to the most elementary notions of common sense as well as of religion.

XI. Spirits of illustrious men and obscure men

Others object that it seems odd that we concern ourselves only with the spirits of illustrious personalities, so they wonder why these are the only ones who communicate. Like many other misconceptions, this one comes from a superficial observation. Among the spirits who present themselves spontaneously, much more numerous than those who are famous are those who are unknown to us, who take a plain name, or one that is metaphorical or suggests a characteristic they want to emphasize. Regarding those whom we evoke, except for relatives or friends, it is quite natural that we would choose to address those we know rather than those we do not know. As for illustrious personalities, they are the ones who make a more vivid impression, therefore attracting more attention.

Yet others challenge the notion that the spirits of eminent men answer so casually to our calls, and that they sometimes concern themselves with issues that seem too trivial in comparison with what they accomplished during their lifetime. But that is not at all surprising to those who know that the power and respect those men commanded on Earth do not automatically warrant them any authority in the spirit world.

The Spirits confirm the words from the Gospel: "He that exalts himself shall be humbled, and he that humbles himself shall be exalted." [h] This should be understood in terms of the position that each one of us will have relative to others in the spirit world. Thus, he who was first on Earth may find himself among the last; he before whom we bow our heads in this life may later rank below the humblest laborer among us, for when he quits his earthly life, he leaves all his grandeur behind as well, and the most powerful monarch might find himself below his lowest-ranking soldier.

XII. On the identity of spirits

A fact demonstrated by observation and confirmed by the Spirits themselves is that spirits of inferior degree often present themselves using well-known and respected names. Therefore, how can we be certain that those who say they have been, for example, Socrates, Julius Caesar, Charlemagne, Fénelon [i], Napoleon, Washington, and so on, really once were those individuals? This doubt exists even among some enthusiastic followers of Spiritism; who accept the intervention and manifestation of spirits but ask what certainty we may have over their identity. Such certainty can indeed be very difficult to obtain, but although identities cannot be established as positively as by means of a birth certificate, they may nonetheless at least be inferred from certain evidence.

When the spirits of those we have personally known—such as relatives or friends, especially if they have only recently passed away—present themselves, their language is usually in perfect accord with the characteristic traits known to us, something which in itself is an evidence of identity. But any lingering doubts cannot remain when such spirits speak of private affairs or recall family matters known only to the interviewer. A son could hardly be mistaken about the language of his father or mother, nor parents about that of their child. Sometimes, during such intimate evocations, the most fascinating incidents occur, able to convince even the most incredulous person. Hardened skeptics are often disconcerted by the unexpected revelations that are made to them.

Another rather characteristic feature of this type of communication is often enough to verify a spirit's identity. As we have stated, a medium's handwriting generally changes according to the spirit who is evoked, being reproduced exactly the same way each time the same spirit communicates. It has been demonstrated many times, especially in cases involving people who have recently deceased, that the handwriting displays striking similarities to that of the person during life; we have in fact seen perfectly identical signatures. We are far from suggesting that this is commonly the case, and certainly do not claim that it always happens. We simply mention the fact as an occurrence worthy of note.

Only those spirits who have reached a certain degree of development are completely free from all corporeal influences. As long as they are not yet completely dematerialized (this is the expression they use), they keep most of the ideas, leanings, and even *eccentricities* they had on Earth, and this is another means of recognition. Above all, however, identity can be established through a multitude of details that only attentive and continuous observation can reveal. We have seen writers discussing their own works or doctrines, approving or condemning certain parts of them. Others remember unknown or little-known circumstances concerning their life or death—in a word, things which constitute moral evidence of identity, the only type we can count on when dealing with such abstract matters.

Thus, if the identity of an evoked spirit may be established to a certain extent in some cases, then there is no reason why it cannot be established in others. And even if we do not have the same means of identification in the case of people who died a very long time ago, we can always analyze their language and character, for assuredly, the spirit of a good man will never communicate like the spirit of an evil or immoral one. As for spirits who falsely take on respectable names, they soon betray themselves by their language and ideas. For instance, a spirit claiming to be Fénelon, but who offends common sense and good morals, even if only by accident, would thereby expose his ploy. But if the thoughts expressed are always noble, without contradiction, and consistently display a character worthy of Fénelon's standing, there would be no reason to doubt the spirit's identity. Otherwise, one would have to believe that a spirit who preaches nothing but the good could at the same time deliberately resort to falsehoods, and that without any practical purpose.

Experience has taught us that spirits of the same degree and character, and who are driven by similar feelings, are united into groups and families. With that in mind, the number of spirits is incalculable, and we are far from knowing them all. The vast majority are, in fact, nameless to us.

A spirit of the same rank as Fénelon may therefore come in his name or may even be sent by him as a representative, presenting himself under Fénelon's name because he is his equal and may stand in for him, and because we need a name as a reference in order to absorb the instructions.

But in the end, what does it really matter in this case if the spirit is indeed Fénelon himself? As the spirit only says good things in a way in which Fénelon himself would have spoken, it is a good spirit. The name used does not matter and is frequently no more than a tool to help us register the teachings. But that would not apply to intimate evocations, because, as we have said, in such cases an identity can be established by means of evidence that is, so to speak, unmistakable.

There is no doubt that the use of representatives may create misunderstandings and result in mistakes, or even deceit. Such is one of the difficulties of *practical Spiritism*. Nevertheless, we have never said that this science is easy, or that it may be learned haphazardly, any more than any other science. We cannot repeat too often that Spiritism demands assiduous and often lengthy study. Since we cannot produce these phenomena at will, we must wait for them to happen on their own. Frequently they are triggered by the least-expected circumstances. For the attentive and patient observer, facts are plentiful, as one can discover thousands of distinct nuances that are like rays of light. The same applies to established sciences: while the superficial observer sees in a flower only an elegant form, the scientist sees in it a treasure trove of knowledge.

XIII. Alleged inconsistencies

The foregoing observations prompt us to say a few words on another difficulty, the one which stems from the inconsistency in the language of spirits.

As spirits are very different from one another in knowledge and morality, it is unsurprising that contradictory answers may be given to one same question, according to the advancement of the spirit who responds, much like if we were to pose that question consecutively to a scientist, to a simpleton, and to a prankster. The essential point, as we have said, is to know to whom we address our question.

"But," one may ask, "how is it possible that even spirits from higher orders do not always agree with one another?" May we say first that, aside from the factors we have just pointed out, there are others that may have a certain influence on the nature of the responses, independent of the spirit's advancement. This is a crucial point that an in-depth study clarifies, only to reinforce our recommendation for constant, careful observation, in addition to—as with every other science—method and perseverance.

Years are required to train even a mediocre physician, and almost an entire lifetime for someone to become truly learned, yet some people fancy that a few hours will be enough to acquire the science of the infinite! Let there be no mistake in that regard: the study of Spiritism is vast, involving every issue of metaphysics and the social order, representing a whole new world that opens up before us. Why is it so surprising that a great deal of time is required to understand it?

In addition, such contradictions are not always as real as they may at first seem. Do we not constantly see scientists who research the same field diverge in their definitions of a given topic, using different terminology or considering the subject from different viewpoints, although the underlying subject is one and the same? Try to count how many definitions can be given to the concept of grammar! We must add that the form of an answer often depends on the form of the question. It would be silly to see a contradiction where there is more often than not only a difference of words. Superior spirits do not concern themselves with form at all. For them, the underlying idea is all that matters.

Let us take a look at the definition of *soul*, for example. Since this word does not have a unique definition, Spirits may use it with different implied meanings, just like we do. One may say that it is the principle of life, another may call it the animistic spark, a third may say it is internal while a fourth may say it is external, and so on. And all will be correct according to their own point of view. We might even be led to believe that some among them profess materialistic theories, yet such is not the case.

The same applies with respect to the word *God*, which the spirits could variously define as "the principle of all things," "the Creator of the universe," "the Supreme Intelligence," "the Infinite," "the Great Spirit," and so on, but ultimately, God is always God.

We should mention the classification of spirits as another last example. They form a continuous chain from the lowest to the highest degree; categorizing them is thus arbitrary. One spirit might divide them into three classes—another into five, ten, or any other number—without being incorrect for saying that. All scientific fields offer similar examples, with each researcher developing a different system. Now, systems vary, but the science remains the same. Whether we study botany according to the system of Linnaeus, of Jussieu, or of Tournefort, [j] what we learn is always botany. Let us thus stop attributing to purely conventional issues more importance than they deserve, and let us devote ourselves only to what is truly relevant. Then, often, upon reflection, we shall realize that things which seemed most contradictory display a similarity that eluded us in our first analysis.

XIV. Spelling issues

We would only quickly glance over the objection raised by certain skeptics as to the issue of spelling errors made by some spirits, were it not for the fact that it provides us with an essential insight. One must agree that the spirits' spelling is not always perfect, but only a lack of arguments could make it the object of serious criticism by claiming that, if spirits know everything, they should know how to spell. We could point out the numerous mistakes of this kind that are made by famous scholars, mistakes which in no way diminish their merit—but this fact involves a more serious issue.

For spirits, and especially for more advanced ones, the idea is everything—the form is nothing. Since they are free from matter, their communication is as fast as thought, because thought itself is communicated without intermediary means. Thus, they must find it very uncomfortable being forced, when communicating with us, to use the tedious and cumbersome structures of human language, particularly with its imperfections and insufficiency to articulate all their ideas—they themselves have alluded to this fact.

It is also interesting to observe the means they use to diminish such an inconvenience. It would be the same with us if we had to express ourselves in a language composed of longer words and more convoluted sentence structures, or poorer in vocabulary than our native tongue. It is the type of exasperation that a man of genius experiences when he grows impatient with the slowness of his quill, always much behind his train of thought.

One can therefore understand why spirits give little importance to spelling issues, especially when dealing with a deep and serious subject. Moreover, is the fact that they are able to express themselves with equal ease in all languages (and understand all languages) not awe-inspiring? But we must not conclude from this that they are unfamiliar with linguistic rigor, as they observe it whenever they consider it necessary. Such is the case, for instance, with the poetry they dictate, which almost always defies the criticism of the most demanding perfectionist—and that *in spite of ignorance of literary matters on the part of the medium.*

XV. Mental illness and its causes

Next, there are those who see danger everywhere and in everything they are unfamiliar with. For this reason, there are many who have drawn unfavorable conclusions about Spiritism from the fact that some people have lost their reason after devoting themselves to its study. But how could reasonable people see in this a serious objection? Does the same not apply to any intellectual pursuit when undertaken by a weak-minded individual?

How many mentally challenged people exist as a result of the study of mathematics, medicine, music, philosophy, and so on? Should we therefore ban those disciplines? What does that prove, after all? Through physical labor one can harm one's arms and legs, the instruments of physical action; through mental work one can harm the brain, which is the instrument of thought. However, even if the instrument is broken, the spirit is not, as it remains intact. And once freed from matter, it will regain the use of its faculties in their entirety. In a way, such an individual can be seen as a martyr to work.

Any intense intellectual pursuit may result in mental illness: the sciences, the arts and even religion all have produced it. Insanity has as its primary cause an organic predisposition of the brain, making it more or less vulnerable to certain influences. If a predisposition to mental disorders exists, it shows up in a person's main concern, turning that into a fixation. The fixation may be about spirits—for those who study them—or it may just as easily involve God, angels, the Devil, riches, power, a specific art or science, motherhood, or a political or social system. If a man is fixated on religion, he would probably have a fixation on Spiritism if that had been his main interest instead, just as a mentally ill Spiritist would express his handicap under other forms if circumstances were different.

We therefore claim that Spiritism is not especially privileged in this respect. However, we shall go further still, and state that Spiritism, when rightly understood, is a safeguard against mental illness.

Among the most usual causes of mental overexcitement are traumas (such as disappointments, misfortunes, and broken hearts), which are also the most frequent causes of suicide. But true Spiritists see things of this world from such a higher vantage point that those tribulations seem tiny and petty in light of the future that awaits them, and life seems so short and fleeting that its troubles are nothing more than unpleasant incidents along a journey. That which in other people would stir violent emotions affects them but slightly, for they know that life's afflictions are trials that pave the way for their advancement—if they undergo them without lamentation—and that they will be rewarded according to the fortitude with which they have endured such trials.

Their convictions give them a fortitude that shields them from despair, a common cause of mental disorders and suicide. Furthermore, through spirit communication, Spiritists know the terrible fate of those who intentionally shorten their days, and this image is sufficient to give them pause. For this reason, the number of those who have been rescued from the edge of the precipice of suicide is significant: this is one of the results of Spiritism. The incredulous may laugh at it all they want; we only wish them the consolations that Spiritism affords to all who have taken the time to probe its intricate workings.

Fear must also be included among the causes of insanity. Fear of the Devil has indeed deranged countless minds. How can we know how many victims have been made by impressing their frail imaginings with a picture made ever more terrifying with details of all sorts? Some will say that the idea of the Devil can only scare little children, that it is a way to rein them in. Yes, just as the boogeyman and werewolves also serve that purpose; but once children no longer fear the Devil, they are much worse than before. And to such dubious success one must add the cases of epilepsy or other mental conditions triggered by the trauma inflicted on such delicate minds.

Religion would be quite vulnerable if fear had to be one of the pillars of its strength. Fortunately, such is not the case, as other means exist to persuade souls, and Spiritism makes more effective and accurate tools available, if religion knew how to put them to use. Spiritism discloses the reality of things, neutralizing the terrible effects of overblown fear.

XVI. The animal magnetism and reflective theories

There remain two objections to be considered, the only ones really deserving of the name, because they are based on reasoned-out theories. Both accept the reality of all the material and intelligent phenomena, but dispute the intervention of spirits.

According to the first theory, all the manifestations attributed to spirits are merely effects of animal magnetism. [k] Mediums would then be in a state known as waking somnambulism, a phenomenon witnessed by anyone who has studied magnetism. In this state, the intellectual faculties expand to an exceptional degree, and the reach of the medium's intuitive perception is extended beyond the limits of what is typical. At that point, the argument goes, mediums would be able to find in themselves, and with their own lucidity, all they say and all the ideas they transmit, even on matters that are completely foreign to them in their normal state.

We will not contest the power of somnambulism, as we have witnessed its wonders and have studied all its aspects for over thirty-five years. We admit that many spirit manifestations may indeed be explained by it. However, sustained and careful observation has shown us a great number of occurrences in which any intervention on the part of the medium, other than as a passive instrument, is materially impossible. To those who share this opinion we will say, as to all others: "Watch and observe, for you have certainly not seen everything yet."

We then shall contrast two considerations that arise from their own hypothesis. Where did the Spiritist theory come from? Is it a theory imagined by a few men in order to explain the facts? Not at all. But then who revealed it? The very mediums whose lucidity these critics extol. However, if this lucidity is as great as they claim it to be, why would these mediums have attributed to spirits what came from themselves? How could they have given such precise, logical, and sublime information regarding the nature of extra-human intelligences?

One of two things is happening here: either they are lucid or they are not. If they are, and if we can rely on their testimony, then it would be contradictory to claim that they do not speak the truth. Second, if all the phenomena derive from mediums themselves, they should always be identical in the case of each individual, and we would not observe the same person adopting disparate styles, or alternately expressing contradictory opinions. This lack of uniformity in the manifestations obtained by the same medium proves the diversity of their sources, and since we cannot find all these sources in the medium, it must be sought elsewhere.

According to a different interpretation, the medium really is the source of the manifestations, but instead of deriving their content from within, the medium draws it from the environment. The medium would be a type of mirror, reflecting all the ideas, thoughts, and knowledge from those in the vicinity, and as a result, the medium would not say anything not known at least to some of them.

We cannot deny, as it is indeed one of the tenets of the Doctrine, the influence exerted by participants on the nature of manifestations. But this influence is much different from what it is claimed to be in this case, and very far from indicating that the medium merely echoes the thoughts of people around them, for the reason that thousands of occurrences have positively established just the opposite. Therefore, this theory contains a serious error, which once again proves the danger of drawing premature conclusions.

Those who subscribe to this theory cannot deny the existence of a phenomenon that ordinary science is unable to explain, but because they are not willing to accept the intervention of spirits, they explain it in their own way. Their theory would seem plausible if it could explain all the facts, but that is not so. Yet, when it becomes abundantly clear that some of the communications obtained through the medium are completely foreign to the thoughts, knowledge, and even the opinions of anyone present, and are also often spontaneous and contradict all preconceived ideas, these critics are not discouraged by so slight an obstacle. They reply that the radiation of thought goes far beyond the immediate circle surrounding us, and that mediums are a reflection of all mankind. Thus, if they cannot draw their inspiration from their immediate vicinity, mediums surely search for it outside, be it in the city, in the countryside, in the entire world, or even on other spheres.

We do not find in this theory a simpler and more plausible explanation than the one provided by Spiritism, because it supposes a much more marvelous cause. The notion that universal space is full of beings who are in permanent contact with us and who communicate their thoughts to us is no more shocking to our reason than the supposition of a widespread radiation of thought coming from every point of the universe and converging on the brain of one single individual.

Again—and this is a crucial issue we cannot stress enough—the somnambulism theory described above and this one that we may call the *reflective theory*, are conjectures formulated by a number of people to explain a phenomenon, while the Doctrine of the Spirits is not a human conception. It was revealed by the manifesting intelligences themselves when no one had even dreamed about it, and when the general opinion in fact opposed it. Therefore, we must ask, first, where did mediums procure a doctrine that did not exist in the thoughts of anyone on Earth? Secondly, is it not a rather strange coincidence that thousands of mediums all over the planet—mediums unknown to one another—all agreed to say the same thing? If the first medium who appeared in France was influenced by opinions already endorsed in America, by what odd ways did this medium seek ideas many thousands of miles across the ocean and among a people of foreign habits and language, instead of drawing them from the medium's immediate vicinity?

There is another circumstance that has not been sufficiently considered, however. The first manifestations in both France and America did not take place in the form of written or verbal communication, but in the form of raps that corresponded to letters of the alphabet, thus forming words and sentences. This was how the manifesting intelligences declared themselves to be spirits. So, even assuming the intervention of the medium's own thought in verbal or written communications, the same cannot apply to raps, as their meaning could not have been known beforehand.

We might cite as evidence a number of facts that demonstrate, in the intelligences that manifest, the presence of an evident individuality and an absolutely independent will. We therefore urge those who dispute this to observe more carefully, and if they are to ponder without prejudice, and not draw any conclusions before having seen it all, they will recognize that their theory is unable to account for all the facts.

We shall limit ourselves to posing the following questions: Why does the manifesting intelligence, whatever it may be, refuse to answer certain questions on subjects that are perfectly well-known to the mediums or others in the room—for example, the name and age of the interviewers, what they have in their hands, what they did the day before, their plans for the following day, and so on? If the medium is the mirror that reflects the thoughts of those present, nothing should be easier to answer.

Our adversaries rebut this argument by asking in turn why the spirits, who should know everything, cannot answer such simple questions, since, as the dictum goes, whoever can do more can do less. From which they conclude that the intelligences are not spirits. Now, what would happen if a foolish or ignorant person appeared before a group of scientists and asked, for example, why is it daytime at noon? Would the scientists bother to answer such a question seriously, and would it be logical to conclude from the silence or disdain directed at the interviewer that the scientists are all fools?

It is precisely because such spirits are of a higher order that they are not willing to respond to idle or silly questions, and much less to be treated like a defendant summoned to an arraignment hearing. That is why they remain silent or state that they will only concern themselves with judicious questions.

Finally, we ask why spirits often come and go at any given moment, and why, once they are gone, no prayer or pleading is able to bring them back? If the medium only acts under the mental influence of those present, it would seem evident that in such circumstances the contribution of all their combined wills should be able to stimulate the medium's clairvoyance.

Therefore, if a medium cannot comply with the directive of the other participants, which are aligned with the intention of the medium himself, it is because the latter is subject to an influence which is foreign to both the medium and those around him, thereby demonstrating its independence and individuality.

XVII. Filling the cosmic void

Skepticism about Spiritism, when not the result of a self-serving systematic opposition, almost always originates from an incomplete knowledge of the facts, something which does not seem to prevent certain people from adjudicating on the issue as though they understood it perfectly. One can be highly clever, highly learned, and yet lack common sense; and one of the first signs of poor judgment is to believe one's own to be infallible. Many people, too, see in spirit manifestations only an object of curiosity. We hope that reading this book will help them find in such wondrous phenomena something more than a mere pastime.

The Spiritist science consists of two aspects: one is the experimental aspect which deals with manifestations in general, while the philosophical aspect deals with intelligent manifestations. Whoever has only observed the first aspect is like someone whose only knowledge of physics comes from recreational experiments, never penetrating the depths of that science. The true Spiritist Doctrine rests on the teachings transmitted by the Spirits, and the knowledge those teachings entail is far too serious to be acquired in any way other than through a detailed and continuous study—a study carried out in silence and recollection, because only under such conditions can one observe a great number of facts and details that normally go unnoticed by the superficial observer, but that constitute the basis of an informed opinion.

It would be enough if this book had no other result than showing the serious aspect of the subject and stimulating its investigation. And we would be glad to have been chosen to carry out a work in which we ourselves claim no personal merit, as its underlying principles are not our own creation: the merit goes entirely to the Spirits who have dictated such principles. We hope that this work may also produce the additional result of guiding those desirous of learning by showing them, in their studies, the grand and sublime goal of individual and social progress, and by pointing out to them the road to follow for its achievement.

Let us wind up these introductory remarks with a final consideration. When probing the depths of outer space, astronomers discovered, in the distribution of celestial bodies, unexpected gaps at variance with the laws governing the ensemble of the Solar System. They therefore speculated that such vacant spots were occupied by bodies that had escaped their observation. In addition, they observed certain disturbances of unknown origin, and they said to themselves: "There must be a world there because such a gap should not exist and because such disturbances must have a cause." Then, by inferring the cause from the effects, they were able to calculate the orbital position of a new planet, a prediction later confirmed by actual observations. [1]

Let us apply this same reasoning to another order of ideas. If we observe the series of living beings, we will realize that they form a continuous chain, from crude matter up to the most intelligent man. But between men and God—the alpha and omega of all things—what an immense gap! Is it reasonable to suppose that the links of this chain stop with man, who would then be able to bridge, without interruption, the gap that separates him from the Infinite?

Reason tells us that there must be intermediate steps between man and God, just as it showed astronomers that between known planets there should be a yet undiscovered one. Which philosophy has filled this immense gap? Spiritism shows that it is occupied by the beings of all ranks in the invisible world, and that these beings are none other than the spirits of men who have reached the successive degrees that lead up to perfection.

Therefore, everything is linked together, forming a chain from the alpha to the omega. Let him who denies the existence of spirits then attempt to fill the gap they occupy; and let him who scoffs at them scoff thereby at the work of God and His almighty power!

Allan Kardec

■■■

[a] In the original French text, Kardec had not included titles for the sections of the Introduction (which had simply been numbered with Roman numerals). J. Herculano Pires, in his Portuguese translation, was the first to devise a title for each section, a practice which was followed by other translators as well (see the editorial observations in Appendix 1). Given the fact that the Introduction is somewhat long, encompassing many different topics in its seventeen sections, we believe that the section titles constitute a useful paratext that helps readers navigate through this part more easily. This is all the more true considering that Kardec, in this Introduction, answers most of the objections normally raised by critics in what still is a remarkably valid and up-to-date argumentation, in spite of the more than one hundred sixty years that have passed since the text was written. We adopt this practice and include an adapted translation of Herculano Pires's section titles here. —Trans.

[b] Luigi Galvani (1737–1798) was an Italian scientist who discovered the phenomenon he called *animal electricity* while dissecting a frog. His assistant touched the frog's exposed sciatic nerve with a metal scalpel that had picked up an electrical charge from a nearby Leyden jar, causing the frog's leg to flex as though it were still alive. This discovery led to the invention of the first electrical batteries and the development of a whole new branch of physics. Kardec refers to it as the *dance of the frogs*, implying that a phenomenon worthy of serious study may be considered a trifling matter when not investigated with the required commitment and seriousness. —Trans.

[c] "E pur si muove" (and yet, it moves) is a phrase attributed to the Italian physicist and mathematician Galileo Galilei (1564–1642). Accused of heresy by the Church, he was forced to recant his claim that it is the Earth that circles the Sun, rather than the other way around. This expression is normally used as a pithy form of argumentation implying that, despite someone's beliefs, facts show that the opposite is true. Kardec uses it here as a play on words, as in this case the expression can also be interpreted in its literal sense, in that tables do move during certain spirit manifestations. —Trans.

[d] A small triangular device supported by two casters and a pencil, used to write on a surface when moved by the fingertips of two or more people. —Trans.

[e] In *The Mediums' Book*, Kardec called this process *psychography*, which can be *direct*, when a medium holds a pen directly, or *indirect*, when a basket or other intermediary tool is used. —Trans.

[f] The expression *the Spirits* (with a capital S) refers to the superior spirits involved in the development of the Spiritist Doctrine. —Trans.

[g] In Greek mythology, Proteus is an early sea-god capable of telling the future and changing shapes. —Trans.

[h] Matthew 23:12. —Trans.

[i] François Fénelon, French theologian and writer, 1651–1715. —Trans.

[j] See question #100 and the respective translator's note. —Trans.

[k] The use of the word *magnetism* here refers to the concept of *animal magnetism*, also known as *mesmerism*, a theory advanced by the German doctor Franz Mesmer (1734–1815). His theory was that all living creatures produce the so-called *animal magnetism* (*lebensmagnetismus*, literally, *magnetism of the living*), an invisible natural force that could produce physical effects, induce trances, and even promote healing. *Hypnotism*, in fact, is a designation coined by the Scottish surgeon James Braid after studying the phenomenon of animal magnetism. Those who are

able to induce a magnetic trance are called *magnetizers*. The word *magnetism* continues to be used in this particular sense within the Spiritist community and elsewhere, especially in spiritual healing practices, being closely associated with the Eastern concepts of *prana* and *qi*. See Gilson Roberto, MD, "Magnetic healing, prayer, and energy passes," in Emma Bragdon, PhD, Editor, *Spiritism and Mental Health* (Philadelphia: Singing Dragon, 2012). The use of the word *magnetism* in this context should therefore not be confused with the altogether different concept of (*electro*)*magnetism* in the physical sciences. —Trans.

[l] This is a reference to the planet Neptune, discovered in 1846 by John Galle in the orbital position predicted by Urbain Le Verrier, who, in turn, had inferred the presence of a new planet from the gravitational perturbations observed in the orbit of Uranus. —Trans.

Preface

Phenomena that escape the laws of ordinary science are occurring everywhere, revealing as their cause the action of a free and intelligent will.

Reason dictates that an intelligent effect must have as its cause an intelligent agent, and facts have shown that this agent can communicate with men through physical means.

When questioned about its nature, this agent has declared itself to belong to the world of spirit beings who have shed their human corporeal envelope. This is how the doctrine of the Spirits was revealed.

The communication between the spirit world and the corporeal world is in the nature of things, and there is nothing supernatural about it. That is why signs of it can be found among all peoples and throughout the ages. Nowadays it has become widespread and evident to the whole world.

The Spirits announce that the time appointed by Providence for a universal manifestation has now come, and that, as ministers of God and instruments of His divine will, their mission is to instruct and enlighten mankind, ushering in a new era for the regeneration of humanity.

This book is a compilation of their teachings. It has been written at the order and from the dictation of superior spirits, so as to establish the foundations of a rational philosophy free from the prejudices of sectarianism and preconceived ideas. It does not contain anything that is not the expression of their thought or that has not undergone their scrutiny. The ordering and methodical arrangement of the contents, as well as comments and the form of certain parts of the text, are the only contributions from the one who received the mission of publishing it.

Among the Spirits who have contributed to the completion of this work, there are many who have lived at different times on Earth, preaching and practicing virtue and wisdom. Others do not bear names of characters whose records have been kept by history, but their elevated spiritual standing is attested to by the purity of their doctrine and their union with those who bear venerated names.

The following are the words they wrote with the assistance of several mediums, when the mission of preparing this book was assigned to us:

"Be zealous and persevering in the work you have undertaken with our assistance, for this work is ours. In it we have laid the foundations of the new rising edifice destined someday to unite all mankind in one common sentiment of love and charity. However, before publishing it, we shall review it together, so as to assure its accuracy.

"We shall be with you whenever you request, as well as to assist you in the rest of your efforts, for this is only one part of the mission which has been entrusted to you, as it has already been revealed by one of us.

"Among the teachings given to you, there are some that must be kept solely to yourself until further notice; we will tell you when the time has come to publish them. Meanwhile, meditate on them, so as to be ready when we notify you.

"Place at the beginning of the book the vine branch that we have drawn[1] because it is the emblem of the work of the Creator. All the material principles that best represent the body and the spirit are brought together in it: the body is the stem; spirit is the juice; the soul or spirit connected to the body is the fruit. Man distils his spirit through labor, and you know that it is only through the toil of an earthly life that the spirit acquires knowledge.

"Do not allow yourself to be discouraged by criticism. You will face relentless opponents, especially among those who profit from

---

[1] The vine branch at the beginning of the Preface is a facsimile of the one drawn by the Spirits. —Auth.

exploitation. You will find them even among spirits, because those who are not completely disengaged from the pull of matter often seek to sow the seeds of doubt out of malice or ignorance. Carry on, nonetheless. Believe in God and boldly forge ahead: we shall be there to support you. The time is close at hand when the truth will shine forth all around.

"The vanity of those men who believe they know everything and are able to explain everything in their own way will give rise to dissenting opinions. However, all who have the grand principle of Jesus in mind will gather around the same sentiment of love of the good and will be united by a fraternal bond that will embrace the entire world. Putting aside the senseless disputes of words, they shall concern themselves solely with essential matters, and the doctrine will always be the same in substance for all who receive communications from superior spirits.

"By persevering, you shall reap the fruit of your efforts. The contentment you will feel in seeing the dissemination of the doctrine and its correct comprehension will be a reward, the full value of which you shall perhaps witness more in the future than in the present. Do not be troubled because of the thorns and rocks that the skeptic or the spiteful will cast in your path. Hold onto your confidence: through it you shall reach your goal, and you shall always be deserving of our help.

"Remember that good spirits only aid those who serve God with humility and disinterestedness. They reject anyone who uses heavenly gifts as a stepping-stone to earthly possessions; they eschew the proud and greedy. Pride and greed will always be barriers between man and God, as they make man blind to the celestial splendors, and God cannot employ the blind to expound on light." (Saint John the Evangelist, Saint Augustine, Saint Vincent de Paul, Saint Louis, The Spirit of Truth, Socrates, Plato, Fénelon, Franklin, Swedenborg, et al.)

Allan Kardec
[Paris, 1857]

■■■

Note: The principles contained in this book result either from the replies given by the Spirits directly to questions posed to them at various times and through a great number of mediums, or from the teachings they spontaneously gave to us and to other persons concerning the matter at hand. The entire work has been organized so as to present a regular and methodical whole and was submitted for publication only after it was carefully reviewed and corrected by the Spirits themselves. This second edition has been the object of a new and detailed examination on their part as well. The text between quotation marks following each question [in the body of the book] is the literal answer given by the Spirits. The text written in either a different type or in a different paragraph formatting represents comments added by the author that were equally subject to the Spirits' examination. —Auth.

Part 1:
First Causes

Chapter 1:
God

1. God and the infinite

1.   What is God?

"God is the supreme intelligence, the first cause of all things."[1] [a]

2.   What is to be understood by the infinite? [b]

"That which has neither beginning nor end: the unknown. All which is unknown is infinite."

3.   Could we say that God is the infinite?

"That would be an incomplete definition. The deficiency of human language makes it insufficient to define that which is above human intelligence."

God is infinite in His perfections, but the infinite itself is an abstraction. To say that God is the *infinite* is to mistake the attribute for the thing itself, and to define one thing that is not known in terms of another thing that is not known either.

2. Proofs of the existence of God

4.   Where may we find proof of the existence of God?

---

[1] The text within quotation marks after each question is the actual answer provided by the Spirits. Comments and explanations added by the author were printed in smaller type, whenever they might be confused with the text of the answer. When the author's comments comprise an entire chapter or section, however, no confusion is possible, so normal type is used in these cases. —Auth.

"In an axiom you apply in your sciences: 'There is no effect without a cause.' Look for the cause of all that which is not the work of man, and your reason will answer you."

To believe in God, it is enough to cast our eyes on the works of creation. The universe exists; therefore, it must have a cause. To doubt God's existence would be to deny that every effect has a cause and to claim that something could have come from nothing.

5.   What can we infer from the intuitive feeling that all men have within themselves of God's existence?

"That God exists; otherwise, where would such a feeling come from, if it were not based on something real? This still is a consequence of the principle that there is no effect without a cause."

6.   Couldn't the intuition about the existence of God that we have within ourselves be the consequence of education, the product of acquired ideas?

"If that were the case, why would your primitive men have this intuition?"

If the sentiment of the existence of a supreme being were only the product of education, it would not be universal. Like the knowledge of science, it would only exist among those who received such education.

7.   Could we find the first cause of the formation of things in the intrinsic properties of matter?

"But, then, what would be the cause of those properties? There must always be a first cause."

To attribute the first formation of things to the intrinsic properties of matter would be to mistake the effect for the cause, since such properties are themselves an effect that must have a prior cause.

8.   What about the opinion of those who ascribe the initial formation of all things to an accidental combination of matter, in other words, to chance?

"Another absurdity! What reasonable man would consider chance to be an intelligent agent? Besides, what is chance? Nothing."

The harmony that governs the workings of the universe reveals certain determined combinations and designs, and thus an intelligent power. To ascribe the first formation of things to chance would be nonsense, because chance is blind and cannot produce intelligent effects. If chance were intelligent, it would no longer be chance.

9.   Where may we see in the first cause an intelligence which is absolute and superior to all other intelligences?

"You have a proverb that says, 'The workman is known by his work.' Well then, look at the work and search for the workman! Pride is what engenders incredulity. A conceited man cannot imagine anything above himself, believing himself to be an independent freethinker. Poor creature, who could be brought down by a mere breath from God!"

We judge the power of an intelligence by its works. Since no human being could create that which is the product of nature, the first cause must be an intelligence superior to mankind.

Whatever may be the prodigies accomplished by human intelligence, such intelligence itself must have a cause, and the greater its accomplishments, the greater the first cause must be. That intelligence is the first cause of all things, however one may call it.

3. Attributes of the Divinity

10.   Can man comprehend God's intrinsic nature?

"No, that is an aptitude that he lacks."

11.   Will man ever be able to fathom the mystery of the Divinity?

"When his spirit is no longer clouded by matter, and, by perfecting himself, he has brought himself closer to God, then he will see and understand Him."

The inferior quality of his faculties makes it impossible for man to fathom God's intrinsic nature. When mankind is in its infancy, men often confuse God with His creatures, whose imperfections they ascribe to Him. But as man's intellect develops, he better understands the nature of things and is therefore able to have a more accurate and rational idea of God, though always incomplete.

12.   Though we cannot understand God's intrinsic nature, can we have an idea of some of the His perfections?

"Yes, of some of them. Man understands them better as he raises himself above matter; he catches glimpses of them through his thought."

13.   When we say that God is eternal, infinite, immutable, immaterial, unique, all-powerful, and supremely just and good, do we not have a complete idea of His attributes?

"Yes, from your point of view, because you believe you have summed up everything in such terms; but you must understand that there are things which transcend the intelligence of the most intelligent person, things that your language cannot articulate, as it is bound by your thoughts and sensations. Effectively, reason tells you that God must have those perfections to the greatest degree, for if any one of them were lacking, or if He did not possess them to an infinite degree, He would not be superior to all, and consequently would not be God. In order to be superior to everything else, God must not be subject to any change and must not have any imperfection conceivable by your imagination."

God is *eternal*. If God had a beginning, then either He would have sprung from nothing or He would have been created by a prior being. In this way we gradually arrive at the idea of infinity and eternity.

God is *immutable*. If He were subject to change, then the laws that govern the universe would have no stability.

God is *immaterial*. This means that God's nature differs from everything we call matter; otherwise, He would not be immutable, as He would be subject to the transformations of matter.

God is *unique*. If there were several gods, then there would be neither unity of plan nor unity of power in the organization of the universe.

God is *all-powerful* because He is unique. If He did not possess sovereign power, there would be something more powerful than Him, or at least as powerful. He would not have created all things and those which He had not created would be the work of another God.

God is *supremely just and good*. The providential wisdom of the Divine laws is revealed both in the smallest as well as in the largest things, and this wisdom prevents us from doubting either His justice or His goodness.

4. Pantheism

14. Is God a distinct being, or is He, according to the opinion of some people, the result of all the forces and all the intelligences of the universe combined?

"If the latter were the case, God would not be God, for He would be the effect and not the cause; He cannot be both at the same time.

"God exists. You cannot doubt it; that is the essential point. Believe me and do not try to go beyond that. Do not get lost in a maze from which you will not be able to exit. Doing so will not make you any better, but perhaps only a little more conceited, as you would believe you know something, when in reality you know nothing at all. Therefore, let go of all your elaborate constructs in that regard. You have enough issues that concern you much more directly, beginning with yourselves. Study your own imperfections in order to get rid of them; that will be far more useful to you than attempting to penetrate the impenetrable."

15. What should we think of the opinion that all the bodies in nature—all the beings, stars, and planets in the universe—are parts of the Divinity, and, taken as a whole, comprise the Divinity itself? Or in other words, what are we to think of the pantheistic doctrine?

"Not being able to become God himself, man wishes to be at least a part of God."

16. Those who profess this theory claim that it confirms some of God's attributes: since there are an infinite number of worlds, then God is infinite; since void, or the absolute nothingness, exists nowhere, then God is everywhere. God being everywhere, because everything is an integral part of God, He imparts an intelligent purpose to all phenomena of nature. How can we counter this argument?

"With your reason. Reflect on it carefully and you will have no difficulty in realizing how absurd it is."

Pantheism views God as a material being who, even though equipped with supreme intelligence, would simply be on a large scale what we are on a small one. Moreover, since matter undergoes transformations incessantly, then God would have no stability and would be subject to all the vicissitudes and even all the needs of mankind. God would thus lack one of the essential attributes of the Divinity: immutability.

The properties of matter cannot be attributed to God without downgrading the conception we have of Him, and no deceptive subtlety will ever be able to solve the issue of His essential nature. We do not know all that God is, but we do know what God cannot *not* be. The pantheistic thesis contradicts the most essential properties of God; it confuses the Creator with the creature, much like imagining that an ingenious machine could be part of the engineer who designed it.

God's works reveal His intelligence, just like a painting reveals the intelligence of an artist; but God's works are no more God Himself than the painting is the artist who conceived and painted it.

■■■

[a] In order to distinguish the different types of notes, we have used Arabic numerals to indicate the original notes written by the author and have marked them "Auth." Notes prepared by the translator are identified as "Trans." and are notated using lowercase Latin letters. —Trans.

[b] In here Allan Kardec is confronting the Spirits with the Cartesian *Ontological Argument* of *God as the Infinite* (René Descartes, *Meditations on First Philosophy*, Fifth Meditation), and Spinoza's idea of *God as the infinite substance* (B. Spinoza, *Ethics*, Part 1, definition 6). The latter ties back to the concept of *apeiron* (ἄπειρον), a central tenet of the cosmological theory proposed by the pre-Socratic Greek philosopher Anaximander. According to this principle, the ultimate reality, apeiron, is eternal, boundless, and infinite, continuously generating all known forms, which in turn are then destroyed and return to apeiron. —Trans.

Chapter 2:
General Elements of the Universe

1. Knowledge of the origin of things

17.   Can man know the origin of things?

"No. God does not allow everything to be revealed to man on Earth."

18.   Will man ever penetrate the mystery of things that are now hidden from him?

"The veil is lifted as he perfects himself, but in order to grasp certain things he needs faculties he does not yet possess."

19.   Cannot man penetrate some of the secrets of nature through scientific investigation?

"Science has been given to him for his advancement in all matters, but he cannot go beyond the limits set by God."

The more man is allowed to further understand those mysteries, the greater should be his admiration for the power and wisdom of the Creator. However, whether due to pride or weakness, his own intelligence often makes him a victim of illusion. He then heaps theory upon theory, only to see, without respite, how many errors he has mistaken for truths and how many truths he has dismissed as errors. These are further setbacks for his pride.

20.   In addition to scientific investigation, is man allowed to receive communications from higher spheres on that which eludes the abilities of his senses?

"Yes, if God deems it useful, He may reveal what science cannot yet discover."

It is through such communications that man can obtain, to a certain degree, knowledge about his past and his future destiny.

2. Spirit and matter

21.   Has matter existed from all eternity like God, or was it created by Him at some specific time in the past?

"Only God knows. However, one thing that your reason should tell you is that God, the utmost model of love and charity, has never been inactive. However far off in the past you might imagine the onset of His action, could you possibly conceive of God as ever having been inactive for even a single moment?"

22.   Matter is generally defined as that which has extension, that which can impress our senses, and that which is impenetrable. Are these definitions correct?

"From your own point of view, they are correct because you can only discuss that which you know. Matter, however, also exists in states that are unknown to you. For example, it may be so ethereal and subtle as to not make any impression upon your senses; and yet, it is still matter, even though you do not see it as such." [a]

—   Then what definition can you give of matter?

"Matter is the link that binds spirit; [b] it is the instrument that spirit uses and upon which it simultaneously exerts its action."

From this viewpoint, one could say that matter is the agent or intermediary that enables spirit to act while at the same time being acted upon by spirit.

23.   What is spirit?

"The intelligent principle of the universe."

—   What is the intrinsic nature of spirit?

"It is not easy to explain spirit in your language. For you, it is nothing because it is not tangible; for us, however, it is something. Realize that nothing is void, the Void does not exist."

24.   Is spirit synonymous with intelligence?

"Intelligence is one of the essential attributes of spirit, but both merge into a common principle, so that, for you, they are one and the same thing."

25. Is spirit independent of matter, or is it only a property of matter, as colors are properties of light and as sound is a property of air?

"They are distinct from each other, but the union of spirit and matter is necessary to impart intelligence to matter."

— Is this union equally necessary for the manifestation of spirit? (Here *spirit* refers to the intelligent principle, rather than to the individual entities normally designated by this word elsewhere in this book).

"It is necessary for you, because you are not designed to perceive spirit apart from matter. Your senses are not developed for that."

26. Can we conceive of spirit apart from matter, and matter apart from spirit?

"Certainly, through thought."

27. Is it correct to say, then, that there are two general elements in the universe, matter and spirit?

"Yes, and above them both is God, the creator and author of all. The three of them are the principle of all that exists, the universal trinity. However, to the material element must be added the universal fluid, which plays an intermediary role between spirit and matter strictly speaking, which is too dense for spirit to be able to act upon.

"Although from a certain point of view this fluid may be regarded as a type of material element, it distinguishes itself through special properties. If it were absolute matter, there would be no reason for spirit not to be matter as well. It is placed between spirit and matter; it is a fluid, just as matter is matter. Through innumerable combinations with matter, and under the agency of spirit, the universal fluid is capable of producing an infinite variety of things, of which you only know a small fraction. By being the agent employed by spirit, this universal, primitive, or elementary fluid is the principle without which matter would forever stay in a state of dispersion, and would never acquire the properties given to it by gravity."

—   Is this fluid what we call electricity?

"We have stated that it is capable of countless combinations. What you call electric and magnetic fluids are both modifications of the universal fluid, which is only, strictly speaking, a more refined, subtler matter that is independent of matter per se."

28.   Since spirit itself is something, wouldn't it be more exact and less subject to confusion to name these two general elements *inert matter* and *intelligent matter*?

"Words are not of much importance to us. It is up to you to formulate your expressions so as to understand one another. Your disputes almost always derive from the fact that you cannot agree on your words, and because your language lacks the terminology for things that do not impress your senses."

One evident fact impinges on all hypotheses: we see matter which is not intelligent, and we see an intelligent principle that is independent of matter. Their origin and connection are unknown to us. If they have a common origin or necessary points of contact, if intelligence exists independently on its own, or if it is only a property or effect, or even, as some claim, if it is an emanation of the Divinity—all of it is unknown to us. Matter and intelligence appear to us as distinct, and, as such, we regard them as representing the two constituent principles of the universe. Above them, however, we see an intelligence that exceeds and governs all others, distinguishing itself from them through its essential attributes: this supreme intelligence is what we call God.

3. Properties of matter

29.   Is weight an essential attribute of matter?

"Of matter as you understand it, yes, but not of matter considered as the universal fluid. The ethereal and subtle matter that forms this fluid is imponderable to you, and yet it is the very principle of your ponderable matter." [c]

Weight is a relative property. Outside the sphere of gravitational action of celestial bodies, there is no weight, just as there is no up or down.

30.   Does matter consist of one or many elements?

"One single primitive element. The elements you regard as simple are not true elements, but transformations of the one primitive matter."

31.   Where do the different properties of matter come from?

"From the modifications that the elementary particles [d] undergo as a result of their combination within certain conditions."

32.   According to that, flavors, scents, colors, sounds and the poisonous or healing properties of certain substances are only modifications of the one and the same primitive substance?

"Yes, of course; and they only exist owing to the disposition of the organs that are meant to perceive them."

This principle is confirmed by the fact that not all people perceive the qualities of substances in the same way: what one person finds pleasing to one's palate, another might find repulsive; what appears blue to one person may appear as red to another; something that is poisonous to some might be harmless or even beneficial to others.

33.   Is the same elementary matter capable of undergoing all possible modifications and acquiring all possible properties?

"Yes, and this is what should be understood when we say that 'everything is in everything.' "[1] [e]

Oxygen, hydrogen, nitrogen, carbon and all the other elements we consider to be simple, are only modifications of the one primitive substance. As it is still

---

[1] This principle explains the phenomenon known by all magnetizers, which consists of using willpower to confer very different properties upon any given substance—water, for instance—a specific flavor or even the active qualities of other substances. Since there is but one primitive element, and since the properties of different bodies are but modifications of this one element, it follows that the most innocuous substance has the same underlying principle as the most harmful substance. Thus, water is made up of one part oxygen and two parts hydrogen but becomes corrosive if the proportion of oxygen is doubled. An analogous transformation may be produced through magnetic action directed by the human will. —Auth.

impossible for us to explore this substance except by hypothesizing about it, the elements are truly elementary to us, and without major consequence, we can consider them as such until further notice.

—   This theory seems to endorse the opinion of those who do not believe in more than only two essential properties for matter—force and movement—and who believe that all the other properties are only secondary effects that vary according to the intensity of the force and direction of the movement, is that not so?

"This opinion is correct. But it should be added that those properties also vary according to the arrangement of the particles, as you verify, for example, in the case of an opaque body that may become transparent, and vice versa."

34.   Do particles have a defined form?

"Certainly, particles do have a form, but it is indiscernible to you."

—   Is this form constant or variable?

"Constant for the primitive elementary particles but variable for the secondary ones, which are only aggregations of the former. However, what you call *particle* is still very far from being the elementary particle."

4. Universal space

35.   Is universal space infinite or limited?

"Infinite. If it had boundaries, what would be beyond them? I know this is puzzling to you, yet reason itself tells you that it cannot be otherwise. The same can be said of the idea of infinity; you cannot yet understand it from your narrow vantage point."

If we suppose the existence of a limit to space, however far out our thought may imagine it, reason tells us that there must still be something beyond that limit, and step by step we arrive at the idea of infinity. Even if there were only an absolute void beyond that limit, there would still be space.

36.   Does the absolute Void exist in any part of space?

"No, the Void does not exist. What appears to you to be void is actually occupied by matter that cannot be detected by your senses or instruments." [f]

•••

[a] The Spirits' answer is rather prescient. John Dalton had advanced the idea of the atom in 1803 (to explain the law of multiple proportions), but the Atomic Theory had not been fully confirmed yet. At the time the book was published (1857) fewer than sixty elements were known, and it would not be until 1864 that Lothar Meyer arranged the elements into families according to their valence, and not until 1869 that Dmitri Mendeleev discovered the Periodic Law. Not only did the Spirits confirm the still-provisional Atomic Theory, but they went further, predicting the existence of particles smaller than the atom, something which was only verified in 1897, when J. J. Thomson confirmed the existence of the electron, a constituent particle of the atom. Latter discoveries (such as radioactivity and quantum physics) finished proving the limitations of the classical concept of matter (that is, any substance that has mass and takes up space), in accordance with the foresight of the Spirits. —Trans.

[b] Here the author refers to *spirit* as the general intelligent principle (as opposed to *matter*), not as individual souls (the latter being the usual meaning of the word elsewhere in the book). Kardec himself clarifies this point in question 25. —Trans.

[c] This question is surprisingly insightful in that it predicts the existence of massless particles, something confirmed by science only in the twentieth century. —Trans.

[d] The original French text reads "des modifications des molécules élémentaires." The word *molécule* was at the time still commonly used in the sense of *particle* or *corpuscle*. The current usual definition of "the simplest unit of a chemical compound, consisting of two or more atoms chemically bound together" was first proposed by Amedeo Avogadro in 1809, but did not come into widespread use until much later in that century. Effectively, the word *molecule* is the diminutive of the Latin noun *mole* (mass), meaning "small portion of mass," or *particle*, as translated here. This is important to highlight, as the Spirits had to use the existing vocabulary of that time in order to describe things which had yet to be discovered or fully explained by science. —Trans.

[e] The expression *everything is in everything* can be traced back to the Pre-Socratic Greek philosopher Anaxagoras of Clazomenae (ca. 500–480 BC). Noticeably, String Theory (which at this point is only a theoretical framework attempting to describe gravity as a quantum phenomenon, eventually allowing for a unified explanation of all forces that are known in nature) speculates that one-dimensional entities called

strings are the ultimate constituents of matter, or the *elementary matter* as Kardec hypothesizes. —Trans.

[f] This is yet another surprising premonitory statement verified by science later on. The discovery of electromagnetic fields and radiation rendered the concept of a completely empty space unrealistic. More puzzling still is the current realization that over 95% of the mass-energy in the universe cannot be accounted for by standard cosmological models. —Trans.

Chapter 3:
Creation

1. Formation of worlds

The universe comprises the multitude of worlds we can see and those we cannot see, all animate and inanimate beings, all the heavenly bodies that move through space, as well as the fluids that fill it.

37. Was the universe created or has it existed from all eternity, like God?

"Undoubtedly, the universe did not create itself, and if it had existed from all eternity like God, then it could not be God's work."

Reason tells us the universe cannot possibly have created itself, and, as it cannot be the work of chance, it must be the work of God.

38. How did God create the universe?

"To borrow an expression: by His will. Nothing can better depict the all-powerful will than these majestic words from the Book of Genesis: 'God said, "Let there be light," and there was light.' "

39. Can we know how worlds are formed?

"All that we may say that you can understand is that worlds are formed by the condensation of matter scattered throughout space." [a]

40. Would comets be, as currently imagined, the beginning of the aggregation of matter, and worlds in the process of formation?

"That is correct, but it would absurd to believe in their influence. I refer to the influence commonly attributed to them, for all the heavenly bodies exert a certain influence in a number of physical phenomena."

41.   Could a completely formed world disappear, and the matter that makes it up be once again scattered in space?

"Yes. God renews worlds just as He renews living beings." [b]

42.   Can we know how long it took for worlds to be formed—Earth, for instance?

"I cannot answer that, for only the Creator knows. It would be rather imprudent to pretend to know how many eons it took for them to be formed." [c]

2. Formation of living beings

43.   When did the Earth begin being populated?

"In the beginning, all was chaos; the elements were all mixed up. Little by little, each thing settled into its proper place. Living beings appropriate for the state of the planet then appeared."

44.   Where did these living beings come from in order to appear on the earth?

"The Earth already contained their prototypes, [d] which had been waiting for the favorable moment in order to develop. The organic components began to gather once the force that held them apart waned, thereby forming the source of all living beings. This remained latent and inert, like a chrysalis or seed, until the appropriate time for each species to emerge. Then, the beings of each species came together and reproduced."

45.   Where were the organic elements before the Earth's formation?

"They were, as it were, in a fluidic or immaterial state in space, among the spirits or on other planets, waiting for the creation of the Earth in order to start a new existence on a new world."

Chemistry shows us that the molecules of inorganic elements unite to form crystals of consistent regularity, according to their specific type, if the required conditions are in place. However, the slightest disturbance of these conditions is enough to prevent the combination of the elements, or at least the regular arrangement that makes up the crystal. Why would the same not apply to organic elements? [e] We store seeds of plants and animals for many years, but they do not develop except when provided with the appropriate temperature and environment. We have seen grains of wheat germinate after many centuries. Thus, there is a *latent* element of vitality in these seeds that only waits for a favorable moment in order to develop. Could this everyday occurrence not have existed since the planet's origin? Does the creation of living beings out of chaos by the very forces of nature detract in any way from the glory of God? On the contrary, this view is more in accord with the notion that the divine power is exerted over infinite worlds through eternal laws. [f] It is true that this theory does not solve the problem of the origin of the life elements themselves, but God guards His secrets and has set limits to our investigations.

46. Are there still creatures that come into being spontaneously?

"Yes, but their embryonic seeds already existed in a latent state. You witness this phenomenon every day. Doesn't human and animal tissue contain the germs of a multitude of microorganisms that wait the necessary decomposition process to emerge? It is a minuscule world that slumbers and then flourishes."

47. Was the human species among the organic elements on the terrestrial globe?

"Yes, and it emerged at the appropriate time. Hence the dictum that man was made from the dust of the earth."

48. Can we know the time when man and other living beings first appeared on Earth?

"No, your calculations are entirely illusory." [g]

49. If the prototype of the human species was to be found among the organic elements of the planet, why don't humans continue to appear spontaneously, as they did when they first came into being?

"The beginning of things is one of God's secrets. We can say, however, that once men began to spread out over the Earth, they absorbed into themselves the elements needed for their formation in order to pass those elements down, according to the laws of reproduction. The same applies to all the different species of living beings."

3. Populating of the Earth: Adam

50. Did the human species begin with one single man?

"No, the man you call Adam was neither the first nor the only one to populate the Earth."

51. Can we know when Adam lived?

"More or less at the time assigned to him, around four thousand years before Christ."

The man traditionally known by the name of Adam was one of those who survived one of the great cataclysms that have disturbed the surface of the planet in different places and at different times. He became the forefather of one of races currently present on the planet. The laws of nature challenge the notion that the progress accomplished by mankind long before the time of Christ, could have taken place in only a few centuries, if man had only lived on Earth since the time assigned to Adam. Some people consider Adam—for good reason, in fact—as a myth or allegory representing the earliest ages of the world.

4. Diversity of human races

52. Where do the physical and intellectual differences that distinguish the various races on Earth come from?

"Climate, lifestyle, and habits. The same would happen with two children from the same mother that, by growing up away from each other and with different upbringings, displayed little intellectual resemblance."

53. Did the human species appear at various points of the globe?

"Yes, and during different periods, which is another cause of the diversity of human races. Later on, spreading throughout different climate zones and interbreeding with other races, mankind gave rise to yet new types. [h]

— Do such differences represent distinct species?

"Certainly not, they are all part one single family. Do the different varieties of a fruit prevent them from belonging to the same species?

54. Since the human species does not derive from a single ancestor, should human beings no longer regard one another as brothers and sisters?

"All are brothers and sisters in God, because they are all animated by the same spirit, and gravitate toward the same goal. You always tend to take matters literally."

5. Plurality of worlds

55. Are all the globes that revolve in space inhabited?

"Yes, and, contrary to his belief, man on Earth is far from being the first in intelligence, goodness, or perfection. There are, however, individuals who think so highly of themselves as to imagine that this little planet is the only one to have the privilege of being inhabited by intelligent beings. Pride and vanity! They fancy that God has created the universe for them alone."

God has populated the worlds with living beings, all contributing to the final goal of Providence. To believe that living beings are limited to the one point in the universe where we live would be to doubt the wisdom of God, who never makes anything without a purpose. He must have assigned to these worlds a more important role than simply to delight our eyes. Besides, there is nothing about the Earth's position, size, or physical structure to provide any reasonable basis for the notion that Earth alone has the privilege of being inhabited, to the exclusion of many thousands of similar worlds. [i]

56. Is the physical composition of the different globes the same?

"No, they do not resemble one another by any means."

57.   Since the physical composition of all the different worlds is not the same, does it follow that the beings that inhabit them have a different physical form?

"Certainly, just as on your world fish are adapted to live in the water and birds in the air."

58.   Are the worlds further away from the sun deprived of light and heat, since the sun would appear to them only as a distant star?

"Do you believe that there are no other sources of light and heat than the sun? You forget about electricity, which plays on some worlds a role unknown to you, and rather more important than the one it plays on Earth. Besides, we have not said that all beings are made of the same matter as you are, and with organs built like yours." [j]

> The conditions of existence of the beings who inhabit different worlds must be suitable for the environment where they must live. If we had never seen fish, we would not conceive that certain beings could live in the water. The same applies to other worlds, which undoubtedly contain elements unknown to us. Do we not see on Earth the long polar nights being lit by the electricity of the aurora borealis? Is it not possible that on other worlds the use of electricity is more widespread than on Earth, playing a more important role, with consequences we cannot fathom? These worlds may therefore contain other sources of light and heat needed by their inhabitants.

6. Considerations on the biblical account of the creation

59.   According to their degree of understanding, nations have conceived widely divergent ideas about creation. With the support of science, reason has recognized the implausibility of some of such theories. The account given by the Spirits, however, confirms the opinion long admitted by more informed individuals.

The objection that can be made to it is that it contradicts the sacred texts. Yet, a careful examination shows that this contradiction is more apparent than real, and that it results from the interpretation given to expressions that frequently have an allegorical meaning.

The issue of the first man, symbolized by Adam, as being the single ancestor of mankind, is not the only religious belief that has had to be revised. The revolution of the Earth seemed at one time so contrary to the scriptures that all sorts of persecution were carried out on that pretext, yet the Earth moves despite all the anathemas, and no one today would dispute the concept without embarrassing himself.

The Bible also says that the world was created in six days, and establishes the time of its creation at about four thousand years before the Christian era. The Earth did not exist before then; it was created out of nothing; the text is categorical. Yet, the evidence of science—inexorable science—has proven otherwise. The history of the formation of the planet is carved in indelible characters into the fossil record, and it has been proven that the six days of creation represent in fact a sequence of periods, each lasting perhaps many hundreds of thousands of years.

This does not represent a dogma, a doctrine, or an isolated opinion. It is as certain a fact as the revolutions of the Earth around the sun, a fact that theology cannot refuse to accept, and a clear proof of the error one may be led into when one takes what is often figurative speech for the literal truth. Should one conclude, therefore, that the Bible is wrong? No, but rather that men were mistaken when interpreting it.

Science has determined the order in which different living beings have appeared on the surface of the Earth by excavating its archives, and this order agrees with the one indicated in the Book of Genesis, the difference being that—instead of having sprung miraculously from the hands of God in only a few hours—the work of creation was accomplished indeed by His will, but according to the laws of natural forces over the course of many millions of years. Is God less grand or less powerful for that? Is His work less sublime for not bearing the seal of instantaneity? Of course not. One must have a very petty conception of the Divinity not to recognize His omnipotence in the eternal laws that He established to govern the universe. Far from detracting from the divine work, science reveals it in a more magnificent light, and more in harmony with the notions we have of God's power and majesty, for the very reason that it was carried out without the need to violate the laws of nature.

In line with the Mosaic account, science places mankind last in the order of the creation of living beings. But Moses puts the universal flood at one thousand six hundred fifty-four years after the creation of the planet, whereas geology shows us that this great cataclysm took place before the advent of man, given that, so far, no evidence either of his presence or of physically similar animals has been found in the primitive layers. Nothing proves this to be impossible, though. Many discoveries have, in fact, already raised doubts about this matter, so it is possible that at any moment the material confirmation of the prior existence of the human race may be established; and in that case, as happened in others, one would recognize that the biblical text represents an allegory. The question remains to determine whether or not the geological cataclysm was the same one as that of Noah. Now, the time needed for the fossil layers to be formed does not allow them to be mistaken one for the other; and so, as soon as any evidence of the existence of man prior to the great catastrophe is found, it will be proven either that Adam was not the first man, or that his creation has been lost in the mists of time. There is no arguing against facts, and this fact would have to be accepted, just like the revolution of the Earth and the geological periods of creation.

Admittedly, the existence of the human race prior to the geological flood is still hypothetical, but ever less so. Supposing that man first appeared upon the Earth four thousand years before Christ. If all of the human race, except for a single family, was annihilated one thousand six hundred fifty years later, it follows that the entire current population of the Earth dates back to the time of Noah, or 2350 BC. But when the Hebrews immigrated to Egypt in the eighteenth century before Christ, they found a densely populated and already highly civilized country. History shows equally that at that time India and many other cultures were flourishing as well; and that is not even considering the chronology of certain nations, which goes back to even more remote ages. Thus, from the twenty-fourth to the eighteenth century BC, an interval of only six hundred years, not only the progeny of a single individual would have to have populated all the vast regions known at that time—supposing that other regions were uninhabited—but also, in such a short time, the human race would have to have been able to lift itself from its original absolute ignorance to a much higher degree of intellectual development, which is against all anthropological laws.

The diversity of human races also endorses the interpretation of the biblical account as an allegory. Climate and customs certainly produce changes in physical characteristics, but only to a certain extent, and physiological study shows the existence among certain races of a number of physical differences which are greater than climate alone could produce. The mixing of races creates intermediary types; it tends to reduce—not to produce—extreme characteristics, simply generating new varieties.

Now, for races to have been mixed, there must have been distinct races in the first place; but how to explain their existence if we attribute them to one common and not-at-all distant origin? How to admit that over the course of only a few centuries a handful of Noah's descendants had been transformed to the point of producing the Ethiopian race, for example? Such a metamorphosis is no more likely than to admit one immediate common origin for wolves and sheep, for elephants and insects, or for birds and fish.

Again, nothing can resist the evidence of facts. On the other hand, all can be explained if we admit the existence of the human species prior to the time commonly assigned to its emergence by the biblical account and the diversity of progenies— and if we also admit that Adam, having lived six thousand years ago, populated an uninhabited region, and that Noah's flood was a localized natural disaster rather than a great geological cataclysm. We must also take into account the allegorical form typical of the Oriental style, a form which can be found in the sacred books of every nation. [k] For this reason, it is prudent not to flippantly dismiss as wrong those doctrines which could, like so many others in the past, prove their opponents wrong. Rather than discrediting them, marching along with science allows for the advancement of religious ideas. This is the only way not to be vulnerable to skepticism.

∎∎∎

[a] Another surprising prediction made by the Spirits, which is in line with prevailing models that describe planetary formation from the collapse of the matter of a nebula into a central star along with its surrounding planets. —Trans.

[b] Again, a piece of information later confirmed by science, as it now posits that our own solar system was formed by the collapse of matter produced by the explosion of previous generations of stars. —Trans.

[c] Science has now established that the Earth was formed about 4.6 billion years ago, along with our solar system. As the spirits mention in question #19, "Science has been given to [man] for his advancement in all matters." —Trans.

[d] The original French text reads "La terre en renfermait les germes." The subsequent question makes it clear that the Spirits are not referring to material structures, which means that the implied meaning of the word *germe* in this case is "principe, source, cause originelle, élément de développement de quelque chose," hence the decision to translate it as *prototype*, in order to avoid any confusion. —Trans.

[e] In 1952, almost a century after Kardec's hypothesis, the Miller-Urey experiment confirmed that conditions on the primitive Earth favored chemical reactions that could produce complex organic compounds from simpler inorganic precursors. —Trans.

[f] This statement is nothing short of revolutionary. At that time, Europeans by and large still believed the literal description of creation provided by Genesis. The suggestion that living beings (including humans) were created by a gradual process based on set natural laws is all the more surprising in that Darwin's *On the Origin of Species*, would only be published two years later (1859). In the first edition of *The Spirits Book* (1857) this comment appears in Kardec's note to question #20. —Trans.

[g] At the time the book came out the prevailing notion was based upon biblical accounts, which established the creation of living beings at around 4000 BC. Currently it is believed that modern *Homo sapiens* appeared in Africa about two hundred thousand years ago. —Trans.

[h] This is another instance where the information provided by the Spirits anticipates scientific confirmation by virtually a century. —Trans.

[i] This represents a revolutionary concept advanced by the Spirits that awaits a definitive confirmation, although government officials from a number of countries acknowledge the occurrence of encounters with extraterrestrial intelligences. Notice that the Spirits mention in question #234 that not all planets are necessarily inhabited by incarnate beings. —Trans.

[j] Another prescient statement, as the onset of the electricity revolution would only begin with the invention of a practical incandescent light bulb in the 1870s, leading to the widespread application of electrical power. —Trans.

[k] Again, Kardec's comments are remarkable: the claim about the existence of the human race prior to biblical times was written before Darwin's theory of evolution was published (1859), and the hypothesis of Noah's flood being a localized event was endorsed by the research of Charles Leonard Wolley in 1929. —Trans.

Chapter 4:
The Vital Principle

1. Organic and inorganic beings

Organic beings are those that have in themselves an intrinsic source of activity that produces life. They are born; grow, reproduce by themselves, and die. They are provided with special organs in order to accomplish the various vital functions that are appropriate for their needs and their survival. Organic beings include men, animals, and plants. Inorganic beings are all those that possess neither vitality nor an intrinsic ability to move, being formed solely by the agglomeration of matter, including minerals, water, air, and so on.

60. Is it the same force that unites the material elements in both organic and inorganic bodies?

"Yes, the law of attraction is the same for all of them."

61. Is there any difference between the matter of organic and inorganic bodies?

"It is always the same matter, but in organic bodies it is vitalized."

62. What is the cause of the vitalization of matter?

"Its union with the vital principle."

63. Does the vital principle reside in some particular agent or is it only a property of organized matter? In other words, is it an effect or a cause?

"It is both. Life is an effect produced by the action of this agent upon matter; this agent, without matter, however, is not life, just as matter cannot be alive without this agent. It gives life to all beings that absorb or assimilate it."

64. We have seen that spirit and matter are two constituent elements of the universe; does the vital principle represent a third one?

"It is certainly one of the elements required in the composition of the universe, but its source lies in the modulation of the one universal matter. For you it is an element, like oxygen or hydrogen, although even these two are not primitive elements, because they all derive from one same principle."

— That seems to suggest that vitality does not result from a separate primitive agent, but rather from a special property of the universal matter, due to certain modifications.

"That follows from what we have just said."

65. Does the vital principle reside in any one of the bodies known to us?

"Its source is in the universal fluid; it is what you call the magnetic fluid or the animalized electric fluid. It is the intermediary or link between spirit and matter."

66. Is the vital principle the same for all organic beings?

"Yes, but modified according to the species. It is this principle that enables all species to move and act and distinguishes them from inert matter. Because the movement of matter itself is not life. Matter is imparted with movement; it does not produce it."

67. Is vitality a permanent attribute of the vital agent, or does it only develop through the activity of the organs?

"It only develops in connection with the body. Have we not already said that without matter this agent by itself is not life? The union of the two is required to produce life."

— Could we say that vitality is in a latent state when the vital agent is not united with a body?

"Yes, precisely."

Taken as a whole, the organs represent a type of mechanism that receives its momentum, as it were, from the internal activity, or vital principle, that exists within them. The vital principle is the driving force behind all living organisms.

At the same time the vital agent imparts impulsion to the organs, the action of the organs maintains and strengthens the vital principle, more or less in the way that friction generates heat.

2. Life and death

68. What causes the death of organic beings?

"The wearing out of their organs."

— Could we compare death to the cessation of movement in a machine that has broken down?

"Yes. If the machine is incorrectly assembled, its engine breaks down; if the body falls ill, life abandons it."

69. Why does a lesion in the heart cause death more often than one in other organs?

"The heart is a life-giving machine. Nevertheless, it is not the only organ the damage of which may lead to death; it is only one of the essential parts of the body."

70. What happens to the matter and the vital principle of organic beings after death?

"The inert matter decomposes and is then recycled; the vital principle returns to the original whole."

Once an organic being dies, the elements that formed its body undergo new combinations to form new beings. These new beings, in turn, draw the principle of life and activity from the universal source; they absorb and assimilate it, only to return it to that source when they, in turn, cease to exist.

The organs are, so to speak, infused with the vital fluid, which gives all the parts of the body a stimulus that restores them when certain lesions occur, reestablishing the functions that were temporarily interrupted. However, when the elements that are essential for the functioning of the organs are destroyed or too deeply compromised, the vital fluid can no longer transmit this life-giving stimulus to them, and the being dies.

A body's organs necessarily react upon one another to a greater or lesser extent, and from the harmony of the whole results their mutual action. When some event destroys this harmony, their functions halt, just as the movement of an engine halts when its essential parts break down, and just as a clock wears out with use, or has some of its parts disconnected by accident, so that the spring is no longer able to keep it running.

An electric battery gives us an even more exact image of life and death. Such a device stores electricity in a latent state, as do all bodies in nature. However, the electric phenomenon does not manifest until the electric current is stimulated by a given cause: only then can we say that the electric circuit comes alive. When the cause of the activity ends, so does the phenomenon: the device goes back to a resting state. Organic bodies may thus be compared to batteries or electric devices in which the activity of the vital fluid produces the phenomenon of life; the cessation of this activity causes death.

The amount of vital fluid is not the same in all organic beings. It varies according to the species, and is not constant in one single individual, or among individuals of the same species. There are those who are, so to speak, saturated with this fluid, while others barely have enough of it. That is why for some people life is more active, more vigorous, and, in a way, overabundant.

The amount of vital fluid may be depleted; it may become insufficient for the preservation life if it is not renewed by the absorption of substances that contain it.

Finally, the vital fluid may be transmitted from one individual to another. Those who have it in greater quantities can give it to those who have less, and, in certain cases, revive a life on the verge of expiring.

3. Intelligence and instinct

71.   Is intelligence an attribute of the vital principle?

"No. Plants are alive but do not think—they only have organic life. Intelligence and matter are independent, as a body may be alive yet lack intelligence. But intelligence can only be expressed through material organs. The union with spirit is necessary to endow animated matter with intelligence."

Intelligence is a special faculty particular to certain classes of organic beings which endows them with thought, with the willpower to act, with the awareness of their own existence and individuality, and, additionally, with the means to interact with the external world and to provide for their own needs.

We may therefore distinguish: first, inanimate beings, formed of matter alone, without vitality or intelligence, represented by inert bodies, such as minerals, for instance; second, animate, non-thinking beings, formed of matter and endowed with vitality, but lacking intelligence; third, animate beings, formed of matter, endowed with vitality and with an intelligent principle that gives them the ability to think.

72. What is the source of intelligence?

"We have said: the universal intelligence."

— Could we say that every intelligent being draws and assimilates a portion of intelligence from the universal source, the same way that it draws and assimilates the principle of material life?

"That comparison would not be exact because intelligence is a faculty specific to each being and constitutes its intellectual individuality. Besides, as you know, there are matters that man is not allowed to penetrate; this is one of them, for now."

73. Is instinct something other than intelligence?

"Not exactly, because it is a type of intelligence. Instinct is a type of non-reasoning intelligence, through which all beings provide for their own needs."

74. Can we draw a line between instinct and intelligence? In other words, can we determine where one ends and the other begins?

"No, for they frequently overlap. However, we can clearly distinguish the actions deriving from instinct from those deriving from intelligence."

75. Is it correct to say that the instinctive faculties decrease as the intellectual faculties develop?

"No, instinct is always present, but man neglects it. Instinct can also lead us in the right direction. It guides us almost always, and sometimes more safely than our reason. It does not go astray."

— Why isn't reason always an infallible guide?

"It would be if it were not distorted by a flawed education, by pride, or by selfishness. Instinct does not reason, whereas reason allows the freedom of choice, endowing man with free will."

Instinct is a rudimentary intelligence, differing from intelligence proper in that its manifestations are almost always spontaneous, while those of intelligence are the result of a thought process and then a deliberate action.

Instinct manifests in various ways according to the species and its needs. In beings with consciousness and the perception of the external world, it is associated with intelligence—in other words, with will and freedom.

■■■

Part 2:
The Spirit World

Chapter 1:
Spirits

1. Origin and nature of spirits

76. How can we define spirits?[1]

"We can say that spirits are the intelligent beings of creation. They populate the universe beyond the material world."

77. Can we say that spirits are beings distinct from the Divinity? Or are spirits only emanations or portions of the Divinity, being called, for this reason, the children of God?

"Goodness! They certainly are God's work. Like in the case of a man who builds a machine, the machine is the man's work but it is not the man himself. You know that when man makes nice and useful things he calls them his children, his creation. Well then, it is the same with God. We are God's children because we are His creation."

78. Did spirits have a beginning or have they existed from all eternity, like God?

"If spirits had had no beginning, they would be equal to God, when in fact they are His creation and subject to His will. God has existed from all eternity—that is indisputable—but we know nothing as to when and

---

[1] The word *spirit* here is used in reference to individual immaterial beings, and no longer to the universal intelligent element. —Auth.

how He created us. You could say that we had no beginning, if by that you mean that, since God is eternal, then He must have created without respite. However, as to when and how each of us was created, I repeat, no one knows: therein lies the mystery."

79.   Since there are two general elements in the universe, the intelligent element and the material element, could we say that spirits are formed from the intelligent element, while inert bodies are formed from the material element?

"Certainly. Spirits are the individualization of the intelligent principle, just as bodies represent the individualization of the material principle. It is the time and mode of this formation that are unknown."

80.   Is the creation of spirits constant or did it only take place at the beginning of time?

"It is constant. That is to say, God has never ceased creating."

81.   Are spirits formed spontaneously or do they proceed from one another?

"God creates them as he creates all other creatures: by his will. But, again, their origin is a mystery."

82.   Is it correct to say that spirits are immaterial?

"How can we define something when we have no terms of comparison and the available language is lacking? Can one who is born blind define light? *Immaterial* is not the right word; *incorporeal* would be more exact, because you ought to understand that, since a spirit is a creation, it must be something. It is matter in quintessential form, [a] but you have nothing analogous to it; it is also so etherealized that your senses cannot perceive it."

We say that spirits are immaterial because their essence differs from everything we call matter. A nation of blind people would not have any words to represent light and its effects. Those who are born blind believe that they perceive everything through the senses of hearing, smell, taste and touch, but they cannot understand the ideas that would result from the sense they lack. Similarly, we are in a way truly blind regarding the essence of spiritual beings.

We can only define them by means of imperfect comparisons, or by an effort of our imagination.

83.   Do spirits have an end? We can understand that the principle from which they emanate is eternal, but what we are asking is whether their individuality will come to an end, and whether, after a more or less extended period of time, the element from which they are formed disintegrates, returning to the mass from which they came, as happens with material bodies. It is difficult to understand that something that had a beginning would not have an end.

"There are many things that you do not understand because your intelligence is limited, but that is not a reason to reject them. A child does not understand everything that his father understands, nor does an ignorant man understand all that a learned man grasps. We tell you that the spirits' existence has no end; that is all we may say for now."

2. Primitive normal world

84.   Do spirits encompass a separate world beyond the one we see?

"Yes—the world of spirits, or incorporeal intelligences."

85.   Which of the two is the main one in the order of things, the spirit world or the corporeal world?

"The spirit world. It preexists and outlasts everything else."

86.   Could the corporeal world cease to exist, or never have existed, without changing the essence of the spirit world?

"Yes. They are independent of each other, but their interaction is continuous because they continuously act in response to each other."

87.   Do spirits occupy a specific and circumscribed region in space?

"Spirits are everywhere. They inhabit the infinite space in infinite numbers. Unbeknownst to you, there are some who are constantly by your side, observing and influencing you. For spirits are one of the powers of nature and one of the instruments that God employs to fulfill His providential designs. But not all spirits may go everywhere, as there are regions forbidden to those who are less advanced.

3. Form and ubiquity of spirits

88.   Do spirits have a specific, limited, and constant form?

"No, not to your eyes. But to ours, yes. You might say they are like a flame, a gleam, or an ethereal spark."

—   Does this flame or spark have a color?

"To you it may range from an opaque tone to the radiance of a ruby, depending on the spirit being more or less pure."

Spirits are ordinarily represented with a flame or a star on their forehead, an allegory alluding to the essential nature of spirits. This symbol is placed at the top of the head because it represents the seat of intelligence.

89.   Does it take any time for spirits to travel across space?

"Yes, but they move as rapidly as thought."

—   Isn't thought the soul itself moving from one place to another?

"Wherever the thought is, there the soul is as well, since it is the soul that does the thinking. Thought is an attribute."

90.   When moving from one place to another, is the spirit conscious of the distance he travels and the space he crosses, or is he suddenly at the place to which he wanted to go?

"One or the other. A spirit may very well be aware of the distance he crosses if he so wishes, or the awareness of the distance may disappear entirely. It depends on his will and also on the degree to which his nature is purified."

91.   Is matter an obstacle to spirits?

"No, they can go through anything: the air, the earth, water, and even fire. All are equally accessible to them."

92.   Do spirits have the gift of ubiquity? In other words, can a single spirit divide itself up or exist at various points all at the same time?

"A spirit cannot be divided; however, each one is a center that radiates in different directions, and that is why it appears to be in many places at the same time. You see the Sun, which is only one, but which radiates nonetheless all around, sending its rays to great distances. Notwithstanding, it does not divide itself up."

— Do all spirits radiate with the same power?

"Far from it. It all depends on their degree of development."

Each spirit is an indivisible unit, but spirits can extend their thought in different directions without dividing themselves. We should understand the gift of ubiquity attributed to spirits only in this sense, like a spark which projects its light far away, being perceived from all points of the horizon. Or perhaps like a man who, without changing places or dividing himself up, can transmit commands, signals, and movements to different points.

4. The perispirit

93.   Is a spirit, properly speaking, without a covering? Or, as some insist, is a spirit surrounded by some kind of substance?

"A spirit is surrounded by a substance that might look vaporous to you, but which is still quite dense to us. Nonetheless, it is sufficiently light to be able to lift itself up into the air and travel to wherever the spirit wants to go."

As the heart is enclosed in the pericardium, the spirit itself is surrounded by an envelope, which, by comparison, may be called the *perispirit*. [b]

94.   Where does a spirit draw this semi-material envelope from?

"From each planet's particular universal fluid. That is why the perispirit is not the same on all worlds. Going from one world to another, spirits change their envelope just as you change your clothes."

— Then, when spirits from more highly evolved worlds come to ours, do they take on a denser perispirit?

"They must clothe themselves with your matter, as we have already said."

95.   Does the spirit's semi-material envelope assume a specific form, and can it become perceptible?

"Yes, a form at the discretion of the spirit, and that is how it sometimes appears to you, be it in dreams or in your waking state, and how it may assume a visible or even tangible form."

5. Different spirit orders

96.   Are all spirits equal or is there some type of hierarchy among them?

"They are of different orders, according to the degree of perfection they have reached."

97.   Are there a fixed number of orders or degrees of perfection among spirits?

"The number is unlimited, because there is no boundary line that acts as a wall between each order. Accordingly, the number of divisions may be expanded or reduced at will. However, if we consider their general characteristics, we may reduce them to three main orders.

"In the first order we may place those who have already reached perfection: the pure spirits. Those of the second order have reached the middle of the hierarchy: their main concern is the desire for the good. Those of the last degree are still at the bottom of the ladder: these are the imperfect spirits, characterized by ignorance, the desire for evil, and all the passions that hinder their advancement."

98.   Do the spirits of the second order only possess the desire for the good, or do they also have the ability to do it?

"They have the ability to do good in accord with their degree of perfection: some have scientific knowledge, while others have wisdom and kindness. All of them, however, have trials they must still endure."

99.   Are all spirits of the third order fundamentally evil?

"No, some of them do neither good nor evil. Others, however, take pleasure in evil and are delighted when they find an opportunity to do it. Still others are frivolous or foolish, more mischievous than mean, reveling in being naughty more than in being downright wicked. They enjoy promoting deceit and causing petty annoyances, at which they laugh."

6. Spirit hierarchy

100. Preliminary observations

The classification of spirits is based on their degree of advancement, the qualities they have acquired, and the imperfections from which they still have to free themselves. But this classification is by no means absolute, as no single category displays a clear-cut expression except as a group. From one degree to the next, the transition is gradual, with distinctions blending together on the boundaries, much like the colors of the rainbow, or even like the different phases of human life. Thus, we may establish a larger or smaller number of classes, according to the vantage point from which we consider the matter.

The same applies to all systems of scientific classification; those systems may be more or less complete, more or less reasonable, or more or less convenient for the intellect. Whatever they may be, however, it does not change the underlying science. The Spirits questioned about this matter may therefore have given a varying number of categories, without that representing any problem. Some people have objected to this apparent contradiction, without considering that the Spirits do not give any importance to what is a mere convention. For them, thought is everything: they leave the form to us, along with the choice of terminology, the categories—in short, the systems.

We should further add another consideration that must never be ignored, namely, that among spirits as among men, there are some who are deeply ignorant. We must therefore always be on our guard against the tendency to believe that they ought to know everything simply because they are spirits. Any categorization requires method, and in-depth analysis and knowledge of the subject. Now, in the spirit world, those with limited knowledge are, much as among men, ignorant and therefore unable to see the forest for the trees, or to formulate any type of system. They can only imperfectly know or understand any classification.

To them, all spirits who are above them belong to the first order, because they cannot distinguish their differences in knowledge, ability, and morality, just as a primitive man would be unable to make any distinction among civilized individuals.

Even those who may be capable of formulating a system can vary in the details according to their own point of view, especially when a division has nothing absolute about it. Linnaeus, Jussieu, and Tournefort [c] had each their own method, but botany did not change because of it; they invented neither plants nor their characteristics, but merely observed the existing common traits, from which they were able to establish groups or classes. That is precisely how we have proceeded: we invented neither spirits nor their characteristics; we have watched and observed, analyzing their discourse and action, then categorized them according to their similarities, taking into account the data they themselves furnished us.

Spirits generally acknowledge three main categories or large divisions. In the last category, at the bottom of the ladder, are the imperfect spirits, characterized by the predominance of matter over spirit, and propensity for evil. Those of the second category are characterized by the predominance of the spirit over matter and their desire for the good: they are the good spirits. Finally, the first category includes the pure spirits, who have reached the highest degree of perfection.

This division seems to us perfectly rational and presents well-defined characteristics, leaving us only to distinguish, through a sufficient number of subcategories, the main nuances of each group. That is what we did with the assistance of the Spirits, whose benevolent instructions have never failed us.

With the aid of the following outline, it will be easy to determine the order and degree of superiority or inferiority of the spirits with whom we may communicate, and, consequently, the degree of trust and regard they deserve. In a way, this represents the key to Spiritist science, because it alone can explain the anomalies that sometimes exist in spirit communications, by shedding light on the intellectual and moral inequalities of spirits. However, we should note that spirits may not belong exclusively to a given class. Their progress being gradual, often occurring in one area more than another, they may display characteristics of more than one category, something which is easy to assess through their language and acts.

6.1. Third order: imperfect spirits

101. General characteristics

This order is characterized by the predominance of matter over spirit and by the propensity for evil. The most common traits of spirits of this order include ignorance, pride, selfishness, and all the evil passions that result from them.

They have an intuition of God, but they do not comprehend Him.

Not all are essentially evil. In some of them there is more of frivolity, thoughtlessness, and mischief than downright wickedness. Some do neither good nor evil, but the very fact that they do no good indicates their inferiority. Others, on the contrary, do take pleasure in evil, and are pleased when they find an opportunity to do it.

With their wickedness or malice, they may associate a degree of intelligence, but regardless of their intellectual development, their ideas are little elevated, and their feelings are more or less corrupt.

Their knowledge about the spirit world is limited, and the little they do know is mixed up with the ideas and prejudices from their corporeal life. They cannot give us more than wrong and incomplete notions, but the attentive observer may frequently find in their communications, though imperfect, the confirmation of certain great truths taught by superior spirits.

Their character is revealed by their language. All spirits who betray an evil thought in their communication may be placed in the third order. Consequently, every evil thought that may be suggested to us comes from a spirit of this order.

They see the joy experienced by the good spirits, a sight that tortures them endlessly, because they experience all the anguish that envy and jealousy can engender.

They also preserve the memory and perception of the sufferings of their corporeal life, and this impression is often more painful than reality itself. They thus truly suffer, either from the harms they endured or from those they inflicted on others. And since they suffer for a long time, they believe they will suffer forever, a belief allowed by God as punishment.

We may divide these spirits into five principal classes.

102.   Tenth class: impure spirits

These are inclined to evil and make it the object of all their concerns. As spirits, they give treacherous advice, incite discord and mistrust, using all sorts of guises to better deceive. They attach themselves to those weak enough to yield to their suggestions, leading them to their ruin, pleased at being able to hinder their advancement by causing them to fail in the trials they undergo.

In their manifestations, we recognize them by their language. Trivial and coarse language, as among humans, is always indicative of moral, if not intellectual, inferiority. Their communications reveal the baseness of their leanings, and if they wish to fool us by speaking in a reasonable way, they are unable to maintain their ploy for very long, and always end up betraying their origin.

Certain cultures have transformed them into maleficent deities, while others have called them demons, wicked genies, or evil spirits.

When incarnate, they are inclined to all the vices that are engendered by vile and degrading passions: sensuality, cruelty, roguery, hypocrisy, and avarice. They do evil for the sheer pleasure of doing it, most often without motivation, and out of their hatred of the good, they almost always choose their victims from among upright people. They are scourges to mankind, no matter a person's social position, and the veneer of civilization does not safeguard them from dishonor and ignominy.

103.   Ninth class: frivolous spirits

They are ignorant, sly, thoughtless, and scornful. They meddle in everything and respond to every question with no regard for the truth. They take pleasure in causing petty annoyances and providing small joys, in creating harassments, and in maliciously leading people into error through deceit and mischief. To this class belong the spirits commonly known as sprites, goblins, gnomes, and elves. They are under the order of superior spirits, who often employ them as we employ servants.

In their communications with people, their language is often spirited and facetious, but almost always lacks depth. They seize upon human flaws and eccentricities, which they point out in scathing and sarcastic remarks. If they take on distinguished names, it is more out of mischief than wickedness.

104. Eighth class: pseudo-wise spirits

Their knowledge is very extensive, but they think they know more than they actually do. Since they have made a certain amount of progress in a number of respects, their language has a serious tone that may give a false impression regarding their abilities and enlightenment. Often this is only a reflection of the prejudices and zealotry that characterized them in their earthly life. Their language mixes a few truths with the most absurd errors, conflating presumption and pride, envy and fanaticism, traits which they have not been able to eliminate.

105. Seventh class: neutral spirits

These are neither virtuous enough to do good nor bad enough to do evil, wavering between the two and not being able to raise themselves above the ordinary human condition, through either their moral or intellectual qualities. They are attached to the things of their earthly life, craving its crude pleasures.

106. Sixth class: poltergeists and disorderly spirits

Strictly speaking, these spirits do not form a distinct class regarding their personal qualities—they may belong to any class of the third order. They frequently make their presence felt through demonstrative physical effects, such as raps, the abnormal displacement of solid objects, agitation of the air, and so on. They appear to be more attached to matter than other spirits, and are apparently the main agents of the transformation of the planet's elements, whether by acting on the atmosphere, water, fire, and solid bodies, or acting in the depths of the Earth. One can recognize that such phenomena are not due to a fortuitous physical cause when there is an intentional and intelligent quality about them. All spirits can produce these phenomena, but superior spirits usually leave the work to subordinate spirits, as these are more suited for material rather than intelligent tasks. When the former deem that manifestations of this type are appropriate, they enlist these spirits as assistants.

6.2. Second order: good spirits

107. General characteristics

The predominance of spirit over matter and the desire for the good characterize spirits of this order. Their qualities and power to do good are in proportion to the degree of advancement they have reached. Some possess knowledge, others wisdom and kindness; the more highly evolved ones combine knowledge with moral qualities. They have not yet completely shed the influence of matter, and depending on their class, they still preserve, to a greater or lesser extent, remnant traits of their corporeal existence through their language and habits, which may even display some of their eccentricities. If it were not for this, they would be pure spirits.

They comprehend God and the infinite, and they already experience the joy of the morally upright. They find happiness in doing good and preventing evil. The love that unites them is a source of ineffable bliss that cannot be marred by either envy or remorse, or any of the other evil passions that trouble imperfect spirits. They must, however, continue to undergo trials until they have reached absolute perfection.

As spirits, they instill good thoughts, turn men away from the path of evil, protect the lives of those who have proved themselves deserving, and neutralize the influence of imperfect spirits on those who do not yield to it.

When incarnate, they are good and benevolent toward their fellow creatures; they are not moved either by pride, by selfishness, or by ambition. They feel neither hatred nor bitterness, neither envy nor jealousy, and do good for its own sake.

To this order belong the spirits commonly called *good genies* or *guardian spirits*. In the ages of ignorance and superstition they were regarded as beneficent deities.

We may divide this order into four principal groups.

108. Fifth class: benevolent spirits

Their dominant quality is kindness. They take pleasure in serving and protecting men, but their knowledge is limited: their progress has occurred more in the moral than in the intellectual dimension.

109. Fourth class: learned spirits

What distinguishes them specifically is the breadth of their knowledge. They are less concerned with moral questions than scientific matters, for which they have a greater aptitude. But they only pursue science for its utility, not tarnishing it with the passions that are the hallmark of imperfect spirits.

110. Third class: wise spirits

Moral qualities of the highest order constitute their distinctive character. Though they do not possess unlimited knowledge, they are endowed with an intellectual capacity that allows them to judge people and situations with clarity.

111. Second class: superior spirits

They combine science, wisdom and goodness. Their language expresses only benevolence and is consistently dignified, elevated, and frequently sublime. Their superior standing renders them more apt than the others to convey to us the most exact notions about things of the incorporeal world, within the limits of what we are allowed to know. They willingly communicate with those who seek truth in good faith, and whose souls are sufficiently freed from earthly influences to understand it. They withdraw, however, from those moved only by curiosity, or who deviate from the practice of good due to the influence of matter.

Under exceptional circumstances, when they incarnate on Earth, they accomplish a mission of progress, offering us an example of the perfection to which mankind can aspire in this world.

6.3. First order: pure spirits

112. General characteristics

Spirits of this order suffer no influence from matter, displaying therefore an absolute intellectual and moral superiority relative to the spirits of the other orders.

113. First and only class

These spirits have gone through all of the degrees of the spiritual hierarchy and have freed themselves from all the influence of matter. Having reached the highest perfection attainable by created beings, they have no more trials or expiations to endure. They are, thus, no longer subject to reincarnation in perishable bodies, living eternal life in the bosom of God.

They enjoy unchanging bliss, as they are no longer subject to the needs or vicissitudes of material life; but such bliss is not a *monotonous idleness lived in perpetual contemplation*. They are the messengers and ministers of God, whose orders they carry out for the preservation of the universal harmony. They direct all the spirits beneath them, help them to perfect themselves, and assign their missions to them. They consider it a pleasing occupation to assist men in their distress, to stimulate them to do good, or to expiate the wrongs that keep them from the supreme bliss. Sometimes these spirits are called angels, archangels or seraphim.

We may communicate with them, but rather presumptuous would be the man who pretends to have them at his beck and call.

7. Progression of spirits

114. Are spirits good or evil by nature, or do they advance through their own efforts?

"Spirits advance by themselves, and, as they do so, they go from a lower to a higher order."

115.   Have some spirits been created good and others evil?

"God has created all spirits simple and ignorant, that is, without knowledge. He has given each of them a mission with the goal of enlightening their minds and making them march progressively toward perfection through the knowledge of the truth, bringing them ever closer to Himself. They shall find eternal and unspoiled bliss in that perfection. Spirits acquire knowledge by experiencing the trials that God has imposed on them. Some accept such trials humbly, and thus arrive more quickly at their destiny; others do not endure them without complaining, thus remaining, by their own fault, removed from the promised perfection and happiness."

—   According to that, is it correct to say that spirits are at their origin like children, ignorant and inexperienced, only gradually acquiring the knowledge they lack, as they go through the different phases of human life?

"Yes, that is an accurate comparison. The rebellious child remains ignorant and imperfect, only advancing in proportion to the docility displayed. However, man's life has a term, whereas that of spirits extends to infinity."

116.   Are there spirits who shall forever remain in the lower orders?

"No, all will become perfect. They change, although slowly. As we once said, a just and merciful father cannot banish his children forever. Do you think that God, who is so grand, so good, and so just, could be worse than you yourselves?"

117.   Does it depend on spirits themselves to hasten their advancement toward perfection?

"Certainly. The amount of time it takes them depends on their desire and submission to God's will. Doesn't the well-behaved child learn more rapidly than the unruly one?"

118. Can spirits retrograde?

"No. As they advance, they gain an understanding of what holds them back from perfection. When a spirit finishes a particular trial, the acquired knowledge is never forgotten. Spirits may remain stationary, but they never retrograde."

119. Could God exempt spirits from the trials that they need to go through in order to reach the first order?

"If they had been created perfect, they would not have the merit to enjoy the benefits of that perfection. Where would be the merit without the struggle? Besides, inequality among the spirits is necessary for their personalities. The missions they accomplish at the different stages reside in the designs of Providence for the harmony of the universe."

> Since it is possible for everyone in our society to reach the highest posts, we might as well then ask why the sovereign of a country does not make a general of every one of his soldiers, why every subordinate employee is not made manager, or why all students are not made teachers. There is also another difference between social life on Earth and spirit life, in that the former is limited, not always allowing everyone to reach the highest positions, whereas the latter is unlimited, offering each one the possibility of ascending to the highest ranks.

120. Must all spirits tread the path of evil before they reach the path of good?

"Not the path of evil, but that of ignorance."

121. Why have some spirits followed the path of good and others the path of evil?

"Don't they have free will? God has not created spirits bad; He has created them simple and ignorant, in other words, with equal aptitude for good and evil. Those who are evil have become so of their own volition."

122. How can spirits have the freedom of choice between good and bad, if they still have no consciousness of themselves at their origin? Is there some seed or some sort of tendency that leads them more toward one path than the other?

"Free will develops as the spirit acquires self-awareness. There would be no freedom if it were the result of a cause independent of the spirit's will. The cause is not within the spirit, but outside, in the influences to which he yields, by virtue of the freedom of his will. This is the grand symbolism of the fall of man and the original sin: some yielded to temptation; others resisted it."

—   Where do the influences that act upon spirits come from?

"From the imperfect spirits who seek to ensnare and dominate them, taking pleasure in making them fail. This is what was intended to be portrayed by the allegory of Satan."

—   Is this influence only exerted upon spirits at their origin?

"It follows spirits over the course of their existence until they have acquired enough self-control, to the point that evil spirits desist from besieging them."

123. Why does God allow spirits to follow the path of evil?

"How dare you demand God to account for His acts? Do you believe you can penetrate God's will? You should realize instead that God's wisdom is to be found in the freedom of choice that has been granted to everyone, so that everyone may have the merit of their own deeds."

124. As there may be spirits who follow the path of the absolute good from the beginning, while others follow the path of absolute evil, there must undoubtedly be gradations between these two extremes, must there not?

"Yes, certainly, and they represent the vast majority."

125. Will the spirits who follow the path of evil be able to arrive at the same degree of perfection as the others?

"Yes, but *the eternities* will be much longer for them."

By the expression *the eternities* we must understand the way in which inferior spirits make out the length of their suffering, the end of which they are not allowed to foresee, a perception renewed every time they fail in a trial.

126. Do spirits who have reached the highest degree after treading the path of evil have any less merit than the others, in the sight of God?

"God looks upon those who have gone astray the same way, and loves all of them with the same affection. They are called evil because they have failed—prior to that, they were no more than simple spirits."

127. Are all spirits created equal in terms of their intellectual faculties?

"They are all created equal, but since they do not know where they come from, it is necessary for them to develop their free will. They progress more or less rapidly both in intelligence and in morality."

Spirits who follow the path the of good from the beginning are not therefore perfect because of it. Though they have no evil leanings, they must still acquire the necessary experience and knowledge to reach perfection. We could compare them to children who, no matter how good their natural instincts are, must still develop and learn, only gradually passing from their tender age into adulthood. Just as there are individuals who are good or evil since their childhood, there are spirits who are good or evil from the start, but with the crucial difference that children possess their instincts already formed, whereas spirits are neither evil nor good when they are first created. Having both tendencies, they take one or the other direction as a result of their own free will.

8. Angels and demons

128. Do the beings we call angels, archangels and seraphim form a special category of a nature different from that of other spirits?

"No, these are the pure spirits, those at the highest degree of the hierarchy and who possess all the virtues."

The word *angel* usually elicits the idea of moral perfection; however, it is frequently used in reference to all beings—good or evil—that are beyond the physical human world. We say a good or bad angel, an angel of light, or the angel of darkness; in this case, the word is synonymous with *spirit*. We use it here in its positive interpretation.

129. Have angels gone through all of the degrees?

"They have gone up through all of them, but as we have already said: some accepted their mission without bemoaning, thus arriving more quickly; others took a longer amount of time to reach perfection."

130. If the opinion that some beings were created perfect and superior to all others from the start is erroneous, how to explain that that belief is present in the tradition of nearly all cultures?

"Understand that your world has not existed from all eternity, and that long before it existed, there already were spirits who had reached the highest degrees; men therefore believed that such spirits had always been perfect."

131. Are there demons in the usual sense of the word?

"If there were demons, they would be the work of God. But would God be just and good in creating unfortunate beings that are eternally dedicated to evil? If there are demons, they reside on your lowly world and on similar ones: they are the hypocritical men who portray a just God as evil and vindictive, and who imagine they can please Him with the horrors they commit in His name."

Only in its modern meaning does the word demon imply the idea of evil spirit, because the Greek word *daimon* (δαίμων), from which it derives, means *genie* or *intelligence*, and was used in reference to all good or evil incorporeal beings, without distinction.

According to the common meaning of the word, demons are essentially maleficent beings, but they would be, like everything else, one of God's creations. Now, God, who is sovereignly just and good, could not have created beings dedicated to evil by their very nature, and thus condemned for eternity. If they were not God's creation, however, they would have existed from all eternity like Him, in which case there would be many sovereign powers.

The first requirement of any theory is to be logical; that of demons, in its absolute sense, lacks this essential foundation. It is conceivable that, in the creeds of primitive cultures—which did not understand the attributes of God, and therefore believed in malefic deities—one also believed in the existence of demons. But for anyone who understands the goodness of God as an attribute par excellence, it would be illogical and contradictory to suppose that He could have created beings dedicated to evil and destined to do it perpetually, as this would negate His goodness.

Proponents of the doctrine of demons seek support in the words of Christ, and we certainly will not be the one to dispute the authority of his teachings, which we would like to see present more in men's hearts than on their lips. But can they be certain of the meaning he attached to the word demon? Do we not know that the allegorical form is one of the distinctive marks of his language? And should everything contained in the Gospels be taken literally, then? We need no further proof beyond this passage: "Immediately after the tribulation of those days shall the sun be darkened, and the moon shall not give her light, and the stars shall fall from heaven, and the powers of the heavens shall be shaken. Verily I say unto you, this generation shall not pass, till all these things be fulfilled." [d]

Have we not seen the *form* of the biblical text contradicted by science where it refers to the creation and movement of the Earth? Could it not be the same with regard to certain figures of speech employed by Christ, who had to speak according to his time and place? Christ could not have consciously said anything false. Therefore, if in his words there are things that seem to affront reason, it is either because we do not understand them, or because we interpret them incorrectly.

Men have done to demons what they have done to angels; just as they have believed in the existence of beings perfect from all eternity, they have taken spirits of lower ranking as perpetually evil beings. The word demon should therefore be understood as referring to impure spirits, who often are no better than the beings normally designated by that name, but with the difference that their state is only transitory. They are the imperfect spirits who rebel against the trials they endure, and, for that reason, will have to endure them for a long time. They will eventually succeed, nonetheless, once they muster the will to do so. We might accept the term *demon* with this restriction, but because it is generally understood according to this exclusive meaning nowadays, it could mistakenly lend credence to the belief in the existence of beings created especially for evil.

As for Satan, it is obviously the personification of evil in allegorical form, as it is impossible to believe in an evil being who fights on equal terms against the Divinity, and whose sole concern is to thwart God's designs. Since man needs images and figures to capture his imagination, he has depicted incorporeal beings under a material guise, endowed with attributes that portray their qualities or flaws. For instance, in their attempt to personify Time, the ancients depicted it as an old man with a scythe and an hour-glass—the figure of a young man would have been nonsensical. The same applies to the allegories of Fortune, Truth, and so on. Modern men have represented the angels—or pure spirits— as radiant entities, endowed with white wings, the symbol of purity; and Satan, with horns, claws and other animal attributes, all symbols of base passions. Common folk, who often interpret things literally, have taken these symbols for real creatures, just as they formerly regarded Saturn as the allegory of Time.

■■■

[a] Quintessence means a subtle and imponderable substance, distinct from matter, and normally associated with the idea of ether. —Trans.

[b] In the French original Kardec says "Comme le germe d'un fruit est entouré du périsperme" (As the germ of a fruit is enclosed in the perisperm). Realizing that in modern botanical terminology the pair *périsperme/perisperm* has been replaced by *endoderme/endoderm*, we used instead the *heart/pericardium* analogy, which is more euphonious and more easily understood by the modern reader, yielding "As the heart is enclosed in the pericardium," in keeping with the intended goal of the author. —Trans.

[c] Joseph Pitton de Tournefort (1656–1708), Carl Linnaeus (1707–1778), and Antoine Laurent de Jussieu (1748–1836) were three scientists who helped to establish modern taxonomy, each of them proposing a somewhat different classification of living beings. Kardec's purpose here is to emphasize that any classification is arbitrary, serving only as an instructional tool. —Trans.

[d] Matthew 24:29,34. —Trans.

Chapter 2:
Incarnation of Spirits

1. Purpose of incarnation

132. What is the purpose of the incarnation of spirits?

"God imposes incarnation with the purpose of leading spirits to perfection: for some, it is an expiation; for others, a mission. But in order to reach this perfection *they must endure all the tribulations of the corporeal existence*—there lies the expiation. Incarnation also has another purpose, which is to enable spirits to take on their role in the work of creation. It is to accomplish this goal that they don, on each world, an instrument that is in harmony with its prevailing matter, so as to carry out the directives of God, from that perspective, in that same world. This way, by contributing to the grand scheme of things, they themselves advance."

> The action of corporeal beings is necessary for the advancement of the universe; but in His wisdom God has willed that, in this very action, they might find a means of progressing and ascending closer to Him. Thus, through the admirable law of His providence, everything is connected, everything is linked by chains of solidarity in nature.

133. Is incarnation necessary for spirits who have followed the path of good from the outset?

"All are created simple and ignorant, acquiring knowledge through the struggles and tribulations of corporeal life. Being just, God could not have created a blessed few who, without trouble and toil, would consequently have no merit either."

—   But then what do spirits have to gain from following the path of good, if by doing so they do not exempt themselves from the hardships of corporeal life?

"They reach their goal more quickly; in addition, the hardships of life are often a consequence of spirits' imperfections—the fewer their imperfections, the fewer their tribulations. Spirits who are not envious, jealous, miserly, or greedy will not have to endure the suffering that results from such flaws."

2. On the soul

134.   What is the soul?

"An incarnate spirit."

—   What was the soul before uniting itself with the body?

"A spirit."

—   Are souls and spirits therefore one and the same thing?

"Yes, souls are no more than spirits. Before uniting itself with the body, a soul constitutes one of the intelligent beings who populate the invisible world, and who temporarily assumes a physical body in order to purify and enlighten itself."

135.   Is there in man anything else aside from the soul and the body?

"There is the link that unites the soul and the body."

—   What is the nature of this link?

"It is semi-material, that is to say, of a nature which is in between the natures of the spirit and the body. This is necessary for the latter two to communicate with one another. It is through this link that the spirit acts upon matter, and vice-versa."

Man is thus formed by three essential parts:
1) The body, or material being analogous to that of animals, animated by the same vital principle;
2) The soul or incarnate spirit, dwelling in the body; and

3) The intermediary principle, or *perispirit*, a semi-material substance that serves as a primary envelope of the spirit, uniting the soul with the body.

Much like a fruit consists of the seed, the flesh, and the skin.

136. Is the soul independent of the vital principle?

"The body is only the envelope, as we repeatedly say."

— Can the body exist without the soul?

"Yes. However, when the body ceases to live, the soul abandons it. Prior to birth, there is not a definitive union between the soul and the body yet, whereas, once this union has been established, only the death of the body can cut the links that unite it with the soul, enabling the latter to leave. Organic life may animate a soulless body, but a soul cannot inhabit a body devoid of organic life."

— What would our body be if it did not have a soul?

"A mass of flesh without intelligence, or anything you might want to name it, except a human being."

137. Can the same spirit incarnate in two different bodies at the same time?

"No. The spirit is indivisible and cannot simultaneously animate two different beings." (See the chapter "Bi-corporeality and transfiguration" in *The Mediums' Book*.)

138. What about the opinion of those who regard the soul as being the principle of material life?

"It is a matter of words—we are unconcerned about it. Start by making yourselves understood by each other."

139. Certain spirits, and a number of philosophers before them, have defined the soul as *an animate spark emanated from the great Whole*. Why the contradiction?

"There is no contradiction; everything depends on the meaning of the words. Why do you not have one word for each thing?"

The word *soul* is used to express very different things. Some call it the principle of life, and, in this sense, it is correct to say *figuratively* that the soul is an animate spark that has emanated from the great Whole. These last words describe the universal source of the vital principle, of which each being absorbs a portion that goes back to the whole after death. This interpretation by no means excludes the idea of a moral being who is distinct from and independent of matter, and whose individuality is preserved. This being is equally called *soul*, and, with this definition, one could say that the soul is an incarnate spirit. In attributing different meanings to the word *soul*, Spirits have spoken according to their use of the word, and according to the terrestrial ideas with which they were still more or less imbued.

All this results from the limitations of human language, which does not have one term for each idea, thus creating a large number of misunderstandings and disputes. For this reason, superior spirits urge us first to reach an agreement on the words we use.[1]

140. What should be thought about the theory that the soul is subdivided into as many parts as there are muscles, each presiding over a different bodily function?

"That will also depend on the meaning attributed to the word *soul*. If by this word we mean the vital fluid, the definition is correct, but it is wrong if we mean the incarnate spirit. We have already said that the spirit is indivisible; it imparts movement to organs through the intermediary fluid without dividing itself in the process."

— Nevertheless, there are spirits who have given this definition.

"Ignorant spirits may take the effect for the cause."

The soul acts through the organs, which in turn are animated by the vital fluid shared among them, and more abundantly in those organs that constitute the centers or focal points of movement. But this explanation is not suitable if by the word *soul* one understands the spirit that inhabits the body during life and leaves it upon death.

141. Is there anything valid in the opinion of those who think the soul is external to the body, surrounding it?

"The soul is not imprisoned in the body like a bird in a cage. Rather, it radiates and manifests externally like light through a glass globe or

---

[1] See the explanation of the word *soul* in section II of the Introduction. —Auth.

sound from a speaker. In that certain sense one may say that it is external, but that does not make it an envelope of the body. The soul has two envelopes: the first is subtle and weightless, the one you called *perispirit*; the other is dense, material, and heavy—the body. The soul is the center of these two envelopes, like a nut in its shell, as we have already said."

142. What about another theory according to which a child's soul continues to complete itself during each stage of life?

"The spirit is only one; it is as integral in the child as it is in the adult. It is the organs—the instruments for the manifestation of the soul—that develop and complete themselves. This is once more taking the effect for the cause."

143. Why don't all spirits define the soul in the same way?

"Spirits are not all equally knowledgeable about these matters. There are spirits who are still limited and who do not understand abstract concepts; they are like the children among you. There are also pseudo-wise spirits, who parade their vocabulary in order to make an impression; again, much like it happens among you. In addition, even enlightened spirits may express themselves using different words, but with the same underlying meaning, especially when it comes to matters that your language is incapable of describing with precision; it is thus necessary to resort to figures of speech and analogies that you end up taking literally."

144. Then what is to be understood by the expression *soul of the world*?

"The soul of the world is the universal principle of life and intelligence from which individualities are born. But those who use this expression frequently do not understand it. The word *soul* is so elastic that everyone interprets it as their whim takes them. At times a soul has even been attributed to Earth itself, but that must be understood to mean the host of devoted spirits who direct your actions in the path of good when you listen to them, and who are, so to speak, lieutenants of God on your planet."

145. How to explain that so many ancient and modern philosophers have discussed psychological science for so long without arriving at the truth?

"These individuals were the forerunners of the eternal truths underlying the Spiritist Doctrine—they have prepared the way. As human beings, they were subject to error, as they have mistaken their own ideas for the light. Their very mistakes, however, helped underscore the truth by contrasting their positive and negative aspects. Besides, great truths can be found among those mistakes, as a comparative study would reveal."

146. Does the soul have a fixed and circumscribed seat in the body?

"No, although it operates more particularly in the head among men of genius, and those who exert their intellect intensely, and in the heart among those with ardent feelings and whose actions concern all humanity."

—   What is to be thought of the opinion of those who place the soul in a given vital center?

"It means that the spirit actuates that part of your physical organization more intensely, because that is the point on which most of your impressions converge. Those who place it in what they consider the center of vitality confuse it with the vital fluid. Nevertheless, one could say that the seat of the soul resides more intensely in the organs through which intellectual and moral qualities manifest."

3. Materialism

147. Why are anatomists, physiologists, and those who specialize in natural sciences in general frequently led into materialism?

"Physiologists relate everything to what they can see. Because of pride, men believe they know everything and cannot admit that something could possibly be beyond their understanding. Their own knowledge makes them presumptuous—they think nature cannot hide anything from them."

148. Isn't it unfortunate that materialism may be a consequence of studies that should instead prove to man the superiority of the intelligence governing the world? Should we then conclude that such studies are dangerous?

"It is not true that materialism is a consequence of such studies. Men may draw wrong conclusions from them, as they can make an incorrect use of anything, including that which is most worthwhile. Besides, the idea of annihilation troubles them more than they would have you believe, and such self-righteous individuals are almost always more braggart than brave. Most of them are materialists only because they have nothing with which to fill that void. However, when on the edge of the abyss that opens before their eyes, throw them a lifeline and they will readily cling to it."

Through a distortion of intelligence, there are those who see nothing in organic beings but the action of matter, to which they ascribe all our actions. They see in the human body only an electrical apparatus, and study the mechanism of life only within the activity of the organs. They have frequently seen life vanish due to the rupture of a vessel, and have seen nothing beyond that vessel. They have tried to find out whether anything else might be left, but since they found nothing but inert matter, and could not see the soul escape, or capture it, they concluded that everything derives from the properties of matter. They therefore also concluded that, upon death, the mind no longer exists.

What a sad outcome if it were true, because, in that case, good and evil would have no meaning; man would be justified in thinking only of himself and in placing the satisfaction of material pleasures above all else. Social ties would be broken, and the holiest affections would be shattered forever. Fortunately, such ideas are far from being the rule; one can even say that they are very circumscribed, representing only individual opinions, as they have not established a doctrine anywhere. A society founded on such a basis would contain the seeds of its own destruction, and its members would tear each other to pieces like vicious beasts.

Man instinctively believes that not all ends for him once life is over; the idea of annihilation terrifies him. Try as he may to become impervious to the idea of a future life, when the supreme moment arrives, only very few will not ask what will become of them, because the idea of departing from life forever is disheartening. Indeed, who could face with indifference the absolute and eternal separation from everything that he has loved? Who could stare without terror at the immense abyss of nothingness opening before him, where all his faculties and hopes shall be engulfed forever, and then say to himself: "So be it! After me, nothing, nothing but the Void; all will be gone, ineluctably. In a few days all memories of me will be erased from the minds of those who survive me. Ere long, there will be no trace of my passage on Earth. Even the good I have done will be forgotten by the ungrateful ones I have indulged. There is nothing to compensate for this, no prospect other than that of my body being devoured by worms!"

Is there not something horrifying, something chilling in this picture? Religion teaches us that it cannot be thus, and reason echoes it. But this vague and undefined future existence does nothing to satisfy our desire for a positive proof, something which has engendered doubt in so many. So, we have a soul, but what is it? Does it have any kind of form or appearance? Is it a limited or undefined being? Some say it is a breath of God, others say it is a spark, while others say that it is part of the great Whole, the principle of life and of intelligence, but what does all this really tell us? What does it matter to us to have a soul if after death it will disappear in the immensity like drops of water in the ocean? Is losing our individuality not the same as the Void? It is also said that the soul is immaterial. However, an immaterial thing would not have defined proportions, so for us it is the same as nothing.

Religion also teaches us that we shall be happy or unhappy according to the good or evil we have done. But what is the happiness that awaits us in the bosom of God? Is it a type of beatitude, an eternal contemplation with no concern other than singing praises to the Creator? Are the flames of hell a reality or only an allegory? The Church itself generally interprets them in the latter sense, but, in that case, what are those sufferings? Where is this place of torture? In short, what do we do and what do we see in that other world that awaits all of us? No one, it is claimed, has ever returned to give us an account. That is a mistake, and the mission of Spiritism is precisely to instruct us regarding that future, to allow us, in a way, to see and touch it, no longer through reason alone, but by means of empirical evidence.

Thanks to spirit communications, the future is no longer a conjecture, a probability that each depicts as he pleases, or that poets embellish with their fantasies or sprinkle with an allegorical imagery that misleads us. It is, instead, reality that emerges before us, because it is the very beings from beyond the grave that come to describe to us their situation and what they do, thus allowing us to watch, as it were, the adventures of their new life, thereby presenting to us the inevitable fate reserved for us according to our merits or demerits. Is there anything against religion in this? On the contrary, skeptics shall find faith in it, and the halfhearted, renewed fervor and confidence. Hence, Spiritism is the most powerful aid of religion. This being the case, it is because God has allowed it; and He allows it in order to rekindle our wavering hope, and to lead us back onto the path of virtue, by providing a perspective of the future.

■■■

Chapter 3:
Return from the Corporeal to the Spirit Life

1. The soul after death and its individuality, eternal life
2. Separation of the soul from the body
3. The spirit's bewilderment after death

1. The soul after death and its individuality, eternal life

149. What happens to the soul at the moment of death?

"It becomes a spirit again, in other words, it returns to the world of spirits that it had temporarily left."

150. Does the soul preserve its individuality after death?

"Yes, it never loses it. What would the soul be if it did not preserve it?"

— How does the soul establish its individuality if it no longer possesses its material body?

"It still has a fluid peculiar to it, which it draws from the surroundings of its planet, and which preserves the appearance of its last incarnation: its perispirit."

— Does the soul take with it anything from this world?

"Nothing other than its memories and the desire to go to a better world. These memories are full of either sweetness or bitterness, according to the use it has made of its earthly life. The more advanced it is, the more it understands the futility of what it has left behind on Earth."

151. What about the opinion that the soul returns to the universal Whole after death?

"Taken as a group, don't spirits make up a whole? Is it not a world of its own? When you are in an assembly, you are an integral part of it, and yet you still preserve your own individuality."

152. What proof do we have of the soul's individuality after death?

"Don't you have such evidence through the communications you receive? If you were not blind, you would see it; if you were not deaf, you would hear it, because often a voice speaks to you, revealing the existence of a being outside yourselves."

Those who think the soul returns to the universal Whole after death are mistaken if by that they mean that it loses its individuality like a drop of water that falls into the ocean. They are correct, however, if by *universal whole* they mean the entire assembly of incorporeal beings, of which each soul or spirit is an element.

If souls were fused together into an aggregate whole, they would possess only the qualities of the whole, and nothing would distinguish them from one another; they would have neither intelligence nor qualities of their own. In fact, in all their communications, they display the consciousness of a *self* and a distinct will. The infinite diversity they show in every respect is the consequence of their individuality. If there were nothing after death except what is called the great Whole absorbing all individualities, that Whole would be uniform, and, therefore, all communications received from the invisible world would be identical.

Since we meet entities that are good or evil, knowledgeable or ignorant, fortunate or unfortunate; as well as beings of all temperaments, joyful and sad, frivolous and serious, and so on, it is obvious that they constitute distinct beings. Their individuality becomes even more obvious when these beings prove their identity through indisputable signs and personal details about their earthly lives that can be verified. In addition, there can be no doubt about such individuality when they manifest in plain sight as in the case of apparitions. The individuality of the soul has been taught to us theoretically, as an article of faith; Spiritism makes it evident, and to a certain extent, material.

153. In what sense should we understand eternal life?

"Only the life of the spirit is eternal; the life of the body is transitory and fleeting. When the body dies, the soul returns to eternal life."

— Wouldn't it be more exact to call *eternal life* the life of pure spirits, who, having attained perfection, no longer have trials to undergo?

"That would be eternal happiness, rather. But this is a matter of words; you may call things as you please, provided you understand each other."

2. Separation of the soul from the body

154. Is the separation of the soul from the body painful?

"No, the body often suffers more during life than at the moment of death; the soul has nothing to do with it. The suffering that a man sometimes experiences at the moment of death provides *satisfaction for his spirit*, in that he sees his exile coming to an end."

> In cases of natural death, that which results from the depletion of the organs due to age, man departs from life without even realizing it, much like the light of a lamp is extinguished when all the oil has been consumed.

155. How does the separation of the soul from the body take place?

"Once the connections that secure the soul are broken, it disengages from the body."

—   Does this separation occur instantly and by an abrupt transition? Is there a well-defined dividing line between life and death?

"No, the soul disengages itself gradually. It does not escape like a captive bird suddenly set free. These two states touch each other and blend together; this way the spirit liberates itself little by little from its ties: *they unravel; they do not break apart.*"

> During life, the spirit is attached to the body by its semi-material envelope, or perispirit. Death brings the destruction of the body only, not of this second envelope, which detaches from the body when organic life ends. Observation demonstrates that, at the moment of death, the disengagement of the perispirit is not accomplished all at once, but occurs only gradually, and at a pace that varies considerably according to the individual. For some, it is rather fast, so that one could say that the moment of death is essentially that of the disengagement, which is completed within a few hours.
>
> For others, on the other hand, particularly in the case of those whose life has been devoted to *mostly material and sensual pleasures*, the disengagement is much slower, taking sometimes days, weeks, or even months. This phenomenon

does not imply that there is any vitality left in the body, or any possibility that it may return to life; it simply demonstrates the affinity that exists between the body and spirit, an affinity that is always due to the importance that the spirit attached to matter during life. In fact, it is only rational to assume that the more a spirit has identified with matter, the more difficult it will be to detach itself from the body.

Conversely, intellectual and moral activity and the elevation of thoughts sets off this disengagement process while the body is still alive, so that, when death finally occurs, the completion of the detachment process is almost instantaneous. All this is the result of studies involving individuals observed at the moment of death. They demonstrate further that the affinity that persists between the soul and the body in some individuals is sometimes very painful, as the spirit may even experience the horrors of the decay of the body. This latter case is exceptional and peculiar to certain lifestyles and certain types of death. It may occur in the case of those who commit suicide.

156. Can the definitive separation between soul and body occur before the complete cessation of organic life?

"During the death throes, the soul sometimes has already left the body, which in this case possesses nothing except organic life. The dying man no longer has any consciousness of himself, and yet a last gasp of life remains. The body is a machine that the heart keeps running, and it continues to live as long as the heart pumps blood through the vessels, and for that it does not need the soul."

157. At the moment of death, does the soul sometimes experience a feeling of longing or rapture that gives it a glimpse into the world to which it is returning?

"The soul often feels that the links that secure it to the body are breaking, and so *it makes every effort to finish breaking them completely.* Already partially liberated from matter, it sees the future unfolding before it, enjoying, in anticipation, the spirit state."

158. Can the example of the caterpillar—which initially crawls up a branch and then locks itself inside its cocoon in apparent death, only to be reborn into a brilliant existence—provide us an idea of terrestrial life, followed by that of the grave, and finally that of our new existence?

"A pale idea. It is a good metaphor, but you must not take it literally, as you frequently do."

159.   What sensation does the soul experience the moment it realizes that it is in the spirit world?

"That is as the case may be. If you have done evil for the sake of evil, you find yourself at first ashamed of what you have done. It is much different in the case of the upright person, who feels relieved of a great burden, and does not fear the most meticulous scrutiny."

160.   Does a spirit immediately find those whom he knew on Earth, and who died before him?

"Yes, depending on the affection they had for one another. They frequently come to receive him on his return to the spirit world, and they *help him disengage from the bonds of matter*. He may also see many whom he lost sight of during his earthly stay. He is able to see those who are in between incarnations, disengaged from a material body. Finally, he visits those who are still incarnate."

161.   In the case of violent or accidental deaths, when the organs are not yet debilitated by age or disease, does the separation of the soul and the cessation of life occur simultaneously?

"It is usually so, but, in any case, the interval between them is very short."

162.   After being beheaded, for example, does a man remain conscious for a few moments?

"He frequently remains so for a few moments, until the organic life is extinguished once and for all. Many times, however, the fear of death makes him lose consciousness before the moment of the execution."

This question refers only to the consciousness that the victim may have of himself as still a living being, through the body—not as a spirit. If he has not lost his consciousness before execution, he may preserve it for a few very short moments, a consciousness which forcibly ends with the extinguishing of the organic life of the brain. This does not mean that the perispirit has completely disengaged from the body. On the contrary, in all cases of violent death, when death is not brought about by the gradual extinction of the vital forces, the links that unite the body and the perispirit are more *persistent*, so that the complete disengagement takes longer.

3. The spirit's bewilderment after death

163. Upon leaving the body, does the soul immediately have consciousness of itself?

"*Immediately* is not the right word; it finds itself in a state of bewilderment for some time."

164. Do all spirits experience the bewilderment that follows the disengagement of the soul from the body to the same degree and for the same amount of time?

"No, it depends on their elevation. Those who are already purified are almost immediately aware of themselves, because they had already detached themselves from matter during their corporeal life. The carnal man, however, whose conscience is not clear, retains the impressions from matter for much longer."

165. Does the knowledge of Spiritism have any influence on the shorter or longer duration of this confusion?

"It has a great influence, in that the spirit understands its situation in advance. The practice of good and a clear conscience have the most influence, however."

At the moment of death, everything seems confusing initially, as the spirit needs some time to recognize himself; he feels bewildered, like a man that wakes up from of a deep sleep and tries to get hold of his situation. The lucidity of ideas and the memory of the past come back as the influence of the matter from which he has just freed himself wanes, and the fog that clouded his thoughts dissipates.

The duration of the bewilderment that follows death varies greatly; it may last a few hours, many months or even years. This period lasts the least in the case of those who have identified themselves with their future condition while still alive, because they can immediately understand their situation then.

This confusion has different aspects according to the character of the person and especially according to the type of death. In violent deaths, such as suicide, torturing, accident, stroke, fatal wounds, and so on, the spirit is surprised and astonished, not even believing himself to be dead, an opinion he stubbornly maintains; yet, he sees his body and knows it belongs to him and cannot reconcile the fact that he is detached from it. He approaches his loved ones and speaks to them, but cannot understand why they do not hear him. This illusion lasts until the complete liberation of the perispirit; only then does he recognize himself, realizing that he is no longer among the living.

This phenomenon is easy to explain. Surprised by the unexpected death, the spirit is stunned by the sudden change that has taken place in him. For him, death is synonymous with destruction and annihilation; now, as he can think, see, and hear, it seems to him that he is not dead. This illusion is reinforced by the fact that he finds himself in a body similar to the one he had before, but the ethereal nature of which he has not had the time to verify yet. He presumes that it is solid and compact like the previous one, and he is astonished not to be able to touch himself when it is pointed out to him that his new body is not tangible. It is a phenomenon similar to that of some inexperienced somnambulists who do not believe that they are asleep. For them, sleep is synonymous with the suspension of the faculties, and since they can freely think and see, they believe not to be sleeping. Certain spirits display this feature, even in cases where death has not occurred suddenly, but it is always more frequent among those who did not expect to die, despite having been ill. This leads to the odd spectacle of spirits who attend their own funeral procession as though it were that of a stranger, speaking of it as though it in no way concerns them, until they grasp the truth.

There is nothing painful about the bewilderment that follows death for the good man; it is tranquil and, in every detail, similar to the process associated with a peaceful awakening. But for he whose conscience is not clear, it is filled with a feeling of anxiety and anguish that grows as he regains consciousness of himself.

In cases of collective death, it has been observed that those who have perished at the same time do not always see one another immediately. In the confusion following death, spirits go each their own way, or are only concerned about those that interest them.

■■■

Chapter 4:
Plurality of Existences

1. On reincarnation

166. How can a soul that has not reached perfection during the corporeal life finalize the process of purification?

"By undergoing the trial of a new existence."

— How does the soul accomplish this new existence? Would it be through its transformation as a spirit?

"In purifying itself, the soul undoubtedly undergoes a transformation, but for that to occur it needs the trial of corporeal life."

— Does the soul then have many corporeal existences?

"Yes, we all live many lives. Those who say otherwise wish to keep you in the ignorance in which they find themselves; that is their desire."

— It seems to follow from this tenet that, after having left one body behind, the soul then takes another; in other words, it reincarnates in a new body. Is this how this principle should be understood?

"Evidently so."

167. What is the purpose of reincarnation?

"Expiation and the progressive improvement of mankind. Without it, how could there be justice?"

168. Is the number of corporeal existences limited, or must a spirit reincarnate endlessly?

"In each new existence, a spirit takes a step forward along the path of progress. When it has shed all impurities, it no longer needs to undergo the trials of a corporeal life."

169. Is the number of incarnations generally the same for all spirits?

"No. He who advances quickly spares himself many trials. Nevertheless, those successive incarnations total a great number, since progress is almost infinite."

170. What does the spirit become after its final incarnation?

"A blissful or pure spirit."

2. Justice of reincarnation

171. On what is the doctrine of reincarnation based?

"On the justice of God and revelation, as we repeatedly tell you: a good father always leaves the door of repentance open to his children. Doesn't reason tell you that it would be unjust to irrevocably deprive of the eternal bliss, those who have not had the opportunity to perfect themselves? Isn't every man a child of God? It is only among selfish men that we find iniquity, implacable hatred, and punishments without reprieve."

All spirits tend toward perfection and God provides them with the means of accomplishing it through the trials of corporeal life. But, in His justice, God permits them to accomplish in new existences *that which they were not able to do or to complete in a previous trial.*

It would not be consistent with God's justice or goodness to punish eternally those who may have encountered obstacles to their advancement independent of their will and from the circumstances in which they found themselves placed. If the fate of man is irrevocably sealed after his death, it would be tantamount to saying that God does not weigh the actions of everyone on the same scale, and that He does not treat them impartially.

The doctrine of reincarnation, which consists of accepting that man has many successive lives, is the only one that is in line with the idea of God's justice with regard to those of a lower moral standing. It is the only one that can explain our future and strengthen our hope, as it offers us the means of atoning for our mistakes through new trials. Reason suggests so, and the Spirits teach so.

The man who is aware of his inferiority finds a reassuring hope in the doctrine of reincarnation. If he truly believes in the justice of God, he cannot expect to be eternally on a level with those who have done better than he has. The thought that his lower standing will not ban him forever from the supreme happiness, and that he will be able to conquer his difficulties through renewed efforts, provides him with hope and restores his courage. Would one not regret, at the end of one's career, having acquired a particular experience too tardily in order to put it to good use? This tardily acquired experience is not lost—one will benefit from it in a new existence.

3. Incarnation on different worlds

172. Do all of our different corporeal existences take place on Earth?

"No, not all of them, but on different worlds. Your existence on this planet is neither the first nor the last, and is, in fact, one of the most material and most removed from perfection."

173. With each new corporeal existence does a soul go from one world to another, or may it live several lives on the same planet?

"It may live many lives on the same planet if it has not evolved sufficiently to graduate to a more advanced world."

—   We may then reappear several times on Earth?

"Certainly."

—   Can we come back to it again after having lived on other worlds?

"Surely; you may have already lived elsewhere and on Earth."

174. Is it a requirement to be reborn on Earth?

"No, but if you do not advance, you may go to another world that is no better, and perhaps even worse."

175. Is there any special advantage in coming back to live on Earth?

"No special advantage, unless you are on a mission; in any event, you shall advance, there or on any other world."

— Wouldn't it be better to remain a spirit?

"Not at all! Then you would remain stationary, whereas you should wish to advance toward God."

176. After having incarnated on other worlds, can spirits incarnate on this one without ever having been here before?

"Yes, just as you may incarnate on others. *All worlds are united in solidarity*. What you have not accomplished on one, you may accomplish on another."

— Then are there men who are now on Earth for the first time?

"There are many, and at various levels."

— Is there any feature that would allow us to recognize that a spirit is on Earth for the first time?

"That would serve no useful purpose."

177. In order to arrive at the perfection and supreme happiness—mankind's final objective—must a spirit live on all the worlds that exist in the entire universe?

"No, because there are many worlds of equivalent degree, where the spirit would not learn anything new."

— Then how can we explain the plurality of existences on the same globe?

"A spirit may find himself each time there in a very different situation, each of which will be a different opportunity to acquire experience."

178. Can spirits be reborn corporeally on a world that is relatively less advanced than the one on which they have already lived?

"Yes, when they have a mission to fulfill in order to foster the progress of that world. They then accept with joy the tribulations of that existence, because it provides them with a means of advancement."

—   May this not occur also as an expiation and may God not send rebellious spirits to inferior worlds?

"Spirits may remain stationary but they do not retrograde, so their punishment consists in not advancing, and in having to restart their squandered lives in an environment suited to their nature."

—   Who are the ones who must restart the same existence?

"Those who have failed in their missions or trials."

179. Are the beings who inhabit each world all at the same degree of perfection?

"No, it is like on Earth—there are some who are more and some who are less advanced."

180. In going from this world to another, does a spirit retain the intelligence it possessed here?

"Certainly, because intelligence is never lost, but the spirit may not have the same means of expressing it, as that depends both on the progress accomplished and the conditions offered by the body that will serve as instrument." (See Part 2, Chapter 7, "Bodily influences")

181. Do the beings who inhabit different worlds have bodies similar to ours?

"Of course they have bodies because the spirit must be clothed with matter in order to act upon it. This envelope, however, is more or less material, according to the level of advancement that the spirit has reached, which determines the differences among the worlds through which we must go. For in our Father's house are many mansions, and therefore many degrees. Some realize this and are aware of it here on Earth, but others know nothing about it."

182. Can we accurately know the physical and moral state of the different worlds?

"We, Spirits, can only answer in accordance with the level at which you find yourselves. This means that we must not reveal these things to everybody because not all are in a position to understand them, and because *such revelations would disturb them.*"

As spirits purify themselves, the bodies that clothe them also approach the spiritual nature. Their matter becomes less dense and they do not need to strenuously plod over the planet anymore; their physical needs are more refined, and they no longer have to kill other living beings in order to feed themselves. They enjoy greater freedom and possess capacities of perception of objects at a distance that are unknown to us, being able to see through their physical eyes that which we can see only through thought.

The purification of spirits is reflected in the moral perfection of the beings in which they are incarnated. Animal passions become weaker, and selfishness gives way to a feeling of brotherhood. It is thus that on worlds more advanced than Earth, wars are unheard of, and there is no reason for hatred and conflict, because no one would dream of harming a fellow being. Their intuition of the future and the assurance provided by a clear conscience mean that death is no longer a cause for apprehension, and its approach is accepted without fear, and as simply a transformation.

The lifespan on different worlds appears to be in proportion to the degree of physical and moral advancement of those worlds, something which is perfectly logical. The less material the body is, the fewer the hardships that may damage it; the more advanced spirits are, the fewer the passions that may pose a risk. This is another display of compassion on the part of the divine Providence, desirous of thus shortening all suffering.

183. In passing from one world to another, must a spirit go through a new childhood?

"Childhood is a necessary transition everywhere, but it is not always as limiting as it is on your world."

184. Can spirits choose the new world they will inhabit?

"Not always, but they may ask for it, and their wish may be granted, if they deserve it; worlds are accessible to spirits only according to their degree of elevation."

—   If a spirit does not express a preference, what determines the world on which he will reincarnate?

"His degree of elevation."

185. Is the physical and moral situation of living beings on each globe perpetually the same?

"No. Worlds are also subject to the law of progress. All began like yours, from an inferior state. Earth itself shall undergo a similar transformation. It will become a terrestrial paradise when all men have become good."

Thus, the race that populates the Earth today will disappear someday and will be replaced gradually by more perfect beings. Such races will succeed the current one, just as the current one succeeded others that were even more primitive.

186. Are there worlds on which the spirit no longer lives in a material body, keeping only the perispirit as an envelope?

"Yes, and that envelope itself becomes so etherealized that to you it is as if it did not exist at all. This is the state of the pure spirits."

—   That seems to imply that there is no precise line separating the state of the final incarnations and that of a pure spirit, is that not so?

"There is no such line. The difference diminishes little by little, finally becoming imperceptible, like the night fades away with the first lights of the day."

187. Is the substance of the perispirit the same on all globes?

"No, it is more or less etherealized. Going from one world to another, a spirit clothes himself with the specific matter of the new world, as fast as a flash of light."

188. Do pure spirits inhabit special worlds, or do they inhabit the universal space without being attached to one rather than another world?

"Pure spirits inhabit certain worlds, but they are not confined to them as people are to Earth. Much more easily than any others, they may be wherever they want to be."[1]

---

[1] According to the Spirits, of all the globes that comprise our solar system, *Earth* is one of those whose inhabitants are the least physically and morally advanced. *Mars* would be even less advanced than Earth, whereas *Jupiter* would be far superior in every respect. The *Sun* would not be inhabited by corporeal beings, but a meeting place for superior spirits, who radiate their thought to other worlds, which they govern through the mediation of less elevated spirits, communicating their directives through the universal fluid. Regarding its physical constitution, the Sun would be an electricity-producing furnace. All the other stars seem to operate identically.

Size and distance from the Sun have no necessary relationship with the degree of advancement of the planets, because it seems that Venus is more advanced than Earth, and Saturn less so than Jupiter.

Many spirits who have animated well-known personalities on Earth are said to have progressed to Jupiter, one of the worlds closest to perfection. It is surprising that on a globe so advanced, persons may be found who might not have been considered very evolved when they lived on Earth. However, this is not so surprising if we consider that certain spirits who inhabit that planet could have been sent to Earth to fulfill missions that did not place them, by our standards, in very important positions. Second, between their earthly existence and their life on Jupiter they may have had intermediate ones in which they progressed further. Thirdly, on that world as on this one, there are different degrees of development, and the existing range may be as wide as the difference separating the primitive from the civilized man on Earth. Thus, the fact that they inhabit Jupiter does not mean they are at the level of the most advanced beings there, just as one is not necessarily at the intellectual level of a Sorbonne professor simply for living in Paris.

Life cycles are also not necessarily the same as they are on Earth, and ages cannot be compared. A person who had died a few years ago was evoked and claimed to have reincarnated just six months before on an undisclosed world, replying that, when the spirit's age was asked, "I cannot say it, because we do not count time like you do; in addition, our way of life is not the same. We grow up much more quickly, so much so that it has been only six of your months since I came here, but my intellectual development is equivalent to that when I had reached about thirty years on Earth."

Many comparable responses have been given by other spirits, and they contain nothing implausible. Do we not see many animal species on Earth that reach

4. Progressive transmigration

189. Do spirits fully enjoy their faculties from the beginning of their creation?

"No. Like a man, a spirit also has an infancy. At their origin, spirits have no more than an instinctive existence, being barely aware of themselves and of their acts. Their intelligence develops only little by little."

190. What is the state of the soul during its first incarnation?

"The state of infancy in corporeal life. Its intelligence is barely beginning to bloom—*it attempts the first steps of living.*"

191. Are the souls of primitive peoples in a state of spiritual infancy?

"A relative infancy. Those souls have already achieved a certain progress, in that they are endowed with passions."

— Are passions an indication of development, then?

"Of development, but not of perfection. They are a sign of activity and awareness of the *self*. In the primitive soul, intelligence and life are in an embryonic state."

The life of a spirit in general goes through the same phases seen in a corporeal life. It gradually goes from the embryonic state to that of childhood, only to reach, over a series of stages, the adult state, which would be that of perfection in the case of a spirit, the difference being that there is no decline or decrepitude as in a corporeal life. Even though a spirit's life had a beginning, it will have no end, and from our vantage point a very long time is required to go from spirit infancy to complete development, a progress accomplished not on one single world alone, but on many of them. The life of a spirit consists therefore of a series of corporeal existences, each representing an opportunity to advance,

adulthood in only a few months? Why could it not be the same with human beings on other planets? In addition, we must notice that the development acquired by a thirty-year old man on Earth may be equivalent to a type of childhood in comparison with what an incarnate spirit should normally reach elsewhere. We would be very narrow-minded, on the one hand, to presume ourselves to be the standard of creation in every way, and, on the other hand, we would be belittling the Divinity if we were to believe that nothing else could have been created by God besides us. —Auth.

much like each corporeal existence consists of a long series of days, each providing man with additional experience and knowledge. However, just as in a man's earthly life there are unproductive days, in the life of a spirit there may be a corporeal existence that produces no results because the spirit failed to put it to good use.

192. Can we leap over every existing level by means of a perfect conduct in this life and thus become pure spirits without going through the intermediate stages?

"No, because what man conceives perfection to be like is actually very far from it. There are qualities that are either unknown to him or that he cannot understand. He may become as perfect as his earthly nature allows, but that would not represent absolute perfection. The same happens to children who, no matter how precocious they may be, must still go through adolescence before they reach maturity. Or perhaps it is like a sick person that must go through a period of convalescence before fully recovering. Additionally, spirits must advance in knowledge as well as in morality, and if they have only progressed in one dimension, they will have to perfect themselves also in the other, so as to reach the top of the hierarchy. However, the more a man advances in his present life, the shorter and less painful his next trials will be."

—   Can man at least assure himself in this life of a less bitter future existence?

"Certainly. He can reduce the length and difficulties of his journey. *Only the neglectful man remains stationary.*"

193. In his new existences, can a man descend to levels lower than the one he has already reached?

"Only in his *social position*, not as a spirit."

194. Can the spirit of an upright man animate the body of an evil person in a new incarnation?

"No, because a spirit cannot retrograde."

—   Can the soul of an evil man become that of an upright man?

"Yes. If he repents, and that would represent a reward."

The journey of spirits is always forward, they never retrograde. They gradually ascend through the hierarchy and do not fall from the rank they have once reached. In their different corporeal lives, they may descend as people but not as spirits. Thus, the soul of a powerful man may later become a humble craftsman, and vice versa, because rankings among men are frequently in the inverse ratio of their morality. Herod was a king, Jesus, a carpenter.

195. Couldn't the possibility of improving oneself in another existence lead some people to persist on the path of evil, as they know they can always correct their conduct later?

"Those who think like that do not really believe in anything at all, and the idea of eternal punishment would not restrain them any further, as their reason would reject it. Besides, such a concept leads them to a general attitude of skepticism. If only reasonable means were used to guide men, there would not be so many skeptics. During his corporeal life, an imperfect spirit may indeed think as you just described. But once liberated from matter, he thinks differently, because he soon understands the great mistake he has made, *and then adopts the opposite attitude in his new existence.* This is how progress is accomplished, and why on Earth there are those who are more advanced than others: some have already had the experiences that others have yet to go through, but which will be acquired little by little. It depends on them alone to hasten their progress or to halt it indefinitely."

The man who finds himself in a difficult situation wishes to change it as fast as possible. He who has convinced himself that the tribulations of this life are the consequence of his own imperfections will seek to assure himself of a new existence that is less painful. This attitude will more effectively keep him away from the path of evil than the threat of eternal fire, in which he does not believe.

196. Since spirits can only advance by undergoing the tribulations of a corporeal existence, does it follow that material life may be seen as a type of *sieve* or *filter* through which the beings of the spirit world must go in order to arrive at perfection?

"That is correct. They progress in such trials by avoiding evil and doing good. However, it is only after many incarnations or successive developments that they reach, within a more or less extended period of time, and *in proportion to their own efforts*, the goal toward which they tend."

— Does the body prompt the spirit to improve itself, or the other way around?

"Your spirit is everything. Your body is a garment that rots, no more."

An analogy can be made between the various degrees of development of the soul and the juice of grapes. Wine contains the liquor, called spirits or alcohol, which is weakened by the large quantity of foreign elements that dilute its essence. Absolute purity is only achieved after several distillations, each removing a fraction of the impurities. The still represents the body, into which the soul must enter to be purified; the foreign elements are like the perispirit, which is also more refined as the spirit approaches perfection.

5. Fate of children after death

197. Is the spirit of a child who dies in infancy as advanced as that of an adult?

"Sometimes much more so, because the child may have lived much more, and therefore may have acquired more experiences, in proportion to the progress achieved."

— Then can the spirit of a child be more evolved than that of the father or mother?

"That is very frequently the case. Haven't you yourself often seen it on Earth?"

198. Does the spirit of a child who dies in infancy, without having had the chance to do any evil, belong to the higher degrees?

"If such a child has done no evil, nothing good was accomplished, either. God does not liberate that spirit from the trials he must undergo. If he is pure, it is not because he was a child, but because he was already more advanced."

199. Why is life so often cut short in childhood?

"The length of a child's life may be, for the incarnate spirit, the complement of a previous life that had been cut short before the appointed term, and the child's death is often *a trial or an atonement for the parents.*"

— What becomes of the spirit of a child who dies very young?

"The spirit begins a new existence."

If man only had one existence, and if after this existence his fate were sealed for all eternity, why would half the human beings, those who die in infancy, deserve to enjoy eternal happiness without having made much effort? And why would they be exempt from the frequently very painful conditions imposed on the other half? Such an order of things could not be in accord with the justice of God. Through reincarnation, justice is allotted equally for all. The future belongs to all, without exception and without any favors, and those who arrive last will have only themselves to blame. Man must have the merit of his actions, the same way that he is responsible for their consequences.

Besides, it is unreasonable to consider childhood as being simply a state of innocence. Do we not see children endowed with the worst instincts at an age at which education could not have yet exerted any influence? Do we not see those who seem to be innately cunning, devious, and treacherous, who even harbor the instinct of theft or killing, despite the good examples around them? The law absolves them from the transgressions committed, by considering that they have acted without judgment. The law is right, in that they have acted more out of instinct than deliberate intent.

But where do such instincts come from in order to vary so widely among children of the same age, brought up under the same conditions and subject to the same influences? Where does such precocious wickedness come from, if not from the imperfections of the spirit, which education cannot have played a role in yet? Those who are really mean have progressed less, and now suffer the consequences, not of the acts from their present childhood, but of those from their previous existences. This way, the law is the same for everyone, and the justice of God reaches everyone.

6. Sex in spirits

200. Do spirits have sex?

"Not as you understand it, because sex depends on the physical makeup. Love and sympathy exist among spirits, but based on the affinity of sentiments."

201. Can the spirit who has animated the body of a man animate the body of a woman in a new existence, and vice versa?

"Yes, the same spirits may animate men and women."

202. As spirits, do we prefer to incarnate in a male or a female body?

"It matters little to the spirit; it depends on the trials that the spirit must undergo."

Because they do not have sex, spirits may incarnate as either men or women. Since they must progress in every aspect, each sex, like each social position, offers them specific trials and duties, as well as the opportunity to acquire more experience. The one who always incarnated as a man would only know what men know.

7. Kinship, filiation

203. Do parents transmit a portion of their soul to their children, or do they only give them the biological life, to which a new soul afterwards adds the moral life?

"Only the biological life, since the soul is indivisible. Parents of limited intellect may have intelligent children, and vice versa."

204. Since we have had many existences, does kinship go back beyond our current existence?

"It could not be otherwise. The series of corporeal existences establishes ties among spirits that go back to previous existences. This is frequently the reason for the affinity between you and some people whom you believe to have met for the first time."

205. What to think of the opinion that the doctrine of reincarnation destroys family ties by making them go back to previous existences?

"Rather than destroying family ties, the doctrine of reincarnation extends them. Since kinship is based on previous affections, the ties that unite members of the same family are less uncertain. Moreover, reincarnation reinforces the importance of brotherly love, because in your neighbor or in your servant you may find a spirit who was formerly related to you by blood."

— It diminishes, however, the importance that some people attach to their family lineage, as one's father may be a spirit who had previously been of a different race, or of a much different social standing. Isn't that so?

"That is true, but such importance is based on pride. Most people honor their ancestors' titles, ranks, and riches. They would be ashamed of their grandfather if he had been an honest shoemaker, but would boast if they had descended from an immoral aristocrat. No matter what people say or do, they will not prevent things from being what they are, for God has not established the laws of nature to satisfy their vanity."

206. As there may be no actual filiation among the spirits of the descendants of a given family, would it be foolish to honor one's ancestors?

"Assuredly not, because they should feel happy to belong to a family in which spirits of higher orders have incarnated. Although spirits do not proceed from one another, they have no less affection for those who are linked to them by family ties, for they are often attracted to this or that family because of affinities or previously existing bonds. You may be very certain that the spirits of your ancestors do not feel honored at all with the respect you render them out of pride. Their merits are of no avail to you unless you strive to follow the good examples they set forth. Only this way can your memories not only be pleasing, but even useful to them."

8. Physical and moral likeness

207. Parents almost always pass their physical likeness down to their children. Do they pass on a moral likeness to them as well?

"No, because they have different souls or spirits. The body proceeds from the body, but the spirit does not proceed from the spirit. Among the descendants of a given race there is only a biological connection."

—   Where does the moral likeness that sometimes exists between parents and children come from?

"From their spiritual sympathy, which attracts them due to their similar inclinations."

208. Don't the spirits of the parents exert an influence on that of their child after birth?

"A very great influence. As we have said, spirits should contribute to one another's progress. This way, the spirits of the parents are entrusted with the mission of developing those of their children through education. This is a task appointed them; *if they fail at it, they will be guilty.*"

209. Why is it that good and virtuous parents sometimes have children of a perverse nature? In other words, why don't the good qualities of parents always attract, out of affinity, good spirits to be their children?

"An imperfect spirit may ask for good parents hoping that their advice will guide him along a better path, and God often grants his wish by entrusting him to such parents."

210. Through their thoughts and prayers, can parents attract a good spirit instead of an imperfect one to be their child?

"No. They can, however, foster the improvement of the spirit of the child that they brought to the world, and who has been entrusted to them—that is, in fact, their duty. Bad children are a trial for the parents."

211. Where does the likeness of character which often exists among siblings come from, especially in the case of twins?

"They are sympathetic spirits who are attracted by their similar feelings, and *who are happy to be together.*"

212. In the case of conjoined twins, those who share some of their organs, are there two spirits, that is, two souls?

"Yes, but their likeness often makes them seem to you as though they are only one."

213. But if spirits incarnate as twins out of sympathy, where does the aversion come from that may sometimes be noted between them?

"There is no irrevocable rule establishing that twins must always be sympathetic souls. Inimical spirits may wish to struggle together in the great drama of life."

214. What should we think of the stories of children fighting in their mother's womb?

"A metaphor! In order to depict their hatred as deep-rooted, one describes it as dating back before birth. In general, you don't make enough allowance for what is simply a figure of speech."

215. Where does the distinctive character that we observe in each nation or people come from?

"Spirits also constitute families that are brought together by the affinity of tendencies, which are more or less refined according to their spiritual advancement. A nation is like a large family where sympathetic spirits congregate. The predisposition that leads members of these families to unite is the source of the likeness that exists within the distinctive character of each people or nation. Do you think that good and humane spirits would seek to live in a nation of crude and unrefined people? Certainly not. Spirits are attracted to like-minded groups, just as they are attracted to like-minded individuals; there, they find themselves in their element."

216. In his new existences, does man preserve any signs of his moral character from previous ones?

"Yes, that can happen. But as he advances, he changes. His social position may not be the same either; if a master becomes a slave, his tastes will be completely different and you would find it rather hard to recognize him. Since a spirit is the same throughout his various incarnations, his manifestations may have certain similarities from one to the next, tempered, however, by the habits acquired in his new situation, up until a sizeable advancement has completely changed his character. From being a proud and cruel man, for instance, he may become humble and humane, if he has repented."

217. In his different incarnations, does man retain any of his physical characteristics from previous existences?

"The body is destroyed and the new one has no connection with the old. Nevertheless, the spirit is reflected in the body. Admittedly, the body is nothing but matter, but it is modeled according to the abilities of the spirit, which imprints certain characteristics on the body, noticeable mainly on the face. It is thus very apt that the eyes have been described as the mirror of the soul, because the soul is indeed most particularly reflected in the visage. As such, a rather unsightly person may, nonetheless, display a pleasing quality when the body harbors a good, wise, and humane soul. Conversely, one may find very beautiful faces that awaken nothing in you, and may even elicit some sort of dislike. You could suppose that only perfectly-carved bodies would shelter spirits of higher standing, when in reality every day you encounter upright souls inhabiting deformed bodies. Although there may not be any marked physical likeness, a similarity of tastes and tendencies could still convey what we call a family likeness."

The body that clothes a soul in a new incarnation does not *necessarily* have any connection with the previous one, as it may proceed from a totally different origin. It would therefore be absurd to deduce a succession of incarnations of one single spirit from a merely fortuitous likeness. Nevertheless, a spirit's qualities almost always modify the organs that are the instrument of the spirit's manifestation, imprinting on the face, and even on the overall demeanor, a signature characteristic. Thus, inside the humblest body one might find expressions of nobility and dignity, while under the luxurious attire of a patrician one can often find corruption and dishonor. Some people who have risen from the lowest ranks acquire the habits and manners of high social ranks with hardly any effort; they seem to have *rediscovered* their natural element, whereas others, in spite of their birth and upbringing, always feel out of place there. How can this fact be explained except as a result of what the spirit had been in previous existences?

9. Innate ideas

218. Do incarnate spirits preserve any trace of the thoughts they had and the knowledge they acquired in their previous lives?

"They retain a vague memory which provides the incarnate spirit with what you call innate ideas."

— Then the theory of innate ideas is not just a fantasy?

"No, the knowledge acquired in each existence is not lost. When liberated from matter, a spirit always recalls such knowledge. While incarnate, this knowledge may be partially and temporarily forgotten, but the intuition that remains of it helps the spirit advance. Without it, he would always have to start anew. In each additional existence, the spirit starts from the point at which he left in the preceding one."

— Must there be then a very close connection between two successive existences?

"Not always as close as you might imagine, because circumstances are frequently very different, and the spirit may have progressed in the interval between two incarnations." (See #216)

219. What is the origin of the extraordinary faculties of those individuals who, without any previous training, seem to have an intuition about certain fields of knowledge, such as languages, mathematics, and so on?

"A memory of the past, of the progress previously accomplished by their souls, of which they now have no awareness, however. Where else do you suppose that such abilities come from? The body changes, but the spirit does not, even if it changes attire."

220. In changing bodies, can one lose certain intellectual faculties, no longer having, for example, a taste for the arts?

"Yes, if one has dishonored or misused it. Additionally, a faculty may remain dormant during an existence because the spirit wishes to exercise an unrelated one. In that case, it remains latent and reappears later."

221. Is it due to a retrospective memory that man, even in primitive cultures, possesses the instinctive sentiment of the existence of God and the presentiment of the future life?

"It is a memory that man has retained of what he knew as a spirit before incarnating; pride often stifles this sentiment, though."

—   Are certain beliefs related to the Spiritist Doctrine—which are to be found in all cultures—due to this same memory?

"This doctrine is as old as the world. That is why we find it everywhere—an evidence of its validity. Preserving an intuition of the spirit state, the incarnate spirit has an instinctive awareness of the invisible world. Frequently, however, prejudices distort this awareness, and ignorance contaminates it with superstition."

■■■

Chapter 5:
Considerations on the Plurality of Existences

222. Some people object that the doctrine of reincarnation is not new, that it is a rehash of the ideas of Pythagoras. We have never said that the Spiritist Doctrine is a modern invention. Its tenets stemming from the laws of nature, the belief in them must have been held since the beginning of time, and we have always sought to show that traces of it may be found in the earliest accounts of antiquity. It is known that Pythagoras was not the creator of the doctrine of metempsychosis; he took it from the Hindu philosophers and the Egyptians, who had believed in it from time immemorial.

The idea of the transmigration of souls was therefore a common belief, accepted by the most eminent men. How did this idea come to them? Was it by revelation or intuition? We do not know, but whatever the case may be, an idea could not have traversed the ages and have been accepted by the most advanced intellects if there were not an element of truth in it. The antiquity of this doctrine should therefore be considered an evidence in its favor rather than against it. But, as it is equally known, between the metempsychosis of the ancients and the modern doctrine of reincarnation there is this one chief difference: Spirits most absolutely reject the transmigration of human souls into animals, and vice versa.

In teaching the doctrine of the plurality of corporeal existences, the Spirits have thus renewed a doctrine that was born during the earliest ages of the world, and which has been kept deeply ingrained in many people's minds. The Spirits have simply presented it from a more rational standpoint, more according to the progressive laws of nature, and more in harmony with the wisdom of the Creator, by divesting it of all the exaggerations of superstition. A point worth noting is that it is not only in this book that they have taught it recently: even before it was published, numerous communications of the same nature had been received in many places, and they have grown considerably since then. It would, perhaps, be a case to examine as to why not all Spirits seem to agree about this point; we shall revisit this point later.

For now, let us examine the issue from another vantage point, not considering any revelations by the Spirits, by putting them aside for the moment, and assuming that this theory did not come from them at all. Let us even suppose that the Spirits were never asked anything about it. Let us instead place ourselves on a neutral ground for the time being, and accept the same degree of likelihood for both hypotheses: that of the plurality of corporeal existences and that of a single existence. Let us then see toward which side reason and our own interests will take us.

Some individuals reject the idea of reincarnation for the simple reason that it is not convenient for them. They say that one existence is quite enough, and that they would not like to restart a similar one. We even know people who are enraged by the mere thought of returning to Earth. We would ask them whether God has asked for their advice or checked their preferences when establishing the laws of the universe. Now, only one of the two possibilities can be true: either reincarnation exists, or it does not. If it does, it matters little that they do not like it; they will have to submit to it, as God shall not ask for their permission. Opposing it would be the same as a sick man saying, "I've already suffered too much today; I don't want to suffer any more tomorrow." No matter how ill-tempered he is, he will not suffer any less tomorrow or in the days that follow until he has recovered.

Likewise, if those individuals must live again corporeally, they will do so; they will reincarnate. They will protest uselessly, like a child who does not want to go to school, or a criminal condemned to prison, because they will have to go through it. Objections of this kind are too childish to merit a more serious examination. In order to reassure them, however, we will state that the Spiritist tenet of reincarnation is not as terrible as they might think, and that if they were to study it in depth, they would have no reason to fear; they would understand that their standing in a new existence only depends on themselves; that it will be happy or unhappy according to what they have done here on Earth, *and that they may, right from their present life, raise themselves high enough so as not to fear falling back into the mire of atonement.*

We presume that we address ourselves to people who believe in some kind of future after death, rather than those who only see annihilation before them, or those who wish to plunge their soul into a universal whole, without preserving their individuality, like drops of rain falling into the ocean, which turns out to be not much different from annihilation. If you believe in any kind of future at all, you certainly do not suppose that it will be the same for everyone, otherwise, why strive to be good? In other words, why should men place any restraint upon themselves? Why should they not satisfy all their passions, all their desires—even at the expense of others—if their future would be neither better nor worse for it? If you believe that your future will be more or less fortunate according to what you have done during your earthly life, would you not wish to make it as happy as possible because it would be for all eternity? Would you, by any chance, have the presumption of being one of the most perfect creatures to have ever lived on Earth, thus acquiring the right to the supreme bliss of the elect?

Probably not. You must then admit that there are those who stand above you and deserve a better situation, although this does not imply that you must be classed among the reprobate. Well then, imagine yourself for a moment in that middle position, at which you admit to be currently placed, and imagine that someone tells you, "You suffer, you are not as happy as you could be, whereas there are others all around you who seem to enjoy perfect happiness. Would you like to trade your situation for theirs?"

"Of course, I would," you reply, "but what would I have to do?" The answer is that you have to do next to nothing; resume the work you have not carried out correctly, and try to do it better. Would you hesitate to accept that, even at the cost of many lifetimes of trial?

Let us make a more ordinary comparison. Suppose you were to say the following to a man who, although not in extreme poverty, is going through a period of hardships due to his limited resources: "There is a huge fortune for you to enjoy; however, you must work hard for it for one minute." If he were the laziest being on Earth, he would not hesitate to say, "I'm willing to work for one minute, two minutes, an hour, a whole day if necessary! What difference would that make if I would later enjoy a life of abundance?" Well then, what does one corporeal life represent in comparison with eternity? Less than a minute, less than a second.

At other times we are faced with the following reasoning: God, who is supremely good, would not impose on us the obligation to recommence another series of wretchedness and tribulations. Is there, by any chance, more kindness in condemning man to eternal suffering because of a few moments of error than in granting him the means to repair his wrongs? Let us say that two craftsmen each had a worker who aspired to become partners with their respective employer, but on one particular workday, both employees spent their working hours in idleness, deserving to be fired. One of the craftsmen actually fired his worker despite the pleas of the latter, who, unable to obtain any other employment, died of want. The other craftsman said to his worker, "You have wasted a whole day so you owe me compensation. You have performed badly, so you owe me reparation; however, I will let you start over tomorrow. Do your work well, and I will keep you, and you will be able to continue aspiring to the promotion I promised you." Is it necessary to ask which of the two craftsmen was more humane? Then would God, who is clemency itself, be more uncompromising than man?

The thought that our fate is forever sealed because of a few years of trial—even though it does not always depend on our efforts to reach perfection on Earth—is rather disheartening; conversely, the opposite idea is eminently consoling, as it rekindles our hope. Therefore, without deciding either for or against the plurality of existences, and without favoring one hypothesis over the other, we will simply say that if the choice could be made, no one would prefer a sentence that could not be appealed.

A philosopher [a] once said that if God did not exist, it would be necessary to invent Him for the satisfaction of mankind. The same could be said of the plurality of existences. As we stated previously, God does not ask for our permission, nor does God check our preferences—things either are or they are not. Based on such considerations, let us see on which side the odds might lie. Let us consider the matter from another point of view—still ignoring the teachings of the Spirits—and only as a philosophical investigation.

If there is no reincarnation, then obviously there can be only one corporeal existence; if there is only one corporeal existence, the soul of each individual must then be created at birth, unless we accept the preexistence of the soul. However, if that were the case, then we would have to ask what the soul was before birth and if such a preexisting state would not comprise an existence of some kind or another. There is no middle ground: either the soul existed before the body, or it did not. If it existed, what was its situation? Did it or did it not possess self-awareness? If it did not, that would be about the same as saying that it did not exist at all; if it did, however, could this individuality progress or was it stationary? In either case, what was its situation when it joined the body? According to the common belief, which assumes that the soul is born at the same time as the body, or, with the same consequences, that before incarnation it possessed only neutral faculties, we must ask the following questions:

1) Why does the soul display aptitudes that are so diverse and independent of the ideas acquired by education?

2) Where do the extraordinary abilities that some very young children possess in a given art or science come from, while others lag behind or remain unexceptional their entire life?

3) Why do some children seem to be endowed with inborn or intuitive ideas that do not exist in others?

4) Why do certain children demonstrate precocious impulses towards vice or virtue, or innate sentiments of virtue or evil, in evident contrast with the environment in which they have been born?

5) Why is it that some individuals, regardless of their education, are more advanced than others?

6) Why are there primitive and civilized men? If we took a Khoikhoi baby at birth, raised and then sent him to one of our most renowned schools, would he become a Laplace or a Newton?

We would ask what philosophy or theosophy can solve these problems. Either souls are equal at birth or they are not—that we cannot doubt. If they are equal, why are there such differences of aptitude? One could claim that it depends on the body, but in that case, we would have the most monstrous and immoral doctrine. Man would be no more than a machine, a victim of matter. He would not be responsible for his actions since everything could be attributed to his physical imperfections. However, if souls are not equal, then it is because God created them so. Then, we must ask, why is that inborn superiority awarded to only a few? Would such a partial treatment be consistent with the justice and love that God grants to all creatures equally?

Conversely, if we admit a succession of previous, progressive existences, everything can be explained. At birth, men bring with them the intuition of what they have already acquired. They are more or less evolved according to the number of existences they have gone through, which will establish how near or how far they are from their starting point—precisely like in a group of individuals of all ages, where they will have developed according to the number of years each one has lived. The series of existences represent for the life of the soul what years represent for the life of the body. Gather one day, for instance, a thousand individuals of ages ranging from one to eighty. Now suppose that a veil has been cast over all their preceding days, so that you unwittingly believe that all of them were born on the same day. You would naturally wonder why some are big and others are little, some look old and others young, some are educated and others still ignorant. Nevertheless, if the cloud hiding their past were lifted, if you suddenly realized that some have lived longer than others, everything would be explained. God, out of His divine justice, could not have created some souls more advanced than others. With the plurality of existences, the inequality that we see has nothing contrary to the strictest equity; the issue is that we can only see the present, not the past.

Does this argument rest upon some arbitrary theory or supposition? No, because we start from an evident, incontestable fact: the inequality of aptitudes, and of intellectual and moral development, and we have found that this fact cannot be explained by any existing system, whereas our theory gives it a simple, natural, and logical explanation. Would it be rational to prefer the one that does not explain this fact over the one that does?

Regarding the sixth question, it will likely be said that Khoikhoi are less advanced. But then we will ask: are they human or not? If they are human, why would God have denied them the privileges granted to Caucasians? And if they are not human, then why try to make them Christians? The Spiritist Doctrine is much more generous than all of that, because it reveals that there are not different human species, but only human beings whose spirits may be more or less advanced, but all subject to reaching perfection. Is this not more in accord with the justice of God?

We have just considered the soul according to its past and its present. However, if we consider it with respect to its future, we shall encounter the same difficulties:

1) If our destiny is to be decided solely by our present existence, what will be the respective situations of those of primitive and of more advanced cultures in the future life? Will they be on equal footing or will there be a difference in their level of eternal happiness?

2) Will the man who has worked his entire life to promote his advancement be on the same level as the one who has lagged behind, not due to his own fault, but because he did not have the time or the opportunity to advance?

3) Is he who has done evil because the means to escape ignorance was not available to him, liable for a state of affairs that did not depend on him?

4) As much as one strives to enlighten, moralize, and civilize mankind, for each one who is touched by such efforts, there are millions

who die every day before light has managed to reach them. What is their fate? Will they be treated as reprobates? If not, what have they done to deserve to be on the same level as the others?

5) What is the fate of children who die at a very early age before having been able to do either good or evil? If they are among the elect, why are they granted such a favor without having done anything to deserve it? And by what privilege are they exempt from the tribulations of a full lifetime?

Is there a doctrine that can reconcile these issues? Admit the existence of successive lives, and everything can be explained in conformity with God's justice. What we could not accomplish in one existence, we can in another. Thus, no one escapes the law of progress, and all will be rewarded according to their *real* individual merit, and no one is excluded from the supreme bliss to which everyone aspires, no matter what obstacles may have been encountered along the way.

Similar questions could be raised endlessly, because the psychological and moral problems that can only be explained by the plurality of existences are countless; we have limited ourselves to the most general only. Nevertheless, it may still be argued that the doctrine of reincarnation has not been accepted by the Church. It would therefore be the subversion of religion. It is not our objective at this juncture to address this issue, since it is sufficient for us to have shown that the doctrine is eminently moral and rational. Furthermore, what is moral and rational cannot be contrary to a religion that proclaims God to be the perfect embodiment of goodness and reason.

What would have become of religion if, contrary to the universal opinion and the testimony of science, it had denied the evidence and expelled anyone who did not believe in the movement of the Sun and the six days of creation? What credit would religion deserve, and what authority would it have among enlightened nations, if it were based on such obvious errors that were once articles of faith? Whenever evidence has been established conclusively, the Church has wisely sided with it. If it is proven that things exist which would be impossible without reincarnation, if certain points of religious dogma cannot be explained except by such means, then it will be necessary to accept this doctrine and realize that the discrepancy between it and religious tenets is only apparent. Later, we shall demonstrate that religion is perhaps less distanced from this doctrine than one would imagine, and that it would suffer no more in accepting it than it suffered from the discovery of the orbiting of the Earth around the Sun and of the geological periods, which at first also seemed to contradict the sacred texts. In addition, the principle of reincarnation appears in many passages of the scriptures, and is found explicitly formulated in the gospels (Matthew 17:9-13):

> "As they were coming down from the mountain, Jesus charged them, 'Tell no one about the vision until the Son of Man has been raised from the dead.' Then, his disciples asked him, 'Why do the scribes say that Elijah must come first?' He said in reply, 'Elijah will indeed come and restore all things. But I tell you that Elijah has already come, and, they did not recognize him, but did to him whatever they pleased. So also will the Son of Man suffer at their hands.' Then the disciples understood that he spoke of John the Baptist."

Since John the Baptist was Elijah, he must have been the reincarnation of the spirit of Elijah in the body of John the Baptist.

Besides, whatever may be our opinion of reincarnation, whether we accept it or not, we are subject to it if it is real, despite our beliefs to the contrary. The essential point is that the teachings of the Spirits are eminently Christian, resting upon the immortality of the soul, future punishments and rewards, God's justice, human free will, and the Christ's moral code; it is therefore not anti-religious.

As mentioned before, we have so far argued without any reference to the Spirits' teachings, which for some people carry no authority. If we, as so many others, have adopted the tenet of the plurality of existences, it is not only because it comes from the Spirits, but because it has seemed to us to be the most logical, and the only one that solves issues that were until now insoluble. If it had come to us from a mere mortal, we would have adopted it just the same, not hesitating to give up our own ideas. The moment an error is exposed, our self-esteem has more to lose than to gain from holding on to it.

Likewise, we would have rejected it, although coming from the Spirits, if the idea had seemed to us to be contrary to reason, just as we have rejected so many others. We know from experience that we must not blindly accept everything that comes from spirits, just as we cannot accept everything that comes from men. The first of its merits, in our opinion, therefore, is that this doctrine is logical. But it also has another merit, that of being confirmed by the facts—positive, material facts, so to speak, which an attentive and well-reasoned study reveal to anyone who strives to study them with patience and perseverance, and before which doubt is no longer tenable. Once these facts become widely known, like the formation of the planet and its orbit around the Sun, it will be necessary to surrender to the evidence, and the opponents of the doctrine of reincarnation will have raised their objections in vain.

Summing up, we recognize the fact that the doctrine of the plurality of existences is the only one that can explain what would be unexplainable without it; that it is eminently consoling and conforms to the strictest justice; and finally, that it is for men the lifeline that God, out of His divine mercy, has thrown to them.

The words of Jesus himself leave no doubt about it. As we read in the third chapter, verses 3–5 of the gospel according to Saint John:

> Jesus answered him, "Verily, verily, I say unto you, *except a man be born again*, he cannot see the kingdom of God." Nicodemus said unto him, "How can a man be born when he is old? Can he enter a second time into his mother's womb and be born?" Jesus answered, "Verily, verily, I say unto you, except a man be born of water and of spirit, he cannot enter into the kingdom of God. That which is born of the flesh is flesh; and that which is born of the spirit is spirit." Marvel not that I said unto you, *you must be born again*." (See the section "Resurrection of the Flesh" below, #1010).

■■■

[a] This refers to the quote by Voltaire (François-Marie Arouet, 1694–1778), "Si Dieu n'existait pas, il faudrait l'inventer" (If God did not exist, it would be necessary to invent Him), from the *Épître à l'Auteur du Livre des Trois Imposteurs* (1770-11-10). —Trans.

Chapter 6:
Spirit Life

1. Spirit life in between incarnations

223. Does the soul reincarnate immediately after separation from the body?

"Sometimes immediately, but most often after an interval of longer or shorter duration. On more highly evolved worlds, reincarnation is almost always immediate; as the corporeal matter of those worlds is less coarse, an incarnate spirit enjoys nearly all of its spirit faculties. Its normal state is the same as that of your lucid somnambulists." [a]

224. What happens to the soul in the interval between incarnations?

"During this interval the spirit aspires to a new incarnation; it waits."

— How long may this interval last?

"From a few hours to thousands of centuries. Besides, strictly speaking, there is no maximum length of time that may be stipulated for the interval between consecutive incarnations. It may last for a very long time, but never forever. Sooner or later, a spirit always has the opportunity to begin another existence, which serves for the purification of the preceding ones."

—   Does the length of this interval depend on the spirit's wishes, or can it be imposed as an expiation?

"It is a consequence of the spirit's free will. Spirits understand the consequences of their choices, but for some it may be a punishment inflicted by God. Others ask for it to be extended in order to pursue studies that cannot be carried out productively except in the spirit state."

225. Is the state in between incarnations in itself an indication of the inferiority of spirits?

"No, since there are spirits of every degree in this state. Incarnation is the state that is transitory, as we have already stated. In their normal state, spirits are disengaged from matter."

226. Could we say that all spirits who are not incarnate are in this state?

"Those who must reincarnate, yes, but pure spirits, who have reached perfection, are not between-incarnation spirits: their state is permanent."

Regarding their intrinsic qualities, spirits belong to different orders or degrees, through which they go successively as they purify themselves. Regarding their state as spirits, they may be: *incarnate*, that is, connected to a body; *between-incarnation spirits*, which is to say, disconnected from the material body while awaiting a new incarnation in order to improve themselves; or *pure spirits*, that is, perfected and having no further need of incarnating.

227. How do spirits in the state between incarnations educate themselves? It certainly is not the same way we do.

"They study their past and seek ways to evolve. They watch and observe what happens in the realms they visit. They listen to the explanations of enlightened individuals and the advice of spirits who are more evolved than they are, and all this provides them with notions that they do not yet have."

228. Do spirits retain any of the human passions?

"Upon shedding their material body, more advanced spirits leave their lower passions behind, only keeping the good ones. Low order spirits maintain their baser passions, otherwise, they would belong to the first order."

229. Why don't spirits leave all their lower passions behind upon leaving Earth, as they can then see the problems they cause?

"In your world, there are people who are excessively jealous. Do you believe they will lose that imperfection upon departing? After they leave Earth behind, especially in the case of those who had deeply rooted passions, there remains a type of atmosphere around them, filled with all their lower qualities, as their spirit is not entirely freed from matter. Only occasionally they have a glimpse of the truth, so as to be able to see the right path."

230. Can spirits progress while in between incarnations?

"They may improve themselves significantly, always according to their will and desire. However, it is only during a corporeal life that they put into practice their newly acquired ideas."

231. Are spirits in between incarnations happy or unhappy?

"More or less so according to their merit. They either suffer from the passions the essence of which they have retained, or else they are happy to the extent of their dematerialization. During their interval between corporeal lives, spirits can make out what they still lack in order to be happier, so they look for the means of achieving it. But they are not always allowed to reincarnate at their discretion, something which may represent a punishment."

232. While in the interval between incarnations, can spirits visit every other world?

"That is as the case may be. When a spirit leaves his body, he is still not completely disconnected from matter. He still belongs to the world on which he has lived, or to one of the same degree, unless he has progressed sufficiently during his lifetime. Progress is where his objective must lie, or else he will never be able to perfect himself. He may, however, visit certain superior worlds, but in the role of an outsider. He can only catch glimpses of such worlds, being inspired to improve himself so as to be worthy of the happiness enjoyed there, and eventually to be able to incarnate there."

233. Do spirits who are already purified ever go to less-evolved worlds?

"They frequently go there in order to help those worlds advance. Without that, such worlds would be left to themselves, without guides to direct them."

2. Transitional worlds

234. Are there, as some have stated, worlds that serve as stopovers and resting places for spirits during the interval between incarnations?

"Yes, there are worlds that are meant particularly for spirits during this interval. They may temporally inhabit these worlds, which are a sort of camp where they can rest during a very long interval, which is always somewhat wearisome. These are intermediary positions among worlds, ranked according to the nature of the spirits who have access to them, and where they find more or less enjoyable conditions."

—   Can the spirits who live on those worlds leave as they please?

"Yes, spirits who live on those worlds can leave them to go wherever they need to be. Imagine them to be like migrating birds that have descended on an island, waiting until they have regained their strength in order to reach their destination."

235. Do spirits progress during their stopovers on these transitory worlds?

"Certainly. Those who gather on them do so with the goal of educating themselves and to more easily gain permission to go to more advanced places, until they reach the position of the elect."

236. Are these transitional worlds, due to their special nature, forever destined for spirits between incarnations?

"No, that function is only temporary."

—   Are they simultaneously inhabited by corporeal beings?

"No, their surface is barren. Those who inhabit them do not need anything."

—   Is this barrenness permanent and related to their special nature?

"No, their barrenness is only transitory."

—   Must these worlds then be devoid of natural beauties?

"Nature manifests by the beauties of the immensity, in no way less admirable than what you call natural beauties."

—   Since the state of these worlds is transitory, will Earth be among them one day?

"It has already been."

—   When?

"During its formation."

Nothing in nature is useless; each thing has its purpose, its destination. There is no void, everything is inhabited, and life manifests everywhere. Thus, during the eons that elapsed before the appearance of man on Earth, during the slow periods of transition attested to by the geologic layers, and even before the formation of the first organic beings within that shapeless mass, in that barren chaos in which the elements were mixed together, life was not absent.

Beings who did not have our needs or our physical sensations found a refuge there. Even in that imperfect state, God willed for the Earth to be useful for something. So, who would dare say that among the billions of worlds that orbit through the immensity of space, only a single planet—one of the smallest of them all, lost in the crowd—had the exclusive privilege of being inhabited? What would then be the utility of all the others? Could God have made them merely to regale our eyes? This would be an absurd supposition, incompatible with the wisdom that transpires through all His works, and unacceptable if we imagine all those that we cannot yet see. No one can dispute that, in the idea that worlds still unsuitable for material life are nevertheless populated with beings appropriate for the conditions on them, there is something grand and sublime, where perhaps is to be found the solution to more than one problem.

3. Perceptions, sensations, and sufferings of spirits

237. Once in the spirit world, do souls still have the perceptions they had when alive?

"Yes, as well as others that they did not have because their body was like a veil that obscured their perception. Intelligence is a natural attribute of the spirit, but it expresses itself more freely when it is unhindered."

238. Are the perceptions and knowledge of spirits unlimited? In other words, do they know everything?

"The closer they approach perfection, the more they know. If they are high-order spirits, they know much. Low-order spirits are more or less ignorant on all subjects."

239. Do spirits know the beginning of things?

"That too depends on how evolved and purified they are. Low-order spirits do not know any more than men."

240. Do spirits perceive time as we do?

"No, and that is what makes you not always understand us when it comes to fixing dates or eras."

Spirits live outside of time as we know it; for them time ceases to be, as it were. The centuries, that are so long to us, represent to them only instants that dissolve into eternity, the same way that irregularities of a terrain fade and disappear to someone who looks at it from high above.

241. Do spirits have a more precise and appropriate idea of the present than we do?

"More or less so, just as someone who can see clearly has a more appropriate idea of things than a blind person. Spirits see what you do not see, and they thus judge differently than you; but, once again, that depends on how evolved they are."

242. How do spirits have knowledge about the past? Is such knowledge unlimited for them?

"When we concern ourselves with the past, it becomes like the present, precisely like when you remember something that has impressed you during your life on Earth. Except that, as we are no longer limited by the material veil that clouds your intelligence, we remember things that have vanished from your memory. Spirits, however, do not know everything, their own creation, in the first place."

243. Do spirits know the future?

"Again, it depends on their advancement. Frequently they only have a glimpse of it, *but they do not always have permission to reveal it*. When they do see it, it appears to them to be the present. Spirits see the future more clearly the more they approach God. After death, souls may see and grasp their *past incarnations* immediately, but they cannot see what God has in store for them. For that, it is necessary for them to become one with God, after a great number of existences."

— Do spirits who have reached perfection possess complete knowledge of the future?

"Complete is not the right word, because God alone is the sovereign master; no one can be equal to God."

244. Do spirits see God?

"Only superior spirits see and understand Him; spirits of lower orders feel and intuit Him."

— When a low-order spirit says that a thing is forbidden or permitted to him by God, how does he know that the order actually comes from Him?

"He does not see God but senses His sovereignty; when a certain thing must not be done or when a certain word must not be spoken, he receives a sort of intuition or invisible warning that keeps him from proceeding. Don't you have presentiments that secretly warn you to do or not do certain things? The same happens to us, but to a higher degree. Understand that, as the essence of spirits is subtler than yours, we can more easily receive the divine warnings."

— Is the order transmitted by God directly or through other spirits?

"It does not come from God directly, because to communicate with Him directly one must be worthy of it. God transmits His orders through spirits that are more advanced in perfection and knowledge."

245. Is the sight of spirits circumscribed as it is in corporeal beings?

"No, it resides within the spirits themselves."

246. Do spirits need light in order to see?

"They see on their own, without the need of external light. There is no darkness for them, except that in which they may find themselves as an expiation."

247. Do spirits need to transport themselves in order to see in two different places? For instance, can they see simultaneously the two hemispheres of the globe?

"As spirits travel at the speed of thought, we may say that they see everywhere all at once. Their thought can radiate and be present at many different points at the same time, but this faculty depends on their advancement; the less pure they are, the more limited is their sight. Only superior spirits can take in a whole at a single glance."

Among spirits, the sense of sight is inherent in their nature and permeates their whole being like light in a luminous object, constituting a type of universal lucidity that extends to everything, simultaneously embracing space, time, and things, and for which there is no darkness or material obstacle. One must understand that it ought to be this way; in the case of man, the sense of sight operates through an organ that is stimulated by light; without light man cannot see. In the case of spirits, however, as their sense of sight is an inherent attribute, independent of any outside agent, it does not depend on the availability of light. (See "Ubiquity," #92)

248. Do spirits see things as distinctly as we do?

"Even more distinctly, because their sight penetrates that which yours cannot. Nothing hampers it."

249. Do spirits perceive sounds?

"Yes, and they perceive even those sounds that your imperfect senses are not able to detect."

— Is the hearing faculty, like that of sight, in their whole being?

"All perceptions are attributes of their nature, and are thus part of their being. When a spirit is clothed with a material body, perceptions are only registered through specific organic systems. When free from matter, however, they are no longer localized."

250. Since the perceptions are attributes of the spirits themselves, can they refrain from registering them?

"Spirits only see and hear what they want to; at least this is generally the case, especially for more evolved spirits, because those still quite imperfect frequently must hear and see what may be useful for their advancement, often against their will."

251. Are spirits sensitive to music?

"Do you mean your earthly music? What is that kind of music when compared to the music of the celestial spheres, that harmony of which nothing on Earth can give you the remotest idea? One is to the other what the chant of the primitive man is when compared with a tender orchestral melody. Nevertheless, ordinary spirits may take a certain pleasure in listening to your music because they are not yet able to appreciate a more sublime form of music. For spirits, music has infinite enchantments, due to their highly developed sensitive qualities. Of course, I refer to the music of the celestial spheres, of a beauty and delicacy that only the most perfect spiritual imagination is able to conceive."

252. Are spirits sensitive to natural beauties?

"The natural beauties of the different worlds are so diverse that spirits are far from knowing them all. Yes, they are sensitive to them according to their ability to appreciate and understand them. In the case of highly evolved spirits, the perception of the beauties of the ensemble is such that the beauties of the details fade in comparison."

253. Do spirits experience our physical needs and sufferings?

"They *know* them, because they have endured them, but they do not experience them physically as you do—they are spirits."

254.   Do spirits feel fatigue and the need to rest?

"They cannot feel fatigue as you understand it, and therefore they do not need your type of physical rest, because they do not have organs that require their energies to be restored. However, spirits do rest, in the sense that they are not in a state of constant activity. They do not act in a physical way, because their action is entirely intellectual and their rest is entirely mental. There are moments when their thought is not so active, and is no longer directed to an object in particular. This is a true rest for them, but it cannot be compared to that of the body. The type of fatigue that spirits may experience is owing to their lack of advancement; the more perfect they are, the less they need to rest."

255.   When spirits say that they suffer, what is the nature of the suffering they experience?

"A mental anguish which tortures them more acutely than physical suffering."

256.   Why then do some spirits complain about suffering from cold or heat?

"It is a recollection of what they suffered during their lifetime, a feeling sometimes as painful as the actual suffering. Frequently, they use it as a comparison to describe their situation, for the lack of a more suitable description. When they remember their body, they experience a sensation similar to when you take off a heavy coat, but feel as if you were still wearing it a little later."

4. Theoretical essay on sensation in spirits

257.   The body is the instrument of pain; if not its first cause, it is at least its immediate cause. The soul has the perception of such pain, and this perception is the effect. The memory that it preserves of it can be very painful, but this does not imply a physical action. In reality, neither cold nor heat can hurt the soul's tissues, for a soul can neither freeze nor burn.

Do we not often see either the memory or the fear of physical pain produce real effects, even to the point of causing death? We all know that amputees may still feel pain in the limb that no longer exists. The limb is obviously neither the site nor the starting point of the pain; the brain has preserved the impression, simply. Likewise, we can assume there is a similar process in the suffering of spirits after death. The perispirit plays an important role in all spirit phenomena, including vaporous or tangible apparitions, the state of the spirit at the moment of death, the so-frequent perception of still being alive, the terrifying situation of suicides, as well as those who have undergone capital punishment and those who have overindulged in material pleasures, and so on. An in-depth study of the perispirit has therefore shed light on the question of sensation in spirits, providing the explanations which we summarize below.

The perispirit is the link that unites the spirit with the matter of the body. It is drawn from the universal fluid of the surrounding environment. At the same time, it contains electricity, magnetic fluid, and to a certain extent, inert matter. We could say that it is the quintessence of matter. It is the essential element of organic life but not of intellectual life, as the latter rests in the spirit. The perispirit is also the agent of external perceptions. In the body, these sensorial perceptions are localized in the organs that serve as channels for them. When the body is destroyed, the sensations become generalized, and that is why spirits do not generally say that their head hurts more than their feet, for instance.

Also, we have to be careful not to confuse the sensations of the perispirit, once disengaged and independent, with the sensations of the body; we can only take the latter as a comparison, not as a perfect equivalent. Liberated from the body, the spirit may suffer, but this suffering is not the same as that of the body. It is not, however, an exclusively mental or moral suffering either, such as the feeling of remorse, because the spirit may complain of being hot or cold. Spirits suffer no more in the summer than in the winter, we have seen spirits go through flames without experiencing any pain at all, demonstrating that high temperatures have no effect on them. The pain they eventually feel is thus not physical, exactly, but rather a vague inner sensorial perception, of which the spirit is not always aware, because the pain is not localized or produced by external agents. It is a memory rather than a reality, but a very painful memory nonetheless. However, sometimes it may be more than a memory, as we shall see.

Experience has taught us that, at the moment of death, the perispirit disengages itself more or less slowly from the body. In the first few moments, the spirit does not understand the new situation, not believing himself to be dead, but feeling alive, rather. The spirit sees the body by his side and knows that it is his own, but does not understand why he is separated from it. This state lasts as long as there is a link between the body and the perispirit. One who had committed suicide once told us, "No, I'm not dead," and added, "yet, I can feel the worms devouring me." Of course, the worms were not devouring the perispirit, let alone the spirit, but only the body. Since the separation between the body and the perispirit was not yet complete, there continued to be a mental repercussion of sorts that conveyed to him the sensation of what occurred to the body. Repercussion may not be the exact term, however, as it may imply an effect of too physical a nature. It was rather the sight of what was happening within the body, to which the perispirit was still attached, producing an illusion which the spirit took as being real. It was not therefore the memory of a past occurrence, as he had never been devoured by worms during his lifetime; it was rather an attending sensation.

We can therefore draw certain conclusions from the attentive observation of these facts. When alive, the body receives external stimuli and transmits them to the spirit through the perispirit, which is likely what is called the neural fluid. When dead, the body no longer feels anything because it does not have an attending spirit or perispirit. When disengaged from the body, the perispirit has sensorial perceptions, but because such perceptions no longer reach it via a specific channel, they are generalized.

Now, as in reality the perispirit is only an agent of transmission—because it is the spirit that is endowed with consciousness—it follows that if the perispirit could exist without the spirit, the perispirit would feel no more than the body once devoid of life. Similarly, without an attending perispirit, the spirit by itself would be inaccessible to all painful sensation, which is what happens in the case of completely purified spirits. We know that the more a spirit advances in perfection, the more etherealized becomes the essence of the perispirit, which means that material influences diminish as the spirit progresses, that is, as the perispirit itself becomes less coarse.

One may say, however, that if pleasant sensations are transmitted to the spirit via the perispirit, so are unpleasant ones, and if a pure spirit is inaccessible to some, he must be equally inaccessible to others. Yes, certainly, but only to those sensations that derive from the influence of matter as we know it. The sound of our instruments and the smell of our flowers make no impression whatsoever on a pure spirit, yet he enjoys inner perceptions of indefinable enchantment, of which we cannot have the slightest idea, because we are, with that regard, like someone who is blind from birth with regard to light. We know that it exists, but how? This is where our knowledge stops. We know that spirits have perceptions, sensations, hearing, and sight and that these faculties are attributes of the whole being—not only of certain organs—as is the case with incarnate human beings. But once again, how is this so? That is what we do not know. Spirits themselves cannot explain it to us, because our language was not made to express ideas that we cannot conceive of, just as in the language of primitive tribes there are no terms for the expression of our arts, sciences, and philosophical studies.

In saying that spirits are inaccessible to the impressions of matter, we are referring to the most advanced spirits, whose etherealized envelopes find no analogy in this world. It is different with spirits whose perispirit is denser, because these are able to perceive our sounds and scents, but not through a specific part of their being, as when alive. We may say that molecular vibrations are felt throughout their entire being and are then transmitted to their *sensorium commune*, the spirit itself, albeit in a different manner, and perhaps producing a different impression, which may cause a modification in their perception. They hear the sound of our voice, and yet they can understand us without the aid of speech, merely through the transmission of thought.

This confirms something we have mentioned, that the more dematerialized spirits are, the greater their mental perception. Their sense of sight is independent of our light. The ability to see is an essential attribute of the soul, for whom darkness does not exist. It is also more extensive and more penetrating among those who are more purified. Therefore, souls or spirits have within themselves the faculty of all perceptions. During the corporeal life, these perceptions are hampered by the coarseness of our organs; during the extra-corporeal life, they are less obstructed, as the semi-material envelope becomes more refined.

The perispiritual envelope, drawn from the surrounding environment, varies according to the nature of the different worlds. As they go from one world to another, spirits change that envelope as we change our clothes when we go from summer to winter, or from the poles to the equator. When they come visit us, more evolved spirits assume an earthly perispirit, and with that their perceptions operate like those of other spirits of our world; however, all spirits, of lower or higher advancement, only hear and feel that which they want. Since they do not have sensorial organs, they can render their perceptions active or dormant at will, although there is one thing they are compelled to hear: the advice of good spirits. Their sight is always active but they can become invisible to one another. Depending on their rank, they may hide themselves from those who are below them, but not from those who are more advanced. In the first moments following death, a spirit's sight is always blurred and confused, but becomes clearer as the spirit is liberated from the body, and may regain the same clarity as when the spirit was alive, in addition to the possibility of seeing through objects that are normally opaque to us. As for the extension of a spirit's vision through space, and into the future and the past, it all depends on the degree of the spirit's purity and advancement.

One might say, "This whole theory is hardly reassuring. We had thought that, once freed from our dense envelope, the instrument of our suffering, we would no longer suffer. Now you tell us that we suffer, still; whether it is one way or another, it is suffering all the same." Alas, yes, we can still suffer a great deal, and for a long time, but we may also no longer experience any suffering at all, perhaps right from the moment we leave our corporeal life behind.

The sufferings of this world may sometimes not depend on us, but many are the consequences of our own choice. If we trace them back to their origin, we will see that most of them are the result of causes that we could have avoided. How many misfortunes, how many illnesses, does man owe solely to his excesses and ambition, in a word, to his passions? The man who lives soberly in all respects, who never runs into excesses of any kind, who is always simple in his tastes and modest in his desires, spares himself many tribulations. The same applies to spirits, as the sufferings they endure always result from the way they lived on Earth. While they will certainly not suffer from gout or arthritis, they will experience other types of suffering that are no less painful. We have seen that such suffering is the result of the links that still exist between the spirit and matter, that the more the spirit is disengaged from the influence of matter—that is, the more dematerialized he is—the fewer painful sensations he will experience. It is up to himself to break free from this influence, starting with his corporeal life, because he is endowed with free will, and has therefore the ability to choose to act one way or the other. Let the spirit subdue his animal passions; let him entertain no hatred, no envy, no jealousy, no pride; let him liberate himself from the yoke of selfishness; let him purify his soul by nurturing noble sentiments; let him do good; let him not attach to earthly things any more importance than they deserve. In so doing, even while in his corporeal envelope, he will have already purified himself, already detached himself from matter, and when he leaves his body behind, he will no longer suffer its influence. The physical hardships he endured shall leave no painful memory, no unpleasant impression, because they only affect the body, not the spirit. He will then be happy to be relieved of them, and his peace of mind will exempt him from any mental anguish. We have asked thousands of spirits about these matters, spirits of every social rank and extraction. We have studied them at every stage of their spirit life, from the moment they shed their physical body. We have followed them step by step in that life beyond the grave, so as to observe the changes that took place in them, in their ideas and sensations; in this regard, the most ordinary individuals provided us with the most precious objects of study. We have always verified that their suffering is always connected to their past behavior, the consequences of which they must endure; and that their new existence is a source of ineffable happiness for those who have followed the right path. From which it follows that those who suffer, suffer because they have so chosen, and have only themselves to thank for it, in the other world, as in this one.

5. Choice of trials

258. In between incarnations and before starting a new corporeal existence, does a spirit have the awareness and foresight of what will happen to him during his new earthly life?

"The spirit himself chooses the types of trials he wishes to endure. In that consists his free will."

— Then it is not God who imposes the tribulations of life on him as a punishment?

"Nothing happens without God's permission, because it was He who established all the laws that govern the universe. You may as well ask why God made such and such a law rather than some other one. In giving a spirit freedom of choice, God leaves to him the entire responsibility for his acts and ensuing consequences. Nothing stands in the way of his future. Open to him is the path of good, as is the path of evil. But if the spirit fails in his trials, there is still the consolation that not everything is lost, as God, out of His kindness, allows the spirit to start over from the point where he failed. It is necessary to distinguish between that which is the work of God's will and that which is man's. If a danger threatens you, it is not you who created it, but God. However, you have chosen to expose yourself to it, because you saw it as a way to advance, and God has allowed it to happen."

259.   If as spirits we are able to choose the kinds of trials we shall undergo, does it follow that all tribulations of life are foreseen and chosen by us?

"Not all of them, because it cannot be said that you have chosen and foreseen everything that happens to you in the world, down to every minute detail. You have chosen the kinds of trials; the details are a consequence of your position, and, frequently, of your own actions. If a spirit chose to be born among evildoers, for example, he knew what types of temptation he would expose himself to, but not every single act he would carry out. Those acts are the result of his volition or free will. In choosing a particular path, a spirit knows the type of struggle he will endure; he therefore knows the nature of the tribulations he will encounter, but he does not know whether these will present themselves in one form or another. The details stem from circumstances and the force of things. Only the major events, those that will influence his destiny, are foreseen. If you walk down a path full of ruts, you know you must be very cautious because you run the risk of tripping, but you do not know when you will trip, and maybe you will not trip at all if you are cautious enough. If you are walking down the sidewalk and a tile falls on your head, you should not believe that 'it was written', as the saying goes." [b]

260.   Why would a spirit want to be born among evildoers?

"He ought to be sent to the environment in which he can experience the trials he requested. Well, then, to that end he must be in a situation where the corresponding predispositions are to be found; for example, in order to overcome his tendency to steal, he must find himself among thieves."

—   If there were no longer evil people on Earth, would spirits not be able to find the necessary conditions for certain trials?

"Would it be reason to regret? That is what takes place on superior worlds, to which evil has no access. That is why only good spirits dwell on them. Strive so as to make that happen on your planet sooner rather than later."

261.   In the trials he must undergo to reach perfection, must a spirit experience every type of temptation possible? In other words, will he have to go through all the circumstances that may elicit pride, jealousy, greed, lust, and so on?

"Of course not. You should be aware that there are those who from the beginning have taken a road that has spared them many trials; those, however, who allow themselves to be led along the road of evil expose themselves to all its dangers. For instance, a spirit may ask for wealth and it may be granted to him. Then, depending on his character, he may become greedy or wasteful, selfish or generous, or he may indulge in all the pleasures of sensuality. This, however, does not mean that he had forcibly to experience each and every one of those tendencies."

262. How can a spirit, who at his origin is simple, ignorant, and inexperienced, consciously choose an existence and be responsible for the choices made?

"God makes up for his inexperience by tracing out for him the path he should follow, as you do for an infant from the cradle. However, as the spirit's free will develops, God gradually leaves him the freedom to choose his path. It is at this point that the spirit will choose the wrong path if he does not listen to the advice of good spirits. That is what we may call 'the fall of man.' "

—   When a spirit exercises his free will, does the choice of his corporeal existence always depend only on his own will, or can the new existence be imposed on him by God as an expiation?

"God knows how to wait; He does not need to hasten the process of expiation. However, God may impose an existence on a spirit when he is not able to understand what would be most advantageous to him, owing to his inferiority or unwillingness, and when God sees that such an existence could be useful for the spirit's purification and advancement, at the same time that it may serve as an expiation."

263. Do spirits make their choice immediately after death?

"No, because many of them believe in eternal punishment, a fact that, as we have told you, is in itself a punishment."

264. What directs a spirit in the choice of the trials he wishes to endure?

"He chooses what may serve as an expiation according to the nature of his mistakes, and may enable him to advance more quickly. Some spirits may impose on themselves a life of poverty and hardships, and attempt to bear it with courage. Others may wish to experience the temptations of fortune and power, which are much more dangerous than poverty, because of the abuse and misuse that may be made of them, and because of the base passions they may stimulate. Others, finally, may wish to be tested by struggling against various vices with which they may come in contact."

265. If certain spirits choose contact with vice as a trial, are there those who choose it out of affinity and out of a desire to live in an environment in conformity with their tastes, or where they may give free rein to their sensual leanings?

"There are, certainly, but only among those whose moral sense is still little developed; *the trial comes by itself, and they shall endure it for a longer period of time.* Sooner or later, they realize that indulging in their base passions has dire consequences which they will have to suffer for what will seem to them to be like an eternity. God may leave them in this state until they have understood their mistake, and ask for the means of atoning for it through suitable trials."

266. Wouldn't it be natural for a spirit to choose the least painful trials?

"For you, perhaps, but not for the spirit. Once the spirit is free from matter, the veil of illusion is lifted and he thinks differently."

Man on Earth, subject as he is to the influence of matter, only sees the painful aspect of his trials. That is why it seems natural for him to choose those which, from his standpoint, may be compatible with the enjoyment of material pleasures. However, in the spirit life, he compares such fleeting and crude pleasures with the unchanging happiness of which he can now catch a glimpse; what then do a few temporary hardships represent? A spirit may therefore choose the hardest trial, and consequently the most painful existence, hoping to reach a better state more quickly, just as a patient often chooses the bitterest medicine in order to recover more promptly. He who aspires to immortalize his name by the discovery of an unknown land does not seek a flowery road—he knows the dangers he will have to face but he also knows what glory awaits him if he succeeds.

The idea that we are free to choose our existences and the trials we must endure does not seem unusual when we consider the fact that, when spirits are disengaged from matter, they appreciate things differently than we do as incarnate souls. They envisage their ultimate goal, far more important to them than the short-lived pleasures of the world. After each existence, they see the strides already made, understanding what they still lack in perfection in order to reach that goal. That is the reason why they willingly submit to all the tribulations of corporeal life, even requesting the ones that will help them reach their goal more quickly, and it should come as no surprise to know that a spirit does not prefer a life of comfort instead. A life completely free of woes is unattainable so long as spirits remain imperfect, but, as they catch a glimpse of such a life, they strive to perfect themselves in order to reach it.

Besides, do we not see similar instances all the time? Isn't the man who works part of his life without respite in order to save for his retirement one example of a self-imposed task for the purpose of a better future? What do soldiers who volunteer for a dangerous mission and explorers who confront dangers no less formidable for the sake of science or riches, represent, if not examples of voluntary trials that shall bring them honor and profit if they succeed? What will man not endure for his own profit or glory? Are not all entrance examinations voluntary trials to which men subject themselves in order to advance in the career of their choice? No one arrives at a position of importance in the sciences, arts, or industry without advancing through the lower ranks, a process which in itself constitutes yet another type of trial.

Human life is thus a replica of the spirit life, where the same twists and turns can be found on a smaller scale. Therefore, if in our earthly life we often choose the hardest trials for the sake of a higher position, why would spirits—who see beyond their bodies, and for whom life on Earth is nothing but a fleeting incident—not choose an existence of hardships and toil, if it will lead them to eternal happiness? Those who claim that they would choose to be princes or millionaires if they had a choice of existence are like the blind who can only see what they touch, or like gluttonous children who, when asked what they want to be when they grow up, reply, "a baker or confectioner."

Similarly, travelers in the depths of a foggy valley can discern neither the length nor the starting and ending points of their journey, but, upon reaching the top of a mountain, they can take in at a glance both the ground they have covered and the distance they have yet to traverse; being able to see their destination and the obstacles they have yet to clear, they arrange in the best way possible the available resources in order to reach their goal. Incarnate spirits are like travelers in the depths of the valley: when liberated from their earthly ties, they have the same ample vision as the traveler who has reached the mountain top. For travelers, the goal is to rest after a strenuous hike; for spirits, the goal is the supreme happiness after enduring tribulations and trials.

All spirits say that in between incarnations they search, study, and observe in order to make their choice. Do we not have an example of this in our corporeal life? Do we not often spend years searching for a career which we finally choose in the belief that it is the most suitable for our goals? If we fail at it, we look for another one. Each career we embrace is a phase, a period of our life. Do we not program every day the activities to be carried out the following day? Well then, what do the different corporeal existences represent for spirits if not only phases, periods, or days in the context of their spirit life, which, as we know, is their normal life, the corporeal life being only transitory and ephemeral?

267. Can a spirit, while incarnated, choose the trials of his subsequent corporeal life?

"His desire may have an influence, depending on his intention. In the spirit state, however, he frequently sees things quite differently. It is only as a spirit that the choice is made, but then again, he may make it during his material life because a spirit always has moments in which he is liberated from the matter he inhabits."

— Are there not many cases where people desire power and wealth, but not as an expiation or a trial?

"Undoubtedly. It is the influence of matter that stimulates the desire for greatness and wealth, but the spirit desires them in order to experience the attending trials."

268. Until he reaches the state of perfect purity, does a spirit have to constantly undergo trials?

"Yes, but they are not as you understand them, for you normally consider trials to comprise only material tribulations. Actually, after reaching a certain degree of perfection, although he may not yet be perfect, a spirit no longer needs to endure material trials. But he still needs to perform certain duties that will help him advance, duties that are not painful, that consist of helping others to perfect themselves."

269. Can a spirit be mistaken as to the effectiveness of a trial he chooses?

"He may choose one that exceeds his strength, and then he fails. He may also choose one that will not be profitable at all, which would be the case if he chooses an idle and useless life. In such a situation, however, upon returning to the spirit world, he realizes that he has gained nothing and asks to make up for the lost time."

270. Why do people have certain vocations or the desire to follow one career instead of another?

"It seems to me that you can answer this question yourself. Is it not the result of everything we have said about the choice of trials and the progress accomplished in preceding existences?"

271. When a spirit in between incarnations studies the conditions that will enable him to progress, how could he possibly imagine he could do so by being born, for instance, among cannibals?

"Spirits who have already advanced are not born among cannibals, only those spirits that are at the same level of cannibals, or even lower."

We know that our cannibals are not at the lowest degree of the spiritual hierarchy, and that there are worlds where brutality and ferocity find no parallel on Earth. Such spirits are therefore lower than the lowest of our world, and to be among our cannibals would represent progress for them, just as it would be progress for our cannibals to exercise a profession among us that would require them to shed blood. If they aim no higher, it is because their moral limitations do not allow them to envisage a more complete progress.

A spirit only advances gradually; he cannot simply bridge the gap between barbarity and civilization in a single leap. In this resides one of the necessities of reincarnation, which is truly in accordance with the justice of God. Otherwise, what would become of the millions of beings who die every day in the lowest state of degradation, if they had no means of ever reaching a higher position? Why would God deprive them of favors granted to others?

272. Can spirits who come from a world that is inferior to Earth, or from a much less advanced people, like cannibals for instance, be born among civilized people?

"Yes, there are those who lead themselves astray by wishing to rise too high, but they are out of place among you, as they display habits and instincts that clash with yours."

Such beings present us with the sad spectacle of ferocity in the midst of civilization. Returning to live among cannibals would not be a demotion for them, because it would be no more than a resumption of their actual position, possibly even to their own gain.

273. Could a person that belongs to a civilized culture reincarnate in a less advanced one as an expiation?

"Yes, but that would depend on the kind of expiation. Masters who had been cruel to their slaves might become slaves themselves and suffer the harsh treatment they used to inflict on others. Those who wielded power at one time may, in a new existence, obey those who formerly bent to their will. This would be an expiation if they used to abuse their power, and God may impose it on them. Furthermore, a good spirit may choose an influential life among people of lesser advancement in order to help them; in that case, it would be a mission."

6. Relationships beyond the grave

274. Do the different orders of spirits establish a hierarchy of powers, with the existence of subordination and authority among them?

"Yes, greatly so. Spirits have authority over one another in proportion to their superiority, which they exert through an irresistible moral ascendancy."

—   Can low-order spirits avoid the authority of those who are their superior?

"As we said—irresistible."

275. Do the power and influence that men enjoy on Earth warrant them any supremacy in the spirit world?

"No, because the humble shall be exalted and the great shall be humbled. Read the Psalms." [c]

—   How should we understand this exalting and humbling?

"You know that spirits belong to different orders according to their merits. Well then, the greatest on Earth may belong to the lowest order of spirits, while their servants may belong to the highest. Can you understand this? Has not Jesus said, 'Whosoever humbles himself shall be exalted, and whosoever exalts himself shall be humbled?' " [d]

276.   He who was great on Earth but finds himself one of the lowliest among spirits must be filled with humiliation, is that not so?

"Frequently, and with great humiliation indeed, especially if he was proud and jealous."

277. After a battle, does a soldier who meets his general in the spirit world still acknowledge him as his superior?

"Titles are meaningless, the actual spiritual superiority is what matters."

278. Are the spirits of different orders mixed together?

"Not exactly. They see each other, but differentiate themselves, approaching or avoiding one another according to the similarities or differences of sentiments, much as it happens among you. *The spirit world is an entire world in itself, of which yours is but a pale reflection.* Those of the same order are drawn together by a sort of affinity, forming groups or families of spirits united by mutual sympathy and the shared objectives they pursue: good spirits, by their desire to do good; evil ones, by their desire to do evil, by the shame of their crimes, and by the need to find themselves among kin."

> This is like a big city, where individuals of all social classes and conditions see and meet one another without mixing together, where groups are formed by similarities of tastes, and where vice and virtue brush against each other without ever speaking.

279. Do all spirits have mutual access to one another?

"Good ones go everywhere, and it must be thus in order for them to exert their influence over the bad ones. However, imperfect spirits are not allowed to go to areas inhabited by the good ones, so as not to disrupt those regions with their evil passions."

280. What is the nature of the relationship between good and bad spirits?

"The good ones strive to fight the evil tendencies of the others *in order to help them advance*—it is a mission."

281. Why do inferior spirits take pleasure in inducing us to evil?

"They do so out of spite for not deserving to be among the good ones. Their desire is to prevent inexperienced spirits, as much as possible, from reaching the supreme good. They want to make others endure what they themselves endure. Don't you see the same among yourselves?"

282. How do spirits communicate with one another?

"They see and understand one another. Speech is material: it is a reflection of the spirit. The universal fluid establishes a constant communication among them; it is the vehicle for the transmission of thought, as the air is for you the vehicle for the transmission of sound. It is a sort of universal telegraph line that connects all worlds, enabling spirits to communicate from one world to another."

283. Can spirits hide their thoughts, or even themselves, from each other?

"No, everything is out in the open for them, especially when they are perfect. They may be far away, but always see each other. This is not an absolute rule, however, as certain spirits may very well make themselves invisible to others, if they deem it useful."

284. Since spirits no longer have a body, how can they establish their individuality and make themselves distinguishable from other spirits around them?

"They establish their individuality by means of their perispirit, which makes them distinct from one another, as do bodies among men."

285. Do spirits recognize each other after having lived together on Earth? Does a son recognize his father and a friend, another friend?

"Yes, and so on and so forth, from generation to generation."

—   How do people who were acquainted on Earth recognize each other in the spirit world?

"We see our past life and read it like a book. As we watch the past of our friends and enemies, we also witness their passage from life to death."

286. Upon leaving their mortal remains behind, do souls immediately see the relatives and friends who preceded them into the spirit world?

"Not quite immediately. As we have already said, they need some time to recognize themselves and shake off the material influence."

287. How are souls received upon their return to the spirit world?

"The soul of the just, as a beloved and long-awaited sibling; the soul of the wicked, as a despised being."

288. What do impure spirits feel upon the arrival of another bad spirit?

"Much as on Earth a criminal is received among his peers, bad spirits are pleased to see another one who resembles them and who is deprived, just as they are, of the infinite bliss."

289. Do our relatives and friends sometimes come to meet us upon our departure from the Earth?

"Yes, they come to meet the souls they love. They welcome you as though you have returned from a journey, congratulating you if you have escaped the dangers of the road; in addition, *they help newly-arrived souls to disengage from their corporeal links.* It is a blessing granted to good spirits when their loved ones come to meet them; on the other hand, the wicked remain isolated, or are surrounded only by spirits like themselves as punishment."

290. Are relatives and friends always reunited after death?

"That depends on how evolved they are and the path they follow for their advancement. If one of them is more advanced and progresses more rapidly than the other, they cannot stay together. They may see each other occasionally, but they will not be reunited until they can march shoulder to shoulder, or when they have reached perfection. In addition, being kept from seeing relatives and friends is sometimes a punishment."

7. Affinities and antipathies among spirits, eternal halves

291. Aside from the general affinity stemming from a correspondence of thoughts and feelings, are there special affections among spirits?

"Yes, just as among men, but the link that unites spirits is stronger in the absence of the body, because they are no longer exposed to the vagaries of passion."

292. Is there hatred among spirits?

"There is hatred only among impure spirits. It is they who spread hostility and dissent among you."

293. Will two beings who were enemies on Earth retain their resentment in the spirit world?

"No, they understand that their hatred was senseless and their motivation childish. Only imperfect spirits retain a sort of animosity until they have perfected themselves. If what kept them apart was an issue of purely material interest, they no longer think about it, no matter how little dematerialized they are. If there is no antipathy between them, and if the cause of their disagreement no longer exists, they can see each other again with pleasure."

Exactly like two schoolboys who, having reached the age of reason, realize the silliness of their juvenile quarrels and no longer hold any resentment.

294. Is the remembrance of the wrongs that two people have committed against each other an obstacle to their sympathy?

"Yes, it tends to keep them apart."

295. What feelings do those whom we have wronged in this world experience after death?

"If they are good, they forgive you as you repent. If they are evil, they may hold on to their resentment and at times even persecute you in a future existence. God may allow this as a punishment."

296. Are spirits' personal affections susceptible to change?

"No, because they cannot be fooled. *They no longer wear the mask behind which hypocrites hide themselves,* and that is why their affections are unchangeable when they are pure. The love that unites them is a source of supreme bliss for them."

297. Does the affection that two beings had for each other on Earth always continue in the spirit world?

"Yes, undoubtedly, if it is based on true affinity; however, if physical attraction has had more influence than spiritual affinity, it will cease with the cause. Affections among spirits are more solid and long-lasting than on Earth, because they are not subject to the whims of material interests and self-importance."

298. Are the souls who ought to be united in affection predestined for such a union from their origin, and does each one of us have, in some part of the universe—our *other half*—to whom we will one day be inevitably reunited?

"No, there is no particular and inexorable union between two souls. There is union among all spirits, but in different degrees, according to their rank—that is, according to how perfect they are. The greater their perfection, the more united they are. All the ills of mankind are born out of discord; from concord results the complete happiness."

299. In what sense should we understand the term *other half*, which certain spirits use to designate sympathetic spirits?

"The expression is inaccurate. If one spirit were the other half of another spirit, they both would be incomplete so long as they were separate from each other."

300. When two perfectly sympathetic spirits are united, will they remain so for all eternity, or can they separate from each other and unite themselves with other spirits?

"All spirits are united among themselves. I refer here to those who have already reached perfection. In less evolved spheres, after a spirit advances, he no longer has the same sympathy for the ones left behind."

301. Are two sympathetic spirits each other's complement, or is such sympathy the result of a perfect identification between them?

"The sympathy that attracts one spirit to another is the result of the perfect agreement of their tendencies and instincts. If one of them were to complete the other, he would lose his individuality."

302. Does the affinity needed for perfect sympathy consist only of the similarity of thoughts and feelings, or does it also consist of a uniformity of the knowledge acquired?

"It consists in their similar degree of advancement."

303. Could spirits who are not sympathetic today become so later?

"Yes, all will be someday. This way, when a spirit who currently belongs to a lower order advances in perfection, he will be able to reach the sphere where the other one dwells. Their reunion will take place faster, however, if the more evolved spirit remains stationary for having failed at his trials."

— May two sympathetic spirits cease to be so?

"Certainly, if one of them advances more slowly."

The theory of "eternal halves" is an allegory representing the union of two sympathetic spirits. It is an expression used even in ordinary speech, and must not be taken literally. Spirits who have used it certainly do not belong to the highest order; the range of their ideas is necessarily limited, and they may express their thoughts using the same terminology that they used in their earthly life. We must therefore reject the idea that two spirits are created for each other, who must inevitably be one day reunited in eternity, after being separated for a more or less long period of time.

8. Recollection of physical existences

304. Do spirits remember their corporeal existence?

"Yes, having lived many times as human beings, they remember what they have been, and I can assure you that they sometimes laugh at their past immaturity."

Like a man who, having reached the age of reason, laughs at the follies of his youth or the silliness of his childhood.

305. Does the memory of his last physical existence completely and unexpectedly return to a spirit after death?

"No, it returns little by little, like an object that emerges from the fog, as he focuses his attention on it."

306. Do spirits remember all the events of their lives in detail, taking in the whole in a single retrospective glance?

"They remember things according to the consequences events have for them as spirits; but you should understand that there are circumstances of their lives to which they attribute no importance whatsoever, and which they do not even attempt to recall."

—   Could they remember them if they so wished?

"They can recall the minutest details and incidents, be they events or even thoughts. But when doing so has no utility, they do not do it."

—   Do they see the purpose of their past earthly life relative to their future life?

"They certainly see and understand it much better than when incarnate. They understand the need for purification in order to reach the infinite, and they know that during each existence they free themselves from a number of imperfections."

307. How does their past life unfold in their memory, through an effort of their imagination, or like a motion picture playing before their eyes?

"Both. All the actions that they wish to remember are as if they were present. The others remain more or less vague in their minds, or are completely forgotten. The more dematerialized they are, the less importance they attach to material things. You often evoke discarnate spirits who have just left Earth and do not remember the names of the people they have loved, or the details that seem important to you, but in fact they are no longer concerned with them, so that those details have fallen into oblivion. What they remember very well, however, are the main events that have been instrumental to their progress."

308. Do spirits remember all the lives that preceded the one they have just left behind?

"Their whole past unfolds before them like the legs already completed of a journey. However, as we have already said, they do not recall all their actions with absolute precision; they only remember them to the extent of the influence such actions have on their present condition. As for their earliest existences, those that may be considered the spirit's infancy, they are dissolved in time, disappearing in the fog of oblivion."

309. How do spirits regard the body they have just left behind?

"As an uncomfortable garment *that has encumbered them*, and which they are happy to dispose of."

— What do they feel when they see their body decomposing?

"Almost always indifference. It is something about which they no longer care."

310. After a certain time, do spirits recognize their remains or other objects that had belonged to them?

"Sometimes, depending on the more or less elevated vantage point from which they consider earthly things."

311. Does the respect we have for the objects that spirits have left behind attract their attention to them, and do they view such respect with pleasure?

"Spirits are always happy to be remembered by those they have left behind. The objects that one keeps which once belonged to them awaken their memory, but it is your thoughts that attract them to you, not the objects themselves."

312. Do spirits hold onto the memory of the sufferings they endured during their last physical existence?

"They frequently do, and this memory allows them to better appreciate the value of the happiness they may now enjoy as spirits."

313. Does the man who was happy on Earth regret the pleasures he left behind?

"Only lower spirits regret the pleasures associated with the imperfections of their nature, for which they atone in their sufferings. For evolved spirits, eternal happiness is a thousand times preferable to the fleeting earthly enjoyments."

As is the case of an adult man who no longer cares about the things that brought him joy in his childhood.

314. Does the man who has begun great enterprises with a useful goal in mind, but who dies before their completion, regret, in the spirit world, having left them unfinished?

"No, because he understands that others are meant to finish them. On the contrary, he strives to influence other individuals to carry them on. His goal on Earth was the wellness of mankind; that aim is the same in the spirit world."

315. Does the man who leaves works of art or literature behind maintain the same interest in them as when he lived?

"According to his spiritual development, he often judges them from a different standpoint, and frequently disapproves of what he most admired."

316. Do spirits still take an interest in the works that are being done on Earth for the progress of the arts and sciences?

"Again, it depends on how advanced they are, or on the mission they may have to fulfill. What appears splendid to you is often in fact a small matter to certain spirits. They admire it like the master admires the work of an apprentice. They examine only that which can demonstrate the elevation and progress of incarnate spirits."

317. After death, do spirits preserve their love for their motherland?

"It is always the same principle: for advanced spirits, their motherland is the universe; on Earth it is the place where they find the greatest number of people with whom they share their affection."

The situation of spirits and their way of looking at things vary infinitely, in accordance with their degree of moral and intellectual development. Spirits of the higher orders generally make only short stopovers on Earth, as everything that is done here is so petty in comparison with the splendors of the infinite. The things to which men attribute the most importance seem so childish to them, that this world hardly offer them any allure, unless they have been called to help with the progress of mankind. Spirits of average advancement stay here more frequently, although they consider things from a higher vantage point than when incarnate. Ordinary spirits are characterized by a certain degree of inertia, and comprise the throngs of spirits that make up the population of the invisible world. They hold on to roughly the same ideas, tastes, and tendencies they had when they donned their physical envelope. They get involved in our gatherings, dealings and amusements, in which they take part more or less actively, according to their character. No longer being able to satisfy their passions directly, they do so vicariously by latching onto those still alive who abandon themselves to their own passions, the indulgence of which these spirits stimulate. But among them there are some who are more serious, and who watch and observe in order to educate and perfect themselves.

318. Do spirits' ideas change in the spirit life?

"Very much so. Their ideas undergo significant changes as they become more dematerialized. They may occasionally dwell on the same notions for a long time, but little by little the influence of matter subsides, and they see things more clearly. It is then that they look for ways to improve themselves."

319. Since a spirit had already lived the spirit life before incarnating, what causes his bewilderment upon returning to the spirit world?

"That is only the effect of the initial moments and the state of confusion that follows the spirit's awakening in the spiritual world. Later, the spirit is able to recognize himself perfectly, as the memory of the past comes back to him, and the impressions of his earthly life wear off." (See #163–164)

9. Commemoration of the dead, funerals

320. Are spirits moved when they are remembered by those they loved on Earth?

"Much more than you would imagine. Being remembered adds to their happiness if they are already happy, or provides solace if they are unhappy."

321. Does All Souls' Day have a more solemn meaning for spirits? Do they prepare to visit those who come pray by their graves?

"Spirits respond to the call of thought on that day as on all others."

—   Does that day represent for them an occasion to gather at their gravesides?

"They gather in greater numbers on that day because more people call to them, but each one of them only attends to their friends, not to the droves of indifferent people."

—   In what guise do they come, and what would their appearance be, if they could render themselves visible?

"The same one you knew them when they were alive."

322. Do the spirits who have been forgotten, and whose graves are not visited by anyone, come in spite of it, and do they lament the fact that no friend remembers them?

"What does the Earth matter to them? Only their hearts link them to it. If love is no longer to be found there, nothing will keep spirits bound to it—they have the whole universe before them."

323. Does a visit made to their grave provide spirits with more satisfaction than a prayer made on their behalf at home?

"A visit to their grave is a way of showing that one thinks about the absent spirits—it is a symbolic gesture. I have already told you that it is the prayer that blesses the act of remembering. The place matters very little, if the prayer comes from the heart."

324. Do the spirits of people to whom statues or monuments are erected attend their inauguration, and do they see them with pleasure?

"Many attend it when they can, but they are less moved by the honors paid to them than by the memories proper."

325. Where does the wish that some people have to be buried in one place rather than in another come from? Do they go back to it more readily after death? And is the importance attached to a physical thing a sign of a spirit's inferiority?

"It shows a spirit's attachment to certain places, and is a sign of moral limitation. What does one piece of earth represent more than another to an evolved spirit? Doesn't he know that his soul will be reunited with his loved ones, even if their remains may be far apart?"

— Should the gathering of the mortal remains of the members of a family be considered a futile act, then?

"No. It is a pious tradition and a testimony of affection toward those that one has loved. If such gatherings mean little to spirits, they are nonetheless useful to men, as their memories are more focused."

326. Upon returning to the spirit life, are souls moved by the honors paid to their mortal remains?

"When spirits have already reached a certain degree of perfection, they are no longer under the influence of earthly vanities, understanding the futility of all these things. You should know, however, that there are spirits who, in the first few moments after death, may take great satisfaction in the honors paid to them, or may be disappointed by the little consideration shown for their dead bodies, because they still display some of the prejudices of this world."

327. Do spirits attend their own funeral?

"They very frequently do, but sometimes they do not realize what is happening, if they are still in the state of confusion."

—   Do they feel flattered by a large attendance at their wake?

"More so or less so, according to the feelings of those gathered there."

328. Do the spirits of those who have recently passed away attend the reading of their wills?

"Almost always. God wishes it to be so for the instruction of spirits and as punishment for those who are guilty. There, spirits are able to judge what their heirs' protestations of affection really are worth. All feelings become obvious to them, and the disenchantment they feel in seeing the rapacity of those fighting over their estate makes the true intentions of the latter very evident. The day of reckoning shall also arrive for their heirs, however."

329. Is the instinctive respect that man has had for the dead in all ages and in all cultures the result of the intuition of a future existence?

"It is its natural consequence. Without it, such respect would have no reason."

■■■

[a] See question #425 and Translator's Note [c] in Part 2, Chapter 8 for a more detailed explanation of the word *somnambulist*. —Trans.

[b] A reference to the Arabic expression *maktub* (it was written). —Trans.

[c] This is a reference to Psalm 138:6, a recurring figure which can also be found in Proverbs 3:34, Matthew 23:12, Luke 1:52, James 4:6, and 1 Peter 5:5. —Trans.

[d] Matthew 23:12. —Trans.

Chapter 7:
Return to Corporeal Life

1. Prelude to the return

330. Do spirits know the time when they will reincarnate?

"They can sense it like a blind man feels the heat from a furnace he is approaching. They know they must once again don a physical body, just as you know you must die someday, but without knowing when it will happen." (See #166)

— Is reincarnation therefore a requirement of spirit life, as death is a requirement of corporeal life?

"It is certainly so."

331. Do all spirits worry about their next reincarnation?

"There are those who never give it a thought, or do not even understand it. It all depends on their degree of advancement. For some, the uncertainty about their future life is a punishment."

332. Can spirits hasten or delay the moment of their reincarnation?

"They may hasten it by means of a strong desire. They may also delay it if they recoil from the upcoming trial, since among spirits there are those who are cowardly and indifferent, but they may not delay it with impunity. They will suffer for doing so, like he who refuses the medicine that would cure him."

333. If a spirit felt quite happy with an average or simply passable situation among other discarnate spirits in between corporeal existences, and had no ambition to advance, could he protract such a state of affairs indefinitely?

"Not indefinitely. Advancement is a necessity, and spirits realize it sooner or later. They all must advance; it is their destiny."

334. Is the union of a soul with a particular body predestined, or is it only at the last moment that the choice is made?

"The spirit is always designated beforehand. When choosing the trials they wish to endure, spirits ask to reincarnate. God, who sees and knows everything, sees and knows in advance which soul in particular will be united with a given body."

335. Do spirits have the choice of the body they will take, or do they only choose the kind of life that will serve them as a trial?

"They may also choose their body, because the imperfections of the body will be the trials that will help in their advancement if they overcome the obstacles that they are bound to face. This choice does not always depend on them, but they may ask for it."

—   Can spirits refuse to enter the chosen body at the last moment?

"If they refuse it, they will suffer much more than one who had not undertaken a new trial in the first place."

336. Could an unborn baby about to be delivered not have a spirit willing to incarnate in it?

"God would provide for it. When a child is to be *born alive*, the body is always predestined to have a soul; nothing is created without a design."

337. Can the union of a spirit with a particular body be imposed by God?

"It may be imposed, just as other different trials, especially when the spirit is not yet able to make a conscious choice about it. As an expiation, a spirit may be compelled to unite with the body of a particular infant who, by birth and owing to the position that the person will have in the world, may be a means of atonement for that spirit."

338. If it happened that several spirits presented themselves to occupy the same body, how would the decision be made among them?

"Many could very well request the same body, but, in such cases, it is God who decides which one is best suited to fulfill the mission for which the infant is destined. But as I have already said, the spirit is designated before the instant in which the spirit is to join the body."

339. Is the moment of incarnation accompanied by a bewilderment similar to the one that follows the spirit's separation from the body?

"The confusion is much greater and above all much longer. At death, the spirit is released from slavery; at birth, the spirit reenters it."

340. Is the moment of incarnation a solemn one for the spirit? Does he effect this act as a grave and important event for him?

"He is like a traveler who embarks on a perilous voyage, not knowing if he will meet his death in the waves he is about to defy."

The traveler who sets sail is aware of the dangers to which he will be exposed, but he does not know whether he will get stranded. The same applies to spirits, as they know the type of trials they will endure, but they do not know if they will fail.

Just as the death of the body is a type of rebirth for the spirit, reincarnation is a type of death, or, rather, a type of exile and confinement. A spirit leaves the spirit world to enter the corporeal world, just as a man leaves the corporeal world to reenter the spirit world. A spirit knows that he will reincarnate, just as a man knows that he will die. But like the latter, a spirit only knows that the appointed time has arrived at the very last moment. Then, in that superlative moment, confusion takes hold of the spirit, like a man in the throes of death, with this distress lasting until the new existence has firmly taken root. Therefore, the onset of the reincarnation process for the spirit is, in a way, similar to the agony of death.

341. The uncertainty with which spirits are filled about the likelihood of successfully enduring the trials they will face in a new corporeal life must be a reason for anxiety before they incarnate, is that not so?

"It is a cause of great anxiety, because the trials of their new existence will either delay or hasten their evolution, depending on whether these trials are withstood well or not."

342. At the moment of their reincarnation, are spirits accompanied by other spirit friends who come to assist with their departure from the spirit world, just as they come to meet them upon their return?

"That depends on the sphere a spirit inhabits. Spirits that pertain to a sphere in which affection predominates are accompanied by other spirits that love them up to the last moment, encouraging them, and frequently even following them into their corporeal life."

343. Are the spirit friends who follow us through life those whom we sometimes see in our dreams, who show us their affection and present themselves in a semblance we do not recognize?

"Quite often they are. They come to visit you as you would visit a captive behind bars."

2. Union of the soul and the body, abortion

344. At what moment is the soul united to the body?

"The union begins at conception, but is only complete at the moment of birth. From the moment of conception, the spirit designated to inhabit a given body is connected to it by a fluidic link, which becomes gradually tighter up until the moment that the baby is born. The cry then uttered announces that the newborn can now be numbered among the living and servants of God."

345. Is the union between the spirit and the body definitive from the moment of conception? In other words, during this initial period, can the spirit refuse to inhabit the body that has been designated for him?

"The union is definitive in the sense that no other spirit can replace the one who has been designated for that body. However, as the links that bind them are very tenuous and can be easily broken, they may be undone by the will of a spirit who recoils from the trial that has been chosen. In that case, the infant does not survive."

346. What happens to a spirit if the chosen body comes to die before the baby is born?

"The spirit chooses another body."

— What could be the usefulness of such premature deaths?

"Organic imperfections are frequently the cause of such deaths."

347. What utility could there be for a spirit to incarnate in a body that dies a few days after birth?

"Spirits in this situation do not have a sufficiently developed consciousness about their existence. The importance of the baby's death is very little, and, as we have already mentioned, such cases are often meant as a trial for the parents."

348. Does a spirit know beforehand that the body that was chosen will have no chance of surviving?

"The spirit knows it sometimes, but if the choice of body was made for that reason, it means that the spirit is recoiling from the trial."

349. When the process of incarnation is not successfully carried out for any reason, is the spirit immediately provided with another attempt?

"Not always immediately. The spirit needs time to make another choice, unless an immediate reincarnation had already been determined beforehand."

350. Once united to the body of an infant, and therefore no longer able to balk at it, do spirits sometimes regret the choice made?

"If you wonder whether, as incarnate men, spirits complain about their life, wishing for a different one, the answer is yes. Now, whether spirits regret the choice made, the answer is no, because the spirits do not even remember having made that choice. Once incarnate, spirits cannot regret a choice of which they are not aware, but they may find the burden to be too heavy, and if they consider it to be beyond their capacity, they might then resort to suicide."

351. In the interval between conception and birth, do spirits enjoy all their faculties?

"More or less so, depending on the stage of pregnancy, because they are not fully incarnated yet, only linked to the body. At the moment of conception, a state of confusion begins to take over the spirit, who is thereby warned that the time has come to start a new existence. This confusion increases until the time of birth. Meanwhile, the spirit's state is more or less that of an incarnate man during sleep. As the moment of birth approaches, the spirit's ideas fade away, as do all past memories, of which he is no longer conscious as an incarnate man, from the moment he has initiated a new corporeal life. But these memories gradually come back to him in the spirit state."

352. At the moment of birth, do spirits immediately recover the full possession of their faculties?

"No, their faculties develop gradually as the organs themselves mature. Commencing a new existence, spirits must learn how to use their organic instruments. Their ideas come back little by little, like it happens to a man who wakes up from sleep only to find himself in a different place than the one he was in the day before."

353. As the union of a spirit with the body is not complete and definitely consummated until after birth, can the fetus be considered as having a soul?

"The spirit who must animate it exists outside of it, as it were. Therefore, strictly speaking, the fetus does not have a soul, since the current incarnation is only in the process of being brought about. However, the fetus is linked to the soul that ought to inhabit it."

354. How can intrauterine life be explained?

"It is like the life of the plant that vegetates and that of an infant that lives an animal-like life. Man possesses in himself aspects of the animal and the plant life, to which he finally adds the spiritual life, completing the incarnation process, upon birth." [a]

355. As science shows, there are babies who, even in their mother's womb, have no chance of surviving. For what purpose does this occur?

"This is a common occurrence that God permits as a trial, either for the parents, or for the spirit designated to animate the infant's body."

356. Are there stillborn infants who were never meant for the incarnation of a spirit?

"Yes, there are some who never had a spirit designated for their bodies—nothing would have been accomplished in them. It is solely for the parents that such an infant is delivered."

— Can a being of such a nature be carried to term?

"Yes, sometimes, but in such cases it does not survive."

— Therefore, every baby that survives has necessarily a spirit incarnated in it?

"Certainly. Otherwise, what would it be without a spirit? It would not be a human being."

357. What are the consequences of abortion for a spirit?

"It becomes a voided existence that must be restarted."

358. Is an induced abortion a crime, regardless of how far into the pregnancy it occurs?

"Crime occurs whenever you infringe the law of God. The mother, or any other person involved, will always have committed a crime by taking the life of an infant before its birth, because that prevents a soul from experiencing the trials for which the body being formed should have been the instrument."

359. In cases where the life of the mother would be endangered by the delivery of the infant, is it a crime to sacrifice the infant in order to save the mother?

"It is better to sacrifice the being who does not yet exist than the being who already does."

360. Is it rational to treat the fetus with the same respect as the body of an infant who has lived?

"In all of it you should recognize the will of God and His creation. Therefore, do not treat lightly the things you ought to respect. Why not respect all the works of creation, which are sometimes incomplete by the will of the Creator? This ranks among the designs of God, upon which no one is called to judge."

3. Moral and intellectual faculties

361. Where do the moral traits of a person come from, whether good or bad?

"They come from the qualities of the incarnate spirit. The purer the spirit, the more that person is inclined to the good."

— That seems to imply that a good person is the incarnation of a good spirit, and a bad person that of an bad spirit. Is that so?

"Yes, but we should call them *imperfect spirits*. Otherwise, one might believe in the existence of spirits that are eternally bad, those you call *demons*."

362. What is the character of individuals in whom frivolous and foolish spirits are incarnated?

"They are negligent, mischievous, and sometimes wicked beings."

363. Do spirits possess any passions not seen among mankind?

"No. Otherwise, they would have passed those passions on to you."

364. Does the same spirit endow man with both his moral and intellectual qualities?

"Certainly it is one and the same, and that in proportion to the degree of advancement that the spirit has reached. A man does not have two spirits in him."

365. Why can some very intelligent men—their intelligence indicating the presence in them of an advanced spirit—sometimes be extremely cruel at the same time?

"It is because the incarnate spirit is not pure enough, and because man yields to the influence of other spirits who are even worse. A spirit advances in a measured ascending march, but this progress is not accomplished simultaneously in all aspects. In one period a spirit may advance in knowledge; in another, in morality."

366. What should one think of the opinion that a man's various moral and intellectual qualities are the result of many different spirits incarnate in him, each possessing a special aptitude?

"If you think about it carefully, you will realize how absurd it is. A spirit must acquire all aptitudes. But in order to advance, each spirit needs a unified will. If a man were an amalgamation of spirits, this unified will would not exist. He would possess no individuality, because, upon death, all those spirits would be like a flock of birds escaping from a cage. Man often complains about not understanding certain things, but it is rather intriguing to see how he multiplies his problems, when very simple and natural explanations are readily available to him. This is yet another example of taking the effect for the cause. This is attributing to man what pagans attributed to God—they believed in as many deities as there were phenomena in the universe. But, even among the pagans, there were those who were reasonable and understood that those phenomena were only effects with a unique God as their cause."

The physical and moral worlds offer many analogies regarding this matter. We believed in the existence of multiple types of matter when our observations were limited to the outward aspects of physical phenomena. Today we understand that such diverse phenomena might very well be no more than modifications of a unique elementary matter. Also, the diverse faculties are manifestations of one same cause, which is the soul—an incarnate spirit—and not several souls, just as the different sounds of a pipe organ are the result of the same type of air, and not of as many types of air as there are sounds. Such a theory would imply that when a person abandons or acquires certain aptitudes or tendencies, that would be the result of as many spirits leaving or entering the person, who would therefore be a multiple being without individuality, and, thus, without responsibility. In addition, this theory is further disproved by the numerous examples of manifestations in which spirits demonstrate their personality and identity.

4. Bodily influences

367. Upon uniting with the body, does the spirit identify himself with matter?

"Matter is simply the envelope of the spirit, just as clothing is the envelope of the body. Upon uniting with the body, the spirit retains the attributes of his spiritual nature."

368. Are the faculties of a spirit exercised with full freedom after his union with the body?

"The exercise of his faculties depends on the organs that function as his instruments. They are weakened by the crudeness of matter."

— Consequently, would the material envelope be an obstacle to the free manifestation of the spirit's faculties, just as an opaque glass hinders the free propagation of light?

"Yes, and very opaque, indeed."

One may further compare the action of the body's dense matter upon a spirit to that of muddy waters which hamper the free movement of objects immersed in them.

369. Is the free exercise of the faculties of the soul dependent on the development of the physical organs?

"The organs are the instruments for the manifestation of the faculties of the soul. This manifestation depends on the degree of the respective organs' development, as the perfection of an artwork depends on the quality of the tool employed."

370. Could one infer from the influence of the organs a connection between the development of the cerebral structure and the moral and intellectual faculties?

"Do not mistake the effect for the cause. The spirit always retains the faculties that belong to him. It is not the organs that endow him with his faculties, but rather the faculties that promote the development of the organs."

—   Therefore, does the diversity of aptitudes among human beings derive uniquely from the condition of their spirit?

"*Uniquely* is not the exact term. The qualities of the spirit, who may be more or less advanced, are the basis for this diversity. But you must also consider the influence of matter, because it inhibits to a greater or lesser degree the exercise of the faculties."

When a spirit incarnates, he brings with him certain predispositions, and if we accept the idea that there is a corresponding area in the brain for each one of them, then the development of these areas will be seen as an effect and not a cause. If the faculties had their origins in the organs themselves, man would be a machine without free will and without any responsibility for his actions. We would have to admit that the greatest geniuses—including scientists, poets, and artists—were so owing to chance, which has provided them with a special organic arrangement. This would mean that, without such privileged organs, they would not be men of genius. Conversely, any simpleton could have been a Newton, a Virgil, or a Raphael, if he had been provided with a certain organic structure.

The supposition is even more absurd if applied to moral qualities, since, according to it, if Saint Vincent de Paul had been endowed by nature with a specific organic structure, he might have been a scoundrel, whereas the greatest scoundrel would only be missing a particular brain structure in order to be a Saint Vincent de Paul. On the other hand, if we accept the idea that such special structures, if they do exist, are a consequence, that they are developed by the utilization of faculties, much like muscles develop with exercise, then nothing seems irrational. Let us take the following comparison—real, even if commonplace. By certain physical signs one can recognize that someone is addicted to alcohol. Do these traits make the person an alcoholic, or is it alcoholism that produces such traits? Therefore, one may establish that it is the organs that receive the impression from the faculties.

5. Mental disabilities

371. Is there any basis for the opinion that the mentally disabled have less-evolved souls?

"No. They have a human soul, frequently more intelligent than you would suppose, and which suffers from the insufficiency of the means to communicate, just as the mute suffer from the inability to speak."

372. What is the goal of Providence in creating unfortunate beings like the mentally disabled?

"The spirits who dwell in the bodies of the mentally disabled are being punished. They suffer from the limitations imposed on them, and from the impossibility of expressing themselves through undeveloped or defective organs."

— Then is it inaccurate to say that organs have no influence on the faculties?

"We have never said that organs have no influence. They exercise a very great influence on the manifestation of the faculties, but they are not their source; therein lies the difference. A good musician will not make good music if only a defective instrument is available, but that does not mean that the person is not a good musician."

A distinction must be made between the normal and the pathological states. In the normal state, mental ability may overcome difficulties posed by matter. There are cases, however, where matter offers such a challenge that the manifestations are distorted or completely blocked, as it is the case with mental impairment and insanity. These are pathological cases, and in such states the soul is not in full possession of its faculties, which is why human law exempts people in this condition from the responsibility for their actions.

373. What could possibly be the purpose of the existence of beings like the mentally impaired, who can do neither good nor evil, and therefore cannot progress?

"It is an expiation imposed on them for having previously abused certain faculties. It is a temporary pause."

— Therefore, may the body of a mentally impaired person confine a spirit who perhaps animated a man of genius in a previous existence?

"Yes, genius can sometimes be a curse when one abuses it."

Moral perfection is not necessarily achieved in lockstep with intellectual advancement, and the greatest men of genius may have much to expiate. Hence, they may often have an existence that is inferior to one they have previously lived, which represents a cause of great suffering for them. The predicaments that these spirits experience when they try to express themselves are for them like chains that restrain the movements of a robust man. One could say that the mentally disabled have an impairment in their brain, as those who limp have an impairment in their legs, and the blind, in their eyes.

374. In the spirit state, are the mentally disabled aware of their mental condition?

"Yes, very often. They understand that the chains hampering their development are a trial and an expiation."

375. What is the situation of the spirit in the case of insanity?

"When freed from the body, the spirit receives impressions directly, and directly exerts his action upon matter. Once incarnated, however, he finds himself in completely different conditions, and needs to act with the help of special organs. If these organs are partially or entirely compromised, the spirit's actions are disrupted. If the eyes are injured, he becomes blind; if the ears are hurt, he becomes deaf, and so forth and so on. Now, if the organ presiding over the manifestations of intelligence and will is partially or entirely hurt or compromised, you can easily understand that the use of such an impaired organ will result in a disorder of which the spirit is fully aware, but the onset of which he is unable to prevent."

— Then it is always the body and not the spirit that is defective?

"Yes, but you must remember that just as a spirit acts upon matter, matter reacts upon the spirit to a certain degree. Therefore, a spirit may find himself temporarily affected by the disruption of his organs, through which he manifests and receives his impressions. It may happen that, with time, and after insanity has taken hold for a long time, the repetition of the same behavioral pattern ends up exerting on the spirit an influence from which he will not be free until he is completely liberated from every material impression."

376. Why does insanity sometimes lead to suicide?

"The spirit suffers immensely from limitations he endures and from the powerlessness to freely manifest himself. He then seeks in death a means of breaking the ties that bind him to the body."

377. After death, does the spirit of a mentally disabled man still feel the derangement of his faculties?

"He may feel it for some time, until he is completely disengaged from matter, like a man who, upon awakening, still feels the confusion into which sleep has plunged him."

378. How is it possible for an impairment of the brain to affect the spirit after death?

"It is a memory effect. It acts like ballast weighing upon the spirit, and since he is not conscious of everything that took place during his insanity, the spirit requires a certain amount of time to get abreast of the facts. That is why the longer insanity lasts during his corporeal life, the longer the distress and the constrictions will last after death. Disengaged from the body, the spirit continues to feel the impression of these links for a while."

6. On childhood

379. Is the spirit who animates the body of a child as developed as the spirit of an adult?

"The spirit of a child may be even more developed if he has made more progress. Only his undeveloped organs keep him from fully manifesting himself. He acts in accordance with the instrument through which he operates."

380. In the case of an infant, not considering the limitations imposed by the organs on his ability to freely manifest himself, does the spirit think as a child or as an adult?

"As a child, it is natural that the as-yet undeveloped organs of intelligence cannot provide him with all the perceptions of an adult. His intelligence is therefore quite limited until his reason has matured with age. The confusion that accompanies the incarnation process does not cease suddenly at birth. It only dissipates gradually, as the organs develop."

An observation endorses this response: the dreams of a child do not have the character of the dreams of an adult. Their object is almost always childlike, which is an indication of the nature of the spirit's concerns.

381. When the child dies, does the spirit regain his former faculties immediately?

"He should, since he has been liberated from his physical envelope. Nevertheless, he does not regain his former lucidity until the separation is complete, that is to say, until there is no connection left between the spirit and the body."

382. Does the incarnate spirit suffer from the limitations created by the imperfections of his organs during childhood?

"No. Childhood is a necessary stage that is in the order of nature, in harmony with the designs of Providence. *It is a time of rest for the spirit.*"

383. For a spirit, what is the utility of going through childhood?

"Spirits incarnate in order to perfect themselves. During childhood they are more accessible to the impressions they receive, which may help in their progress—a process toward which those in charge of their education ought to contribute."

384. Why is the infant's first manifestation that of crying?

"To stimulate the mother's interest and ensure the care that the baby requires. Don't you understand that if it only had expressions of joy while still unable to speak, those around it would be little concerned about its needs? Therefore, in all of this, learn to admire the wisdom of Providence."

385. What causes the changes in a person's character at a certain age, particularly upon leaving adolescence—is it the spirit that changes?

"In this process the spirit retrieves his nature, showing himself as who he truly was.

"You do not know the secrets that children hide behind their innocence. You know neither what they are, nor what they have been, nor what they will be. Yet, you love and cherish them as though they were a part of you, to such a degree, in fact, that the love of a mother for her child is reputed to be the greatest love that one being may have for another. What is the reason for the sweet affection and tender benevolence that even strangers feel toward a child? Do you know? You do not, and that is precisely what I shall explain to you.

"Children are beings whom God has sent into a new existence. So that God is not known for an excessive severity, God gives them all the appearances of innocence. Even in children of an evil nature, their misdeeds are veiled by the unawareness about their own actions. But this innocence is not really an advancement relative to what they previously were. No, it is a picture of what they ought to be, and if they are not so, they alone shall face the consequences.

"But it is not only for the sake of the children that God has given them such an appearance. It is also, and above all, for the sake of their parents, whose love is crucial in their fragile condition. Such love would be significantly weakened if the parents were faced with a quarrelsome and ill-tempered character—whereas, viewing their children as good and kind, parents give them all their affection and provide them with the most tender care. However, when children no longer need the protection and assistance that has been given to them for fifteen or twenty years, their true individual character reemerges in all its nakedness. Their character remains good if it was fundamentally good originally, but it will always be combined with nuances that were hidden during early infancy.

"Notice that God's ways are always the most perfect; if one has a pure heart, one can easily grasp this explanation.

"Indeed, consider the possibility that the spirit of the child who is born among you may have come from a world on which he had acquired altogether different habits. How would you want this new being to be in your midst with passions much different than yours, inclinations and tastes entirely opposite to yours? How would you want him to incorporate himself into your environment if not the way God has desired, that is, through the filter of infancy? In it are blended all the thoughts, all the characters, and all the varieties of beings engendered by the multitude of worlds on which creatures develop. And you yourselves, upon dying, will also find yourselves in a sort of childhood, in the midst of a new family. In your new, non-terrestrial existence, you will not know the habits, customs, and relationships of that which is a new world to you, in addition to having to utilize with difficulty a language over which you have no command, a language more alive than your thought is today. (See #319)

"Childhood provides yet another purpose: spirits only enter corporeal life in order to perfect and advance themselves. The frailty of infancy renders them supple and open to the advice of experience and of those who ought to promote their progress. That is the time when one can best redirect their character and curb their evil leanings. Such is the duty with which God entrusts parents, the sacred mission for which they will have to answer.

"Thus, childhood is not only useful, necessary, and indispensable, but it is also the natural consequence of the laws established by God to govern the universe."

7. Earthly affinities and antipathies

386. Could two individuals who have already known and loved each other meet in another corporeal existence and recognize one another?

"They would not recognize one another, but they could feel attracted to each other. Frequently, intimate connections founded on sincere affection have no other cause. Two individuals are drawn together by apparently fortuitous circumstances, but it is actually the result of the attraction of two spirits *who search for each other among the crowd*."

—   Would they not find it more pleasurable if they could recognize one another?

"Not always. The recollection of past lives may create greater difficulties than you would imagine. After death, they will recognize one another and will remember the time spent together." (See #392)

387. Is affinity always a result of a previous acquaintance between two spirits?

"No. Two spirits who have affinities are naturally drawn to each other, without necessarily having known each other previously on Earth."

388. Could the encounters which at times happen between people, usually attributed to chance, be the effect of a kind of sympathetic link?

"Among thinking beings there are connections that you do not yet know. Magnetism is the crux of this science, which you will better understand later." [b]

389. What is the cause of the instinctive repulsion that one may feel toward certain individuals when meeting for the first time?

"They are antagonistic spirits who sense and recognize each other, without having to speak to each other."

390. Is instinctive antipathy always a sign of an evil nature?

"Two spirits are not necessarily bad just because they have no affinity. Antipathy may originate from a divergence in the way they think. As they evolve, however, such divergences fade away, and the antipathy disappears."

391. Does the antipathy between two people arise first in the one whose spirit is worse or in the other whose spirit is better?

"It arises in both, but the causes and effects are different. An imperfect spirit feels antipathy toward anyone who may be able to judge and unmask him. Upon seeing a person for the first time, he sees that he will be condemned. This moral distance may then change into hatred and envy, inspiring him with the desire to do evil. The good spirit, on the other hand, is repulsed by the bad one because he knows he will not be understood by the other, and because they do not share the same feelings. However, conscious of his superior moral standing, he feels neither hatred nor jealousy toward the other—it suffices to simply avoid and pity the other one."

8. Forgetfulness of the past

392. Why does an incarnate spirit lose the memory of his past?

"Man neither can nor may know everything. God, in His divine wisdom, wills it so. Without the veil that hides certain things from him, man would be dazzled, like one who passes abruptly from darkness to light. *Through the forgetfulness of the past, man is more fully himself.*"

393. How can a man be responsible for acts and atone for faults of which he has no recollection? How can he profit from the experience acquired in existences fallen into oblivion? We would imagine that the tribulations of life might be a lesson for him, if he recalled what has caused them. But if he does not remember them, each new existence for him is as though it were his first, and he, therefore, must always start over. How is this to be reconciled with the justice of God?

"With each new existence, man acquires more intelligence and can better distinguish between good and evil. Where would his merit be if he remembered his whole past? When a spirit reenters his primitive life (the spirit world), his entire prior life unfolds before him. He sees the wrongs he committed, and which are the cause of his suffering, as well as what could have prevented him from committing them. He understands the fairness of the position now assigned to him, and he then looks for an existence that could make up for the one that has passed. He seeks trials similar to those he has already experienced, or struggles he believes will be appropriate for his advancement, asking spirits who are more advanced than himself for help in the new task that he is about to undertake, for he knows that the spirit who will be assigned to him as his guide in that new existence will try to help him to right his wrongs, giving him a sort of *intuition* about them.

This same intuition is the thought, the evil impulse which frequently assaults you, and which you instinctively resist, most of the time attributing your resistance to the principles you have received from your parents, when in fact it is the voice of your conscience speaking to you, a voice which is a memory of the past, warning you not to make once again the same mistakes you have previously committed. Entering that new existence, if a spirit endures his trials with fortitude and resists them, he advances, ascending in the spirit hierarchy, when he finds himself once again among other spirits."

If during our corporeal life we do not have a precise recollection of what we have been, and of what good or evil we did in our previous existences, we have at least an intuition of them. Our instinctive tendencies are therefore a reminiscence of our past, which our conscience—representing our aspiration to no longer commit the same mistakes—warns us to resist.

394. On worlds more advanced than ours, where one is not subject to all our physical needs and hardships, do men understand that they are happier than we are? Happiness, in general, is relative, in that we feel it in comparison with a less joyful state. Because some of those worlds, though better than ours, have not yet reached perfection, those who inhabit them must be subject to nuisances of their own. The rich among us do not suffer from material needs like the poor do, but they are no less subject to their share of tribulations that also embitter their lives. So do the inhabitants of more advanced worlds feel as unhappy as we do? And do they also complain about their fate, since they do not recollect an inferior existence with which to compare?

"There are two different answers to this question. Among the worlds to which you refer, there are those on which the inhabitants have a clear and exact memory of their past lives. You can therefore understand that these can and do know how to appreciate the happiness that God allows them to enjoy. However, there are other worlds whose inhabitants are, as you say, in better conditions than yours, but who are no less subject to great nuisances, or even misfortunes. They do not appreciate their happiness, because they do not have recollection of an even more unfortunate state. However, even if they do not appreciate their circumstances as incarnate men, they will as spirits."

Is there not, in the forgetfulness of past existences, especially when such existences were filled with pain, a revealing testimony to the divine wisdom? It is only on superior worlds, where the memory of unhappy existences is nothing more than a bad dream, that those memories resurface. On less evolved worlds, however, would not the misfortunes one presently endures be aggravated by the memory of everything one has previously suffered? We may thus recognize that perfection exists in all of God's works. We are not in a position to criticize them, or to say how He ought to have regulated the universe.

The remembrance of our former existences would cause serious inconveniences. It could, in certain cases, be a source of great humiliation; in others, it could exalt our pride and therefore hinder our free will. God has provided us with just that which is necessary and sufficient for our advancement: the voice of our conscience and our instinctive tendencies, keeping us from what could be harmful. We would further add that if we had the remembrance of our own former personal acts, we would also be able to remember those of other people, and such knowledge could have the most unfortunate effects on our social relationships.

As we do not always have reason to be proud of our past, it is frequently convenient that a veil be thrown over it. This is in perfect agreement with the doctrine of the Spirits regarding worlds that are more advanced than ours. On those worlds where virtue reigns, the remembrance of the past is not at all painful. That is why a previous existence there is recalled as easily as we remember what we did the day before. As to the memory of stays that one may have had on inferior worlds, they represent, as we have said, nothing more than a bad dream.

395. Can we obtain any revelations about our previous existences?

"Not always. But many know who they were and what they did. If they were allowed to speak openly, they would make curious revelations about the past."

396. Some people believe they have a vague memory of an unknown past, which presents itself as a fleeting image of a dream, which they try unsuccessfully to hold onto. Wouldn't this belief be only an illusion?

"It is sometimes real. But often it is an illusion against which one should guard oneself, as it could simply be the effect of an overexcited imagination."

397. In corporeal existences of a more advanced nature than ours, is the memory of previous lives more precise?

"Yes, as the body becomes less material, one remembers things more easily. The memory of the past is clearer for those who inhabit higher order worlds."

398. Since man's instinctive tendencies are a reminiscence of his past, does it follow that, by studying these tendencies, he can learn about the faults he committed?

"Certainly, up to a certain point; but one must take into account the improvement that may have taken place in his spirit and the resolutions he made in the interval between incarnations. His present existence may in fact be much better than the preceding one."

— Could it be worse? In other words, could man make, in his present existence, mistakes which he did not make in the preceding one?

"That depends on his advancement. If he does not yet know how to endure certain trials, he may be drawn to commit new wrongs as a consequence of the position he has chosen. But in general, such wrongs indicate a stationary state rather than a regression, because a spirit may advance or remain stationary, but he never retrogrades."

399. As the tribulations of corporeal life are both expiations for past mistakes and trials for the future, does it follow that, from the nature of these tribulations, we may infer the type of our preceding existence?

"Very frequently, as each one is punished according to the mistake made. But do not see in this an absolute rule. The instinctive tendencies are a more accurate indicator, because the trials that a spirit undergoes may relate as much to the future as to the past."

When the end has arrived that Providence has established for a spirit's interval between incarnations, the spirit himself chooses the trials he wants to endure in order to hasten his advancement—in other words, the kind of existence he believes to be most adequate to provide him with the means to evolve, with trials always connected to the wrongs he needs to expiate. If he triumphs over these, he advances; if he fails, he must start over.

A spirit always enjoys his free will. It is by virtue of this freedom that, on the one hand, he chooses the trials of his corporeal life while in the spirit state, and that, on the other hand, he deliberates, when incarnate, what he will or will not do, thus always choosing between good and evil. To deny a man's free will would be to reduce him to a machine.

Having started a new corporeal life, a spirit temporarily loses the recollection of his former existences, as if a veil hid them. However, he sometimes has a vague perception of them, which may even be revealed to him under certain circumstances. But this only occurs with the permission of superior spirits, who may allow it to occur spontaneously with some useful goal in mind, never simply to satisfy an idle curiosity.

Future existences cannot be revealed, as they depend both on the conduct adopted in the present existence, and later choices made by the spirit.

The forgetfulness of previously committed faults is not an obstacle to the advancement of a spirit, because, though he may not have a precise memory of them, the knowledge he had of them in between incarnations—in addition to the desire he then nurtured to make up for them—shall guide him intuitively, and shall inspire him with the thought of resisting evil. This thought is the voice of his conscience, which is seconded by spirits who assist him, if he pays heed to the good inspirations they suggest to him.

Although a man does not know precisely what his conduct was in his former existences, he always knows the kinds of fault of which he is guilty, and what his dominant characteristics were. All he needs is to study himself, and he will be able to infer what he has been, not from what he currently is, but from his tendencies.

The tribulations of corporeal life represent both expiations for past wrongs and trials for the future. Such tribulations purify and elevate us, if we endure them with fortitude and without complaint.

The nature of the trials and tribulations we undergo may also shed light on what we have been and what we have done, as on Earth we may infer the acts of a criminal from the punishment accorded to him by the legal system. Thus, the proud will be punished by the humiliation of a lesser position; the self-indulgent and greedy by poverty; the cruel by the cruelty he himself will suffer; the tyrant by slavery; the bad son by the ingratitude of his own children; the idle by forced labor, and so on.

■■■

[a] This answer should be compared with the answer to question #366, where Kardec tests the Aristotelian notion of the three types of soul in man, the *vegetative soul*, the *sensitive soul*, and the *rational soul*, a concept found in Books II and III of Aristotle's *Περὶ Ψυχῆς* (*Peri Psychēs*, or *On the Soul*). —Trans.

[b] For the meaning of the word *magnetism* in this context, please see note [k] in the Introduction. —Trans.

Chapter 8:
Emancipation of the Soul

1. Sleep and dreams

400. Does an incarnate spirit willingly stay in his corporeal envelope?

"That is like asking a prisoner if he is happy to be incarcerated. An incarnate spirit continuously aspires to be liberated. The denser the envelope, the more he wants to be free of it."

401. During sleep does the soul rest like the body?

"No, the spirit is never inactive. During sleep, the bonds that link him to the body are loosened, and as the body does not need him while sleeping, the spirit travels through space and *enters into a more direct connection with other spirits.*"

402. How can we confirm the fact that a spirit is free during sleep?

"Through dreams. Understand that, while the body rests, the spirit's faculties are more amplified when compared with the waking state. He is able to recall the past and sometimes to catch a glimpse of the future. He acquires more power and is able to communicate with other spirits, *whether on this world or another.* You frequently say, 'I had a bizarre, truly frightening dream, but with no plausibility.' You are mistaken, though; it is frequently a memory of places and things which you have seen, or which you will see in another existence or on another occasion. With the physical senses mostly inactive, the spirit tries to break his chains in order to probe into the past and into the future.

"Poor men! How little you know about the most ordinary events of life! You believe you are very wise, yet the most common things mystify you. What do we do when we sleep? What are dreams? These are questions that all children ask, but to which you are still unable to provide an answer.

"Sleep partially liberates the soul from the body. When you sleep, you briefly find yourself in the state in which you will permanently be after death. Spirits who rapidly liberate themselves from matter upon death had intelligent dreams when alive. Such spirits, while their body is sleeping, connect with those who are more evolved; they travel, talk, and learn with them. They even work on tasks that they find complete upon dying. From all of this you should once more learn not to fear death, because you die daily, as a saint once said. [a]

"All this refers to superior spirits only. In the case of the majority of men, who at death must remain in a state of bewilderment for some time, in the uncertainty we have mentioned, they may go either to worlds even less evolved than Earth, where former affections call to them, or seek out pleasures that are perhaps even baser than those they indulge here. They go on to espouse principles that are viler, more despicable, and more harmful than those they profess among you.

What engenders sympathies on Earth is nothing more than the fact that, upon awakening, one feels linked to the hearts of those with whom one has just spent eight or nine hours of happiness or pleasure. In addition, what explains the insurmountable antipathy we may feel at the bottom of our hearts toward certain individuals, is the fact that they have a character much different than ours, and we recognize them without ever having laid eyes on them. Further, it is what explains your indifference when you do not seek to make new friends, as you realize there are others who love and cherish you elsewhere. In short, the influence of sleep on your life is greater than you think.

"Through sleep, incarnate spirits are always in touch with the spirit world; this is the reason why superior spirits consent to incarnate among you without too much reluctance. God has willed that, in their contact with earthly vices, they can reinvigorate themselves at the source of virtue, so that they—who have come to instruct others—may not themselves fail. Sleep is the door that God opens to them to contact their friends in heaven. It is their break, as it were, after a day of work, as they wait for the great deliverance, the final liberation which shall allow them to be once again in their element.

"A dream is the memory of what your spirit has seen during sleep. Notice, however, that you do not always dream, because you do not always remember what you have seen, or everything that you have seen. As your soul is not in full possession of its faculties, you frequently recall nothing more than the confusion that accompanies your departure and your return, which is mixed with the memory of what you have done, or what worries you while awake. Otherwise, how to explain the absurd dreams that the wise and the fool alike have? Evil spirits also employ dreams to torment weak and cowardly souls.

"Moreover, you shall soon see another type of dream develop; a type as ancient as the kind you already know about, but of which you are ignorant. It is the dream of Joan of Arc, the dream of Jacob, the dream of the Jewish prophets and certain Hindu sages: the dream which constitutes the recollection of the soul when fully disengaged from the body, the memory of that other life about which I have just spoken to you.

"Among the dreams you remember, try hard to differentiate between these two types. Without that, you shall fall into contradictions and errors that could be disastrous for your faith."

Dreams are the result of the emancipation of the soul, which is made more independent through the temporary interruption of activities and social interactions of daily life. From that emerges an indefinable clairvoyance, which extends to the most distant places, to places that have never been seen, and sometimes even to other worlds. It also results in the recollection of events that have taken place in the present existence or in previous ones. The strange images of that which is taking place, or has taken place, on unknown worlds, intertwined with flashes from the present world, form those bizarre and disorderly medleys that seem to have no meaning or connection.

The incoherence of dreams is further explained by the gaps resulting from the incomplete recollection of what we see in them, similar to a narrative from which entire sentences or fragments have been accidentally omitted. Combining the remaining passages would not yield an intelligible text.

403. Why do we not always remember our dreams?

"What you call sleep constitutes only the repose of the body, because the spirit is always active. During sleep, the spirit recovers a little of his freedom, and connects with those who are dear to him, either on this world or on others. But owing to the dense matter of the body, it is difficult for the spirit to retain, upon waking, the impressions received, because they were not received through his bodily organs."

404. What is to be thought of the meanings attributed to dreams?

"Dreams are not true in the sense that fortune tellers, for instance, understand them, for it is absurd to believe that dreaming about one matter necessarily foretells another. Dreams *are* true in the sense that they present real images to the spirit, but these images often have no relation to what occurs in his corporeal life. Also, many times, as we have mentioned, dreams represent a memory of the past. Finally, they may also sometimes be a presentiment of the future, if God allows it, or a vision of what is taking place at that moment in another place to which the soul has been transported. Do you not have numerous examples of people who appear in dreams to warn relatives or friends about what is happening to them? What are these apparitions, if not the soul or spirit of these people communicating with you? When you confirm that what you have seen has really occurred, is it not evidence that your imagination had nothing to do with it, especially if that matter was absolutely not in your thoughts when you were awake?"

405. We often see things in our dreams that seem to be premonitions that do not materialize. Where do these come from?

"They may occur for the spirit, if not for the body, which means that the spirit sees the thing he longs for, *because he goes out to look for it.* You must not forget that, during sleep, the soul is always more or less under the influence of matter, and therefore never completely free from earthly ideas. As a result, the concerns you may have when awake may stamp on that which you see in your dreams the image of longings or fears; this really is what can be called a figment of the imagination. When you are strongly consumed with an idea, you link it to everything you see."

406. When we see living people that are perfectly known to us doing things in a dream which they would absolutely never think of doing in real life, is it not purely our imagination at work?

"How can you know that they would absolutely never consider such things? Their spirit may come to visit yours, as yours may visit theirs, without you necessarily knowing what their thoughts are. Besides, you frequently attribute to individuals familiar to you, and in accord with your wishes, what took place, or is taking place, in other existences."

407. Is complete sleep necessary for the emancipation of the spirit?

"No. The spirit recovers his freedom as soon as he becomes drowsy, taking advantage of every moment of respite that the body offers in order to be liberated. As soon as there is a prostration of the vital forces, the spirit disengages from the body; the weaker the latter is, the freer the spirit will be."

This is why, dozing, or a simple dulling of the senses, often presents the same images as dreaming.

408. Sometimes we seem to hear within ourselves words distinctly pronounced that have no connection with what we are thinking about. Where do such words come from?

"Yes, and even entire sentences, especially when the senses begin to grow numb. It is sometimes the faint echo of a spirit who wants to communicate with you."

409. Often, while we have our eyes shut and we are not yet half-asleep, we see distinct images and figures in the minutest detail. Is this an effect of our vision or of our imagination?

"Once the body is numb, the spirit tries to break free from his chains: he transports himself and sees. If the sleep were complete, it would be a dream."

410. When asleep or half-asleep, we sometimes have ideas that seem very worthwhile, but which, in spite of the efforts we make to recall them, fade away from our memory. Where do these ideas come from?

"They are the result of the freedom of the spirit, who liberates himself and enjoys more powerful faculties at that moment. They may also often be advice given by other spirits."

—   What is the use of such ideas and advice if one cannot recall them and if one cannot benefit from them?

"Such ideas sometimes belong more to the spirit world than to the corporeal one. But more frequently, though the body may forget them, the spirit does not, and the idea reemerges at the appropriate time, as a spontaneous inspiration."

411. When the spirit is disengaged from matter and acts as a spirit, does he know the time of his death?

"He often has the presentiment of it, and sometimes he has a very clear awareness of it, which provides him with an intuition about it in his waking state. That is why some people foresee their own death with great precision."

412. While the body is resting or sleeping, can the activity of the spirit cause the body to be tired?

"Yes, because the spirit is linked to the body like a balloon tied to a post. Well, just like the jerking movements of the balloon cause the post to shake, the activity of the spirit reacts upon the body and may induce fatigue."

2. Visits among the spirits of the living

413. The tenet of the emancipation of the soul during sleep seems to indicate that we live two lives simultaneously: that of the body, or the life of patent relationships, and that of the soul, which represents the life of invisible relationships. Is this accurate?

"In the state of emancipation, the life of the body gives way to that of the soul. But strictly speaking, there are not two lives; there are rather two phases of the same life; for a man does not live a double life."

414. Can two acquaintances visit each other during sleep?

"Yes. Many others as well—who believe not to know each other in their waking state—may gather and talk. Without even suspecting it, you may even have friends in a different country. The phenomenon during sleep in which you visit friends, relatives, acquaintances, and other people who may be of value to you is so frequent, that you experience it almost every night."

415. Of what use are these nightly visits if we do not remember them?

"Normally, upon awakening, an intuition remains that is frequently the source of certain ideas which come up spontaneously, without your being able to explain them, and which are none other than the thoughts you developed in those exchanges."

416. Can man make such spirit visits at will? For example, can he say upon going to bed, "Tonight I wish to meet a given person in spirit, speak with him, and tell him a specific thing?"

"Here is what happens: a man sleeps and his spirit awakens, but the spirit is often very far from following what the man decided while awake, because the earthly life of a person interests the spirit very little, once the spirit is disengaged from matter. This is the case for those who are already fairly evolved, however. The others spend their spirit existence during sleep in an altogether different way, as they may either surrender themselves to their passions or remain totally inactive. Therefore, according to the goal of the planned action, it may happen that the spirit visits the intended people, but the mere desire to do so while awake is not reason enough to make it happen."

417. Can a number of incarnate spirits meet and gather in a group?

"Undoubtedly. The bonds of friendship, old or new, frequently assemble several spirits who feel happy to be together."

The word *old* here refers to the bonds of friendship established in previous existences. We bring back to our waking state an intuition of the ideas we have acquired during such invisible conversations, even though we ignore the source of such ideas.

418. If a man believed his friend to be dead, though the friend is in fact alive, could that man meet his friend in spirit, and therefore know that his friend still lives? In this case, could this man retain an intuition about it upon awaking?

"As a spirit, he can certainly see his friend and know how his friend is. If the belief in the death of his friend was not imposed on him as a trial, he may have the intuition of his friend being alive, just as he may have the intuition of his friend being dead."

3. Concealed transmission of thought

419. Why is it that one same idea, such as a discovery, for instance, sometimes occurs in different places simultaneously?

"We have already said that, in their sleep, spirits communicate with one another. Well then, when the body awakens, the spirit remembers what he has learned, and the person thinks he has invented it. This way, many may discover the same thing at the same time. When you say that an idea is *in the air*, you use a figure of speech that is more accurate than you could imagine. Unsuspectingly, each one contributes to its dissemination."

In this way, as spirits, we ourselves often unknowingly reveal the concerns we have in our waking state to other spirits.

420. Can spirits communicate with each other while the body is completely awake?

"A spirit is not enclosed in his body as if in a box; he radiates around in every direction. He can therefore communicate with other spirits even in his waking state, although he does so with more difficulty."

421. How can two completely awake people often have the same thought at precisely the same time?

"In this case, they are two spirits who are in tune and communicate with each other, being able to see each other's thoughts even when their bodies are not asleep."

When spirits meet, a transmission of thought is established, allowing two people to see and understand each other without the need for outward verbal interchange. We may say that they speak the language of spirits.

4. Coma, catalepsy, apparent death

422. Comatose and cataleptic individuals in general may see and hear what occurs around them, but are unable to express themselves. Do they see and hear through their physical eyes and ears?

"No, they see and hear through the spirit. The spirit is conscious but is unable to communicate."

— Why are they unable to communicate?

"The condition of the body prevents it. The particular state of their organs proves to you that there is something more to a human being than just a body, because, although the body does not function completely, the spirit continues to act."

423. During coma, can the spirit be completely separated from the body in such a way as to give the body all the appearances of death, and then return to it?

"The body is not dead during coma, because there are functions that continue to be active. Vitality remains in a latent state, like in a chrysalis, but it is not extinguished. The spirit is connected to the body so long as the body lives, but once the ties are broken by *actual* death and by the decomposition of the organs, the separation is complete and the spirit no longer returns. When an apparently dead person comes back to life, it is because death had not actually completely occurred."

424. By providing care in a timely fashion, can one restore the links that are about to break, bringing back to life a being who, without such attention, would certainly die?

"Yes, of course. You have evidence of this every day. In such cases, magnetism is often a powerful means, because it provides the body with the vital fluid it required, or else the latter would be insufficient to keep the organs working." [b]

Coma and catalepsy have the same principle, which is the temporary loss of sensitivity and movement, due to a still unexplained physiological cause. They differ from each other in that, in the case of coma, the suspension of the vital forces is generalized and gives the body all the appearances of death; in catalepsy, this suspension is localized, and can affect a larger or smaller portion of the body, leaving the intelligence free to express itself, a fact that clearly differentiates it from death. Coma is always natural; catalepsy is sometimes spontaneous, but it may also be artificially induced and reversed by magnetic action.

5. Somnambulism

425. Does natural somnambulism [c] have any connection to dreams? How can it be explained?

"In it the case of somnambulism, the independence of the soul is more complete than in the case of dreams; its faculties are then more amplified. The soul has perceptions it does not have when dreaming, which is a state of imperfect somnambulism.

"During somnambulism, the spirit is in total possession of itself. The physical organs being in a sort of cataleptic state, they no longer receive *external* impressions. This state manifests especially during sleep, a moment during which the spirit can temporarily leave the body, while the latter surrenders itself to the rest required by its material nature. When somnambulistic phenomena occur, it is because the spirit is preoccupied with a particular issue that requires the use of the body, which is then utilized in the same way a spirit would employ a table or other material object in the phenomenon of physical manifestations, or even a medium's hand in the case of written communications. In dreams in which one is conscious, the sensory organs, including those related to memory, begin to awaken, receiving imperfectly the impressions produced by objects or external factors, and transmitting such impressions to the spirit. The spirit, also in a state of relaxation, only registers confused and often fragmentary perceptions, which, without any apparent reason, are mixed with vague memories of either the present life or previous ones. It is then easy to understand why somnambulists in general have no recollection, and why the dreams they do remember are completely senseless most of the time. I say *most of the time*, because sometimes dreams are the consequence of a precise memory of events from a previous life, and sometimes even a sort of intuition about the future."

426. Does the so-called magnetic somnambulism have any relation to natural somnambulism?

"It is the same thing, except that it is artificially induced."

427. What is the nature of the agent called magnetic fluid?

"It is the vital fluid, or animalized electricity, or modifications of the universal fluid."

428. What is the cause of somnambulistic clairvoyance?

"We have already told you: *it is the soul who sees.*"

429. How can somnambulists see through opaque objects?

"Objects are opaque only to your dense organs. We have already said that matter is not an obstacle to spirits, since they can freely go right through it. Somnambulists frequently tell you that they see through their forehead, through their knee, and so on, because you are entirely immersed in matter and do not understand that they can see without the aid of the organs. However, primed by your preconceptions, they, too, believe they actually need their sensory organs for perception. If left to their own devices, they would understand that they see through all the parts of their body, or rather, that they see independently of their body."

430. Since the clairvoyance of somnambulists is that of their soul or spirit, why cannot they see everything, and why are they so often mistaken?

"First, imperfect spirits are not allowed to see everything and to know everything. You know very well that they still share your faults and prejudices. In addition, while they are attached to matter, they do not enjoy all their spirit faculties. God has given clairvoyance to man for a useful and serious purpose, and not for him to learn that which is forbidden to him. That is why somnambulists may not penetrate everything."

431. What is the source of somnambulists' innate ideas, and how can they speak with such accuracy about things they ignore in their waking state, and which even transcend their intellectual capacity?

"It just so happens that somnambulists may actually have more knowledge than you would imagine. It is dormant, however, as the limitations of their material body prevent them from retrieving that knowledge. What is a somnambulist, after all? They are spirits like us, but incarnated to fulfill a mission; the somnambulistic state into which they enter rescues them from this mental lethargy. We have repeatedly told you that we incarnate many times, a process which makes the knowledge acquired in previous existences materially inaccessible. When they enter a somnambulistic *trance*, spirits recall what they already know, but not always in a complete way. They know, but they cannot say where that knowledge comes from, or how they acquired it. When the trance is over, all the memory of it fades away, and they return to a state of forgetfulness."

> Experience shows that somnambulists also receive communications from other spirits, who transmit to them what they must say and provide them with the knowledge they lack. This is especially seen in cases involving medical prescriptions: the spirit of the somnambulist recognizes the attending affliction, but another spirit indicates the medicine. This double action is sometimes evident, whereas at other times it is revealed through these very frequent expressions: '*They* are telling me to say this,' or '*they* are forbidding me to say that.' In the second example, it is always dangerous to insist on obtaining the information denied, because, otherwise, a door opens to frivolous spirits who talk unscrupulously about everything, without any regard for the truth.

432. How do you explain the remote viewing ability displayed by some somnambulists?

"Doesn't the soul travel during sleep? The same thing happens in the case of somnambulism."

433. Does the greater or lesser development of somnambulistic clairvoyance depend on the physical organization of the body, or on the nature of the incarnate spirit?

"On both. There are physical dispositions that allow the spirit to disengage more or less easily from matter."

434. Are the faculties that the spirit of the somnambulist enjoys the same as those of the spirit after death?

"To a certain extent, but you must take into account the influence of matter, to which the spirit of the somnambulist is still attached."

435. Can somnambulists see other spirits?

"Most can see them very well, but it depends on the nature and degree of their lucidity. But sometimes they do not realize it all at once, and thus mistake them for corporeal beings. This happens especially with those who have no knowledge of Spiritist matters, because they do not yet comprehend the nature of spirits; astonished, they believe they see living creatures."

The same effect is observed at the moment of death among those who think they are still alive. Nothing around them appears to have changed, spirits appear to them as having bodies similar to ours, and they mistake the appearance of their own bodies as being of a physical nature.

436. Do somnambulists who see at a distance do it from the place where their body is located, or from where their soul is?

"Why do you ask, since it is the soul that sees, not the body?"

437. Since it is the soul that transports itself, how can somnambulists experience in their body the sensations of heat or cold from the place where their soul is, sometimes very far from the location of their body?

"Their soul has not entirely left the body. It always remains connected to it by the link that unites them; this link is the conductor of sensorial perceptions. When two people in different cities communicate with one another through an electrical cable, the electricity is the link between their thoughts, allowing them to communicate as though they were right next to each other."

438. Does the use that somnambulists make of their faculties influence the state of their spirit after death?

"Very much so, like the good or bad use of all faculties that God has given to man."

6. Ecstatic trance

439. What is the difference between ecstasy and somnambulism?

"Ecstatic trances are a more refined type of somnambulism. The soul of the ecstatic is even more independent."

440. Do the souls of the ecstatic really visit superior worlds?

"Yes, they see them, understanding the bliss of those who dwell in them, which is why they would like to remain there. However, there are realms inaccessible to spirits who are not sufficiently purified."

441. When ecstatics express the desire to leave the Earth, do they speak sincerely, and are they not held back by their survival instinct?

"That depends on the spirit's degree of purification. If they see that their future situation will be better than their present life, they may make an effort to break the ties that bind them to Earth."

442. If we were to leave ecstatics to themselves during their trances, could their soul quit their body permanently?

"Yes, they could die. That is why it is necessary to call them back by means of everything that might link them to this world, and above all make them understand that, if the chain that holds them here were to be broken, it would be the surest way of preventing them from being in that place where they realize they could experience such bliss."

443. Ecstatics claim to see things that are evidently the product of an imagination marked by earthly beliefs and prejudices. Is what they see, therefore, not always real?

"What they see is real to them, but since their spirit is always under the influence of earthly ideas, they may see it in their own way, or, rather, they may express it in a language in line with their prejudices and with the ideas with which they were brought up, or perhaps in line with your own ideas, in order to make themselves understood more easily. It is especially in this sense that they can misrepresent what they see."

444. What degree of trust can be placed in the revelations of ecstatics?

"Ecstatics can be mistaken quite frequently, especially when they want to grasp what must remain a mystery for man. In such cases, they may surrender to their own ideas, or they may fall prey to dishonest spirits, *who take advantage of their enthusiasm* in order to deceive them."

445. What consequences may be drawn from the phenomena of somnambulism and ecstasy? Would they be a sort of initiation into our future life?

"To put it better, they represent a glimpse into your past and future life. Study these phenomena, and you will find in them the solution to more than one mystery that your reason has tried to penetrate to no avail."

446. Could the phenomena of somnambulism and ecstasy be reconciled with materialism?

"Those who study them in good faith and without preconceived ideas could subscribe to neither materialism, nor atheism."

7. Second sight

447. Does the phenomenon called *second sight* have any connection with dreams and somnambulism?

"All of them represent one and the same thing. What you call *second sight* is, again, the spirit in a state of greater freedom, even though the body is not asleep. Second sight is the sight of the soul."

448. Is second sight permanent?

"The faculty is permanent, but not the ability to exercise it. On worlds that are less material than yours, spirits disengage themselves more easily, and, while not abandoning articulated language, are able to communicate with one another through thought alone. Second sight is also a permanent faculty for most of them. Their normal state may be compared to that of your lucid somnambulists, and that is also why they manifest themselves to you more effortlessly than those who are incarnated in denser bodies."

449. Does second sight develop spontaneously, or by the will of those who possess it?

"Most of the time it is spontaneous, but the will can often play a large role, as well. Take the example of certain individuals that are called fortune tellers, some of whom possess the faculty of second sight, and you will realize that it is their own will that helps them access this faculty, and produce what you call a vision."

450. Can second sight be developed through practice?

"Yes, practice always leads to progress, and the veil that covers things is gradually lifted."

—   Is this faculty linked to one's physical organization?

"Certainly, the physical organization plays a role, and there are organic constitutions that are unsuited for it."

451. Why does second sight seem to be hereditary in certain families?

"First, because of organic similarity, which is passed on like other physical attributes. Second, because of the development of the faculty, through the training that may also be transmitted from person to person."

452. Is it true that certain circumstances can cause second sight to develop?

"Illness, an impending danger, or a large shock may trigger it. In such instances, the body is sometimes in a particular state that allows the spirit to see what you cannot see through your bodily eyes."

Times of crisis and calamities, times of great emotion—in short, everything that causes mental overexcitement—may sometimes trigger the development of second sight. It seems that Providence, in the presence of danger, has given us the means of invoking it. All persecuted sects and groups offer numerous examples of it.

453. Are people endowed with second sight always aware of it?

"Not always. For them it is a completely natural thing, and many believe that if other people paid closer attention to themselves, they would realize they have it, too."

454. May we attribute to a sort of second sight the perceptiveness of certain people who, without appearing to have anything extraordinary about them, judge things with more accuracy than others?

"It always the soul that radiates more freely, being able to judge things better than when under the influence of matter."

— In certain cases, can this faculty provide the foreknowledge of future events?

"Yes. It may also give rise to presentiments, because this faculty manifests to varying degrees, and the same person may display all, or only some of them."

8. Theoretical outline of somnambulism, ecstatic trances, and second sight

455. The phenomenon of natural somnambulism is produced spontaneously, and is independent of any known external cause, but among some people gifted with a special physical organization, it may be induced through the action of a magnetic agent.

The state called *magnetic somnambulism* only differs from natural somnambulism or sleepwalking, in that it is artificially produced, whereas the latter is spontaneous.

Natural somnambulism is a widely known occurrence, and no one questions its reality, despite the marvelous character of the phenomena that if produces. So, why would magnetic somnambulism be any more extraordinary or irrational simply because of the fact that it is produced artificially, like so many other things? One may say that charlatans have exploited it, which is one more reason for it not to be left in their hands. Once science has finally mapped it in its entirety, charlatanism will have much less credit among the masses. Meanwhile, since both natural and artificial somnambulism are facts, and because there is no arguing against facts, they are establishing themselves in spite of the ill-will of some and, penetrating the jurisdiction of science, where it is entering through several side doors, instead of entering through the front entrance. And when the reality of phenomenon is fully established there, it will be necessary to grant it the right of citizenship.

For Spiritism, somnambulism is more than a physiological phenomenon; it is a light shed on psychology. Through it, one can study the soul, because the soul reveals itself undisguised in it. One of the phenomena which characterize the soul is the clairvoyance that occurs independent of the ordinary organs of vision. Those who dispute this fact do so on the grounds that somnambulists are not always able to see as they can with their eyes, and that they are subject to the will of the experimenter. Should we be surprised that the effects are not the same when the means are different? Would it be rational to expect identical effects when the instruments in fact do not exist? The soul has its properties just as the eye has its own, and it is necessary to judge them in their own right, not by analogy.

The cause of clairvoyance in the case of a magnetic somnambulist or a natural somnambulist is identical: *it is an attribute of the soul,* a faculty intrinsic to every part of the incorporeal being that exists in us, and that has no limits other than those assigned to the soul itself. Somnambulists can see wherever their soul may go, whatever the distance may be.

In the case of remote viewing, somnambulists do not see things from the place where their body is, as if through a telescope. They see them as present, as though they were actually at the place where those things exist, because their soul, in reality, is actually there. That is why their body seems to no longer exist and is deprived of sensorial perceptions until the moment in which the soul regains possession of it. This partial separation of the soul from the body is an abnormal state that may last for a shorter or longer time, but not indefinitely. This separation is what causes the fatigue that the body experiences after a certain time, particularly when the soul is dedicated to some active pursuit.

Soul sight or spirit sight is not circumscribed and has no specific locus, which explains why somnambulists cannot assign a particular organ to it. They simply see, without knowing why or how, because vision does not have a specific center for them as spirits. *If they make reference to their body*, they point to the centers where vital activity is more intense, especially the brain, the gastric region, or the organ they perceive to be the *strongest* link point between their spirit and body.

The power of somnambulistic lucidity is not unlimited. Even when completely free, spirits are limited in their faculties and knowledge according to the degree of perfection they have reached. This is ever more the case when they are attached to a material body, being subject to its influence. This is the reason why somnambulistic clairvoyance is neither universal nor infallible. It is less reliable the more it is diverted from its natural purpose and made an object of curiosity and *experimentation*.

When liberated from the body, the spirit of the somnambulist enters into communication more easily with other spirits, *incarnate or discarnate*. This communication is established through the contact of the fluids that make up their perispirits, enabling the transmission of thought, like an electric wire. This way, somnambulists do not need that thoughts be articulated through words, as they can sense and surmise them, something which renders them very sensitive and amenable to the influences of the mental atmosphere around them. That is also why the presence of a large group of spectators, especially of curious onlookers who may be more or less hostile, is very detrimental to the development of somnambulist faculty, which folds in on itself, as it were, and does not unfold with full freedom unless within the intimacy of welcoming surroundings. *The presence of ill-willed or hostile bystanders produces on them an effect akin to that of the contact of a hand on the sensitive plant.* [d]

Somnambulists see at once their own spirit and body. They are, so to speak, two beings that represent the double existence—spiritual and corporeal—which are nevertheless merged together by the ties that unite them. Somnambulists do not always realize this situation, and this *duality* frequently makes them speak of themselves as though they were speaking of a stranger. In such cases, in a given moment, the corporeal being speaks to the spiritual being, and in the next moment, the other way around.

The spirit acquires more knowledge and experience in each new corporeal existence and partially forgets them when reincarnated in a dense, material body, *but is able to recall them as a spirit*. That is how certain somnambulists display a knowledge beyond their education and even beyond their apparent intellectual capacity. The intellectual and scientific limitations of somnambulists in their waking state, however, does not allow one to predict anything about the knowledge they may reveal in their lucid, somnambular state. According to circumstances and the goal one has in mind, they may draw this knowledge from their own experience, from the clairvoyance of surrounding conditions, or from the advice they receive from other spirits. But because their own spirit may be more or less advanced, they may relay more or less accurate information.

Through the phenomenon of somnambulism, whether natural or induced through magnetism, Providence provides us with undeniable evidence of the existence and independence of the soul, allowing us to witness the sublime spectacle of its emancipation. Through this phenomenon, Providence opens up to us the book of our destiny. When a somnambulist describes what is occurring remotely, it is obvious that he really is seeing it, but not through the eyes of his body. He sees himself at that place, and feels himself being transported there, where a part of himself is then present, and since that part of him is not his body, it can only be his soul or spirit. While man is led astray by the subtleties of an abstract and unintelligible metaphysics, in the pursuit of the causes of our mental existence, God routinely places in front of his eyes and within reach of his hands the most unassuming and most patent means for the study of experimental psychology.

The ecstatic trance is the state in which the independence between the soul and body is expressed in the most delicate way, and becomes, in a sense, palpable.

In both dreams and somnambulism, the somnambulists' souls wander through terrestrial worlds, whereas in ecstasy, they enter unknown worlds, those of ethereal spirits, with whom they communicate, without, however, overstepping certain limits: if they did, their souls would completely break the ties connecting them to their bodies. A resplendent and entirely new radiance surrounds them, harmonies unknown on Earth enrapture them, and an ineffable comfort pervades them—they enjoy in advance a sample of celestial bliss, *and one may say that they have set one foot on the doorstep of eternity.*

In the ecstatic trance, the neutralization of bodily perceptions is almost complete. Only organic life, so to speak, is sustained by the body, and one feels that the soul is connected to it by only a single thread, which could be forever broken by a small additional effort.

In this state, all earthly thoughts disappear, yielding to the purest feeling that constitutes the very essence of our immaterial being. Completely enthralled by that sublime contemplation, the ecstatic regards life as a momentary pause. For him, good and evil, as well as the crude joys and woes of this world, are no more than futile incidents in a journey the terminus of which he is pleased to foresee.

As it happens with ecstatics, so it does with somnambulists—their lucidity may be more or less perfect, and they are more apt to know and understand things the greater their degree of advancement. At times, there is more exaltation than true lucidity among ecstatics, or rather, their exaltation hampers their lucidity. That is why their revelations are frequently a combination of truths and errors, of sublime things and absurd—even ridiculous—things. This exaltation is always a source of weakness if ecstatics do not know how to control it, a situation of which spirits of lower orders may frequently take advantage in order to dominate them. To that end, these interfering spirits assume an *appearance* that stimulates the ideas and prejudices of the somnambulist's waking state. This represents an obstacle, but not all cases are similar. It is up to us to judge things carefully, and to subject all revelations to the scrutiny of reason.

The emancipation of the soul occurs sometimes even in the waking state, producing the phenomenon called *second sight*, which provides those endowed with it the ability to see, hear, and feel *beyond the limits of their normal senses.* The action of their soul is extended to remote places, where they can perceive things and they see, so to speak, through their ordinary sight, as a type of mirage.

When the phenomenon of second sight is produced, the seer's physical state is significantly modified. His glance becomes vague, as he looks without seeing, and the whole physiognomy reflects a kind of exaltation. One verifies that the visual organs are not involved in this phenomenon, because the vision may persist despite the eyes being shut.

This faculty seems as natural as that of normal sight for those who are gifted with it. They consider it a normal attribute of their being, and it does not seem at all exceptional to them. Most of the time, forgetfulness follows this temporary lucidity, the remembrance of which becomes increasingly vague, finally disappearing like that of a dream.

The power of second sight ranges from a confused sensation to a clear and distinct perception of things present or absent. In its rudimentary state, it may bestow upon some people a more refined perception and insight, a kind of assurance in their actions which we may call *the precision of the moral glance.* When this second sight is more developed, it awakens presentiments, and, when further developed still, it may reveal events that have already happened or that are about to happen.

Natural and artificial somnambulism, ecstasy, and second sight are no more than variations or modifications of one single source. Like dreams, such phenomena belong to the natural order of things, and that is why they have always existed. History shows us that they have been known and even exploited since the most remote antiquity, and in them one may find the explanation for countless events that prejudice has regarded as supernatural.

■■■

[a] Saint Paul (1 Cor. 15:31). —Trans.

[b] For the meaning of the word *magnetism* in this context, please see note [k] in the Introduction. —Trans.

[c] The word *somnambulism* here refers to a trance-like state that may occur spontaneously, or be induced by a so-called *magnetizer*. In this state, the somnambulist may experience a type of clairvoyance that enables remote viewing and other psychic abilities or, in modern parlance, *extra-sensorial perceptions.* See note [k] in the Introduction, as well as The Marchioness of San Milan Tecmen, *Facts and testimonials in favour of Somnambulism and Clairvoyance with Mesmeric Influence* (London: Cheltenham, 1847); and Edwin Lee, *Report upon the Phenomena of Clairvoyance or Lucid Somnambulism* (London: John Churchill, 1843). An interesting account of a recent decade-long, government-sponsored research program of remote viewing and other psychic abilities can be found in Russell Targ, PhD, *The Reality of ESP: A Physicist's Proof of Psychic Abilities* (Wheaton, IL: Quest Books, 2012). One of Targ's lectures on the topic can be found on https://www.youtube.com/watch?v=hBl0cwyn5GY, last accessed December 21, 2018. —Trans.

[d] *Mimosa pudica*, a tropical plant from the Fabaceae family whose compound leaves fold inward and droop when touched or shaken as a natural mechanism to defend themselves from harm. —Trans.

Chapter 9:
Intervention of Spirits
in the Corporeal World

1. Probing of our thoughts by spirits

456. Can spirits see everything we do?

"They can, because you are constantly surrounded by them. However, they only see those things on which they focus their attention, because they do not busy themselves with matters to which they are indifferent."

457. Can spirits know our most secret thoughts?

"They frequently know about that which you would like to conceal from yourselves. Neither actions nor thoughts can be hidden from them."

— So, is it easier to conceal something from a person who is still alive, than to do so after the person has died?

"Certainly, and when you fancy yourselves in absolute privacy, you often have a throng of spirits by your side, watching you."

458. What do the spirits who surround and observe us think about us?

"That is as the case may be. Frivolous spirits laugh at the petty annoyances they cause you and scoff at your impatience. Serious spirits pity your imperfections and try to help you."

2. Concealed influence of spirits on our thoughts and actions

459. Do spirits have any influence on our thoughts and actions?

"In this regard, their influence is much greater than you would believe, for very frequently it is they who drive you."

460. Do we have thoughts that are our own, and others that are suggested to us?

"Your soul is a spirit who thinks on its own; but you must have noticed that many thoughts occur to you all at the same time, regarding the same subject, and that they frequently contradict one another. Well then, in that you have a combination of your own ideas and ours, and this is what makes you confused, as you have different ideas in your mind, fighting one another."

461. How can we distinguish between our own thoughts and those that are suggested to us?

"When a thought is suggested to you, it is like a voice speaking to you. Your own thoughts are usually those that occur first. But in any case, there is not much to gain from such a distinction, and it is often more useful not to know about it, as then you act more freely. If you make the right decision, you do so more spontaneously; if you choose the wrong path, you have greater responsibility."

462. Do men of intelligence and genius always draw their ideas from within themselves?

"Their ideas sometimes derive from their own spirit, but frequently they are suggested to them by other spirits who deem them capable of understanding and worthy of conveying such ideas. When they cannot find ideas within themselves, they appeal to inspiration—they make an evocation, unsuspectingly."

> If it were useful for us to be able to distinguish between our own thoughts and those suggested to us, God would have given us the means to do so, just as He has given us the means to distinguish between day and night. When an issue seems vague, it must be so for our own good.

463. It is sometimes said that the first impulse is always the best. Is this correct?

"It can be good or bad, according to the nature of the incarnate spirit. It is always good in the case of he who listens to good inspirations."

464. How can we tell if a suggested thought comes from a good or an bad spirit?

"Study the matter. Good spirits give only good advice; it is upon you to make the distinction."

465. For what purpose do imperfect spirits induce us to evil?

"To make you suffer as they themselves do."

—   Does that lessen their suffering?

"No, but they do so anyway, out of envy at seeing beings who are happier."

—   What kinds of suffering do they wish to inflict on us?

"Those that result from belonging to a lower order and from being removed from God."

466. Why does God permit spirits to incite us to evil?

"Imperfect spirits are meant as instruments to test the faith and constancy of men in the practice of the good. As a spirit, you must progress in the science of the infinite, and for that reason you go through the trials of evil in order to reach the good. Our mission is to lead you to the path of virtue. When evil influences act on you, it is you yourselves who call to them, out of your desire for evil. Inferior spirits then come to aid you in the accomplishment of evil deeds, when you are intent on committing them. However, they can only help you in your evil pursuits if you actually want them to do that. If you are inclined to murder, alas, there will be a swarm of spirits who will stimulate that thought in your mind. However, there will also be others who will try to influence you to do good, leveling the scales, as it were, leaving you master of your destiny."

It is thus that God leaves to our conscience the choice of the course we must follow, and the freedom to yield to either one of the opposing influences acting upon us.

467. Can we escape the influence of spirits who incite us to evil?

"Yes, because they only attach themselves to those who solicit them with their desires, or attract them through their thoughts."

468. Do spirits whose influence is repelled by a person's will eventually give up on their attempts?

"What else could they do? When they find their efforts are fruitless, they leave. But they lie in wait for a favorable moment, as a cat attentively waits to ambush the mouse."

469. By what means can we neutralize the influence of evil spirits?

"By doing good and placing all your trust in God, you repel the influence of inferior spirits and you destroy the dominion they wish to establish over you. Guard yourselves against listening to the suggestions of spirits who stimulate evil thoughts in your mind, those who provoke disagreement and elicit in you any evil passion. Distrust particularly those spirits who flatter your pride, for, in so doing, they attack you at your weakest point. That is why Jesus teaches you to recite in the Lord's Prayer, 'Lord, do not let us fall into temptation, but deliver us from evil.' "

470. If a spirit seeks to lead us into evil and thus puts our moral fiber to the test, could this spirit have received a mission to do this, and if so, will he be responsible for carrying out such a mission?

"A spirit never receives a mission to do evil. When he carries out evil deeds, it is by his own will, and he shall, therefore, suffer the consequences. God may let him test you, but never directly orders him to do it; it is up to you to repel him."

471. When we experience a sensation of anguish, an inexplicable anxiety, or an inner satisfaction without a known cause, does it result uniquely from our physical condition?

"It is almost always the result of communications you have established with spirits without being aware of it, or that you had with them during sleep."

472. Are spirits who want to incite us to evil limited to taking advantage of the circumstances in which we find ourselves, or can they create such circumstances?

"They may take advantage of a circumstance, but frequently they cause it, pushing you, without your being aware of it, toward the object of your desire. For example, a man may find a certain amount of money by the road. Spirits did not place that money there, but they may have suggested to him the thought of going that way. Then, they suggest he keep the money, while others suggest he return it to its rightful owner. The same sort of thing happens with all other temptations."

3. Spirit possession

473. Can a spirit temporarily take over the corporeal envelope of a living person? In other words, can the spirit enter an animate body and replace the spirit incarnated in it?

"A spirit does not enter a body as you enter a house. Instead, it associates with an incarnate spirit who has the same flaws and qualities, so that they can jointly act. But it is always the incarnate spirit who acts upon the matter enveloping him, according to his own volition. A spirit cannot replace the one who is incarnate because the incarnate spirit is connected to the body until the time set for the end of that material existence."

474. If there is no such thing as possession per se, that is, the cohabitation of two spirits in the same body, may an incarnate soul nonetheless be under the powerful influence of another spirit, so as to become *subjugated* by him, to such a degree that his own will is, in a way, paralyzed?

"Yes, and these are the truly possessed. You must understand, however, that this kind of domination never occurs without the participation of the one who suffers it, *either through his weakness* or through his desire. Epileptics and insane individuals have often been considered to be possessed, when in fact they needed a physician, rather than an exorcist."

> In its common meaning, the word possession presumes the existence of demons—a category of beings of an evil nature—and the cohabitation of one of these beings with the soul of an individual in his body. But, because there are no demons *in this particular sense*, and since two spirits cannot simultaneously inhabit the same body, there can be no one who is possessed according to the idea normally attached to the word. By the expression *possessed*, one should understand the absolute subjection of a soul to an imperfect spirit.

475. Can one repel bad spirits all by oneself, so as to escape their domination?

"You can always rid yourself of a burden if you have a firm will."

476. Could it happen that the fascination exerted by an evil spirit is such, that the subjugated person does not even perceive it? In addition, could a third person put an end to the subjection, and in that case, what conditions must this person satisfy to that end?

"An upright man may help, through his will power, by appealing to the assistance of good spirits, because the better a person is, the more power this person has over imperfect spirits in order to repel them, and over good ones in order to attract them. However, the good person would be powerless in this case, if he who is *subjugated* is not amenable to be assisted; there are those who revel in a subjection that panders to their tastes and desires. In any case, however, he who does not have a pure heart does not have any influence whatsoever, as good spirits reject such individuals, and evil ones do not fear them."

477. Are formulas of exorcism at all effective against evil spirits?

"No. When spirits see anyone who takes such formulas seriously, they laugh and persist in their endeavor."

478. There are those who are well-intentioned, but who are under the influence of bad spirits nonetheless. What is the best way to free oneself from this influence?

"Tiring their patience, paying no heed to their suggestions, and showing them that they waste their time. Then, as they realize that their efforts are in vain, they quit."

479. Is prayer effective in extinguishing the influence of evil spirits?

"Prayer is of powerful assistance in everything, but you must realize that it is not enough to simply mutter a few choice words to obtain what you desire. God helps those who act, not those who limit themselves merely to asking. In other words, those who are under the influence of bad spirits must do their part in order to extinguish in themselves the cause that attracts such spirits."

480. What should be thought of the casting out of demons mentioned in the gospels?

"That depends on the interpretation. If by *demons* you mean evil spirits who may subjugate an individual, when the spirits' influence is undone, they are truly expelled. If you attribute some sickness to a demon, when you have cured it, you will also claim to have chased the demon away. A thing may be true or false according to the meaning attributed to words. The greatest truths may seem absurd when one focuses on the form alone, or when one takes an allegory for reality. Understand this well and bear it in mind, for this is a principle of universal application."

4. Convulsionaries

481. Do spirits play a role in the phenomena that characterize the so-called convulsionaries? [a]

"Yes, a very large one, as does magnetism, [b] which represents the phenomena's primary source. But charlatans have frequently abused and exaggerated these phenomena, thereby making them the object of ridicule."

—   In general, what is the nature of the spirits who participate in these phenomena?

"They are little advanced. Do you believe that superior spirits would indulge in such practices?"

482. How can the abnormal state of convulsionaries and hysterical people suddenly extend to a whole group?

"Through sympathetic resonance. Mental dispositions are communicated more easily in certain cases. You are familiar enough with the effects of magnetism to understand this, as well as the part that certain spirits play in this phenomenon, through a mechanism of affinity with those who produce it." [c]

Among the peculiar faculties displayed by convulsionaries that are also commonly found in the phenomena of somnambulism and animal magnetism, one could include induced analgesia, mind reading, empathetic induction of pain, and so on. Thus, one cannot doubt that hysterical and convulsionary individuals are in a type of awakened somnambulistic state caused by the influence they exert on one another. Unwittingly, they are both magnetizers and magnetized at the same time.

483. What is the cause of the analgesia, or physical insensibility, that can be observed in the case of certain convulsionaries and in some individuals submitted to the most atrocious tortures?

"In some cases, it is exclusively a magnetic effect that works on the nervous system as certain substances do. In other cases, mental overexcitement deadens physical sensibility because life seems to be withdrawn from the body and transferred to the spirit. Don't you know that when the spirit is intensely concerned with something, the body does not feel, hear or see anything?"

The fervor and fanatic exaltation of a person subject to torture may often provide an example of a calmness and composure that would never be able to triumph over such excruciating pain unless the physical sensibility has been neutralized by some kind of anesthetic effect. We also know that often, in the heat of combat, a serious wound is often not felt at all, whereas under normal circumstances a simple scratch might cause tears.

As these phenomena depend on a physical cause and on the action of spirits, one may wonder how, in certain cases, civil authorities were able to make them stop; the reason is simple. The action of spirits here is secondary; they do nothing more than take advantage of a natural tendency. These authorities did not suppress the predisposition itself, but rather the cause that stimulated and maintained it, switching it from an active to a latent state. They had reason to act this way because the event resulted in abuse and scandal. We know, furthermore, that such intervention is powerless when the action of spirits is direct and spontaneous.

5. Affection of spirits for certain people

484. Do spirits take a liking to certain people specifically?

"Good spirits sympathize with those who are good or who at least are inclined to improve themselves—inferior spirits, with evil individuals or those who may become such. Their bonds, therefore, result from their affinity of character."

485. Is the affection of spirits for certain people exclusively spiritual?

"True affection has nothing material about it, but when a spirit is attached to a particular person, it is not always out of affection. A recollection of their human habits may play a role in it."

486. Do spirits take an interest in our afflictions and triumphs? Are those who wish us well grieved by the woes we endure in life?

"Good spirits do all the good they can and rejoice with all your victories. They grieve over your tribulations if you do not bear them with equanimity, as these trials yield no positive results for you when you behave like the patient who rejects the bitter medicine that shall bring about the cure."

487. Which type of suffering causes the most grief to spirits: physical or moral suffering?

"Your selfishness and intolerance, as everything else derives from them. They smile at all your imaginary troubles born out of pride and ambition, but they rejoice in those that shall abbreviate your trial."

Knowing that our corporeal life is only transitory and that the tribulations accompanying it are the means that leads to a better position, spirits are more concerned about the moral issues that drive us away from our improvement, than about physical afflictions, which are merely transitory.

Spirits do not worry about setbacks that only affect our worldly concerns, as we do not worry about the puerile setbacks of children.

Spirits who realize that the afflictions of life are a means for our advancement consider them as a momentary crisis that shall restore us to health. They feel sorry for our sufferings just as we feel sorry for the sufferings of a friend. But seeing things from a higher vantage point, they perceive them differently from us, and while good spirits stimulate our courage in furtherance of our future, evil spirits try to endanger it by inciting us to despair.

488. Do relatives and friends who have preceded us into the spirit life have more consideration for us than spirits who do not know us?

"Undoubtedly, and as spirits they often protect you according to their capacity."

—   Do they value our affection for them?

"Very much so, but they forget those who forget them."

6. Guardian angels, spirit guides, familial or sympathetic spirits

489. Are there spirits who associate themselves with particular individuals in order to protect them?

"Yes, they are spiritual siblings, or what you call a benevolent or guardian spirit."

490. What should be understood by *guardian angel*?

"A spirit guide of an advanced order."

491. What is the mission of spirit guides?

"That of parents toward their children: to guide their wards along the right path, to help them with their advice, to console them in their afflictions, and to stimulate their courage in the trials of life."

492. Is a spirit guide attached to a particular individual from birth?

"From birth to death, frequently accompanying him after death into the spirit world, and even through numerous corporeal existences, as these existences are only very brief chapters considering the overall life of a spirit."

493. Is the mission of a spirit guide voluntary or mandatory?

"Spirit guides are compelled to watch over you once they have pledged to do so; but they are allowed to choose those who have affinities with them. For some, it is an enjoyment, for others, a mission or a duty."

— Once watching over a person, do spirit guides forego protecting other individuals?

"No, but they do so less exclusively."

494. Are spirit guides irrevocably attached to those who have been entrusted to their care?

"It often happens that certain spirits leave their position to fulfill other missions, but, in such cases, they are relieved by other guides."

495. Do spirit guides sometimes abandon their protégés when the latter rebel against their advice?

"They withdraw when their advice is ignored, and when the will of their wards to yield to the influence of inferior spirits is more powerful. But they do not withdraw completely, and always try to make themselves heard. This way, their protégés are the ones who close their ears. Their guides return upon being called.

"If there is an idea that should convert the most incredulous by its beauty and grace, it is that of guardian angels. Is it not a very reassuring idea to know that you always have by your side beings who are more advanced than you, who are always there to provide good advice, to encourage and help you in climbing up the steep mountain of virtue, who are more reliable and devoted than the most intimate friends you may have on Earth? These beings are under the directive of God, who has placed them there, at your side. They are there out of love for Him, fulfilling a beautiful but arduous mission along with you. Yes, wherever you may be, they will be there with you—in a prison or in a hospital, in dissipation or in solitude, nothing separates you from that friend whom you cannot see, but from whom your soul receives the most loving inspirations and hears the wisest advice.

"May you more fully understand this truth! How many times it would help you in moments of crisis and how many times it would save you from bad spirits! But on the day of reckoning, this angel of virtue might often say to you, 'Did I not offer you advice? Yet, you did not follow it! Did I not show you the abyss? Yet, you flung yourself into it! Did I not make the voice of truth resound in your conscience? Yet, you yielded to the allure of deceit!' Oh, summon your guardian angels, establishing with them that tender intimacy that exists between best friends. Do not think of hiding anything from them, for they are the eyes of God, and you cannot deceive them. Visualize the future, seeking to advance in this life, and your trials will be shorter and your life more joyful. Come and take heart! Once and for all, cast away your prejudices and reservations! Embark upon the new road that opens up before you! March forward! You have your guides, so follow them—your goal cannot fail you, for the goal is God Himself.

"To those who would believe it impossible for truly advanced spirits to continuously devote themselves to such a laborious task, we shall say that we can indeed influence your souls, even though we may be millions of miles away from you. Space does not exist for us, and even while living on another world, our spirits are connected to you. We count on faculties that you cannot understand, but you can be certain that God has not imposed on us a task above our strength, or that God has abandoned you alone on Earth without friends or support. All guardian angels have their protégés, whom they protect as fathers protect their children. They feel happy when they see their wards on the path of virtue, but mourn when their counsels are ignored.

"Do not fear wearing us with your questions. Instead, remain in permanent contact with us—this way you will be stronger and happier. The communication between men and their familial spirit is what makes all individuals mediums—mediums ignored today, but who will emerge later, spreading out like an ocean without shores that sweeps away incredulity and ignorance. People of learning, teach! People of talent, raise your brethren! Unwittingly, by doing so you accomplish the very work of Christ, which is the work that God has assigned to you. Why has God endowed you with intelligence and knowledge, if not to share them with your brothers and sisters, and to enable them to advance along the path of joy and eternal bliss?"

Saint Louis, Saint Augustine

The doctrine of guardian angels watching over their pupils, in spite of the distance that separates worlds, has nothing surprising about it; on the contrary, it is grand and sublime. Do we not often see on Earth a father, although far away, watch over his children, helping them with his wise counsels through the mail? Why should we wonder that there are spirits who, from one world to the other, are able to guide those whom they have taken under their protection, since, to them, the distance that separates the two worlds is less than that which separates continents? Do they not have the universal fluid that links all worlds, uniting them in solidarity with one another, an immense medium for the transmission of thought, as the air is for us the medium for the transmission of sound?

496. If a spirit abandons his ward, no longer doing him any good, can he do him harm instead?

"Good spirits never do evil. They leave that to those who take their place, and then you blame fate for the misfortunes that beset you, whereas you yourselves are the ones to blame."

497. Can spirit guides leave their wards to the mercy of spirits who might want to do harm to them?

"Evil spirits unite to neutralize the action of the good ones, but if wards so wish, they can restore the rule of their good spirits, who may find elsewhere another person amenable to their aid in the meantime, employing their time usefully, as they wait for their ward to return to their influence."

498. When spirit protectors allow their wards to be led astray in life, is it because they are powerless to confront maleficent spirits?

"That is not because they are powerless to confront them, but because they choose not to. Their wards emerge from their trials more perfected and more knowledgeable. Their spirit protectors assist them with their advice through the good thoughts they inspire, but which, unfortunately, are not always heard. It is nothing but human weakness, thoughtlessness, and pride that gives bad spirits any influence. Their power over you comes only from the fact that you do not offer them any resistance."

499. Is a spirit protector with his protégé at all times? Are there not certain circumstances in which a spirit guide may lose sight of his ward, without abandoning him?

"There are circumstances in which the presence of the spirit protector next to his protégé is not necessary."

500. Does a time come in which a spirit no longer needs a guardian angel?

"Yes, when he reaches the level at which he can guide himself, just as the time comes in which the student no longer needs a master. But this stage is not reached on Earth."

501. Why is the action of spirits in our lives so covert? When they protect us, why don't they do so explicitly?

"If you always counted on their support, you would not act by yourselves and your spirit would not progress. In order for you to advance, you need experience, which must be acquired on your own. You must exert your own strength; otherwise, you would be like children who are not allowed to walk by themselves. The action of the spirits who wish you well always occurs in a way so as not to hamper your free will, for if you did not have any responsibility, you would not advance along the path that will lead you to God. Not seeing who is helping them, humans rely on their own efforts. Their guides watch over them, however, and from time to time warn them about dangers."

502. Do spirit protectors who succeed in leading their charges down the right path experience any benefit themselves?

"It is a merit that will be taken into consideration, whether for their advancement or for their happiness. They feel happy when they see their efforts crowned with success. It is a triumph for them, as when a master rejoices in the success of his disciple."

—   Are they responsible if their efforts are unsuccessful?

"No, because they have done everything within their reach."

503. Don't spirit guides suffer when they see their wards following the wrong path despite their warnings, and doesn't it upset their own happiness?

"They suffer from their wards' errors, pitying them, but this suffering has none of the anguish of earthly parenthood, because they know that there is a remedy for any evil, and that whatever is not accomplished today will be accomplished tomorrow."

504. Can we know the name of our spirit guide or guardian angel?

"Why do you want to know names that are irrelevant to you? Do you think there are only spirits with whom you are acquainted?"

—   But how can we invoke them if we do not know their name?

"Call them any name you please, that of a superior spirit for whom you have sympathy or veneration. Your spirit guide will answer that call, for all good spirits are kith and kin, thus mutually assisting one another."

505. Are spirit guides who take well-known names always those who bore those names?

"No, but they are spirits with whom they have an affinity, and who often come under their directive. You need a name, they then take one that inspires your trust. When you cannot personally carry out a task, you send someone to replace you, who acts in your name."

506. Upon returning to the spirit world, do we recognize our spirit guide?

"Yes, because you frequently knew him before reincarnating."

507. Do all spirit protectors belong to the order of superior spirits? Can they sometimes be found among those of average advancement? Can a father, for example, become the spirit protector of his child?

"He can, but protection presupposes a certain degree of elevation, as well as a power or quality accorded by God. A father who protects his child may himself be assisted by a more advanced spirit."

508. Can spirits who have left Earth under favorable circumstances always protect those whom they loved and who survive them?

"Their power is more or less limited. The position in which they find themselves does not always confer them a complete freedom of action."

509. Do primitive men or those of lower moral standing also have spirit guides? If so, are these spirits of as high an order as those of men who are more advanced?

"All people have a spirit who watches over them, but such a mission is in proportion to its purpose. You do not assign a professor of philosophy to a child who is just learning to read. The progress of the familial spirit follows that of the spirit who is being protected. Though having a superior spirit who watches over you, you in turn may become the protector of a spirit who is less advanced than you, and the progress you help that spirit achieve will contribute to your own advancement. God does not require from a spirit more than permitted by the spirit's nature and degree of advancement."

510. When a father who has been watching over his child reincarnates, does he still continue to do watch over his child?

"That would be harder, but, in a moment of liberation from his body, he may ask that a sympathetic spirit assist him in this mission. Besides, spirits only accept missions that they can carry out to the end.

"Incarnate spirits, especially on worlds where the physical existence is of a denser nature, are much too restricted by their bodies to be able to devote themselves entirely to others by assisting them personally. That is why those who are not sufficiently advanced are themselves assisted by spirits of higher development, so that if one spirit fails, for whatever reason, he is replaced by another."

511. Aside from our spirit guide, is there a bad spirit attached to each one of us for the purpose of leading us into evil, thus giving us an opportunity to struggle between good and evil?

"Attached is not the appropriate word. It is certainly true that bad spirits try to draw you away from the virtuous path when they have a chance. However, when one of them attaches himself to an individual, he does so of his own accord because he hopes to be heard. This gives rise to a struggle between the guardian angel and the bad spirit. The one that prevails is the one whose rule the person accepts."

512. May we have several protector spirits?

"All men have a number of kindred spirits of varying degrees of advancement, who regard them with affection and who take an interest in them, as there are also those who help them in their evil pursuits."

513. Do like-minded spirits act in virtue of a mission?

"Sometimes they may have a temporary mission, but generally they are only attracted due to a similarity of thoughts and feelings in good as well as in evil."

—   Is it correct then to infer that like-minded spirits may be good or bad?

"Yes, humans will always encounter spirits who identify with them, whatever their character may be."

514. Are familial spirits the same as kindred spirits or spirit protectors?

"There are many degrees of protection and affinity. Give them whatever names you desire. But the familial spirit, in general, is a friend of the household."

From the explanations above and from observations made of the nature of spirits who attach themselves to incarnate individuals, we may derive the conclusions below:

The spirit protector, spirit guide, or guardian angel is the one whose mission is to follow each man through the course of his life, and to aid him to progress. His degree of advancement is always superior to that of his ward.

Familial spirits attach themselves to certain people through bonds of varying duration to help them within the limits of their power, often rather limited. They are good spirits, but sometimes scarcely advanced and even a little frivolous. They voluntarily busy themselves with the details of an individual's personal life, and only act under the order of or with permission of spirit protectors.

Like-minded spirits are those whom we attract through particular affections and a certain similarity in tastes and feelings, both in good and in evil. The duration of these relationships almost always depends on circumstances.

An evil spirit is an imperfect or maleficent spirit who may attach himself to an individual to divert him from the road of virtue, but in doing so, he acts of his own accord, and not in virtue of a mission. His resolve is proportional to the more or less difficult access granted to him. The incarnate individual is always free to listen to him or to fend off his calls.

515. What should be thought of him who attaches himself to others in order to lead them to their downfall, or, conversely, to guide them along the right path?

"Some people do in fact exert a type of fascination over others that seems irresistible. When this happens for evil purposes, there are in fact evil spirits at work, employing incarnate evil spirits in order to better control their victims. God may permit this in order to test you."

516. Could our good spirit or an evil one incarnate in order to follow us more directly in life?

"This sometimes happens, but they frequently entrust this task to other like-minded spirits who are incarnate."

517. Are there spirits who attach themselves to an entire family in order to protect it?

"Some spirits attach themselves to the members of one same family who live together and are united in affection. But do not ascribe to spirit protectors any type of racial pride."

518. As spirits are attracted to individuals based on affinity, are they attracted to groups of people interested in particular causes as well?

"Spirits go preferably to places where there are like-minded people, where they can be more at ease and are more likely to be heard. Man attracts spirits because of his tendencies, whether as an individual, or as a collective unity, a society, a city, or a nation. Therefore, there are societies, cities and nations that are assisted by spirits of greater or lesser advancement, according to their character and the passions that move them. Imperfect spirits shun those who repel them, and, as a result, the moral perfection of a *collective whole*, as that of individuals, tends to repel bad spirits and attract good ones, who stimulate and maintain a sense of rectitude in the masses, as others may spread the worst passions among them."

519. Do groups of people such as societies, cities, and nations have their own special protector spirits?

"Yes, because such groups are collective unities that work toward a common goal, having, therefore, a need for higher direction."

520. Are the spirit guides of larger groups of people of a more advanced nature than those who are attached to individuals?

"Everything is in proportion to the degree of advancement, that of groups as well as of individuals."

521. May certain spirits assist in the advancement of the arts by watching over those involved in them?

"There are special spirit protectors who assist those who invoke them, and whom they deem worthy of their help. But what do you expect them to do for those who believe themselves to have a gift which they, in reality, do not have? They cannot make the blind see or the deaf hear."

The ancients made special deities out of these spirits. The Muses were the allegorical personification of the spirit protectors of the arts and sciences, just as spirit protectors of families were designated by the names of *lares* and *penates*. Among more modern cultures, the arts and the different industries, cities, and countries also have their own protecting patrons, who are superior spirits, but under other names.

As every man has his group of kindred spirits, it follows that in any *collective whole* the general character of these spirits corresponds to the overall character of the individuals in them. Foreign spirits are attracted to such groups owing to a similarity of tastes and thoughts. That is to say, groups, as well as their members, are surrounded, assisted, and influenced by spirit protectors of a more or less advanced standing in accord with the nature of the prevailing thoughts of the majority.

Among nations, the attraction of spirits is caused by their customs, habits, their dominant character, and above all, their laws, for the character of a nation is reflected in its laws. Those who ensure that justice reigns among them fight the influence of evil spirits. Wherever laws institutionalize injustices and are opposed to humane principles, good spirits are in a minority. The swarm of evil ones flocks in, keeping that nation under its dominion and neutralizing any occasional good influence, which is then lost in the crowd, like an isolated stalk of wheat in the midst of thorny bushes. By studying the customs of nations or of any group of people, it is easy to have an idea of the invisible population that interferes with their thoughts and actions.

7. Presentiments

522. Is a presentiment always a warning from a spirit protector?

"A presentiment can be the intimate and secret advice of a spirit who wishes you well. It can also be an intuition about a choice previously made, the voice of instinct. Before incarnating, a spirit has knowledge of the main phases of his upcoming existence, that is, the kind of trials he will endure. When such trials have a prominent character, he preserves a type of impression in his inner consciousness, and this impression, which is the voice of instinct, awakens when the moment draws near, becoming what we call a presentiment."

523. Presentiments and the voice of instinct are always somewhat vague. What should we do when we are unsure?

"When in doubt, invoke your good spirit or pray to God, the master of us all, to send you one of His messengers, one of us."

524. Do the warnings of our spirit guides concern our moral conduct alone, or our conduct regarding things of our private life as well?

"Everything. They seek to enable you to live in the best way possible, but you frequently shut your ears to their good warnings, making yourselves unhappy by your own fault."

Our protector spirits help us with their advice through the voice of conscience, which they awaken in us. But as we do not always give them the importance they deserve, they offer us more direct advice through the people around us. If we reflect upon the many happy and unhappy circumstances of our lives, we will see that, on many occasions, we received warnings that we did not always heed, but which would have spared us much trouble, if we had listened to them.

8. Influence of spirits on the events of life

525. Do spirits exercise any influence on the events of life?

"They certainly do, as they give you advice."

—   Do they exercise this influence in any way other than the thoughts they suggest? In other words, do they act directly in the course of life events?

"Yes, but they never act outside natural laws."

We mistakenly think that the action of spirits must only manifest through extraordinary phenomena. We would like them to come to our aid through miracles, and we always imagine them wielding some sort of magic wand. But that is not the case, and that is why their intervention seems to be invisible, and that which is accomplished through their intervention seems completely natural. Therefore, for example, they cause the meeting of two people who seem to have met by accident, by inspiring one of them with the thought of going by a certain place. They call a person's attention to a specific issue if it will lead to the result they envision, so that man, believing to have only followed his own impulse, always maintains his free will.

526. As spirits can act upon matter, can they cause certain effects in order to provoke a specific outcome? For example, a man is supposed to die; he climbs a ladder, the ladder breaks and he is killed. Did spirits cause the ladder to break, so as to fulfill the man's fate?

"It is certainly true that spirits have an influence on matter, but always in accordance with the laws of nature, never through the production of unexpected events that violate those laws. In the example you mention, the ladder breaks because the wood is rotting, or because it is not strong enough to support the man's weight. If it were the man's fate to die in such a way, spirits would inspire him with the thought of climbing the ladder, which would then break under his weight. Thus, his death would derive from a natural cause, without a miracle being necessary to that end."

527.   Let us take another example where material circumstances are not relevant. A man is destined to die struck by lightning; he seeks refuge under a tree, lightning strikes it and he dies. Could spirits have provoked the lightning, directing it at him?

"It is still the same situation. The lightning struck the tree at that particular moment because the event happened in accordance with the laws of nature. The lightning was not directed at the tree because the man was under it, but he was inspired to take refuge under the tree where lightning would strike. The tree would have been struck regardless of whether the man had been under it or not."

528.   An ill-intentioned man shoots a bullet that homes in on another man, but misses him. Could a benevolent spirit have deflected the shot?

"If the individual was not meant to be struck, the benevolent spirit may have inspired him with the thought of moving out of the trajectory of the bullet, or he may have confused the man's enemy in such a way as to make him miss his shot. Once in flight, however, the bullet must follow its trajectory."

529.   What is to be thought of magic bullets which according to certain legends must infallibly reach their target?

"It is purely imagination. Man delights in the marvelous but is never satisfied with the wonders of nature."

—   May the spirits who direct the events of life be thwarted by spirits who wish the contrary?

"What God has willed must be. If there is any delay or obstacle, it is His will."

530. Cannot frivolous and mocking spirits create the many little difficulties that derail our projects and upset our plans? In a word, are they not responsible for what we commonly call the petty troubles of human life?

"They take pleasure in causing such hassles, which are trials meant to test your patience; but they stop when they see that they are unsuccessful. However, it would be neither just nor correct to blame them for all your disappointments, of which you yourselves are the main authors through your own negligence. Thus, if you break your porcelain, it is more likely due to your own clumsiness, than owing to the action of spirits."

—   Do spirits who create hassles behave in such a way as the result of personal animosity, or do they attack the first person they encounter, without a set motive, and simply out of malice?

"They act for both reasons. Sometimes they are enemies you made in this life or in a previous one, and who pursue you as a result. At other times, there is no prior motive."

531. Is the resentment of the beings who have harmed us on Earth extinguished with their corporeal life?

"They often realize their injustice and the wrong they have done, but if God permits, they continue pursuing you in their hatred, in order to test you further."

—   Can we put an end to it, and if so, by what means?

"Yes, by praying for them and by returning good for evil. That way they end up realizing their error. In all cases, if you know how to place yourselves above their machinations, they will stop when they see that they gain nothing from tormenting you."

Experience shows that certain spirits carry on their vengeance from one existence to the next, and that sooner or later one must expiate the harm one may have done to another person.

532. Do spirits have the power to divert hardships from certain people and to attract good fortune to them instead?

"Not entirely, because there are misfortunes that are in the plans of Providence. But they can lessen your pain by imbuing you with patience and fortitude.

"Also, be aware that it often depends only on yourselves to divert such hardships, or at least to mitigate them, as God has endowed you with intelligence so that you may use it. It is in this way especially that spirits help you, by suggesting beneficial thoughts, but they only help those who know how to help themselves. That is the meaning of the words, 'Seek, and you shall find; knock, and it shall be opened to you.' [d]

"Realize further that what looks like misfortune to you is not always such. Frequently, something good shall result from it that is far superior than the apparent misfortune, but that is what you do not understand, because you think only of the present moment, or of your own selves."

533. Can spirits enable us to obtain riches if we ask them to?

"Sometimes, as a trial. But most often they will refuse it, just as you would refuse a thoughtless demand made by a child."

— Are they good spirits or evil ones who grant such favors?

"Either, it all depends on their intention, but more frequently they are spirits who wish to lead you into evil, and who find an easy means of doing so in the enjoyments that riches afford."

534. When obstacles seem to fatally obstruct our projects, is it because of the influence of a spirit?

"It may sometimes be because of a spirit. Other times, and more frequently so, it is because of your poor management skills. Position and character play a large role in it, and if you persist in following a path that is not right for you, spirits have no part in it. You become your own evil genie."

535. When something auspicious happens to us, should we thank our protector spirit?

"Above all, thank God, without whose permission nothing takes place, and then the good spirits, who were His agents."

—   What would happen if we forgot to thank them?

"That which happens to the ungrateful."

—   Nevertheless, there are many people who neither pray nor give thanks, but who succeed in all their endeavors.

"Yes, but you must see to the end. They will pay dearly for the short-lived happiness that they do not deserve, because 'from everyone who has been given much, much will be demanded.' " [e]

9. Spirits' action on natural phenomena

536. Are the great natural phenomena, those considered as perturbations of the elements, due to accidental causes or do they all have a providential purpose?

"There is a reason for everything, and nothing occurs without God's permission."

—   Do these phenomena always have a purpose related to mankind?

"Sometimes they may be directly related to mankind, but most often they have no other purpose than to reestablish the balance and harmony of the physical forces of nature."

—   We can perfectly conceive that God's will is the primary cause in these as in all things, but since we know that spirits can in fact act upon matter, and that they are agents of God's will, are there not among them some spirits who might exert an influence over the elements in order to stir, calm, or direct them?

"That is evident, it could not be otherwise. God does not act directly upon matter. He has His devoted agents at every degree in the hierarchy of worlds."

537. Ancient mythology seems largely based on Spiritist ideas, with the difference being that they regarded spirits as deities, representing those gods or spirits by their special attributions. Some were in charge of the wind; others, of the lightning; while others presided over the plant world, and so on. Is this belief without any foundation?

"It is so unfounded as not to have any semblance of truth."

—   By the same reasoning, are there spirits that inhabit the center of the Earth, presiding over geological phenomena?

"Such spirits positively do not inhabit the Earth, but they oversee and direct these phenomena according to their attributions. Someday, you will have the explanation for all these phenomena and understand them better."

538. Do the spirits who preside over the phenomena of nature form a separate category in the spirit world? Are they beings apart, or are they spirits who have been incarnated like us?

"Who will be, or who have been."

—   Are these spirits from a higher or lower order in the spirit hierarchy?

"That depends on whether their role is of a more material or intellectual nature. Some command, others execute. Those in charge of material tasks are always of a lower order, among spirits as among men."

539. In the production of certain phenomena—storms, for example— does a single spirit act, or do they assemble in masses?

"In vast masses."

540. Do the spirits who act upon the phenomena of nature do so with full awareness, and in virtue of their free will, or out of an instinctive and mechanical impulse?

"It may be either way. Let us make a comparison: consider the myriads of animals that little by little build up islands and archipelagos in the ocean. Do you believe that there is no providential purpose in this, and that such a transformation of the surface of the globe is not necessary for its overall harmony? Yet, all this is accomplished by animals of the lowest degree, as they provide for their own needs, unaware of being the instruments of God. Well, then, similarly, the most backward spirits are useful to the general good. As they *risk their first steps in life*, and before having full awareness of their acts and of their free will, they act upon certain phenomena in which they are the unsuspecting agents. At first, they execute; later, when their intelligence is more developed, they will command and direct the matters of the material world. Later still, they will direct the things of the moral world. Therefore, everything serves a purpose. Everything is linked in nature, from the primitive atom to the archangel, who also began as an atom, in an admirable law of harmony, which your limited intellect cannot yet grasp in its entirety!"

10. Spirits during battle

541. In a battle, are there spirits who assist and help each side?

"Yes, and who stimulate their courage."

As in the past the ancients represented the gods as taking the side of one nation or another. Such deities were nothing more than allegorical representations of spirits.

542. In war, justice can only be on one side. How can spirits support the wrong side?

"You know perfectly well that there are spirits who seek only conflict and destruction. For them, war is war. The justice of a cause means little to them."

543. Can certain spirits influence a general in the conception of his plan for a campaign?

"Certainly, spirits can influence them in this as in all cogitations."

544. Can bad spirits inspire them with poor strategies in order to lead them to defeat?

"Yes, but don't the generals have free will? If their judgment does not allow them to distinguish a good idea from a bad one, they will bear the consequences, and would do better obeying rather than commanding."

545. Can a general sometimes be guided by a type of second sight, an intuition that shows him the results of his strategy in advance?

"That is frequently what happens with a man of genius. It is what he calls inspiration, enabling him to act with a type of certainty. This inspiration comes to him from the spirits who guide him, taking advantage of the faculties he is endowed with."

546. In the heat of battle, what happens to the spirits of those who die? Are they still interested in the battle after death?

"Some continue to be interested in it, others retreat."

The same thing happens in battle as in all cases of violent death. At first, spirits are surprised and bewildered. They do not believe themselves to be dead, thinking that they still participate in the action. It is only gradually that reality sets in.

547. Once they die, do the spirits of those who had fought each other while alive still regard one another as enemies and continue to be enraged against each other?

"In such moments, spirits are never calm. At first, they may still hate their enemy and even pursue them, but when they regain their composure, they see that their animosity no longer has any motive. They may retain, however, greater or lesser traces of it, depending on their character."

—   Do they still hear the uproar of battle?

"Yes, perfectly."

548. Do spirits who calmly watch a battle as spectators witness the separation of souls and bodies? How does this phenomenon appear to them?

"Very few deaths are truly instantaneous. Most of the time, a spirit whose body has been mortally wounded is not aware of it at the time. Only when consciousness begins to return can the spirit be seen moving beside the corpse. This appears so natural that the sight of the dead body lying there does not produce any unpleasant impression. All life having been transferred into the spirit, only the spirit attracts any attention; it is the spirit to whom one speaks or gives orders."

11. On pacts

549. Is there any truth to the stories of pacts with evil spirits?

"No, there is no such thing, but there can be affinity between evil spirits and an incarnate man of an evil nature. For example: you want to harass your neighbor, but you do not know how to proceed. You then summon low-order spirits who, like you, desire only evil and who, in return for their help, want you to help them in their own evil schemes. But this does not mean that your neighbor cannot rid himself from the evil spirits by an opposing appeal or through his willpower. He who wishes to do evil, for the simple fact of entertaining such ideas, is calling evil spirits to his aid. He then becomes obliged to serve them reciprocally, because these spirits also need him for the evil they desire to do in turn. Pacts consist only in this."

> The fact that man sometimes finds himself under the subjection of low-order spirits results from his abandoning himself to the evil thoughts inspired by them, and not from any kind of agreement made between that man and the spirits. A pact, in the usual sense of the word, is a symbol of the affinity that exists between a man's evil nature and maleficent spirits.

550. What is the meaning of the fantastic fables according to which certain people would have sold their soul to Satan in exchange for certain favors?

"All fables contain a teaching and a moral. Your mistake is in taking them literally. This one is an allegory that may be explained as follows: he who summons evil spirits to help him acquire the gifts of fortune or other favors, rebels against Providence. He renounces the mission he has received and the trials he must endure in this world, and, consequently, shall suffer the consequences of his attitude in the life to come. This does not mean that his soul is condemned to eternal suffering, but because instead of detaching himself from matter, he immerses himself deeper in it, the enjoyments he had on Earth will no longer be available to him in the spirit world, until he has redeemed himself through new trials, which may perhaps be even greater and more painful. Out of love for material pleasures, he places himself under the subjection of impure spirits, in this way establishing a mutual pact which leads him to ruin, but a pact which will always be easy for him to break with the assistance of good spirits, if he has the firm will to do so."

12. Occult power, talismans, sorcerers

551. Can a bad man, with the aid of a bad spirit who acts upon his orders, cause harm to his neighbor?

"No. God would not allow it."

552. What is to be thought of the belief that some people have the power to cast spells?

"Some people have a very strong magnetic power, which they may use for an evil purpose if their own spirit is evil. In that case, they could be assisted by other bad spirits. But do not believe in the purported magical power that exists only in the imagination of superstitious people, ignorant of the true laws of nature. The events they mention are natural phenomena scantily observed, and above all, poorly understood."

553. What may be the effect of potions and rituals with which certain people claim to control spirits?

"The effect of making them the object of ridicule, if they act in good faith; otherwise, they are scoundrels who deserve to be punished. All such potions and rituals are mere trickery. There are no incantation words, no cabalistic signs, no talismans with any power over spirits, because the latter are only attracted by thoughts, not by material objects."

—   Have not certain spirits sometimes dictated cabalistic formulas themselves?

"Yes, there are spirits who offer you signs and bizarre words, or who prescribe certain rituals which you use to perform what you call conjurations. But rest assured that these spirits are only mocking you and taking advantage of your credulity."

554. Could it be that those who, correctly or not, trust the so-called *power* of a talisman, may attract a spirit by such trust, since it is their thought that operates, while the talisman is only a symbol that helps them to focus their thought?

"That is true, but the nature of the spirit attracted depends on the integrity of intention and the purity of feelings. Now, it is rather rare for those who are naïve enough to believe in the power of a talisman not to have in mind a goal which is more material than moral. In any event, this shows a pettiness of character and weakness of mind that open the door to imperfect and mocking spirits."

555. What should be thought of the so-called *sorcerers*?

"Those you call *sorcerers*, when they act in good faith, are people gifted with certain faculties, such as magnetic power or second-sight, and because they do things that you do not understand, you suppose them to be endowed with some supernatural power. Your scholars and scientists have often been mistaken for sorcerers in the eyes of ignorant men, have they not?"

Spiritism and magnetism give us the key to a number of phenomena around which ignorance has woven many tales, and regarding which the imagination has greatly exaggerated the facts. By demonstrating the reality of things and their legitimate cause, a lucid knowledge of these two sciences, which are one and the same, is the best protection against superstitious ideas. That is because such knowledge shows what is possible or not, what is within the laws of nature, and what is nothing more than a ludicrous fantasy.

556. Do certain individuals really have the gift of healing by touch?

"Their magnetic power may act to that extent when it is assisted by a purity of feelings and an ardent desire to do good, as in that case good spirits come to their aid. It is necessary, however, to keep a wary eye on how such stories are told by gullible or overly enthusiastic people, who are always ready to see the marvelous in the most mundane and natural things. One must also suspect the claims of people who have a vested interest in exploiting credulity for their own profit."

13. Blessings and curses

557. Can blessings and curses attract good or evil to those at whom they are aimed?

"God does not listen to unjust curses, and he who casts them is guilty in God's eyes. As we have two opposing forces, good and evil, there may be a momentary influence as a result, even upon matter, but this influence never occurs without God's permission, and as an additional trial for the one who is the object of the curse. In addition, curses are most often cast upon the wicked, and blessings upon the good. Blessings and curses can never divert Providence from the path of justice, as Providence only strikes those who are cursed if they are evil, and only extends its protection to those who do deserve it."

■■■

[a] The topic of this section refers to the phenomena observed in the case of the *Convulsionaries of Saint-Médard*, a group of 18th-century French religious pilgrims who exhibited convulsions and who largely constituted a minority within the Jansenist Catholic Movement. The ascetic Jansenist deacon François de Pâris was buried at the cemetery of Saint-Médard in Paris in 1727, and his tomb soon became the site of religious pilgrimages, with the report of miracle cures attracting ever-larger numbers of pilgrims. Starting in 1731, several of them started exhibiting convulsions, which led to the closure of the cemetery to the general public in 1732. —Trans.

[b] For the meaning of the word *magnetism* in this context, please see note [k] in the Introduction. —Trans.

[c] The Spirits refer here to the studies of animal magnetism and mesmerism to which Kardec had dedicated himself before he started studying Spiritist phenomena. —Trans.

[d] Matthew 7:7–8; Luke 11:9. —Trans.

[e] Luke 12:48. —Trans.

Chapter 10:
Occupations and Missions of Spirits

558. Do spirits busy themselves with anything other than their own personal advancement?

"They contribute to the harmony of the universe by acting as ministers of God and carrying out His designs. Spirit life represents a continuous occupation, but it is not at all grueling like life on Earth, because it is subject neither to physical fatigue nor to the anguish of bodily wants."

559. Do inferior and imperfect spirits also play a useful role in the universe?

"They all have duties to fulfill. Doesn't the apprentice bricklayer contribute to the construction of a building as much as the architect?" (See #540)

560. Does each spirit have a special assignment?

"All must go through all levels, and acquire knowledge of all things, by successively presiding over functions in all realms of the universe. As mentioned in Ecclesiastes, however, there is a time for everything. Therefore, one currently fulfills his destiny on this world, while another shall accomplish or has already accomplished his destiny at another time, on Earth, in the water, in the air, and so on."

561. Are the functions that spirits perform in the order of things permanent for each spirit, and are such functions exclusive of certain orders?

"All must ascend along the various degrees of the hierarchy in order to perfect themselves. Being just, God could not have endowed some with knowledge without effort, while others only acquired it through tears and toil."

Likewise, among men, no one reaches the highest skill level in any craft without having acquired the necessary knowledge by practicing the most elementary functions in that field.

562. As spirits of the highest level have no skills left to acquire, are they in a state of absolute restfulness, or do they still have other types of occupation?

"What do you expect them to do for all eternity? An eternal idleness would be an eternal torment."

— What is the nature of their occupations?

"Directly receiving God's orders, relaying them throughout the universe, and overseeing their execution."

563. Are spirits' occupations continuous?

"Continuous, yes, if by that we mean that their thought is always active, as they live through their thought. Yet, one must not liken the occupations of spirits with the material occupations of men. Their activity is an enjoyment in itself for them, because they know they are being useful."

— That is conceivable for good spirits, but does the same apply to less evolved ones?

"Less evolved spirits have occupations which are appropriate for their nature. Would you entrust to manual laborers the assignments of doctors?"

564. Are there among spirits those who are idle, or who do not busy themselves with anything useful?

"Yes, but that is a temporary situation, subordinated to the development of their intelligence. Admittedly, there are, as among humans, those who live only for themselves. Such idleness, however, weighs on them, and sooner or later the desire to advance makes them feel the need to work, and they are happy to make themselves useful again. We refer here to spirits who have arrived at a minimum level of awareness about themselves and their free will, because, at their origin, spirits are like newborn children who act more from instinct than out of conscious volition."

565. Do spirits examine our works of art and take an interest in them?

"They examine all that may show the elevation of spirits and their attending progress."

566. Does a spirit who had a field of specialization on Earth, such as a painter or an architect, have a special preference for works in the area of his predilection during life?

"Everything merges into one general goal. If the spirit is good, he will take an interest in them to the extent that they allow him to assist with the advancement of souls toward God. Furthermore, you forget that spirits who developed an art during the existence in which you knew them could have practiced another art in a previous existence, because it is necessary for them to acquire knowledge in all areas in order to perfect themselves. According to their advancement, it may so happen that they do not have a specialization, in reality. This is what I meant when I stated that everything merges into one general goal. Also, you must realize that what is considered sublime in your backward world is nothing more than a naïve accomplishment if compared with more advanced worlds. Why would you imagine that the spirits who inhabit those worlds, where there are arts unknown to you, would admire what would be to them the work of a simple student? As I said, they examine whatever may be an indication of progress."

— We understand why that must be the case of very advanced spirits, but what to say of more ordinary spirits, who have not yet raised themselves above earthly ideas?

"Their case is different, as their point of view is more limited, and they may admire what you yourselves admire as well."

567. Do spirits sometimes meddle in our occupations and pleasures?

"Ordinary spirits, as you call them, yes. They are always around you, and sometimes take a very active part in what you do, according to their nature. It is a good thing that they do it, since this stimulates men in all directions of life, exciting or moderating their passions."

Spirits occupy themselves with the things of this world according to their advancement. Superior spirits undoubtedly have the ability to consider them in their minutest detail, but they only do so to the extent that it is useful for progress. Inferior spirits only give any importance to recollections still present in their memory, and to material ideas they have not yet abandoned.

568. Do spirits who have missions to fulfill do so while in between incarnations or in the incarnate state?

"They may do so in either state. For certain spirits in between incarnations, their mission represents a major occupation."

569. What missions may be entrusted to spirits who are in between incarnations?

"They are so varied that it would be impossible to describe them. Besides, there are some that you would not be able to understand. Spirits fulfill the will of God, and you are not able to penetrate all His designs."

Spirits' missions always have the Good as their goal. Whether as disincarnate spirits or as humans, spirits are in charge of helping the progress of mankind, of nations, or of individuals within a diverse range of ideas, which may be more or less specific, in order to pave the way for certain events, and to supervise the accomplishment of certain tasks. Some have missions that have a narrow scope, perhaps of a personal nature or entirely local (such as helping the sick, the dying, and the afflicted). Some are guides, watching over those who are under their protection, and directing them with their advice and the good thoughts they inspire. One could say that there are as many types of missions as there are areas of interest to watch over, whether in the material or in the moral world. Spirits advance according to how well they perform their tasks.

570. Do spirits always fathom the designs that they are charged with implementing?

"No. There are those who are blind instruments, while others know fully well the goal toward which they work."

571. Are advanced spirits the only ones who have missions to fulfill?

"The importance of a mission is in proportion to the spirit's capacity and advancement. The courier soldier who delivers a letter also fulfills a mission, although it is not equivalent to that of a general."

572. Is the mission of a spirit imposed on him, or does it depend on his will?

"A spirit asks for it and is happy to receive it."

—   May the same mission be requested by many spirits?

"Yes, there are often several candidates, but not all are accepted."

573. What constitutes the mission of incarnate spirits?

"Instructing men, helping them advance, and improving their institutions by direct and material means. Missions may be more or less general and relevant, however: he who plows the land fulfills a mission as much as one who rules or teaches. Everything in nature is linked together. At the same time a spirit perfects himself through incarnation, he is also working to fulfill the designs of Providence. Each human being has a mission in this world, because each one can be useful for something."

574. What could be the mission on Earth of deliberately idle people?

"There really are people who live only for themselves, and who do not know how to make themselves useful for anything. They are poor beings whom we ought to pity, because they shall painfully redress their deliberate idleness, and their punishment frequently begins in their present existence, through weariness and discontent with life."

—   If they had the opportunity to choose, why did they prefer a life that could not be of any advantage to them?

"There are, among spirits, those who are lazy and shrink from a life of labor. God allows them to be this way, because they will understand the disadvantages of a life of idleness later on, and at their own expense, and they will be the first to ask to make up for the lost time. Also, they may have perhaps chosen a more useful life to begin with, but once having started on their mission, they may have lost heart, allowing themselves to be misled by the suggestions of spirits who stimulated their idleness."

575. Ordinary occupations would seem to be duties rather than actual missions. According to the idea normally associated with the word, a mission has an aspect of importance that is less exclusive, and, particularly, less personal. From that point of view, how can we tell if a man has a real mission on Earth?

"By the great things he does and by the progress he helps his fellow men accomplish."

576. Are those who have important missions predestined for them before birth, and do they have knowledge of this?

"Yes, at times, but more often they are unaware. They only have a vague notion of their mission upon arriving on Earth. Their mission emerges after they are born, and in accord with circumstances. God drives them along the path they must tread to fulfill His designs."

577. When a man does something valuable, is it always owing to a previously predestined mission, or might he have received an unexpected assignment?

"Not everything that a man does is the consequence of a predestined mission. He is frequently the instrument that a spirit uses in order to carry out a task that is considered useful. For example, a certain spirit thinks it would be valuable to write a book, which the spirit himself would write if he were incarnate, so he seeks out the writer most capable of understanding his thinking and of executing it. The spirit inspires a man with the idea and supervises its execution. This way, this man did not originally come to Earth with the mission of writing this particular book. The same thing applies to certain works of art and inventions. It should be further noted that during his body's sleep, an incarnate man communicates directly with disincarnate spirits in order to discuss how his mission is to be carried out."

578. Can spirits fail in their mission by their own fault?

"Yes, if they are not high-order spirits."

—   What are the consequences for them?

"They will have to start their task over—that is their punishment. And then, they will suffer the consequences of the harm they caused."

579. As a spirit receives his mission from God, how could God entrust a mission at once important and of general interest to a spirit who may fail?

"Does God not know if one of His marshals will conquer or be conquered? Rest assured that He knows, and that His plans, *when critical*, do not depend on those who shall abandon the work in the middle of it. The whole issue for you is the knowledge of the future, which God possesses, but which is not made available to you."

580. Does a spirit who incarnates to fulfill a mission have the same apprehensions as the one who incarnates to undergo a trial?

"No. He has experience."

581. Those who are the beacons of mankind and enlighten other men with their genius evidently have a mission. But among them are those who are mistaken, and who, in addition to great truths, spread great errors. How should we view their mission?

"As having been ruined by they themselves. They are beneath the task they have assumed. One must take circumstances into account, however. Men of genius must speak according to the strictures of their time, so that a teaching that later seems mistaken or foolish, may have been adequate originally."

582. Can parenthood be considered a mission?

"It is, without question, a mission. It is, at the same time, a very great duty with a more important responsibility for the future than parents realize. God has placed children under the guidance of their parents so that they may lead them to the path of righteousness, and has made their task easier by making children frail and delicate, amenable to all sorts of influences.

"But there are those who are more concerned with pruning the trees in their orchards and making them produce fine fruit, than with straightening up the character of their children. If their children fail due to their neglect, parents will have to face the punishment, and the sufferings of their children will fall back on them in a future life, because they did not do what was incumbent upon them for the advancement of their children along the path of virtue."

583. If a child flounders, in spite of the efforts of the parents, are they still responsible?

"No. The more a child leans toward evil, the harder the parent's task is, but at the same time the greater will be their merit if they manage to turn their child away from the path of evil."

—   If a child becomes a good adult, in spite of the negligence or bad examples of the parents, do the parents reap any benefit from it?

"God is just."

584. What could be the nature of the mission of a conqueror whose only goal is to satisfy his ambition, and who, in order to reach it, does not refrain from wreaking havoc along the way?

"Most of the time, such men are no more than instruments used by God to fulfill His designs. Such devastations are often a means to enable a people to advance more rapidly."

—   If those who are the instruments of such temporary calamities are unaware of the good that may result from them because they inflicted such devastations with a personal goal in mind, will they still benefit from the eventual good that may spring from them?

"All are rewarded in accord with their deeds, the good they *intended* to do, and the rectitude of their intentions."

Incarnate spirits have occupations pertinent to the purpose of their corporeal existence. During the interval between incarnations, their occupations are commensurate with their degree of advancement.

Some journey through the many worlds, learning and preparing for a new incarnation.

Others, more advanced, devote themselves to general progress by presiding over events and suggesting thoughts conducive to a good end; they assist men of genius who contribute to the advancement of mankind.

Others reincarnate on a mission to foster progress.

Still others take under their care individuals, families, villages, cities and nations, becoming their guardian angels, spirit guides, and familial spirits.

Finally, others preside over the phenomena of nature, of which they are the direct agents.

Ordinary spirits meddle in our occupations and diversions.

Impure or imperfect spirits dwell in suffering and anguish, until the moment when it pleases God to grant them the means of advancing. If they do evil, it is because of their resentment at the happiness they are not yet able to enjoy.

■■■

Chapter 11:
The Three Kingdoms

1. Minerals and plants
2. Animals and human beings
3. Metempsychosis

1. Minerals and plants

585. What do you think of the division of nature into three kingdoms—the mineral, plant, and animal kingdoms, to which some people add the human species as a fourth? Others divide nature into two classes—organic and inorganic beings. Which system is preferable?

"They are all reasonable. It depends on one's point of view: from a material point of view, there are only inorganic and organic beings. From the point of view of intelligence, however, there are obviously four degrees."

These four degrees have, as a matter of fact, well-defined characteristics, although their boundaries seem to merge into each other. Inert matter, which comprises the mineral kingdom, displays no more than physiochemical properties. Plants, although composed of inert matter, are endowed with vitality. Animals, made of inert matter and endowed with vitality, have, in addition, a kind of instinctive, limited intelligence, with an awareness of their existence and individuality. Finally, human beings have all that exists in plants and animals and dominate all the other classes through a special intelligence with no set limits, providing them with the awareness of the future, the perception of extra-material things, and the knowledge of God.

586. Do plants have any awareness of their existence?

"No, they do not think; they only have organic life."

587. Are plants sentient beings? Do they suffer when mutilated?

"Plants receive the physical impressions that act upon matter, but they do not have perceptions; consequently, they do not feel the sensation of pain."

588. Is the force that attracts plants toward each other independent of their will?

"Yes, because they do not think. It is a mechanical force of matter acting upon matter, which they cannot oppose.

589. Plants like the mimosa[a] and the Venus flytrap[b] display movements that indicate great sensitivity, and in some cases, a kind of will, like the Venus flytrap, whose lobes seize the fly that lands on it, in order to suck its juices, seeming to have set up a snare to kill it. Are these plants endowed with the faculty of thought? Do they have a will, and do they form an intermediary class between the plant and animal kingdoms, representing a transition from the one to the other?

"Everything in nature is in transition by the very fact that no two things are perfectly equal, but everything is linked together. Plants do not think, and consequently have no will. The oyster, which opens itself, and all other zoophytes do not think—they have nothing more than a blind, natural instinct."

> The human body provides us with examples of analogous functions that do not involve any participation of the will, such as the digestive and circulatory systems. The pylorus closes itself upon contact with certain substances in order to refuse them passage. The same applies to the mimosa, whose movements do not imply the existence of any perception, much less of a will.

590. Is there not in plants, as well as in animals, a survival instinct that leads them to seek what may be useful to them, avoiding that which may cause them harm?

"There is, if you wish, a sort of instinct. It depends on the extent of the meaning you attach to the word, but it is mechanical only. When you see two bodies combine in a chemical reaction, it is because they harmonize with each other—that is, there is an affinity between them, but you do not call it instinct."

591. On more highly evolved worlds, are plants, like other beings, more perfect in nature?

"Everything is more perfect, but plants are always plants, just as animals are always animals, and human beings always human beings."

2. Animals and human beings

592. If we compare human beings with animals in terms of intelligence, it seems difficult to establish a line of demarcation, because certain animals, in certain aspects, are obviously superior to humans. Can such a line of demarcation be established in any precise manner?

"Your philosophers are not in much agreement about this subject. Some would like for humans to be animals, and others for animals to be human. Both are wrong. Humans are beings apart, who sometimes plunge into the basest depths, or who may sometimes ascend very high. In their physical constitution, humans are like animals, and less well-endowed than many of them, as nature has provided animals with everything that humans are forced *to invent with their intelligence*, in order to provide for their own needs and survival. Their body is destroyed like that of the animals, it is true, but their spirit has a destiny that they alone can grasp, because they alone are completely free. Poor humans, who lower yourselves below the beasts! Can you not tell yourselves apart from them? You may recognize human beings through their ability to conceive God."

593. Could we say that animals act only out of instinct?

"That again is a theory. It is quite true that instinct dominates most animals, but do you not see some that act from a determined will? This is a manifestation of intelligence, limited as it may be."

Aside from instinct, one could not deny that certain animals display a complex behavior that denotes the will to act in a determined sense and according to environmental variables. In that sense, there is in them a kind of intelligence, but its exercise is exclusively focused on the satisfaction of their physical needs and on providing for their survival. They do not invent and perfect things. Whatever may be the skill that we admire in their behavior, that which they did yesterday is the same as what they do today, no better or worse, according to unchanging forms and proportions.

Offspring separated from their species do not fail to build their nest according to the same model, without having been taught. If some animals are capable of learning to a certain degree, such mental development is always restricted within narrow limits, and is a result of human action on a pliable nature. They cannot make any progress on their own, and when they do make progress, it is ephemeral and purely individual, because, left to their own devices, they quickly return to the limits traced out for them by nature.

594. Do animals have a language?

"If you mean a language made up of words and syllables, no, but if you mean a way of communicating among themselves, then, yes. They say much more than you might suppose, but their language is limited to their needs, as are their thoughts."

— There are animals that possess no voice. Does that mean that they have no language?

"They make themselves understood by other means. Do you not have ways other than speech to communicate with one another, as happens in the case of mutes, for instance? Since animals interact with one another, they have means of warning each other and of expressing the sensations they experience. Do you think that fish do not understand each other? Human beings do not have the exclusive privilege of language, but the language of animals is instinctive and limited exclusively to the circle of their own needs and thoughts, while that of humans is perfectible, lending itself to all the conceptions of their intelligence."

Indeed, fish—schooling in large numbers, like swallows following a leader that guides them—must have a way to warn, understand, and inform one another. Perhaps their sight is acute enough for them to perceive signals they send to each other, or perhaps the water is a means for the mutual transmission of vibrations. Whatever the case may be, it is undeniable that they have the means available to understand one another, in the same way as all animals deprived of voice perform group activities. Should one be surprised, in view of such facts, that spirits are able to communicate with one another without recourse to articulated speech? (See #282)

595. Do animals have free will?

"They are not mere machines as you might believe, but their freedom of action is restricted to their needs, and cannot be compared to the freedom enjoyed by man. Since they are far less evolved than him, they do not have the same obligations. Their freedom is limited to the actions of their material life."

596. Where does the aptitude that certain animals have to imitate human language come from, and why is this aptitude found more often among birds than among apes, for example, whose physical anatomy is much closer to that of man?

"From the particular conformation of the vocal organs, in conjunction with the instinct of imitation. Apes imitate gestures; certain birds imitate the human voice."

597. As animals have an intelligence that gives them a certain freedom of action, is there in them a principle independent of matter?

"Yes, and which survives their body."

—   Is this principle a soul similar to that of man?

"It is a soul, if you like. *It all depends on the meaning you attach to the word.* Their soul is much less developed than that of man, however. Between the souls of animals and those of humans, there is as great a difference as there is between the human soul and God."

598. Does the animal soul preserve its individuality and awareness of itself after death?

"It preserves its individuality, but not the awareness of a *self*. Its intelligent life remains in a latent state."

599. Can an animal soul choose the species in which it prefers to incarnate?

"No. It does not have free will."

600. Since the animal soul survives the body, does it remain in a type of interim state like the human soul after death?

"It remains in a type of interim state because it is not united to a body, but it is not like *spirits in between human incarnations*. The latter are beings who think and act out of their own free will. Spirits of animals do not have the same faculty. Self-awareness constitutes the main attribute of the human spirit. After its death, the animal soul is categorized by the spirits in charge, being sent to a new corporeal existence almost immediately. It is not given the chance to connect with other creatures."

601. Do animals follow a law of progress like humans?

"Yes, and that is why on superior worlds, where humans are more advanced, animals are also more advanced, and are endowed with more developed means of communication. However, they are always below humans, and subject to them, becoming their intelligent servants."

There is nothing extraordinary about this. Let us imagine that our more intelligent animals, such as the dog, the elephant, and the horse, were endowed with a physical constitution appropriate for manual labor. What would they not be able to accomplish under human guidance?

602. Do animals progress by their will, like man, or by the force of things?

"By the force of things. That is why there is no expiation for them."

603. On superior worlds, do animals know about God?

"No. Man is a god to them, as spirits were once gods to men."

604. Since animals, even those that are more perfect on superior worlds, are always ranked below man, would this not imply that God has created intelligent beings perpetually condemned to inferiority, something which would seem to conflict with the unity of conception and progress apparent in all of God's works?

"Everything in nature is connected by links that you cannot yet discern, and the most apparently discrepant things have points of contact that man will never manage to understand in his current state. He may catch a glimpse of them through an intellectual effort, but only when his intelligence has reached its full development and has freed itself from the prejudices of pride and ignorance, will he be able to see clearly into the works of God. Until then, his limited ideas will cause him to look at everything from a petty and narrow vantage point. Realize that God does not contradict Himself, and that everything in nature is reconciled by general laws that never deviate from the sublime wisdom of the Creator."

—   Then intelligence is a common attribute, a point of contact between the souls of animals and humans?

"Yes, but animals only have the intelligence of material life; in humans, intelligence produces a moral life."

605.   If we examined all the points of contact between man and animals, could we not consider that man possesses two souls: an animal soul and a spiritual soul, and that if he did not have the latter, he would live as a brute, only? In other words, isn't the animal a being similar to man, except for the spiritual soul? If so, wouldn't the good and evil instincts of man be the effect of the predominance of one of these two souls?

"No, man does not have two souls, but the body has its instincts, which result from the sensations of the organs. There is in man only a dual nature: the animal nature and the spiritual nature. Through his body, he shares the nature and instincts of animals. Through his soul, he shares the nature of spirits."

—   Thus, aside from getting rid of their own imperfections, must spirits also fight against the influence of matter?

"Yes, the less evolved they are, the tighter are the ties between spirit and matter. Can you not see it? No, humans do not have two souls; the soul is always one in each individual. The soul of an animal and that of a man are so very different from each other that the soul of one cannot animate the body created for the other. But if man does not have an animal soul, something which would place him at a level with animals, he has, nevertheless, an animal body, which often reduces him down to their level, a body endowed with vitality and its attendant instincts, all of which are unintelligent and restricted to providing for its own physical survival."

When a spirit incarnates into a human body, he brings to it the intellectual and moral principle that places him on a higher level than animals. The two natures that exist in man constitute two distinct sources of passions for him: some stem from the instincts of nature; others, from the imperfections of the incarnate spirit, which sympathizes to a greater or lesser degree with lowly animal appetites. In purifying himself, a spirit is gradually liberated from the influence of matter. Under such influence, man brings himself closer to the nature of animals; freed from such influence, he raises himself toward his true destiny.

606. Where do animals get the intelligent principle that characterizes the particular kind of soul with which they are endowed?

"From the universal intelligent element."

—   Then the intelligence of both man and animals emanates from a single source?

"Certainly, but in man it has gone through a process of improvement that brings it above that of the animals."

607. You have said that, at its origin, the human soul is in a state similar to that of human infancy, in that its intelligence is only beginning to blossom, attempting its first steps in life. (See #190) Where does the soul accomplish this initial phase?

"In a series of existences preceding the period you call humanhood."

—   Does that imply that the soul was the intelligent principle of the less advanced beings of creation?

"As we said, everything in nature is connected and tends toward unity. It is in those beings, that you are far from fully understanding, that the intelligent principle is refined, gradually individualized, and prepared for life, as mentioned. In a way, it is a preparatory work like that of germination, after which the intelligent principle undergoes a transformation and becomes *spirit*. It is then that the period of humanhood begins, and, with it, awareness of the future, the ability to distinguish between good and evil, and the responsibility for one's actions—the same way that childhood comes before adolescence, and finally adulthood.

"There is nothing humiliating about this origin. Do the greatest men of genius feel humiliated for having been formless fetuses in their mothers' womb? If anything ought to humiliate man, it is his low standing before God, and his inability to probe the depths of His designs and the wisdom of the laws ordering the universe. Recognize the greatness of God in the marvelous harmony that establishes the solidarity of all things in nature. To believe that God could have made anything without a purpose, creating sentient beings without a future, would be to blaspheme against His goodness, which embraces all His creation."

— Does the period of humanhood begin on Earth?

"The Earth is not the starting point of early human incarnations. The period of humanhood usually begins on worlds even less evolved. This, however, is not an absolute rule and it may happen that a spirit initiating the human phase may be suited to live on Earth. Such a case is not frequent and would be an exception rather than the rule."

608. After death, does a human spirit have any awareness of the existences that preceded its period of humanhood?

"No, because life as spirit for him did not begin at that period. A spirit in fact can hardly recall its first human existences, just as a man no longer remembers the earliest days of his childhood, and much less the time he spent in his mother's womb. That is why spirits may tell you that they do not know how they began." (See #78)

609. Having entered the human phase, do spirits retain traces of what they had previously been, in other words, of the state in which they found themselves in the period that one could call pre-human?

"That depends on the distance separating the two phases and the progress the spirit has accomplished. For a few generations he may preserve a more or less pronounced reflection of the primitive state, for nothing in nature occurs through an abrupt transition. There are always links connecting the end of the chain of beings or events. But such traces fade away with the development of free will. The initial progress is accomplished slowly because spirits are not yet assisted by their will. But once having acquired a more perfect awareness of themselves, they are able to accelerate their progress."

610. Therefore, are those spirits who have said that man is a being apart from the rest of creation mistaken?

"No, but the subject has not been fully developed, and, besides, there are things that can only be made known at the appointed time. Man is effectively a being apart, for he has faculties that distinguish him from all others, and he has another destiny. The human species is the one that God selected for the incarnation of the beings *who are capable of knowing Him.*"

3. Metempsychosis

611. Isn't the common origin of the intelligent principle in living beings a validation of the doctrine of metempsychosis?

"Two things may have the same origin, and yet not resemble each other at all later on. Who would recognize the tree, its leaves, flowers, and fruit in the shapeless germ contained in the seed from which it sprang? From the moment when the intelligent principle reaches the degree required to become a spirit and to enter the period of humanhood, it no longer has any relationship to its primitive state, and it is not the soul of the animal any more than the tree is a seed. In man, from the animal there remains only the body, the passions that arise from the body's influence, and the survival instinct inherent in matter. Therefore, one cannot say that a given person is the incarnation of a particular animal. As a result, the doctrine of metempsychosis, as commonly understood, is incorrect."

612. Could a spirit that has animated a human body incarnate in an animal?

"That would be a regression, and a spirit does not regress. The river does not flow back to is source." (See #118)

613. However flawed may be the idea of metempsychosis, couldn't it be a result of the intuitive sentiment of a person's different existences?

"This intuitive sentiment can be recognized in this belief as in many others, but, like most intuitive ideas, man has distorted it."

Metempsychosis would be correct if one understood it to mean the progression of the soul from a lower to a superior state, achieving the developments that will transform its nature. It is false, however, if understood to mean the direct transmigration from an animal to a human and vice versa, which would imply the idea of regression or fusion. Interbreeding cannot take place between corporeal beings of two different species, indicating that their natures are not compatible, and the same must apply to the spirits that animate them. If the same spirit could animate them alternately, it would result in an identity of nature, and this would translate into the possibility of material reproduction.

Reincarnation as taught by the Spirits, on the contrary, is founded upon the ascending march of nature and the progression of man within his own species, which in no way diminishes his dignity. What degrades him is the bad use he makes of the faculties that God has given him for his advancement. Be that as it may, the old and universal character of the doctrine of metempsychosis and the number of eminent men who have professed it prove that the principle of reincarnation has its roots in nature itself. These are arguments in its favor rather than against it.

The starting point of spirits is one of those issues connected to the origin of things, and among the secrets of God. It has not been given to man to know them entirely, and man can only make suppositions, elaborating more or less likely hypotheses about them. Spirits themselves are far from knowing everything, and concerning what they do not know, they may also have personal opinions which are more or less reasonable.

Accordingly, not all spirits agree about the connections between man and animals, for instance. To some, a spirit only arrives at the human period after having been prepared and individualized in the different degrees of the inferior beings of creation. According to others, the human spirit would have always belonged to the human race without having gone through the animal stage. The first of these theories has the advantage of giving a future purpose to animals, which would then constitute the first links of the chain of sentient beings. The second is more in conformance with the dignity of man, and can be summed up below. [c]

According to this second opinion, the different species of animals do not proceed *intellectually* from one another by means of a progression. Thus, the spirit of the oyster does not subsequently become that of the fish, the bird, the quadruped and, finally, primates. Each species is an *absolute* type, physically and intellectually. Each of its individuals draws from the universal source the required amount of the intelligent principle, in line with the perfection of its organs and the work it must perform in the phenomena of nature. It is then restored to the general pool upon death. Those of worlds more advanced than ours (See #188) would also constitute distinct species of animals, appropriate to the requirements of those worlds, and to the level of advancement of the humans they assist—but not proceeding from Earth species, spiritually speaking.

The same does not apply to man, however. From the physical point of view, man evidently represents a link in the chain of living beings; from the intellectual point of view, however, there is a chasm between man and animals. Only man possesses a soul or spirit, a divine spark that gives him a moral sense and an intellectual reach that animals do not have; it represents in him the main being, preexisting and outlasting the body, all the while preserving its individuality.

What is the origin of the spirit? Where is the spirit's starting point? Is the spirit formed by the individualization of the intelligent principle? This is a mystery that would be useless to try to penetrate, and on which, as mentioned, we can only create theories. What is certain and is inferred from both reason and experience is the survival of the spirit, the preservation of the spirit's individuality after death, the ability to advance, the happy or unhappy situation commensurate with the spirit's advancement along the path of virtue, and all the moral consequences that follow from this principle. With regard to the mysterious connection between man and animals, that constitutes, we repeat, one of God's secrets, the knowledge of which *at this juncture*—as happens with many other issues—is not essential for our advancement, and upon which it would be useless to dwell.

■■■

[a] *Mimosa pudica*, a tropical plant whose leaves fold when touched. —Trans.

[b] *Dionaea muscipula*, a carnivorous plant native to the subtropical wetlands of the United States that catches small insects and spiders in a trapping structure formed by a pair of modified leaves. —Trans.

[c] From the answers provided by the Spirits up to this point, it is clear that the first hypothesis—that "a spirit only arrives at the human period after having been prepared and individualized in the different degrees of the inferior beings of creation"—is the one that they sanction. Kardec prefers to leave the question still open at this point, but he settles the matter unequivocally in his last book, *La Genèse, les miracles et les prédictions selon le Spiritisme* (Paris, 1868), Chapter VI, item 19: "L'Esprit n'arrive point à recevoir l'illumination divine qui lui donne, en même temps que le libre arbitre et la conscience, la notion de ses hautes destinées, sans avoir passé par la série divinement fatale des êtres inférieurs, parmi lesquels s'élabore lentement l'œuvre de son individualité ; c'est seulement à dater du jour où le Seigneur imprime sur son front son auguste type, que l'Esprit prend rang parmi les humanités." (The spirit does not receive the divine spark—which endows him, on the one hand, with free will and consciousness, and, on the other hand, with the awareness of his higher destination—without having gone through the divinely inevitable ranks of inferior beings, among which the process of the spirit's individualization is slowly elaborated. Only from the moment that the Creator imprints on his front His august mark, does the spirit join the ranks of humanhood). —Trans.

Part 3:
Moral Laws

Chapter 1:
Divine or Natural Law

1. Characteristics of natural law

614. What should be understood by natural law? [a]

"Natural law is the law of God. It is the only one appropriate for the happiness of man; it indicates what he ought to do or not do. Man is unhappy only when he gets estranged from it."

615. Is God's law eternal?

"It is eternal and immutable as God Himself."

616. Could God have prescribed for mankind in one age what He had forbidden in another?

"God does not make mistakes. It is man who is forced to change his laws because they are imperfect—unlike God's laws, which are perfect. The harmony ruling both the material and moral worlds is founded on laws established by God from all eternity."

617. What matters are encompassed by the divine laws? Do they concern anything other than moral conduct?

"All laws of nature are divine because God is the author of all things. The scientist studies the laws of the material world, whereas the virtuous person studies those of the soul and practices them."

—   Is man granted the ability to understand both?

"Yes, but a single existence is not enough."

What, indeed, are a few years for the acquisition of all that is necessary in order to reach perfection, if we consider the distance that separates primitive from civilized man? The longest possible lifespan is insufficient, all the more so when it is cut short, as often happens to a large number of people.

Among the divine laws, some regulate the properties of matter. These are the physical laws, and their study falls within the domain of science.

Other laws specifically concern man himself, as well as his relationship with God and with his fellow creatures. These laws govern both his earthly and his spiritual life. These are the moral laws.

618. Are the divine laws the same for all worlds?

"Reason tells you they must be suitable for the nature of each world and in proportion to the degree of advancement of the beings that inhabit them."

2. Origin and knowledge of natural law

619. Has God given all men the means of knowing His law?

"All may know it, but not all understand it. Those who understand it the best are men of virtue, as well as those who sincerely look for it. All shall one day understand it, however, for progress must be accomplished."

The justice of multiple incarnations is a consequence of this principle, because in each new existence man's intelligence becomes more developed and he better differentiates good and evil. If everything had to be accomplished in a single existence, what would be the fate of the many millions who die every day in degrading viciousness, or in the darkness of ignorance, without ever having a chance to educate themselves? (See #171–222)

620. Before its union with the body, does the soul understand God's law more clearly than after incarnating?

"It understands God's law according to the degree of perfection it has attained, and it preserves an intuitive recollection of it after its union with the body. But then, man's evil instincts often cause him to forget it."

621. Where is God's law written?

"In the conscience."

— Since man carries God's law in his conscience, why the need for revealing it to him?

"He has forgotten and ignored it: God has willed that he be reminded of it."

622. Has God assigned to certain men the mission of revealing His law?

"Yes, certainly. Throughout the ages certain men have received this mission. These are superior spirits who have incarnated with the purpose of furthering the progress of mankind."

623. Haven't those who intended to instruct mankind in God's law fallen at times into error, and haven't they often led others astray through false doctrines?

"Those who were not inspired by God and those who claimed, out of ambition, a mission not assigned to them may have led others into error. Nevertheless, many of them were undeniably men of genius, and even amidst the errors they taught, one can often find great truths."

624. What are the characteristics of true prophets?

"True prophets are men of virtue inspired by God. You can recognize them by their words and deeds. God does not use the mouth of a liar to teach the truth."

625. What is the most perfect example that God has offered man as guide and model?

"Jesus."

Jesus represents the example of moral perfection that mankind may aspire to on Earth. God offers him as the most perfect model, and his teachings represent the best expression of God's law, because he was animated by the divine spirit and was the purest being to ever appear on the planet.

If some of those who intended to teach God's law to man sometimes led him astray with false doctrines, it is because they had let themselves be overtaken by strong earthly sentiments, and because they had mixed up the laws that regulate the life of the soul with those that regulate the life of the body. Many of them promoted as divine certain laws that were nothing but human laws created to serve their passions and to dominate men.

626. Have the divine or natural laws been revealed to mankind by Jesus alone, the knowledge of them prior to him being accessible only through intuition?

"Have we not said that they are written everywhere? All who have pondered upon matters of wisdom have been able to understand and teach these laws since the most ancient times. Though incomplete, their teachings have prepared the ground to receive the seed. As the divine laws are written in the book of nature, man was able to discern them as soon as he decided to look for them. That is why the principles they uphold have been asserted by virtuous men in all ages, and why their elements can be found in the moral code of every society lifted out of barbarity, even if incomplete or tainted by ignorance and superstition." [b]

627. Since Jesus has already taught the true laws of God, what is the use of teachings conveyed by the spirits? Do they have anything more to teach us?

"The discourse of Jesus was frequently allegorical and in the form of parables, because he spoke according to his time and place. Today truth must be made intelligible for all. It is therefore imperative that these laws be explained and expanded upon, because so few people understand them, and even fewer practice them. Our mission is to strike eyes and ears in order to confound the proud and expose the hypocrites—those who mimic outward displays of virtue and religiousness in order to hide their wickedness.

"The teachings of the Spirits must be clear and unequivocal, so that no one may claim ignorance as an excuse, and so that all may judge and evaluate them through reason. We are in charge of preparing for the reign of the good announced by Jesus. For this reason, we must let no man be able to interpret the law of God according to his own passions, or to distort the meaning of a law that is wholly love and charity."

628. Why hasn't truth always been brought within the reach of everyone?

"Each thing must happen in its own time. Truth is like light: you must adapt to it little by little; otherwise, it dazzles you.

"Thus far, never has God allowed man to receive messages as complete and instructive as those he is allowed to receive today. As you know, in ancient times there were indeed a few individuals who were in possession of what they considered a sacred science, and out of which they made a mystery to those they regarded as unholy. You must understand, from what you know of the laws governing these phenomena, that those individuals only received a few scattered truths within an ambiguous and, for the most part, symbolic whole.

"Today, however, the studious man should not disregard any bygone philosophical system, tradition or religion, because they all contain the seeds of great truths, even if they seem to contradict one another, scattered as these truths are among unfounded adornments. Nowadays they can easily be reconciled through the key made available to you by Spiritism, elucidating countless issues which may have up until now seemed unreasonable, but the reality of which has been irrefutably demonstrated today. Consequently, do not neglect such materials as objects of study, as they are very rich and may greatly contribute to your instruction."

3. Good and evil

629. How may one define morality?

"Morality is the rule of good conduct, that is to say, the rule that distinguishes between good and evil. It is founded on the observance of God's law. Man behaves rightly when he does everything for the good of all, because he then complies with God's law."

630. How can we distinguish between good and evil?

"Good is everything that is in keeping with God's law, and evil is everything that deviates from it. As a result, to do good is to conform to God's law. To do evil is to violate that law."

631. Does man have the means to distinguish by himself between good and evil?

"Yes, when he believes in God and wishes to know Him. God has provided man with intelligence in order to differentiate the one from the other."

632. Being prone to error, cannot man be mistaken when distinguishing between good and evil, and believe he is doing what is right, when in reality he is doing wrong?

"Jesus told you, 'Do unto others what you would want them do unto you.' All is in there; you will not go wrong."

633. The golden rule, which may be called the rule of *reciprocity* or *solidarity*, does not apply to man's personal conduct toward himself. Can he find the rule for such conduct in natural law, so as to serve as his reliable guide?

"Eating too much hurts you. Well, this is God's way of demonstrating the limit of how much you actually need. If you go beyond it, you are punished. It is the same with everything else. Natural law draws the limit of man's needs, and when he exceeds this limit, he is punished with suffering. If in all situations man paid heed to the voice that warns him, *'Enough!'* he would avoid most of the ills of which he accuses nature."

634. Why is evil to be found in the very nature of things? I speak of moral evil. Couldn't God have created mankind under better conditions?

"We have already told you: spirits are created simple and ignorant (See #115). God leaves man to choose his own path, so much the worse for him if he takes the wrong one—his pilgrimage will be all the longer. If there were no mountains, man would not understand that he can go up and down; if there were no rocks, he would not understand that there are hard and sharp objects. The spirit must acquire experience, and to that end he must know both good and evil. For that reason, the union of spirit and body is established." (See #119)

635. Different social positions create additional needs that are not the same for everyone. Wouldn't natural law, then, seem not to be a uniform rule?

"Such different positions exist in nature itself and are consistent with the law of progress. That does not invalidate the unity of natural law, which applies to everything."

The conditions of man's existence change according to time and place, resulting in different needs for him, as well as in social positions suitable to such needs. Since such diversity is in the very order of things, it is in conformity with God's law, which nonetheless remains one in principle. It is up to reason to distinguish between real needs and those that are artificial or conventional.

636. Are good and evil absolute for everyone?

"God's law is the same for everyone, but evil depends particularly on the desire one has to commit it. Good is always good, and evil is always evil, whatever a man's position may be; the difference lies in the degree of his responsibility."

637. Is a cannibal guilty when he yields to his instinct and feeds on human flesh?

"As mentioned, evil depends on the will. Man is therefore more culpable the more he understands his actions."

Circumstances ascribe to good and evil relative degrees of significance. Man frequently makes mistakes that, despite resulting from his social position, are nonetheless reprehensible. But his responsibility is proportional his ability to know the difference between good and evil. Thus, the enlightened man who commits a mere injustice may be more culpable before God than the ignorant savage who abandons himself to his base instincts.

638. Occasionally, evil seems to be a consequence of circumstances. That is the case, for instance, in the necessity of destruction, even that of a fellow man. Can one say there is a breach of God's law in such cases?

"Evil is no less evil, even when it may be necessary, but such necessity disappears as the soul becomes purer, in passing from one existence to another. And then man is even more culpable when he does something evil, because he better comprehends it."

639. The evil we commit is frequently a result of the position where others have placed us in. Who is more culpable in such case?

"The responsibility lies with the one who has caused it. As a result, he who is led into evil by circumstances forced upon him is less culpable than those who created such circumstances in the first place. Thus, each and every man shall bear the punishment not only for the wrongs he himself committed, but also for those he induced others to commit."

640. Is he who does not do evil himself, but profits from the evil committed by others, culpable to the same degree?

"It is as though he had committed it himself—partaking of the fruits of evil is taking part in evil. Maybe he would have hesitated to commit it, but if he, upon finding the wrongful deed already consummated, goes on to take advantage of it, it is because he approves of it, and would have committed it himself if he had had the opportunity—*or the courage*—to do it."

641. Is the desire for evil as blameworthy as evil itself?

"That is as the case may be. There is virtue in willfully resisting doing evil if one harbors the desire to commit it, especially when in possession of the means to bring one's plans to fruition. However, a man is already guilty if all that he lacks is the opportunity to carry out his plans."

642. Is it enough for us not to do evil in order to be pleasing to God, and to guarantee our standing in the future?

"No, you must also do good to the extent of your powers. For you shall answer for all the evil *resulting from the good you failed to do*."

643. Are there people who, owing to their position, have no possibility of doing good?

"There is nobody unable to do good: only the selfish person never finds an opportunity to do it. Being in contact with others is enough to provide you with a chance of doing good, and every day of your life offers you such a possibility, so long as you are not blinded by selfishness. Doing good goes beyond being charitable. It also includes being useful to the full extent of your powers, whenever your assistance may be necessary."

644. Isn't the environment into which a man is born the foremost cause for much of his involvement with vice and crime?

"Yes, but even then, it is the result of a trial that he chose in his between-incarnations state, as a spirit. He wanted to expose himself to temptation in order to earn the credit for resisting it."

645. When a man is immersed in an atmosphere of vice, doesn't evil come to be an almost irresistible seduction?

"A seduction, indeed, but not irresistible. For, in the midst of such an atmosphere of vice, you may sometimes find individuals of great virtue. These are spirits who have the strength to resist and who simultaneously have the mission of exerting a good influence on their fellow beings."

646. Is the merit of the good that one does contingent upon certain conditions? In other words, does the good one accomplishes have varying degrees of merit?

"The merit of the good accomplished depends on its difficulty. There is hardly any merit in the good accomplished without any sacrifice or cost. God regards more highly the poor man who shares his last slice of bread than the rich man who only dispenses with his leftovers. Jesus taught you this lesson in the parable of the widow's mite." [c]

4. Division of natural law

647. Is God's law completely contained in the maxim of loving one's neighbor, as taught by Jesus?

"This maxim certainly contains all men's duties toward one another. But it is necessary to show men the maxim's application, otherwise they will neglect their duties, as they currently do. Moreover, natural law encompasses all the circumstances of life, and this particular maxim only deals with a part of it. Men need precise rules. General and overly vague precepts leave too many doors open to interpretation."

648. What do you think of the division of natural law into ten parts, including the laws of *worship; labor; reproduction; preservation;*

destruction; society; progress; equality; freedom; and finally, the law of justice; love, and charity?

"The division of God's law into ten parts is that of Moses and is able to encompass all the circumstances of life, which is the essential point. You may therefore follow such division, keeping in mind that there is nothing absolute in it, any more than in any other methodology dependent on the standpoint from which a subject is considered. The last law is the most important—through it man is able to advance most rapidly on his spiritual path, as this law summarizes all the others."

■■■

[a] The concept of *natural law* or *law of nature* was common currency in France during the eighteenth and nineteenth centuries, to the point of meriting an entry in the *Encyclopédie* of Diderot and d'Alembert: "*Law of nature*, or *natural law*; in its most extended sense, refers to certain principles inspired only by nature that are common to men and to animals. On this law are based the union of male and female, the procreation of children and concern for their education, the love of liberty, the conservation of one's own person, and the effort each man makes to defend himself when attacked by others..." Website Encyclopédie Project, the University of Chicago; accessed December 25, 2017, http://encyclopedie.uchicago.edu/ . Kardec adapts this concept to the Mosaic Decalogue in order to establish the framework for the extensive coverage of *ethics* presented in Part 3 of *The Spirits' Book*. —Trans.

[b] The presence of luminaries all around the world before the birth of Christ—from Lao-Tse and Confucius in China to Buddha and Vyasa in India, from Moses and Daniel in the Middle East to Socrates and Plato in Greece—is a testimony to the fact that God has always sent His emissaries to instruct humankind in His laws and hasten its advancement. —Trans.

[c] Mark 12:41–44, Luke 21:1–4. —Trans.

Chapter 2:
The Law of Worship

1. Purpose of worship

649. What is worship?

"Worship is raising the thoughts toward God. Through worship one draws one's soul closer to Him."

650. Is worship the result of an innate sentiment or the product of education?

"The result of an innate sentiment, like the innate sentiment regarding the Divinity. The awareness of his weakness compels man to bow before the One who can protect him."

651. Has there ever been a people completely devoid of the sentiment of worship?

"No, because there has never been an atheistic people. All peoples have understood that there is a Supreme Being above them."

652. May we consider worship's origin to be in natural law?

"Worship is part of natural law because it is the result of an innate sentiment in man. That is why we find it among all peoples, even if in different forms."

2. Outward worship

653. Does worship require outward demonstrations?

"True worship lies in the heart. Always keep in mind that a Master observes you in all your actions."

—   Is the outward display of worship useful nonetheless?

"Yes, if it is not a vain pretense. It is always useful to provide a good example. However, if those who do it are purely motivated by affectation and pride, contradicting their ostensible piety by their conduct, they set a bad example rather than a good one, and do more harm than they can imagine."

654. Does God prefer those who worship him in any particular fashion?

"God prefers those who worship Him from the heart, with sincerity, doing good and avoiding evil, to those who think they honor Him through rituals that do not make them any better toward their fellow beings.

"All creatures are siblings, children of the same God. He summons all those who follow His laws, whichever way they do it.

"He whose piety is nothing but an outward display is a hypocrite. He whose worship is an affectation in contradiction with his conduct sets a bad example.

"He who professes to worship Christ, but who is proud, envious and jealous; who is hard and merciless toward others; or who covets earthly possessions, has religion only on his lips, not in his heart. God, who sees everything, shall say: 'He who knows the truth is a hundredfold more culpable for the evil he does than the rude primitive man in the desert, and shall be treated accordingly on the day of reckoning.' If a blind man passing by happens to hit you by accident, you forgive him. But, instead, if it is a man with perfect vision who does it, you shall protest, and rightly so.

"So, do not ask which form of worship is the most suitable, for that would be tantamount to asking whether it is more pleasing to God to worship Him in one language or another. Let me reiterate: your chants only reach God when sung through the gates of the heart."

655. Is it wrong to practice a religion one does not sincerely believe in, when one does it in order not to be stigmatized and not to offend those who think differently?

"Intention is the yardstick to be used in this instance, as in so many others. Those whose sole aim is to show respect for the beliefs of others do no wrong. They do better in fact than those who would ridicule the beliefs of others, since that would be a lack of kindness. But those who do it out of self-interest or ambition are despicable in the eyes of God and of their fellow men. God could not be pleased with those who pretend to humble themselves before Him only in order to win the approval of others."

656. Is it preferable to worship in a group, rather than individually?

"When men gather united by thought and sentiment, they have more power to plead for the presence of good spirits. The same applies when they gather to worship God. But do not believe that individual worship is therefore less adequate, for every man is able to worship God by raising his thoughts to Him."

3. Life of contemplation

657. Do those who dedicate themselves to a life of contemplation, doing no evil and thinking only of God, have any merit in His eyes?

"No, for even though they do no evil, they do no good, either, and are therefore worthless. Moreover, not doing good is in itself an evil. God wants you to think about Him, but not that alone, for He has given man duties to discharge on Earth. He who spends all his time in meditation and contemplation does nothing meritorious in the eyes of God, since his life is self-centered and of no use to mankind, and God shall ask him to account for the good he failed to do." (See #640)

4. On prayer

658. Is prayer pleasing to God?

"A prayer is always pleasing to God when offered from the heart, for intention is everything to Him. A prayer from the heart is preferable to one you may read, no matter how beautiful it may be, if you read more with your lips than with your thought. Prayer is pleasing to God when it is offered with faith, fervor, and sincerity. Also, do not believe that God is touched by the prayer of the vain, proud, or selfish man, unless his prayer represents an act of sincere repentance and true humility."

659. What is the general character of prayer?

"Prayer is an act of adoration. Praying to God is thinking of Him, drawing nearer to Him, putting oneself in communication with Him. Through prayer one may accomplish three things: give praise, make a request, and express gratitude."

660. Does prayer make man better?

"Yes, because he who prays fervently and confidently becomes stronger to resist the temptations of evil, and God sends good spirits to assist him. Prayer represents an assistance which is never refused when sincerely requested."

—   Why is it that certain people who pray much have nevertheless a very evil, jealous, envious, and irritable character, lacking in benevolence and forbearance, being even cruel sometimes?

"The essential thing is not to pray much, but to pray correctly. Such people think that the merit lies in the length of their prayer, shutting their eyes to their own faults. For them, prayer is an occupation, a pastime, but not *a moment for self-examination*. It is not the remedy that is ineffective, but how it is used."

661. Is it useful to ask God to forgive us our faults?

"God knows how to distinguish between good and evil—praying does not hide sins. He who asks God to forgive his sins does not receive forgiveness unless he changes his conduct. Good deeds are the best prayers, for deeds are worth more than words."

662. Is it useful to pray for others?

"The spirit of he who prays acts through his determination to do good. Through prayer, he attracts good spirits who cooperate in the good he wants to do."

> In our thought and will we possess an inner power that extends far beyond the limits of our physical dimension. A prayer for others is an expression of that will. If it is ardent and sincere, it can attract to their aid the presence of good spirits, who, in turn, may suggest good thoughts and provide those we wish to help with the needed physical and spiritual strength. But here, again, a prayer sprung from the heart is everything; a prayer recited with the lips is nothing.

663. Can the prayers we offer for ourselves change the nature of our trials and change their course?

"Your trials are in God's hands, and there are trials that must be endured to their term. God, however, always takes equanimity into account. Prayer brings good spirits to your side, who provide you with the strength to endure your trials with courage, making them seem less hard. As we have said, a prayer is never useless when offered properly, because it provides strength, already a very good outcome of itself. Heaven helps those who help themselves—you know that.

"In addition, God could not change the workings of nature to suit the whims of each man, since that which may be a great evil from your narrow point of view, which only takes into account your ephemeral life, is often a great good within the great scheme of things.

"Furthermore, how many misfortunes are caused by people themselves through their own carelessness or wrongdoing? They are punished for their own individual mistakes. However, your fair requests are heard more often than you would suppose. You think that God has not heard your prayer because no miracle was performed for you, while you have in fact received the divine assistance through means so natural that it seems to have happened by chance or as a matter of course. Most frequently, God suggests the thought needed for you to get out of your difficulties on your own."

664. Is it of any use to pray for the dead and for spirits who suffer, and, if so, how can our prayers provide them with solace and shorten their sufferings? Do our prayers have the power to sway the justice of God?

"Prayer has no effect in changing God's designs, but the souls for whom you offer a prayer experience relief, because it represents a testimony to the interest you have in them, and because unhappy souls always find solace when they encounter charitable souls who have compassion for their suffering. On the other hand, through prayer you stimulate them to repent and to do what they must in order to be happier. It is in this sense that you can shorten their affliction, if for their part they assist with their own goodwill. The motivation to advance that is stimulated by prayer attracts to the suffering spirits the presence of more advanced ones who come to enlighten, console and give them hope. Jesus prayed for the sheep gone astray. In doing so, he showed that you are at fault for not praying for those who have the greatest need."

665. What is to be thought of the opinion that rejects praying for the dead because it is not prescribed in the Gospels?

"Christ said to all men, 'Love one another.' This recommendation implies using all possible means to demonstrate love toward others, but without specifying the way to reach this goal. If it is true that nothing can turn God aside from applying His justice—of which He represents the perfect example—to every one of a spirit's actions, it is no less true that the prayer you address to God for those who inspire your love is a testimony to your memory that certainly helps to relieve their sufferings and console them. Once they display the slightest sign of repentance—*and only then*—they are assisted. But it will never be forgotten that a sympathetic soul was concerned about them, imbuing them with the tender notion that your intercession was beneficial to them. This naturally elicits in them a feeling of recognition and affection for the one who has shown this proof of friendship and piety. Consequently, the love recommended to mankind by Christ grows between them. In this way, all have obeyed the law of love and union of all beings, the divine law that must lead to unity—the Spirit's goal and destination."[1]

666. May we pray to spirits?

"You may pray to good spirits, as they are the messengers of God and the executors of His designs. Nevertheless, their power is in proportion to their degree of evolution, and always emanates from the Master of all things, without whose permission nothing is accomplished. For this reason, the prayers that we address to them are only effective inasmuch as they are pleasing to God."

5. Polytheism

667. Why is polytheism one of the most ancient and widespread beliefs, in view of the fact that it is false?

"The idea of a single God could only emerge among men as the result of the development of their intellect. Incapable, in their ignorance, of conceiving of an immaterial being without a determined form and who acted upon matter, they ascribed to God the attributes of a material nature, that is, a form and a face. From then on, everything that seemed to go beyond the normal range of common intelligence became a deity of sorts to them. Whatever they could not understand had to be the work of a supernatural power, and it only took a small step from that point to believing in as many distinct powers as the effects they could see. Nonetheless, in all ages there have been enlightened individuals who have understood the impossibility of such a multitude of powers governing the world without one superior rule, thus refining their thought in the direction of a single God."

668. Since spirit phenomena have always occurred and have been known from the earliest ages, couldn't they have led to the belief in the plurality of gods?

---

[1] This answer was provided by the Spirit of M. Monod, the Protestant pastor of Paris, who died in 1856. The preceding reply, #664, was given by Saint Louis's Spirit. —Auth.

"Undoubtedly, because men labeled *god* everything that was above their human abilities, and spirits thus became gods to them. Likewise, whenever a man distinguished himself among others by his actions, by his genius, or by a secret power incomprehensible to the common folk, he would also be granted the status of a god, and would be worshipped after death." (See #603)

The word *god* had a wide range of meanings among the ancients. It was not, as nowadays, the embodiment of the Master of nature, but was a generic name given to any being above the normal human level. When spirit manifestations revealed to them the existence of incorporeal beings acting as powers of nature, they called them *gods*, just as we call them *spirits*. It is a mere question of words, but with the difference that in their ignorance—maintained on purpose by those who had a vested interest—they built very lucrative temples and altars. For us, on the other hand, spirits are merely creatures similar to us—some of them being more perfect than others—who have shed their earthly envelope. If we carefully study the various attributes of the pagan deities, we can easily recognize all those who characterize the spirits at each degree of the spirit hierarchy, their physical state on more highly evolved worlds, all the properties of their perispirit, and the role they play in earthly affairs.

When Christianity came to illumine the world with its divine light, it could not destroy something which was in nature itself, but redirected this worship, instead, toward the One to whom it is due. As for the spirits, their memory has been perpetuated under different names, in each different culture. Their manifestations, in addition, have never ceased, and have been variously interpreted, and frequently exploited under a cloak of mystery. While religion has identified spirit manifestations as miraculous phenomena, skeptics have taken them as trickery. Nowadays, however, thanks to the serious study carried out in broad daylight under the aegis of Spiritism, unfettered from the superstition that had obscured it throughout the ages, one of the greatest and most sublime principles of nature is thus revealed to us.

6. Sacrifices

669. The practice of human sacrifice dates back to remotest antiquity. Why could man believe that such a thing could be pleasing to God?

"First, because men did not understand that God is the source of all goodness. Amid primitive peoples, matter prevailed over spirit. They yielded to their brutish instincts, and were therefore cruel in general, as their sense of morality had not been developed yet. Second, primitive men naturally believed that a living creature had much more value in God's eyes than an inert object. This is what led them to immolate animals initially, and humans subsequently, because, in their erroneous belief, they imagined that the value of a sacrifice was proportional to the importance of the victim. The usual practice in your earthly life is that, whenever you buy a gift for somebody, you select one with as much value as the affection and consideration you wish to demonstrate. The same happened to primitive men with respect to God."

— Did the sacrificing of animals, then, precede that of human beings?

"That's undoubtedly the case."

— According to that explanation, didn't human sacrifice originate from a sentiment of cruelty?

"No, but from a mistaken notion of being pleasing to God. Take the case of Abraham [a], for instance. In time, men began to commit the abuse of immolating the enemies of their tribes, and then even their personal enemies. But, God has never demanded sacrifices, neither of animals nor of men. God can never be honored by the useless destruction of His own creatures."

670. Could human sacrifices ever have been pleasing to God if performed with pious intentions?

"No, never, but God does judge the intention. Those men, ignorant as they were, may have believed they were performing a laudable act in immolating one of their fellow beings. In that case, God would have focused on the thought, not the action. As they advanced, men had to recognize their error and reject such sacrifices, no longer acceptable to informed spirits. I say *informed* because, back then, spirits were under the influence of matter. Through their free will, however, they were able to catch a glimpse of their origin and destination. Many, in fact, already intuitively understood the evil they committed, but would not refrain from doing it in order to satisfy their passions."

671. What should we think of so-called holy wars? The sentiment that leads fanatical nations to think they are pleasing God by exterminating the greatest possible number of those who do not share their beliefs could have the same origin as the sentiment that formerly led men to sacrifice their fellow human beings, could it not?

"Such nations are driven by evil spirits. By waging war on their fellow beings, they act against the will of God, who establishes that one must love one's neighbors as oneself. Every religion, or, rather, every nation, worships the same God by one name or another. Why wage a war of extermination because a nation's religion is different, or has not yet attained the religious progress typical of more advanced cultures?

"Nations may be excused for not believing in the word of the one who was animated by the Spirit of God and sent by Him, especially those who have neither seen him nor witnessed his deeds. But how could you possibly expect them to believe in a message of peace when you seek to deliver it while bearing a sword? They must be instructed, and we must help them understand God's teachings through persuasion and kindness, rather than by might and blood. For the most part you do not believe in our communications with certain mortals, so how would you expect strangers to believe in your words when your actions contradict the principles you preach?"

672. Did the offering of the fruits of the Earth have more merit in the eyes of God than the sacrificing of animals?

"I have already answered that by saying that God judges the intention; the action itself has little importance. Offering the fruits of the Earth rather than the blood of victims would obviously be more pleasing to God. As we have told you and continue to repeat, a prayer said from the bottom of the heart is a hundred times more pleasing to God than all the offerings you could make. I repeat: the intention here is everything; the act itself, nothing."

673. Could there not have been a way of making those offerings more pleasing to God, by offering them to the relief of those who lack the basic necessities of life? And in that case, might not the sacrificing of animals, performed toward such a useful goal, have been more meritorious than an abusive sacrifice that had no useful purpose, or when it benefited only those who did not need anything? Would there not be something truly godly in pledging to the poor the first fruits of the Earth granted to us by God?

"God always blesses those who do good. Helping the poor and the afflicted is the best means of honoring God. I do not mean that God disapproves of the ceremonies you use for prayer. However, many of the resources spent on such ceremonies could be employed more usefully elsewhere. God loves simplicity in all things. He who attaches importance to external acts and not to those of the heart is a narrow-minded spirit. Judge for yourselves as to whether God should be more concerned with form than with content."

■■■

[a] In Genesis 22:1–19 it is described how Abraham agreed to offer his son Isaac in sacrifice. —Trans.

Chapter 3:
The Law of Labor

1. Need for work

674. Is the need for work a law of nature?

"Labor is a law of nature, and as such it is a necessity. Additionally, civilization compels man to work more, by increasing his needs and enjoyments."

675. Should we understand labor or work to mean only material occupations?

"No. The spirit labors as much as the body. Every useful occupation is labor."

676. Why has labor been imposed on mankind?

"It is a consequence of man's physical nature. It is a means of expiation and at the same time a means of perfecting man's intelligence. Without labor, man would remain in the infancy of his intellect. Therefore, he must obtain his food, safety, and welfare through his own labor and activity. At times, God may have granted more intelligence to certain people in order to compensate for their physical weakness, but that represents labor nonetheless."

677. Why does nature itself provide for all the needs of animals?

"Everything in nature toils. Animals labor as you do, but their work, like their intelligence, is limited to providing for their survival. That is why labor does not directly lead to progress in their case, while among men it has a double objective: the preservation of life and the development of the intellect, the latter also being a necessity, raising men's intelligence to ever higher degrees. When I say that the labor of animals is limited to their survival, I mean the goal at which their labor is aimed. But while devoted entirely to providing for their physical needs, they are also, unwittingly, agents that collaborate in the designs of the Creator. Their labor contributes no less to the final goal of nature, although very frequently you do not realize its result immediately."

678. On more perfect worlds, does man also need to work?

"The type of work is in accord with his needs. The less material his needs, the less material is the labor required. But do not believe that man would eventually become inactive and useless. Idleness would be a torment rather than a benefit."

679. Is the man who possesses plenty of assets that ensure his well-being, liberated from the law of labor?

"From physical labor, perhaps, but not from the obligation to make himself useful according to his possibilities, and to advance his own intelligence as well as that of others, as this also constitutes labor. If the man to whom God has granted enough possessions to ensure his existence is not forced to win his bread from the sweat of his brow, the obligation of being useful to his fellow creatures is all the greater in his case, because the material surplus given to him in advance allows for more free time to do good."

680. Aren't there those who are incapable of working at absolutely anything, and whose existence serves no purpose?

"God is just, only condemning him who voluntarily leads a purposeless life, living at the expense of others, off of their labor. God wills that each man should make himself useful according to his faculties." (See #643)

681. Does the law of nature impose upon children the obligation to provide for their parents?

"Certainly, just as parents must provide for their children. That is why God has made filial and parental love natural sentiments, so that, by such mutual love, members of the same family would be led to help one another mutually, something often ignored by your society today." (See #205)

2. Limit of work, rest

682. Since rest is needed after work, isn't it therefore a law of nature?

"Unquestionably. Rest serves to restore the strength of the body; it is also needed to give a little more freedom to the intelligence, which is then able to raise itself above matter."

683. What is the limit of labor?

"The limit of one's strength. In this regard God leaves man free to decide."

684. What is to be thought of those who abuse their authority by imposing excessive work on their subordinates?

"It is one of the worst actions they could take. Those in a position of command are responsible for any excessive work they impose on their subordinates, constituting a transgression of the law of God." (See #273)

685. Does man have the right to retire in old age?

"Yes. No one is required to labor beyond his capacity."

—   But what options do senior people have available when they must earn a living while not being able to do so?

"The strong should work for the weak. In the absence of a family to provide for them, society should take its place. That is the law of charity."

It is not enough to tell people they must work; it is also necessary for those who make their living from their labor to actually be able to find employment, but this does not always happen. Whenever unemployment is widespread, it reaches the level of a calamity, much like a famine. Economic science seeks a solution in the balance between supply and demand, but this balance—supposing that it is possible—will always experience cycles, and, during the down trends, workers must still make a living.

There is an element that has not been sufficiently considered, but without which economic science is nothing more than theory: *education*—not intellectual education but moral education—and not moral education through books, but moral education that consists in the *art of forming character*, moral education that *creates habits* because *education is the sum of acquired habits.*

When one considers the great numbers of people who are daily thrown into the torrent of the world, without principles, without restraints, and at the mercy of their own instincts, we should not be surprised at the disastrous consequences that ensue. When the art of education is recognized, understood, and practiced, all individuals in the world will develop habits of *order and forethought* for themselves and their dependents. They will *respect whatever is respectable* and will have habits that allow them to less painfully endure the unavoidable days of adversity. Lack of discipline and forethought are two ills that only a *sound* education can cure. That is the starting point, the key to welfare, the guarantee of security for *all.*

■■■

Chapter 4:
The Law of Reproduction

1. World population

686. Is the reproduction of living beings a law of nature?

"Evidently so; without reproduction the corporeal world would disappear."

687. If the population keeps growing at the going rate, will a time come when the Earth can no longer support all of humanity?

"No. God provides for such matters, always maintaining everything in balance. He does nothing that is useless. Man sees but a corner of the universal panorama, being therefore unable to grasp the harmony of the whole."

2. Succession and advancement of races

688. At this moment, there are certain races among men that are clearly diminishing. Will a time come when they will have completely disappeared from Earth?

"Yes, but that is because other races have taken their place, just as still others will someday take yours."

689. Are current human beings a new creation, or are they the perfected descendants of primitive beings?

"They are the same spirits who have *returned* to perfect themselves in new bodies, but who are still far from perfection. Thus, the present human race, which, as it grows, tends to occupy the whole Earth and to replace the races that are vanishing, will also go through its own period of decline and extinction. Other more perfected races will replace it. These will have descended from the present ones, just as the civilized human beings of the present day have descended from the brutish and savage beings of primitive ages."

690. From a purely physical point of view, are the bodies of the present human race a special creation, or have they evolved from more primitive bodies by way of reproduction?

"The origin of the human race is lost in the night of time, but since all belong to one great human family, whatever the primitive roots of each race were, they have since been able to mix with one another and produce new types."

691. From a physical standpoint, what is the distinctive and dominant characteristic of primitive races?

"The exertion of brute force at the expense of intellectual power. The opposite occurs nowadays: man acts more through his intelligence than through his physical strength. And yet, he accomplishes a hundred times more because he has placed the forces of nature at his service, something that animals cannot do."

692. Is the improvement of animal and plant species through science contrary to natural law? Would it be more in accord with natural law to allow things to follow their normal course?

"All efforts must be made to achieve perfection, and man himself is an instrument that God utilizes to accomplish His goals. Perfection being the destiny toward which nature tends, to contribute to such perfection is to be in harmony with God's designs."

—   But in his efforts to improve various species, man is generally motivated by a personal interest that has no other goal than to increase his own enjoyments. Does this not diminish his merit?

"What does it matter that his merit is void, provided that progress is accomplished? It is up to him to make his work meritorious through his intention. Besides, through his work he exercises and develops his intelligence, and it is from this perspective that he derives the greatest benefit."

3. Obstacles to reproduction

693. Are the human laws and customs that have as their objective or as their result, the creation of obstacles to reproduction, contrary to the law of nature?

"Everything that hinders nature in its course is contrary to the general law."

— Nevertheless, there are species of living beings—both animals and plants—whose unrestrained reproduction would be detrimental to other species, and of which man himself would soon be a victim. Would it be reprehensible to limit their reproduction?

"God has given man, above all other living creatures, a power that he should use for the general good, but which he should not abuse. He may regulate reproduction according to his needs, but he should not limit it unnecessarily. The intelligent action of mankind is a counterweight established by God among the forces of nature to restore their balance, and this further distinguishes men from animals, because man does such action with full awareness. But animals, too, contribute to this equilibrium, because the instinct of destruction has been given to them Aside from providing for their own survival, this instinct causes them to control the excessive and perhaps dangerous overpopulation of animal and plant species on which they feed."

694. What should be thought of methods meant to prevent reproduction for the purpose of satisfying sensuality?

"It demonstrates the predominance of the body over the soul, and how deeply man is influenced by matter."

4. Marriage and celibacy

695. Is marriage—the permanent union of two human beings—contrary to the law of nature?

"It represents progress in the journey of humanity."

696. What would be the effect of the abolition of marriage on human society?

"A return to the life of beasts."

The free and casual union of the sexes belongs to the state of nature. Marriage is one of the first signs of progress in human society, because it establishes a fraternal solidarity, being found in all cultures in various forms. Abolishing marriage would represent, therefore, the return of mankind to its infancy, and would place man even below certain animal species which provide him with examples of steady unions.

697. Does the absolute indissolubility of marriage belong to the laws of nature or is it only a human law?

"It is a human law that is quite contrary to the law of nature. But man may modify his laws; only those of nature cannot be changed." [a]

698. Is voluntary celibacy a state of perfection that is meritorious in God's sight?

"No, and those who live that way out of selfishness displease God and mislead others."

699. Isn't celibacy a sacrifice in the case of those people who wish to devote themselves entirely to the service of humanity?

"That is a very different case. I said 'out of selfishness.' Every personal sacrifice is meritorious when made for the general good. The greater the sacrifice, the greater the merit."

God cannot contradict Himself, nor regard as evil what He Himself has made, and consequently, He cannot attribute any merit to a violation of His law. Although celibacy in itself is not beneficial, it becomes so when it represents a sacrifice made on behalf of mankind, by the renunciation of the joys of family life. Every personal sacrifice made for the general good, and *without selfish ulterior motives*, raises man above his material condition.

5. Polygamy

700. Do the approximately equivalent sizes of male and female populations represent an indication of the proportion in which they ought to unite?

"Yes, for everything in nature has a purpose."

701. Which of the two, polygamy or monogamy, is more in accord with the laws of nature?

"Polygamy is a human law the abolition of which indicates social progress. In God's eyes, marriage should be based on the affection between two creatures who join in wedlock. In polygamy there is no true affection. There is only sensuality."

If polygamy were in accord with the laws of nature, it would be universal, something that would be materially impossible due to the roughly equivalent size of male and female populations. Polygamy must be considered as a use or legal institution appropriate to certain cultures, but which will gradually disappear with social progress.

■■■

[a] This is a notable foresight on the part of the Spirits. Divorce laws were uncommon in Europe at the time, and some countries would only enact such laws much later. Italy, for instance, would only introduce its first divorce legislation in 1970, more than a hundred years after *The Spirits' Book*. —Trans.

Chapter 5:
The Law of Preservation

1. Survival instinct

702. Is the survival instinct a law of nature?

"Without a doubt. All living creatures have it, regardless of their degree of intelligence. For some it is purely instinctual; for others it is intellectually internalized."

703. Why has God endowed all living beings with the survival instinct?

"Because all creatures must contribute to the designs of Providence. That is the reason why God has endowed them with the will to live. Besides, life is necessary for the perfecting of all beings; they sense this instinctively, without realizing it."

2. Means of survival

704. In giving man the will to live, has God always provided him with the means for that?

"Yes, and if man does not find those means, it is because he fails to recognize them. God could not have given man the need to live without also providing him with the means. He has thus endowed the Earth with the capacity to provide for all its inhabitants. Only that which is necessary is useful; that which is superfluous never is."

705. Why doesn't the Earth always produce enough to provide for man's needs?

"Ungrateful as he is, man neglects such an excellent mother! Frequently, he blames nature for the result of his own ineptitude or improvidence. The Earth would always produce what is needed if man knew how to be content with his lot. If the Earth does not provide for all his needs, it is because he wastes with extravagant whims many resources that should be employed in what is actually needed. Look at the Bedouin in the desert. He always finds enough to live on because he does not create imaginary needs. But when half of all that is produced is wasted on satisfying his fantasies, should man be surprised to find himself empty handed on the following day, and is there any reason for him to complain if he is to be found poverty-stricken in times of shortages? In truth, I tell you that nature is not improvident; it is man who does not know how to live in moderation."

706. By the expression *fruits of the Earth*, should we understand merely the products of the soil?

"The soil is the original source from which all other resources derive, because, ultimately, such resources are only a transformation of the products of the soil. For this reason you should understand *fruits of the Earth* to mean everything that man can enjoy on the planet."

707. The means of subsistence are frequently lacking for certain individuals, even as they are surrounded by abundance. Why is that the case?

"It is owing primarily to the selfishness of men, who do not always do what they should. Next, and most often, it is due to those individuals themselves. The expression 'seek and you shall find' does not mean that it is enough to simply cast your eyes around in order to find what you want. Instead, you must seek with ardor and perseverance, without laziness and without allowing yourselves to be discouraged by obstacles that are quite often no more than a way of putting your perseverance, patience and resolve to the test." (See #534)

If civilization multiplies our needs, it also multiplies our options of work and means of living, but one must agree that in this sense there is still much to be done. When civilization has accomplished its task, man will not be able to say that he lacks what he needs except due his own fault. Often, misfortune happens when people choose a path that nature has not traced out for them—and that is when they lack the intelligence required to succeed. There is a place in the sun for all, but on the condition that all take their own place and not that of others. Nature cannot be held responsible for the distortions of social organization and for the effects of greed and vanity.

We would have to be blind, however, if we did not recognize the progress that the most advanced nations have made in this sense. Thanks to the laudable efforts that philanthropy and science together have unceasingly put forth for the improvement of mankind's material conditions, and notwithstanding the constant increase in population, shortfalls in production have been for the most part attenuated. The most calamitous years bear no comparison to what they were in the past. Public sanitation, an element so essential to public health and welfare, but which was unknown to our ancestors, is now the object of careful attention. The unfortunate and suffering find shelter, and science and technology are now employed everywhere, increasing everyone's well-being. Can we say that we have finally reached perfection? Certainly not. But what has been accomplished so far gives us an idea of what can be done with determination, if man is sensible enough to seek contentment in the satisfaction of real and serious needs, rather than in the utopias that cause him to go back instead of forward.

708. Aren't there situations in which the means of subsistence do not depend simply on man's will, and where lack of the barest necessities is a result of circumstance?

"These situations are frequently cruel trials which man must endure, and to which he knows he will be exposed. His merit lies in his submission to God's will, if his intelligence does not provide him with the means to overcome such difficulties. If death must touch him, he should submit to it without murmuring, remembering that the hour of his deliverance has arrived, and *that despair at the final moment may cause him to forfeit the prize of his acceptance.*"

709. Have those who, in critical circumstances, found themselves forced to sacrifice their fellow beings to placate their hunger, committed a crime?

If it was a crime, was its gravity mitigated by the imperative to stay alive imposed by the survival instinct?

"I have already responded by saying that there is more merit in withstanding all the trials of life with courage and selflessness. In this case, there is a homicide and a crime against nature that shall be doubly punished."

710. On worlds where their physical constitution is more refined, do living beings need food?

"Yes, but their food is consistent with their nature. Their food would not be substantial enough for your crude digestive system. Similarly, they would not be able to assimilate yours."

3. Enjoyment of earthly goods

711. Is the use of earthly goods a right of all men?

"That right is a consequence of the need to stay alive. God would not impose a duty without providing the means to fulfill it."

712. Why has God made the enjoyment of material things attractive?

"To lead man to fulfill his mission, and also to test him with temptation."

— What is the purpose of such temptation?

"To develop his reason, so that it may steer him away from excesses."

If man had only been driven to use the fruits of the Earth because of their utility, his indifference could have jeopardized the harmony of the universe. God has given him the enticement of pleasure, and this in turn stimulates him to carry out the designs of Providence. However, through this same enticement, God also tests him with temptations that may lead him to abuse, something against which his reason must protect him.

713. Do enjoyments have boundaries established by nature?

"Yes, in order to show you the limit of what is necessary. By exceeding such limits, you go beyond the point of satiety, and end up punishing yourselves."

714. What should be thought of the man who seeks to satisfy his appetites through all kinds of excesses?

"Unfortunate creature! He should be pitied rather than envied, because he is very close to death."

— Is it physical or moral death that he is close to?

"Both."

He who seeks to satisfy his appetites through excesses of all kinds places himself below the level of the brute, who knows to stop when his needs have been satisfied. He disregards the reasoning capacity that God has given him for his guidance, and the greater his excesses, the greater is the dominion he allows his animal nature to exert over his spiritual nature. Simultaneously, illnesses, injuries, and the even the eventual death that may result from such abuse constitute punishments for this transgression of God's law.

4. Necessary and superfluous things

715. How can man know the limit of what is necessary?

"Those who are wise know it intuitively, but many only know it through costly experience."

716. Hasn't nature established the limit of what is necessary in our own physical organization?

"Yes, but man is insatiable. Nature has set the limits of his needs in his physical organization, but his vices alter his own constitution, creating for him needs which are not real or natural."

717. What should be thought of those who control the production of fruits of the earth and use them to provide for their own superfluous needs, at the expense of others who lack life's necessities?

"They do not understand God's law and will have to answer for the privations they inflicted on others."

The line between what is necessary and what is superfluous is not at all absolute. Civilization has created needs which do not exist in humanity's primitive phases, and the Spirits who dictated these precepts do not mean for civilized man to live like his primitive ancestors. Everything is relative, and it is up to reason to designate everything its proper place. Civilization develops the sense of morality, and, at the same time, the sentiment of charity, which leads people to mutually assist one another. Those whose lives impose privations on others take advantage of the benefits of civilization for their own profit. They only possess the varnish of civilization, just as there are people who possess merely the posturing of religion.

5. Voluntary privations, mortifications

718. Does the law of self-preservation drive us to provide for our own physical needs?

"Yes. Without energy and health, it is impossible to work."

719. Is man to blame for seeking his own welfare?

"Welfare is a natural desire. God only forbids abuse, because it is contrary to self-preservation. God does not consider it a crime for you to seek your own well-being, if it is not acquired at the expense of another, and if it does not weaken your moral or physical power."

720. Do voluntary privations for the purpose of an equally voluntary expiation have any merit in the eyes of God?

"Do good to others, and your merit shall be greater."

— Are there any meritorious voluntary privations?

"Yes, the privation of useless pleasures, because it disengages you from the pull of matter and lifts your soul. Merit lies in resisting the temptations that lead you to excesses and to the enjoyment of useless things. It also lies in taking from your own necessities in order to help those in greater need. If your privation is only a vain pretense, it is nothing but a mockery."

721. Ascetic mortifications have been practiced since ancient times, and among different cultures. Are they meritorious from any standpoint?

"Ask yourselves to *whom* a life of that sort is useful, and you will have your answer. If it only serves the one who practices it and if it hinders him from doing good to others, it represents selfishness, whatever pretext is used to embellish it. Enduring privation and working for others is the true mortification in accord with Christian charity."

722. Is the abstention from certain foods as prescribed in various cultures based on reason?

"Everything from which man can feed himself without harming his health is permitted. Legislators, however, may have prohibited certain foods with a useful objective in mind, and in order to lend greater credence to their laws, they have presented them as coming from God."

723. Does the consumption of meat or other products of animal slaughter go against the law of nature?

"Man's physical constitution requires that flesh nourishes flesh, otherwise man would perish. The law of self-preservation imposes on man the duty to preserve his energies and health, so that he may comply with the law of labor. Man should therefore eat according to the needs of his body."

724. Is the abstention from foods—animal or otherwise—meritorious as an expiation?

"Yes, if you abstain from something for the sake of others. But God cannot accept a mortification when there is no *serious* and *useful* privation. For this reason, those whose privation is merely an outward display are hypocrites." (See #720)

725. What are we to think of the mutilations practiced on the body of humans or animals?

"Why such a question? Ask yourselves again if such a thing is useful. What is useless cannot be pleasing to God, and what is harmful is always displeasing. You can be very sure that God is receptive only to sentiments that raise the soul toward Him. It is by practicing His laws, not by infringing them, that you can free yourselves from the yoke of matter."

726. If the sufferings of this world allow us to advance according to how well we endure them, may we also evolve through sufferings that we impose voluntarily on ourselves?

"Sufferings that can elevate you are only those which come upon you naturally, because they come from God. Voluntary sufferings serve no purpose if they do not entail any benefit for others. Do you believe that those who cut their lives short through superhuman hardships—like bonzes, fakirs, and fanatics of various sects—advance their progress thereby? Why don't they work for the benefit of their fellow creatures instead? Let them clothe the destitute, comfort those who mourn, work for those who are sick, and endure privations for the sake of the unfortunate; then their life will be useful and pleasing to God. When you only have yourselves in mind in the intentional hardships to which you subject yourselves, it denotes selfishness. When you suffer for others, it is the practice of charity. Such are the instructions of Christ."

727.   Since we should not voluntarily impose on ourselves sufferings that are of no use to others, should we nevertheless protect ourselves from those that we foresee or from those that threaten us?

"The survival instinct has been granted to all creatures in order to protect them from dangers and sufferings. Flog your spirit and not your body; mortify your pride and stifle your selfishness—this serpent that eats into your heart—and you will do more for your progress than through physical renouncements that do not belong in this century."

■■■

Chapter 6:
The Law of Destruction

1. Necessary and abusive destruction

728. Is destruction a law of nature?

"It is necessary for everything to be destroyed in order to be reborn and regenerated. What you call destruction is only a transformation the objective of which is the renovation and improvement of living creatures."

— Has the destruction instinct, then, been given to living beings for providential purposes?

"God's creatures are the instruments which He uses to accomplish His designs. Living beings kill each other for food, a process which accomplishes the double goal of maintaining the balance among populations—which might otherwise become excessive—as well as providing a use for the constituents of their external envelope. But it is only this envelope that is ever destroyed, and this envelope is only an accessory; the essential part of those beings lies in the intelligent principle which is indestructible and is refined in the course of the various transformations that it goes through."

729. If destruction is necessary for the regeneration of beings, why does nature surround them with the means of survival and preservation?

"To prevent their destruction from occurring before the appropriate time. Any destruction that occurs too soon delays the development of the intelligent principle. That is why God has endowed each being with the urge to stay alive and reproduce."

730. Since death should lead us to a better life and deliver us from the hardships of the present one, and since death should therefore be longed for rather than feared, why does man have an instinctive fear of death, thinking of it with apprehension?

"We have already said that man should seek to prolong his life in order to carry out his mission. That is why God has given him the survival instinct, which sustains him in his trials. Without it he would frequently yield to despondency. The secret voice that tells him to avoid death also says that he may yet do something more for his progress. Whenever danger threatens him, it warns him that he must take advantage of the time God has granted him. But the ungrateful more frequently thanks their lucky stars rather than their Creator."

731. Why has nature placed the agents of destruction side by side with the means of survival?

"The malady and the remedy are placed side by side. As we have already said, this is so in order to maintain equilibrium and to act as a counterbalance."

732. Is the need for destruction the same on all worlds?

"It is proportional to the material nature of each particular world, ceasing altogether on worlds of purer physical and moral standing. On worlds more advanced than yours, the conditions of existence are completely different."

733. Will the need of destruction always exist among men on Earth?

"The need of destruction diminishes among men as their spirit gains ascendancy over matter. That is why the aversion to destruction grows in tandem with intellectual and moral development."

734. In his present state, does man have an unlimited right to kill animals?

"That right is limited to the need of providing for his own food and safety. Abuse has never been a right."

735. What about destruction that exceeds the limits of need and safety: hunting, for instance, when it has no other objective than the pleasure of destroying needlessly?

"It is a predominance of man's animal nature over his spiritual nature. All destruction that exceeds the limits of necessity is a violation of the law of God. Animals only kill to satisfy their needs, but man, who possesses free will, destroys without need. He shall be called to account for abusing the freedom that was granted to him, because he yields to evil instincts in such instances."

736. Do those cultures that carry their scrupulousness regarding the destruction of animals to an extreme have any special merit?

"This behavior represents an exaggeration of a sentiment that is in itself laudable, but it may become detrimental, and its merit may end up being offset by other kinds of abuse that ensue. They act more out of superstitious fear than true kindness."

2. Natural disasters

737. For what purpose does God inflict natural disasters on mankind?

"To compel mankind to advance more quickly. Haven't we said that destruction is necessary for the moral regeneration of spirits, who reach a new level of perfection with each new existence? You must see the end in order to appreciate the results. You only judge such things from your own personal vantage point, and you call them calamities because of the damage they cause you. However, these hardships are often necessary in order to make things arrive at a better state of affairs more quickly, accomplishing in a few years that which would otherwise require many centuries." (See #744)

738. Couldn't God employ other methods instead of destructive disasters for the improvement of mankind?

"Yes, and He employs them every day, since God has given each man the means of advancing through knowledge of good and evil. It is man who does not take advantage of the opportunities, deserving to be chastised in his pride and to be made aware of his own weakness."

—   But in such disasters the good man perishes alongside the wicked. Is that just?

"During life man relates everything to his physical life, but after death he thinks differently. As we have already stated, the life of the body is almost nothing: a century in your world is but *a flash in eternity*. Therefore, sufferings that may last a few of your months or days are nothing, representing only a lesson that will be useful for you in the future. The spirit world is the real one, preexisting and outlasting everything else. (See #85) Spirits represent the progeny of God and are the objects of His concern. Bodies are no more than guises they don when making their appearance in the world. Great calamities that decimate men are similar to times of war, when soldiers' uniforms are worn out, torn, or lost. A general is concerned about his soldiers, not about their uniforms."

—   But aren't the victims of these disasters actual victims nonetheless?

"If you considered life itself, and how insignificant it is in comparison with the infinite, you would attach less importance to this existence. In another life, those victims will find abundant compensation for their sufferings, if they endure them without complaining."

> Whether death results from a calamity or from an ordinary cause, we cannot escape it when the hour of our departure has arrived. The only difference is that, in the case of the former, a greater number of souls depart at the same time.
>
> If we could raise our thought so as to encompass all mankind in a single glance, such terrible disasters would seem no more than short-lived storms in the journey of the world.

739. Are natural disasters useful from a physical point of view, notwithstanding the hardships they entail?

"Yes, they sometimes modify the conditions of a region, but the good they bring about is usually only felt by future generations."

740. Couldn't disasters also represent moral trials for mankind, by exposing men to the most difficult needs?

"Disasters are trials that provide man with an opportunity to use his intelligence and to demonstrate his patience and fortitude before the will of God. At the same time, calamities enable him to develop the sentiments of selflessness, detachment, and love for his neighbor, if he is not dominated by selfishness."

741. Is man able to avert the calamities that afflict him?

"Yes, some of them, but not as is generally believed. Many calamities are the consequences of man's own negligence. As he acquires knowledge and experience, he is able to avert them, that is, to prevent them if he is able to figure out their cause. Among the ills that afflict mankind, however, there are those of a general nature that belong to the designs of Providence, and from which all individuals receive, to a greater or lesser extent, the share for which they are responsible. They can do nothing about them except show acceptance before the will of God. But man often aggravates his suffering through his carelessness."

> Among the destructive calamities which are natural and independent of human action we can count, first of all, plagues, famine, floods, and crop-destroying storms. But isn't it true that mankind found the means to prevent, or at least mitigate, such disasters, in science and technology, in agricultural improvements such as irrigation and crop rotation, and in the widespread implementation of public sanitation? Aren't certain regions that were formerly regularly affected by terrible disasters largely safe nowadays? Therefore, what will man not accomplish toward his material well-being when he learns to make use of all the potential of his intelligence, and when, caring for his own survival, he learns to combine it with a sentiment of true charity for his fellow beings? (See #707)

3. Wars

742. What leads man to war?

"The predominance of the animal over the spiritual nature, and the yielding to his passions. In the state of barbarity, nations only know the right of the strongest, and that is why war is a normal state for them. As man evolves, war becomes less frequent, as he avoids its causes, and when war does become necessary, he knows how to temper it with compassion."

743. Will war someday disappear from Earth?

"Yes, when men understand justice and practice God's law. Then, people of all nations will live as brothers and sisters."

744. What has been the goal of Providence in making war necessary?

"Freedom and progress."

—   If war is meant to bring freedom, why is it that enslavement has frequently been its goal and result?

"Such enslavement is temporary and *challenges* a nation, making it evolve more quickly."

745. What is to be thought of the one who incites war for his own profit?

"He is truly guilty and will need *many incarnations* to expiate all the murders he is responsible for, because he will have to answer for every man killed to satisfy his ambition."

4. Murder

746. Is murder a crime in God's sight?

"Yes, a great crime. For he who takes the life of his fellow creature cuts short *a life of expiation or mission*. Therein is the evil.

747. Is there always the same degree of guilt in murder?

"We have already said: 'God is just.' He judges the intention rather than the deed."

748. Does God excuse murder in cases of self-defense?

"A true necessity alone can serve as an excuse. However, if one can save one's life without having to take that of the aggressor, one must do so."

749. Is man culpable for the murders he commits during war?

"Not when compelled by the force of circumstance. But he is responsible for the cruelties he commits. Similarly, his acts of compassion will also be taken into account."

750. Which one is a more serious crime in the eyes of God, parricide or infanticide?

"They are equally serious, for all crime is crime."

751. Why is infanticide a custom endorsed by the legislation of certain nations that are already intellectually advanced?

"Intellectual development does not necessarily go hand-in-hand with moral development. A spirit of superior intelligence may be evil, if he has lived many lives developing his intellect but without purifying his soul: all he has acquired is knowledge."

5. Cruelty

752. May we associate cruelty with the instinct of destruction?

"It is the instinct of destruction in its worst form. Even though destruction may be at times necessary, cruelty never is. It is always the result of an evil nature."

753. Why is cruelty the dominant characteristic of primitive cultures?

"Among primitive cultures—as you call them—matter prevails over spirit. They yield to their brutish instincts, and since they do not have other needs beyond those of the body, they only care about their own survival. This is what makes them cruel in general. Moreover, nations of imperfect development are under the dominion of equally imperfect spirits, who remain sympathetic to them, until more highly advanced nations come to extinguish or weaken their influence."

754. Doesn't cruelty result from the absence of the sense of morality?

"You may say that the sense of morality is not developed, but do not say that it is absent, because it exists in principle in all human beings. [a] This sense of morality is what will later transform them into good and humane individuals. Therefore, it does exist in primitive man, but incipient as the scent of a flower bud before it comes into full bloom."

All faculties exist in men in a rudimentary or latent state. They develop as circumstances are more or less favorable to them. The excessive development of some of them inhibits or neutralizes the development of others. The overexcitement of material instincts stifles, as it were, the moral sense. Conversely, the development of the moral sense gradually weakens those instincts which are purely animal.

755. Why do we sometimes find people as cruel as a savage in the midst of the most advanced civilizations?

"For the same reason that on a tree laden with good fruit there may be a withered few. They may be considered savages who have nothing of civilization except for the outward appearance. They are wolves who have strayed into the midst of the sheep. They are backward spirits, typical of lower orders, who may incarnate among advanced people hoping to advance themselves in turn. However, if the trial proves too challenging, their primitive nature prevails."

756. Will the society of the good someday be purged of evildoers?

"Mankind is evolving. Those who are under the dominion of evil instincts, and who are out of place among good people, will gradually disappear, as the defective grain is separated from the good when wheat is winnowed. They shall be born again in another corporeal envelope, and, as they acquire more experience, they will arrive at a better understanding of good and evil. You have an example of this in the plants and animals which man has learned to perfect, by imparting new qualities to them. Accordingly, it is only after many generations that perfection is achieved. This illustrates man's many existences."

6. Dueling

757. Can dueling be considered a legitimate case of self-defense?

"No, it is murder, an absurd practice worthy of barbarians. In a more advanced and *moral* civilization, people will understand that dueling is as foolish as the trial by combat of ancient times, which was considered to be 'the judgment of God.' " [b]

758. Can dueling be considered murder on the part of him who, aware of his own weakness, is almost certain to be killed?

"It is suicide."

— And when the odds are equal, is it murder or suicide?

"It is both."

In all cases, even in those in which the odds are equal, the dueler is guilty. First, because he makes an attempt on the life of a fellow man in a coldblooded and deliberate fashion. Second, because he exposes his own life unnecessarily, and without benefit to anyone.

759. In dueling, what is the value of what is called *the point of honor*?

"That of pride and vanity, two ulcers of mankind."

— But aren't there cases where honor really is at stake, and where refusal would represent cowardice?

"It depends on customs and uses. Each country and age has a different way of seeing such matters. However, when men have advanced morally, they will understand that the true point of honor lies above earthly passions, and that it is neither by killing nor by being killed that one can right a wrong."

There is more dignity and true honor in recognizing our wrongdoing if we are wrong, or in forgiving the opponent if we are right, and, in all cases, in not paying heed to insults that cannot affect us.

7. Death penalty

760. Will capital punishment ever be abolished by human law?

"The death penalty will assuredly disappear and its suppression will mark progress for mankind. When men become better informed, capital punishment will be completely abolished on Earth. Men will no longer need to judge each other. I speak of a time which is still a long way ahead of you."

Social progress still leaves much to be desired, but it would be unfair to modern society if we did not recognize progress in the restrictions imposed on the death penalty in more advanced nations, and the crimes to which its application is restricted. If we compare the safeguards of due process, put in place to protect the accused, and the relative compassion with which the accused are treated even when found guilty, with the practices of a not-too-distant past, we cannot fail to recognize the progress made by mankind.

761. The law of preservation gives man the right to defend his life. Doesn't this right apply when a dangerous member of society is eliminated?

"There are means of protecting yourselves from danger other than killing. Besides, it is necessary to open the door of repentance to the offender, rather than close it."

762. Capital punishment may be one day banned from civilized societies, but was it not necessary in less-advanced ages?

"*Necessary* is not the right word. Man always believes that something is necessary when he cannot find anything more appropriate. But as he becomes more knowledgeable, he better understands that which is just or unjust, and then rejects the excesses committed in the name of justice in times of ignorance."

763. Are the restrictions on the cases in which the death penalty is applied an indication of the progress of civilization?

"Can you doubt it? Doesn't your mind revolt on reading the recital of human butcheries that were formerly carried out in the name of justice, and often in honor of God? Are you not disgusted by the tortures inflicted on the condemned, or even on the accused, in order to wring from him, through excruciating pain, the confession of a crime which he very often did not commit? Well, if you had lived in those times, you would have considered this very natural; and, had you been a judge, you would perhaps have done the same. It is thus that what seemed to be right at a given time seems barbaric at another. The laws of God alone are eternal. Human laws change with progress, and they will change still, up until they have been brought in harmony with the laws of God."

764. Jesus said, "Whoever kills by the sword shall perish by the sword." Don't these words represent an endorsement of the "eye for an eye" principle? And isn't the death imposed on the murderer an application of this penalty?

"Beware, because you are as mistaken about these words *as you are about many others.* The law of retaliation is God's justice alone. It is God Himself who applies it. You all suffer this penalty at every moment because you are punished as you have erred, either in this life *or in another.* He who has caused his fellow men to suffer shall be in a situation in which he himself will face the same suffering. This is the meaning of Jesus's words.

"Didn't he also tell you to forgive your enemies? And didn't he teach you to pray that God may forgive your trespasses as you forgive those who have trespassed against you? That is to say, exactly *in proportion as you have forgiven?* Understand this well."

765. What is to be thought of the infliction of the death penalty in the name of God?

"It is usurping God's place in the practice of justice. Those who act that way reveal how far they are from knowing God, and how much they still have to atone for. The death penalty is a crime when it is applied in the name of God, and those who apply it will be held accountable for such murders."

■■■

[a] This remark precedes by more than a century the study of inequity aversion that confirmed the existence of such an inborn sense of morality in infants, and even in certain higher mammals. See S. Sloane, R. Baillargeon, and D. Premack, "Do Infants Have a Sense of Fairness?," *Psychological Science* 23, no. 2 (January, 2012): 196–204; and S. F. Brosnan and F. B. M. de Waal, "Monkeys reject unequal pay," *Nature*, no. 425 (September 2003): 297–299. —Trans.

[b] A duel is an arranged engagement in combat between two people, with matched weapons, fought with swords or pistols. Duels were fought not so much in order to kill an opponent as to gain *satisfaction*, in other words, to restore one's honor by demonstrating the disposition to risk one's life for it, and, as such, the tradition of

dueling was originally reserved for the male members of nobility, extending to those of the upper classes in general, in the modern era. Dueling became rarer after the turn of the twentieth century, having being outlawed in most Western democracies before WWI. France was one of the last countries to ban it, the last known duel having taken place there in 1967, between two members of the parliament. —Trans.

Chapter 7:
The Law of Society

1. Necessity of life in society

766. Is life in society a natural law?

"Certainly. God has created man to live in society. Otherwise, it would have been pointless for God to have endowed him with speech and all the other faculties necessary for a life of relationship."

767. Is absolute isolation contrary to the law of nature?

"Yes, because men instinctively seek to live in society, and because everybody must cooperate in the progress of mankind by mutually helping each other."

768. In seeking to live in society, does man simply obey a personal drive, or is there a wider providential purpose in it?

"Man must progress. He cannot do so alone, however, because there are faculties that he lacks, creating the need for the exchange of experiences with others. In isolation, man becomes stultified and languishes."

No single person possesses all the abilities needed. It is through social interaction that individuals complete one another in order to ensure their own well-being and to advance. Thus, by depending on one another, all individuals have been created to live in society, and not in isolation.

2. Life of isolation, vow of silence

769. We can understand that, as a general principle, life in society is founded on the laws of nature. But since all tastes are also natural, why should the inclination for absolute isolation be condemned if someone finds satisfaction in it?

"Satisfaction of the selfish. There are also those who find satisfaction in getting drunk. Do you approve of that? God cannot consider as pleasing the life in which a man condemns himself to being useful to no one."

770. What is to be thought of those who live in absolute seclusion in order to escape pernicious contact with the world?

"They are doubly selfish."

—   But if such seclusion has as its purpose atonement through the imposition of harsh privations, would it not be meritorious?

"Doing mostly good rather than evil is the best atonement. Through such seclusion they avoid one evil only to fall into another, since they neglect the law of love and charity."

771. What to think of those who renounce the world in order to devote themselves to the relief of those who suffer?

"They raise themselves through humility. They have the double merit of placing themselves above material pleasures, and of doing good by fulfilling the law of labor."

—   How about those who withdraw to seek the quietude required for certain types of labor?

"That is not the absolute withdrawal of the selfish individual. They do not isolate themselves from society, but rather work for it."

772. What is to be thought of the vow of silence that has been prescribed by certain sects since the earliest eras?

"You might as well ask whether speech is natural, and why God has made it available. God condemns the abuse rather than the use of the faculties granted by Him. Nonetheless, silence can be useful at times, because it facilitates your inner recollection. Your spirit becomes freer and can then enter into communication with good spirits. A *vow* of silence, however, is foolishness. Undoubtedly, those who regard such privations as virtuous acts have good intentions, but they are mistaken by not sufficiently understanding the true laws of God."

The vow of absolute silence, like the vow of isolation, deprives man of the social interactions that can provide him with opportunities to do good and to comply with the law of progress.

3. Family ties

773. Why is it that, among animals, parents and offspring do not recognize one another when the latter no longer need care?

"Animals live a material life, not a moral life. A mother's tenderness for her litter derives from the urge to protect the creatures she gave birth to. When they become self-sufficient, her task is complete, and nature requires no more of her. She thus abandons them in order to take care of her future offspring."

774. There are people who infer from the fact that animals abandon their offspring that family ties among humans are merely a result of social customs and not a law of nature. What should be thought of this?

"Man has a destiny which is different from that of animals, so why do you always want to rank them together? For humans, there is something beyond physical needs; there is the need to progress. Social ties are necessary for progress, and family ties strengthen social ties. Family ties are therefore a law of nature. God has thus willed that humans learn to love one another as brothers and sisters." (See #205)

775. What would be the effect on society of the weakening of family ties?

"The resurgence of selfishness."

■■■

Chapter 8:
The Law of Progress

1. State of nature

776. Are the *state of nature* and *natural law* the same thing? [a]

"No, the state of nature is the primitive state. Civilization is not compatible with the state of nature, whereas natural law contributes to the progress of humanity."

> The state of nature represents the infancy of humanity, the starting point for its intellectual and moral development. Being perfectible and containing the seed of his own improvement within himself, man is not meant to live forever in the state of nature, just as he is not meant to live forever in infancy. The state of nature is transitory, and man outgrows it through progress and civilization. Natural law, on the other hand, rules humanity as a whole, and man advances as he better grasps and practices this law.

777. Having fewer needs in the state of nature, man does not suffer all the tribulations that he creates for himself in a more advanced state. What should we think of the opinion of those who regard the state of nature as the state of perfect happiness on Earth?

"So it goes! That would represent the happiness of the brute—there are those who understand no other type of happiness. That would mean to be happy in the fashion of beasts. Children, too, are happier than grownups."

778. Could man go back to the state of nature?

"No, man must progress incessantly; he cannot return to his infancy. He advances, because God has willed it so. To believe that he could go back to his primitive condition would be to contradict the law of progress."

2. March of progress

779. Does man find in himself the power to move onwards, or is progress nothing more than the result of education?

"He advances naturally by himself, but not everybody advances at the same rate or in the same way. The most advanced ought to help others to progress, through social interaction."

780. Does moral progress always follow intellectual progress?

"It is its consequence, but it does not always follow it *immediately*." (See #192 and #365)

—   How can intellectual progress lead to moral progress?

"By making man understand good and evil, because then he can choose between the two. The development of free will follows the development of intelligence, increasing man's responsibility for his acts."

—   Then how can it be that the most developed nations are often the most perverted?

"Reaching a complete progress is the goal, but nations, like individuals, only achieve it gradually. Until they have developed their moral sense, they may still use their intelligence to do evil. Morality and intelligence are two forces that only balance each other over time." (See #365 and #751)

781. Is man ever allowed to halt the march of progress?

"No, but he may hinder it sometimes."

—   What is to be thought of those who attempt to halt the march of progress and cause mankind to move backwards?

"Sorry souls that will be punished by God! They shall be overthrown by the very torrent they attempt to arrest."

Because progress is a condition of human nature, no one has the power to oppose it. It is a *living force* that flawed laws may hinder, but not suppress. When these laws become incompatible with progress, it destroys them, along with all of those who attempt to uphold the superseded legislation. This will continue to be the case until man harmonizes his laws with the laws of God, which aim at the good of all, as opposed to those laws that are made to favor the strong at the expense of the weak.

782. Aren't there those who thwart progress out of good faith, in the belief that they are helping it instead, because from their own point of view they often see progress where it does not in fact exist?

"They represent a small stone under the wheel of a large carriage, unable to prevent it from advancing."

783. Does the perfecting of mankind always follow a progressive and slow march?

"There is the regular and slow progress that results from the force of things. However, when a nation does not advance quickly enough, God may occasionally produce a physical or moral shock that hastens its transformation."

Man cannot remain perpetually in ignorance, because he must reach the goal marked out for him by Providence; he is enlightened by the force of things. Moral and social revolutions are prepared by the gradual diffusion of ideas. They go on to take root, and in time suddenly burst forth, toppling the crumbling edifice of the past, which is no longer in harmony with the new needs and aspirations.

Man does not usually perceive in such commotions anything other than the momentary disorder and confusion that affect his own material interests. But he who extends his vision beyond the circle of his immediate interest admires the providential workings that bring good out of evil, like storms that cleanse the atmosphere after having disturbed it.

784. Man's perversity is rather great. Does it not seem that he is going backwards instead of advancing, at least from a moral standpoint?

"You are mistaken. Observe the whole attentively and you will see that mankind advances through a better understanding of what constitutes evil, constantly curtailing existing excesses. The persistence of evil is instrumental in making understood the necessity of doing good and promoting reforms."

785. What is the greatest obstacle to progress?

"Pride and selfishness. I refer to moral progress, since intellectual progress is always happening. Intellectual progress, indeed, seems at first to give redoubled activity to those vices, by stimulating ambition and the love of riches, which in turn, however, motivate man to carry out the studies that enlighten his spirit. It is thus that all things are linked together, in the moral world as in the physical world, and that good can be born even from evil. But this state of things shall only last for a while. It will change as man better understands that, beyond the enjoyment of earthly possessions, lies an infinitely greater and longer-lasting bliss." (See "Selfishness", chapter 12)

> There are two kinds of progress that mutually reinforce each other, but which do not necessarily advance at the same pace: intellectual progress and moral progress. In this century, intellectual progress among civilized nations has received every conceivable incentive. It has thus reached an unprecedented development. Much is needed for moral progress to reach the same level, but if we compare social mores of today to those of a few centuries ago, we must acknowledge the progress accomplished. Then why should the upward trend of moral progress be interrupted any more than that of intelligence? Why should there not be as great a difference in morality between the nineteenth and twenty-fourth centuries as between the morality of the fourteenth and nineteenth? To doubt this would be to assume that humanity has reached the apex of perfection—which would be absurd—or that it is not morally perfectible—which is disproved by experience.

3. Nations in decline

786. History shows many nations which, after being subject to deranging shocks, relapsed into barbarity. Where is progress to be found in such cases?

"When your house risks collapsing, you tear it down in order to build one which is stronger and more comfortable. Until it is rebuilt, however, there is trouble and confusion in your dwelling.

"Understand it further: suppose you were poor and lived in a hut. But later you became rich and moved to a mansion. Then comes this old fellow, poor as you formerly were, and takes your place in the hut, rather pleased in so doing, for, previously, he had no shelter. Similarly, the spirits now incarnated in those declining nations are no longer those who were part of them during their time of splendor. Those who have progressed moved into more perfect dwellings, while less advanced spirits have taken their place. In time, the latter too shall eventually leave."

787. Aren't there nations that by their very nature rebel against progress?

"Yes, but they gradually disappear, *physically*."

—   What will be the fate of the souls who animate them?

"Like all other souls, they will finally arrive at perfection by going through many existences. God rejects no one."

—   So, the most civilized men may have been savages and cannibals, then?

"You, yourself have been such, more than once, before becoming who you are now."

788. A people or nation is a collective individuality that goes through childhood, adulthood, and decrepitude. Shouldn't this truth confirmed by history make us think that the most advanced nations of this century will decline and end, just as those of the past?

"Nations that only live a material existence, and whose greatness is based only on power and territorial expansion, are born, grow, and die out, because the strength of a nation is depleted just like that of an individual. If their selfish laws obstruct the light of wisdom and charity, nations die out, because light eliminates darkness and charity overthrows selfishness. But there is for nations, as for an individual, the life of the soul. Those whose laws are in harmony with the eternal laws of the Creator shall live on and become torchbearers for other nations."

789. Will progress eventually unite all the peoples of the Earth into a single nation?

"Not into a single nation, as that would be impossible, because the diversity of climates gives rise to the numerous customs and needs that characterize different cultures. Each shall require laws appropriate to its particular habits and needs. But charity knows nothing of latitudes, and makes no distinction between the various shades of skin. When the law of God becomes the foundation of human law, charity will be practiced among nations, as among men. All shall then live in peaceful happiness, because no man will try to deceive his neighbor, or to live at his expense."

Humanity progresses by means of individuals who gradually advance, educating themselves. As these individuals grow in number, they take the lead and bring others along. Men of genius arise among them from time to time and provide a further impulse forward, followed by individuals invested with authority, instruments of God that they are, allowing mankind to advance in just a few years the equivalent of many centuries.

The progress of nations further underscores the justice of reincarnation. The admirable efforts of its leading men help a nation advance morally and intellectually. The nation thus transformed will surely be happier both in this world and in the next. However, during its slow journey through the centuries, thousands of individuals die every day. What is the fate of all of those who perish along the way? Does their relative inferiority deprive them of the joy reserved for those who arrive last? Or is their happiness relative? The justice of God could not endorse such an inequity. Through the plurality of existences, the right to happiness is available to all, for no one is denied the ability to advance. Those who lived in primitive eras are able to come back in the course of the development of civilization, either in the same nation or in another one. In this way, all may benefit from the march forward.

But there is another problem posed by the concept of one single existence. According to this theory, the soul is created at the moment of birth. If a man is more advanced than others, it is because God has created a more advanced soul for him. Why such a favor? Why would this individual, who has not lived any longer than anyone else—and often less time, in fact—deserve to be awarded superior abilities?

But the main hurdle is not there. A nation goes, over the period of a thousand years, from barbarity to civilization. If men could live a thousand years, one could conceive that over that interval they would have time to progress. Continuously, however, men of all ages die, their numbers being renewed incessantly, so that multitudes appear and disappear every day. After a thousand years, no trace remains of the old inhabitants. The primitive nation is now civilized. Who has accomplished progress in this process? The individuals who used to be barbarians? But those already died long ago. Is it the newly-arrived? But if their souls were created at the time of their birth, they could not have existed during the time of barbarity, and we would consequently have to recognize that *the efforts made to civilize a people do not have the power to improve imperfect souls, but only to induce God to create souls that are more advanced.*

Let us compare this theory of progress with the one proposed by the Spirits. The souls that come into a nation in its period of civilization have had their infancy, like all the others, but *they have lived already*, and have brought with them the progress previously accomplished. They come attracted by an environment they have affinity with, suited to their present degree of advancement. Consequently, the enterprise of civilization results not in the creation of souls of a better quality, but in the attraction of the souls that have already improved, be it by having lived in that particular nation in its earlier stages, or by having advanced elsewhere. Here rests the key to the progress of all humanity. When all nations reach the same sense of rectitude, the Earth will be the abode solely of good spirits living in fraternal unity, whereas bad spirits, having fallen behind, will have been driven to less evolved worlds, in search of an environment that suits them, until they make themselves worthy to come back to our transformed world.

The usual theory has the additional consequence that social development efforts only benefit current and future generations, but are meaningless for past generations, who were unfortunate for having arrived too soon, accomplishing whatever they could within an environment of barbarity. According to the teachings of the Spirits, however, any progress accomplished later on also benefits those earlier generations, who are reborn into better conditions, and can then perfect themselves in the midst of civilization.

4. Civilization

790. Does civilization represent progress or, as some philosophers claim, the decadence of humanity?

"Incomplete progress. Man does not go abruptly from infancy to adulthood."

— Is it reasonable to condemn civilization?

"Instead, condemn those who abuse it, rather than the work of God."

791. Will civilization reach one day a level of perfection where the evils it has produced will disappear?

"Yes, when the sense of morality is as developed as that of intelligence. The fruit cannot come before the flower."

792. Why doesn't civilization immediately bring about all the good it may produce?

"Because men are not as yet either ready or willing to achieve that good."

— Wouldn't it also be because, by creating new needs, civilization stimulates new passions?

"Yes, and because the faculties of a spirit do not develop simultaneously—everything takes time. You cannot expect perfect results from an incomplete civilization." (See #751–780)

793. By what signs may one recognize a completed civilization?

"You may recognize it by its moral development. You believe yourselves to be very advanced because you have made great discoveries and wonderful inventions, and because you are better lodged and better clothed than primitive men. However, you will only have the right to truly call yourselves civilized when you have finally banished from your society the vices that dishonor it, and when you finally live as brothers and sisters by practicing Christian charity. Until then, you are really no more than relatively educated nations that have only gone through the first phase of civilization."

Civilization has its degrees like everything else. An incomplete civilization is in a state of transition that engenders particular types of evil, unknown in the primitive state. But it constitutes nonetheless a natural and necessary progress, which brings with itself the remedy for the very evils it creates. As civilization perfects itself, it extinguishes some of the evils it has produced, and all remaining evils shall eventually disappear with moral progress.

Of two nations that have reached the top of the social hierarchy, the one that may be called the more civilized, in the true sense of the word, is the one where selfishness, greed, and pride are to be found least frequently. Where interests are more intellectual and moral than material. Where intelligence can develop with more freedom, and where there is more kindness, generosity, good faith, and mutual benevolence. Where the prejudices of caste and birth are not entrenched, for such prejudices are incompatible with true love for one's neighbor. Where laws do not grant any special privilege, and are the same for everyone irrespective of their social standing. Where justice is applied most impartially and where the weak always find protection against the strong. Where human life, beliefs, and opinions are better respected. Where there are fewer unhappy individuals. Finally, where men of goodwill are always sure they will not lack the minimum necessary to live.

5. Progress of human legislation

794. Could society be governed by natural law alone, without having to resort to human laws?

"It could, if men understood natural law well enough, and if they had the will to practice it, then such law would be sufficient. Society has its demands, however, resulting in the need for special laws."

795. What causes the instability of human laws?

"In times of barbarity, the strongest are the ones who make the laws, and they do it to their own advantage. It becomes necessary to modify those laws as men better understand justice. Human laws become more stable as they move toward true justice, that is to say, to the extent that they become more equitable, conforming to natural law."

Civilization has created for men new demands that are related to the social position they occupy. It has been necessary to regulate the rights and duties of such positions through human laws. Under the influence of their passions, however, men have often created imaginary rights and duties that go against natural law. Such artificial rights and duties are repealed from their legislation, as society progresses. Natural law is unchangeable and is always the same for everyone. Human law is variable and temporary, this being the only reason why it could have endorsed the right of the strongest during the infancy of mankind.

796. Aren't stringent criminal laws a necessity in the present state of society?

"A depraved society certainly needs more stringent laws. Unfortunately, such laws are meant to punish a crime after it has already been committed, rather than to eliminate its root cause. Only education can reform mankind, which will then no longer need such severe laws."

797. How can mankind be driven to reform its legislation?

"This will happen naturally by the force of circumstances and by the influence of virtuous people who shall guide it along the path of progress. Much of it has already been improved, and still much more of it shall be renewed in the future. Wait!"

6. Influence of Spiritism on progress

798. Will Spiritism become a common belief or will it be shared only by a few?

"It will certainly become a common belief and will mark a new era in the history of humanity, for it belongs to the natural order of things, and the time has come for it to rank among the fields of human knowledge. It will nevertheless have to withstand great battles, more against personal interests than against conviction, because it's clear that there are people interested in opposing it, some out of self-importance, others from purely material reasons. Its adversaries, however, becoming more and more isolated, will eventually concede, lest they risk ridicule."

Ideas are only transformed in the long run, never abruptly. They weaken from generation to generation, and end up disappearing along with those who have professed them, who in their turn are replaced by other individuals imbued with new principles, as happens with political ideas. Consider, for example, paganism. There are few today who profess such religious ideas; nevertheless, many centuries after the advent of Christianity, there were still traces of paganism left that only the complete renewal of nations was able to erase. It will be the same with Spiritism. It has made considerable progress, but for a number of generations there will still be a wave of incredulity that only time will erase. However, its journey will be faster than that of Christianity, because it is Christianity itself that opens the way and provides support for Spiritism. Christianity had to destroy; Spiritism has only to build.

799. How can Spiritism contribute to progress?

"By destroying materialism, one of the sores of society, it makes men understand where their true interests lie. The future life being no longer veiled by doubt, man will understand more clearly that he can guarantee his future through his current conduct. By destroying the prejudices of sects, castes, and colors, it teaches people the great solidarity that must unite them as brothers and sisters."

800. Should we not fear that Spiritism may not be able to triumph over man's negligence and over his attachment to material things?

"It would be to know very little about men to suppose that any cause could transform them as if by magic. Ideas change little by little, according to each individual, and several generations are needed to completely erase old habits. Transformation, therefore, can only be realized with time, gradually and progressively. With each new generation a part of the veil is lifted, and Spiritism has now come to tear it apart completely. But meanwhile, if it should do no more than correct one man's imperfection, it would lead him to take a step forward, and would thus do him a great good, because taking that first step makes all his subsequent steps easier."

801. Why haven't the Spirits taught from the earliest times what they teach today?

"You do not teach children the same things you teach adults, just as you do not give newborns food they cannot digest. There is a time for everything. Spirits have taught many things that men either did not understand or misconstrued, but which they are now capable of understanding. Their teachings, although incomplete, prepared the ground to receive the seed which is now about to bear fruit."

802. Since Spiritism must represent a milestone in the progress of humanity, why don't the Spirits accelerate this process through manifestations so widespread and evident that the most incredulous would be convinced?

"You wish for miracles, but God sows miracles by the handful right under your feet, yet you still have many who reject them. Did Christ himself convince his contemporaries by the wonders he performed? Don't you see, even today, those who deny the most obvious facts occurring under their very eyes? Aren't there those who say that they would not believe something, even if they saw it with their eyes? No, it is not by the production of miracles that God wishes to guide mankind. In his goodness, God wishes to leave to each one the merit of being convinced through reason."

■■■

[a] This is a direct inquiry into the validity of the concept of *state of nature*, variously defined by a number of philosophers, including Thomas Hobbes (1588–1679), John Locke (1632–1704), Montesquieu (1689–1755), David Hume (1711–1776) and Jean-Jacques Rousseau (1712–1778). The concept of *state of nature* is used in philosophy and political theory to denote the hypothetical conditions of human life before civil societies were structured. —Trans.

Chapter 9:
The Law of Equality

1. Natural equality

803. Are all men equal before God?

"Yes, all tend toward the same goal, and God has made His laws for everyone. You often say, 'The sun shines on everyone,' and, in so doing, you enunciate a greater and more general truth than you might think."

All are subject to the same laws of nature, born equally fragile and subject to the same sufferings. The body of the rich decomposes like that of the poor. Therefore, God has not granted a natural superiority to anyone in regard to either birth or death: all are equal before God.

2. Inequality of aptitudes

804. Why hasn't God endowed everyone with the same aptitudes?

"God has created all spirits equal, but each has lived over a longer or shorter period of time, and has consequently developed their aptitudes to varying degrees. The difference stems from the amount of experience acquired and their degree of resolve—their free will. Thus, some advance more rapidly, developing a wider range of aptitudes. A combination of aptitudes is necessary so that all may contribute to the designs of Providence within the limits of their physical and intellectual powers: the task that cannot be undertaken by one person is carried out by another, so that everyone has a useful role to play. Furthermore, since all worlds *are united in solidarity*, it is necessary for the inhabitants of more highly evolved worlds, created in general before yours, to come and live here in order to set an example for you." (See #361)

805. In passing from a superior world to a less-evolved one, does a spirit keep all his acquired faculties intact?

"Yes, we have already told you that the spirit cannot go back in the progress accomplished. In his spirit state he may choose a cruder envelope or a position which is more precarious than one he had before, but always to serve him as a lesson and to help him advance." (See #180)

Thus, the diversity of aptitudes among individuals is not related to the intrinsic nature of their creation, but to the degree of perfection they have reached as spirits throughout several incarnations. God has not, therefore, created an inequality of faculties, but has allowed spirits of different degrees of development to be in contact with one another, so that those who are more evolved can help in the progress of the less advanced, and also so that all men, realizing that they mutually need one another, may appreciate the law of charity that is to unite them.

3. Social inequality

806. Is the inequality of social conditions a law of nature?

"No, it is the work of man, not of God."

— Will this inequality disappear someday?

"Nothing is eternal except for God's laws. Do you not see that inequalities decline gradually every day? They are destined to disappear as the predominance of pride and selfishness wanes as well, leaving only that inequality that derives from merit. A day will come when the children of the great family of God will no longer consider each other as being of blood more or less pure, because only the spirit is more or less pure, and that is not at all related to social position."

807. What about those who abuse the superiority of their social position in order to oppress the weak to their benefit?

"They should be deplored, and misfortune shall befall them! They will be oppressed in their turn and *will be reborn* into an existence in which they shall suffer everything they inflicted on others." (See #684)

4. Economic inequality

808. Doesn't economic inequality originate in the inequality of faculties, resulting in some people having more means of acquiring riches than others?

"Yes and no. What do you say of swindle and theft?"

—   How about inherited wealth? For that is not the fruit of evil deeds.

"What do you know about it? Go back to its origin to find out if it is untainted. Do you know whether it was originally the fruit of plundering or another injustice? But aside from its possible dishonest origin, do you believe that the yearning for riches, even those honestly acquired, and the secret longing to obtain them as soon as possible are commendable feelings? That is what God judges, and I assure you that His judgment is more severe than that of men."

809. If a fortune has been dishonestly acquired at its origin, are those who later inherit it responsible in any way?

"They certainly are not responsible for the wrong that others committed, provided they are not aware of the fact. But you should know that a fortune is often destined for a certain individual in order to provide him the opportunity to make up for an injustice. Happy is he who understands this! If he rights a wrong in the name of the one who committed it in the first place, the reparation will be taken into account for them both, because often it is the original wrongdoer who inspires such action."

810. Within legal limits, we may dispose of our assets more or less equitably, without breaking the law. Are we responsible after death for the measures we put in place?

"Every action bears its fruit. The fruit of good deeds is sweet, the fruit of evil deeds is always bitter. *Always*—keep that in mind."

811. Is the absolute equality of wealth possible and has it ever existed?

"No, it is not possible. The diversity of faculties and characters opposes it."

— There are those, however, who believe it to be the remedy for all social ills. What do you think of that? [a]

"They are either dogmatic or greedy and jealous. They do not understand that the equality they dream of would be quickly undone by the very force of things. Fight selfishness, for that is your social cancer. Do not pursue utopias."

812. If equality of wealth is not possible, does the same apply to well-being?

"No, but well-being is relative and everyone could enjoy it if people could live in harmony with each other, for true well-being consists in employing one's time according to one's liking, and not in working at something that provides no enjoyment. Since everyone has different aptitudes, no useful work would be left undone. There exists equilibrium in everything, it is man who upsets it."

— Is mutual understanding achievable?

"Human beings will understand each other when they practice the law of justice."

813. There are people who fall into destitution through their own fault. May society be held responsible for this?

"Yes, we have already told you that society is frequently the chief reason for such problems. Besides, shouldn't society take care of people's moral education? It is often a deficient education that distorts people's judgment, instead of curbing their negative leanings." (See #685)

5. Trials of wealth and poverty

814. Why has God granted wealth and power to some and poverty to others?

"In order to test each one in a different way. In addition, as you know, it is the spirits themselves who have chosen those trials in which they often fail."

815. Which of the two trials is riskier to man: poverty or wealth?

"They are equally risky. Poverty leads to complaining about Providence, whereas wealth stimulates all types of excesses."

816. If the rich man undergoes more temptations, doesn't he also have more means of doing good?

"That is precisely what he does not always do. He becomes selfish, proud, and insatiable. His needs increase with his fortune, and he never believes he has amassed enough for himself."

A prominent position in this world and authority over fellow human beings are trials as great and slippery as poverty, for the wealthier and more powerful we are, *the more obligations we have to fulfill*, and the greater are the means at our disposal to do good and evil. God tests the poor man through equanimity and the rich man through the use he makes of his wealth and power.

Wealth and power awaken all the passions that bind us to matter and keep us from spiritual perfection. That is why Jesus said: "Verily I tell you, it is easier for a camel to go through the eye of a needle than for someone who is rich to enter the kingdom of Heaven." [b] (See #266)

6. Equality of rights of men and women

817. Are men and women equal before God and do they have the same rights?

"Hasn't God given them both the knowledge of good and evil and the faculties to progress?"

818. Where does the lesser social standing of women in certain nations come from?

"From the unjust and cruel dominion that men have exerted over them. It is a result of social institutions and the abuse of the strong over the weak. Among men who are little advanced morally, might makes right."

819. Why are women physically weaker than men in general?

"Because they may be assigned particular functions. Men can do heavier work, as they are normally stronger; whereas women may focus on lighter work. But both ought to mutually help each other in the trials of a life full of hardships."

820. Doesn't women's physical weakness make them naturally dependent on men?

"God has given strength to some in order to protect the weak, not to enslave them."

God has fitted the body of each creature according to the functions that must be performed. If God has endowed women with less physical strength, He has at the same time provided them with greater sensibility with respect to the delicacy of maternal functions and the fragility of the beings entrusted to their care.

821. Are the functions to which women are destined by nature as important as those which are assigned to men?

"Yes, and still more important, as women are the ones that give each human being the first notions of life."

822. All men being equal according to the law of God, should they also be equal before human law?

"This is the first principle of justice: 'Do not do unto others what you do not want them to do unto you.' "

— Accordingly, in order for legislation to be perfectly just, should it also establish the equality of rights between men and women?

"Equality of rights, yes, but not of duties. Roles shall be assigned according to each one's aptitude, which means that men will more frequently busy themselves with material aspects of life and women with its inner side. In order to be fair, human law must sanction the equality of rights between men and women. Any special privilege granted to one and not the other is contrary to justice. *The emancipation of women heralds the progress of civilization*; their servitude is an indication of barbarity. Moreover, the sexes exist through the physical organization, and since spirits can take either form, there are no differences between them in this respect. Consequently, they should enjoy the same rights." [c]

7. Equality in death

823. Where does the desire to perpetuate one's memory through funeral monuments come from?

"From a last act of pride."

— But isn't the opulence of funeral monuments most frequently the result of the relatives' desire to honor the memory of the deceased, rather than the desire of the deceased himself?

"It is the result of the pride of the relatives who want to honor themselves. Indeed, it is not always for the deceased that all such displays are made, but to gratify their own pride, to make a grandstanding impression, and to parade their wealth. Do you believe that the memory of a loved one will not last as long in the heart of the poor just because all they can afford is to place a humble flower on their relative's grave? Do you believe that a marble mausoleum can save from oblivion the one whose life on Earth was utterly useless?"

824. Is funeral pomp to be condemned under all circumstances?

"No. When it honors the memory of a virtuous person it is just and sets a good example."

The grave is the meeting place for all mankind. All human distinctions end mercilessly there. The rich try in vain to perpetuate their memory by erecting magnificent monuments. Time will destroy both their tombs and their bodies: nature has so willed it. The memory of their good and evil deeds will outlast their sepulchers, and the splendor of their funerals will neither cleanse them from their wickedness, nor raise them a single step on the ladder of the spiritual hierarchy. (See #320–329)

...

[a] This is a clear reference to the socialist doctrines which emerged in Europe in the nineteenth century. Authors that developed socialist philosophies include Henri de Saint-Simon (1760–1825), Charles Fourier (1772–1837), as well as Karl Marx (1818–1883) and Friedrich Engels (1820–1895). The latter two published their famous *Communist Manifesto* in London nine years before the first edition of *The Spirits' Book*. In that first edition, this subject is discussed in question #409 with the exact same wording. —Trans.

[b] Matthew 19:24, Mark 10:25, Luke 18:25. —Trans.

[c] Such a forceful defense of the equality of rights of men and women was revolutionary at the time *The Spirits' Book* was first published (1857). Women's rights were severely lacking in all areas back then: the right to work, to vote, to enter into legal contracts, to own property, to receive education, to be paid fair wages, etc. In the case of voting rights, for instance, the first European nation to enact women's suffrage was Finland in 1907, fifty years after the publishing of this book. Canada adopted women's suffrage in 1917, Britain and Germany in 1918, the United States in 1920, and France would only adopt it in 1944. In the book's first edition this topic is treated in question #416. —Trans.

Chapter 10:
The Law of Freedom

1. Natural liberty

825. Are there situations in the world in which people can pride themselves on enjoying absolute freedom?

"No, because all of you need one another, the least as well as the greatest."

826. In what condition could man enjoy absolute freedom?

"In that of a hermit in the desert. As soon as two individuals find themselves together, they have reciprocal rights to respect, and therefore they no longer have absolute freedom."

827. Does the obligation to respect the rights of others deprive man of the right of belonging to himself?

"By no means, for that is a right that he holds from nature."

828. How can we reconcile the liberal opinions of certain men with the despotism they themselves frequently exercise in their own homes and over their subordinates?

"They have the intellectual grasp of natural law, but it is neutralized by pride and selfishness. They understand how things ought to be, but don't behave that way in practice—if and when their principles are not, in fact, an act that they play out of calculation."

—   Will the principles they have professed during this life be of any avail to them in the next?

"The greater the capacity one has to understand a principle, the less excusable it is not to apply it to oneself. Truly, I say to you that the simple but sincere man is farther advanced along the way of God than he who pretends to be what he is not."

2. Slavery

829. Are there men who are destined by nature to be the property of others? [a]

"Every absolute subjection of one man to another is contrary to the law of God. Slavery is an abuse of power that will gradually disappear with progress, as will all other abuses."

> Any human law that upholds slavery is a law against nature because it likens men to animals, degrading them physically and morally.

830. When slavery is to be found among the customs of a people, are those who profit from it to blame, since they simply follow a usage that seems natural to them?

"Evil is always evil, and all your sophistry will not turn an evil action into a good one. But the responsibility for it is commensurate with the means available to understand it. He who profits from the institution of slavery is always guilty of violating the law of nature. But here, as in all things, guilt is relative. Slavery being rooted in the habits of certain peoples, men may have taken advantage of it in good faith, as something which seemed to them altogether natural. But when their reason, becoming more developed and especially enlightened by Christian teachings, eventually demonstrates that a slave is their equal before God, they are no longer excusable."

831. Doesn't the natural inequality of aptitudes place certain races under the sway of the more intelligent ones?

"Yes, but in order to uplift them, not to crush them further under the yoke of servitude. Man has long regarded certain races as domesticated working animals equipped with arms and hands, to the point of believing he has the right to sell them as beasts of burden. He fancies himself to be of purer blood. Preposterous man, who cannot see beyond matter! It is not the blood that is more or less pure, but the spirit." (See #361, #803)

832. There are those who treat their slaves with care, who do not let them suffer any privation, and who believe that freedom would expose them to even greater hardships. What do you say about such individuals?

"I say that they have a very good understanding of their own interests. They also take great care of their cows and horses in order to maximize their profits in the market. They are not as blameworthy as those who abuse their slaves, but they still treat them as possessions, depriving them of the right to belong to themselves."

3. Freedom of thought

833. Is there something in man which escapes all constraints, and in regard to which he enjoys absolute freedom?

"In his thought man enjoys unlimited freedom, for it knows no obstacles. Its expansion may be stalled, but thought itself cannot be eradicated."

834. Is man responsible for his thoughts?

"He is responsible for them before God. God alone being able to see them, condemns or absolves them according to His justice."

4. Freedom of conscience

835. Is freedom of conscience a consequence of freedom of thought?

"Conscience is an intimate thought that belongs to man, like all his other thoughts."

836. Does man have the right to create obstacles to freedom of conscience?

"No more than to freedom of thought, for God alone has the right to judge the conscience. If man regulates the relationship between men and men through his laws, God, through the laws of nature, regulates the relationship between men and God."

837. What is the result of placing obstacles in the way of freedom of conscience?

"Constraining men to act against their own way of thinking is to turn them into hypocrites. Freedom of conscience is one of the hallmarks of true civilization and progress."

838. Should every belief be respected, even when notoriously false?

"Every belief is worthy of respect when it is sincere and leads to the practice of good. Censurable beliefs are those that lead to evil."

839. Is it wrong to deprecate those whose beliefs are not the same as our own?

"It represents a lack of charity and a transgression against freedom of thought."

840. Is it a transgression against freedom of conscience to create obstacles to beliefs that may cause social disruption?

"Acts may be suppressed, but the inner belief is inaccessible."

Restricting external expressions of a belief when they cause harm to others does not infringe on freedom of conscience, for such restriction leaves the belief itself entirely free.

841. Should we, out of respect for freedom of conscience, allow the propagation of harmful doctrines, or may we, without going against that freedom, try to bring back onto the path of truth those who are led astray by false principles?

"Certainly not only you may, but you actually should do so. But following the example of Jesus, you must teach through the use of *gentleness and persuasion*, and never of force, as that would be worse than the belief of the person you wish to convert. If there is something that we are allowed to impose, it is goodness and fraternity. We do not believe, however, that the means for doing so should be violence: conviction cannot be imposed."

842. Given that all doctrines claim to be the unique expression of the truth, by what signs can we recognize the one which has the best claim to present itself as such?

"It will be the one that produces the greatest number of good men and the fewest hypocrites, that is to say, people who practice the law of love and charity in its greatest purity and broadest application. By this sign you will be able to tell that a particular doctrine is good, because every doctrine that spreads disagreement and establishes divisions among the children of God can only be false and harmful."

5. Free will

843. In his actions, does man have free will?

"Since he has freedom of thought, he has freedom of action. Without free will, man would be a machine."

844. Does man possess free will from his birth?

"Freedom of action exists from the moment he has a will to act. In the early stages of life, freedom is generally non-existent. It develops and changes its objectives as faculties develop. A child, whose thoughts are in conformity with the needs of his age, applies his free will to things that are necessary for him."

845. Aren't the instinctive predispositions that man brings with him from birth an obstacle to the exercise of free will?

"Instinctive predispositions are those of the spirit before his incarnation. Depending on how evolved the spirit is, they may incite a man to shameful acts, in which he will be assisted by spirits who sympathize with such dispositions. However, there is no irresistible incitement if the individual has the will to resist. Remember that where there is a will, there is a way." (See #361)

846. Does our body have an influence on the acts of our life, and if so, doesn't it represent an encumbrance on our free will?

"Spirits are certainly influenced by matter, which may encumber their manifestation. That is why, on worlds where bodies are less material than on Earth, faculties can be deployed with more freedom. However, it is not the instrument that imparts faculties to the spirit. Besides, it is necessary in this case to distinguish between moral and intellectual faculties. If a man has an instinct for murder, it is assuredly his own spirit that possesses it and conveys it to him, not his organs. He who silences his thought in order to occupy himself solely with material pursuits is like the brute, or even worse, since he no longer cares to preserve himself against evil. In this lies his guilt, because he acts so out of his own free will." (See #367–370, "Bodily Influences")

847. Can the impairment of mental faculties curtail man's free will?

"He whose intelligence is impaired for any reason is no longer in control of his thoughts, and consequently is no longer free. Such impairments are frequently a punishment for the spirit, who might have been vain and contemptuous, and might have made a bad use of his faculties. He may be reborn in the body of a mentally impaired person, the tyrant in the body of a slave, and the evil rich in that of a beggar. The spirit, however, suffers from such constraints, of which he is perfectly conscious. There lies the influence of matter." (See #371–378)

848. Is the impairment of mental faculties caused by the consumption of alcohol an excuse for wrongful conduct?

"No, because the alcoholic voluntarily trades control of his reason for the satisfaction of his material passion. Rather than one transgression, he commits two."

849. What is the dominant faculty in the primitive man, instinct or free will?

"Instinct, which however does not prevent him from acting with complete freedom in certain circumstances. Like a child, he first applies this freedom to his immediate needs, developing it later through intelligence. Consequently, because you are more knowledgeable than a primitive man, your degree of responsibility for your acts is also greater than his."

850. Isn't social position an obstacle to the complete freedom of action at times?

"The world undoubtedly has its demands. God is just: He takes everything into consideration, but holds you accountable for the little effort you make to overcome such obstacles."

6. Fate

851. Is there fate in the events of life according to the usual meaning attached to the word? In other words, are all events determined in advance, and if so, what becomes of free will?

"Fate only exists in that a spirit chooses to undergo this or that trial upon incarnating. Making the choice of a particular trial, he sets for himself a destiny, as it were, which is the very consequence of the position in which he shall find himself. I speak of physical trials, because, when it comes to moral trials and temptations, the spirit retains his free will to choose between good and evil, which is to say that he is always capable of yielding or resisting. For instance, when good spirits notice that a man's courage wavers, they may rush to assist him, but they cannot influence him to the point of overriding his will. Conversely, an evil or inferior spirit may unsettle and frighten a man by magnifying a physical danger. In any event, however, the incarnate spirit's free will remains unshackled."

852. There are people who seem to be pursued by fate, irrespective of their actions. Is misfortune a part of their destiny?

"Those are perhaps trials that they must undergo, trials they have chosen beforehand. Once again you attempt to ascribe to destiny that which is more often than not a consequence of your own mistakes. When afflicted by hardships, make sure you have a clear conscience. In it you shall find at least a partial solace."

The accurate or inaccurate conceptions we develop of things cause us to succeed or fail according to our character and to our social position. We find it more convenient and less demeaning to our self-esteem to impute our failures to fate than to our own fault. If the influence of spirits may sometimes contribute to this, we can always avoid such influence by warding off the suggested ideas, when they are evil.

853. Certain people escape one mortal danger only to fall into another, seemingly unable to escape death. Isn't there fate in this?

"In the exact meaning of the word, there is fate only as regards the instant of death. When that moment has come, be it one way or another, you cannot escape it."

— It follows then that whatever the danger that threatens us, we will not die if our hour has not yet come?

"No, you will not die, and you have thousands of examples of this. But when your time to depart has arrived, nothing can save you. God knows in advance what kind of death shall mark your departure, and often your spirit is also aware of it, because it was revealed to you when you chose your existence."

854. From the inevitability of the hour of death, does it follow that the precautions taken to avoid it are pointless?

"No, because the precautions you take are suggested to you with the aim of avoiding a premature death that may threaten you. Such precautions are one of the means used to prevent it from occurring."

855. What is the goal of Providence in making us run into dangers that shall have no consequence?

"Your life being threatened constitutes a warning that you yourself have wished for in order to turn you away from evil, and to make you stronger. Once you escape a danger, still under the influence of the risk just incurred, you consider with greater or lesser attention (according to the intensity of the influence of good spirits) the importance of becoming a better person. However, once evil spirits appear (I say *evil* on account of the evil that still exists in them), you think that you can escape other dangers just as easily, and again you give your passions free rein. Through the dangers you incur, God reminds you of your weakness and the fragility of your existence. If one examines the cause and nature of such dangers, one shall realize that most often their consequences would have been a punishment for some fault committed, or for a *duty neglected*. God thus warns you to come to your senses and mend your ways." (See #526–532)

856. Does the spirit know beforehand what type of death he shall suffer?

"He knows that the kind of life he chooses will expose him more likely to certain types of death. But he also knows which struggles he will have to go through in order to prevent such death, and that, God permitting, he will manage to escape."

857. There are men who face the dangers of battle with a conviction that their hour has not yet come. Are there any grounds for such confidence?

"Quite often, man has a presentiment of his end, as he may have the presentiment that he will not die just yet. This presentiment is given to him by his guardian spirit, who desires to warn him to be ready to depart, or in order to stimulate his courage when most necessary. The presentiment may also come to him from his own intuition of the life he has chosen, or of the mission he has accepted and that he knows he ought to fulfill." (See #411–522)

858. Why do those who anticipate their death generally fear death less than others do?

"It is man who fears death, not the spirit. He who anticipates it thinks more as a spirit than as a mortal man. He understands his imminent deliverance and stands by."

859. If death cannot be avoided when the time appointed for it arrives, is it the same with respect to every accident that happens to us over the course of our life?

"They are often small enough issues to allow us to warn you of them, and at times to help you avoid them by directing your thoughts, because we do not like to witness any physical suffering. But all this is of little importance for the life you have chosen. Fate, properly, only applies to the moment you must enter and leave this world."

—   Are there events which must necessarily happen, and which the will of the spirits cannot prevent?

"Yes, but which you, in the spirit state, saw and sensed when you made your choice. However, do not believe that everything that happens to you is *written*, as some say. An event is frequently the consequence of a prior action you have performed out of your own free will, so that if you had not done it, that event would not have taken place. If you burn your finger, it is nothing but a result of your carelessness and the constraints of matter. Only the great sorrows, the pivotal events that are capable of affecting your moral standing, are foreseen by God, because they are useful for your purification and instruction."

860. Can man, through his determination and actions, avert events that were supposed to happen, or cause to happen events that were not supposed to?

"He can, if this apparent departure suits the life he has chosen. In order to do good, as he should, since that is life's single most important goal, he can prevent an evil, especially one that may lead to other still greater evils."

861. A man commits a murder in his present incarnation. Did he know, upon choosing his existence, that he was to become an assassin?

"No. He only knew that, in choosing a life of struggle, he would *run the risk* of killing a fellow man, but he did not know if he would actually do so or not, because almost always he must make the decision in his mind before committing the crime. As such, he who decides on a course of action is always free to do it or not. If the spirit knew beforehand that, as an incarnate man, he would have to commit a murder, it would mean that he was destined to do so. Understand very clearly that no one is ever predestined to commit a crime, and that every crime and every other action are always the result of choice and free will.

"Moreover, you always confuse two very distinct things: the material events of existence and the acts of moral life. If there is fate sometimes, it is only with regard to material events where the cause is outside of you and independent of your will. Concerning the acts of moral life, they always derive from man himself, who consequently always has the freedom of choice. So, there is *never* fate involved in such acts."

862. There are people who never succeed in anything, and who seem to be plagued by an evil genius in all their endeavors. Isn't that what could be called fate?

"It is fate if you would like to call it that, but it results from the choice of the type of existence, as those individuals have elected a life full of disappointments, so that they can exercise their patience and fortitude. However, do not believe that such fate is always inevitable, because it is often only the result of their having taken a wrong path, not consistent with their intelligence and aptitudes. Someone who tries to swim across a river without knowing how to swim stands a very good chance of drowning. The same applies to most events in life. If man only tried to undertake that which is in line with his own aptitudes he would almost always succeed. He fails because of his vanity and greed, which lead him away from his path and make him pursue the satisfaction of his passions. He then fails, and it is his own fault. But rather than blaming himself, he prefers to blame the stars. One who might have been a good workman, making an honorable living, prefers to be a mediocre poet and ends up starving. There would be a place for everyone if each could find the right role."

863. Don't social customs often compel a man to follow a certain path rather than another, making him subject to other people's opinions in his choice of occupation? Isn't the fear of social stigma [b] an obstacle to the exercise of free will?

"Social customs are created by man, not by God. If a man submits to them, it is because they suit him. This is also an act of free will, because if he wanted to, he could disregard them. Why does he complain, then?

He should not blame social customs, but rather his own foolish conceit, which leads him to prefer to die of hunger rather than challenge the prevailing mores. Nobody shall value his sacrifice to public opinion, but God will take into account his sacrifice to his own vanity. This is not to say that he should needlessly defy public opinion, as happens with certain people who are more imbued with eccentricity than with true philosophy. It is just as foolish to parade oneself as an aberration, as it is wise to gracefully step down the social ladder when one can no longer stay atop."

864.   If certain people seem to be plagued by bad luck, others seem to be favored by fate, as everything goes well for them. How to explain this?

"They are usually better at conducting themselves. But it could also be a type of trial, because if they became intoxicated with success, they blindly trust their destiny and later frequently end up paying for their triumphs with ghastly reversals of fortune that could have been avoided with a little caution."

865.   How to explain the run of luck that appears to favor certain people in circumstances that rely neither on will nor on intelligence, as in the case of games of chance, for instance?

"Certain spirits have chosen certain types of pleasure beforehand. The luck that favors them is a temptation. He who wins as a man loses as a spirit: it is a trial for his pride and greed."

866.   Then the fate that seems to preside over the destinies of our material life would still be the result of our free will?

"You yourself have chosen your trials. The harder they are and the better you endure them, the more you advance. Those who spend their lives in the selfish enjoyment of abundance and human pleasures are negligent spirits who remain stationary. Therefore, the hapless greatly outnumber those who are materially fortunate, as the majority of spirits look for those trials that will be most beneficial to them. They see all too clearly the futility of your earthly glories and enjoyments. The happiest life is always agitated, always troubled, if by nothing else, by the absence of sorrows." (See #525–535)

867. Where does the expression *born under a lucky star* come from?

"From the old superstition that associated the stars with the destiny of each person, an allegory that some people foolishly take for literal truth."

7. Knowledge of the future

868. Can the future be revealed to man?

"In general, the future is hidden from him, and only in rare and exceptional cases does God allow it to be revealed."

869. For what purpose is the future hidden from man?

"If man knew the future, he would neglect the present, and he would not act with the same freedom, because he would be swayed by the thought that, if a certain thing must happen, there is no need for him to busy himself with it, or else he would seek to prevent it. God has willed that it should not be thus, so that each may contribute to the accomplishment of things, *even those that man would like to thwart*. In this way, you yourself habitually and unknowingly prepare the events that will come about over the course of your life."

870. Since it is useful that the future be hidden, why does God sometimes allow it to be revealed?

"Because in such cases a prior knowledge of the future helps in the accomplishment of the event at hand, rather than hampering it, prompting into action those who wouldn't do anything otherwise. Moreover, it is frequently a trial. The anticipation of an event may arouse more or less virtuous thoughts. If a man is told, for instance, that he will receive an unexpected inheritance, he may be tempted by greed, by the excitement at the prospect of adding to his earthly pleasures, by the desire to acquire his inheritance sooner, and longing for the death of the one who will leave his estate to him. Or else, such possibility may awaken in the man good feelings and generous thoughts. If the prediction is not fulfilled, there will be the additional trial of how the person in question shall endure the disappointment. He will, nonetheless, have earned the merit or the blame for the good or bad thoughts that the expectation of the event awakened in him."

871. Since God knows everything, He knows whether a man will fail or not in a given trial. Hence, what is the need of that trial, since it cannot reveal anything in addition to what God already knows about that man?

"That's tantamount to asking why God did not create man completely perfect in the first place (See #119) or why man must go through childhood before becoming an adult (See #379). The purpose of that trial is not to inform God about the merits of that man—God knows perfectly well his worthiness—but to leave him the entire responsibility for his acts, since he has the freedom to do as he pleases. The man being able to choose between good and evil, the trial has the purpose of testing him with temptation and leaving him all the merit for resisting it. Now, even though God knows very well beforehand if the man will succeed or not, in His justice, God can neither punish nor reward him for an act that has not been carried out." (See #258)

The same applies to men. However capable a candidate may be, and no matter how certain we are of his success, we do not award him a degree without him taking the prescribed examinations, that is to say, without testing him. Likewise, a judge may only condemn a defendant for a crime that has been actually committed and never on the presumption that he could or would commit such crime.

The more we ponder the consequences that knowledge of the future would have for man, the more we see how wise Providence was to conceal it. The certitude of an auspicious event would cause his inaction; that of an unfortunate event, discouragement. In either case, his forces would be paralyzed. This is why the future is not shown to man except as an *objective* that he must reach through his own efforts, but without knowing the difficulties he must go through in order to reach it. The foreknowledge of all the incidents along the journey would deprive him of his initiative and his free will, as he would let himself be dragged along the inevitable chain of events without exercising his faculties. When the outcome of an event is guaranteed, one no longer worries about it.

8. Theoretical outline of the motivations of human action

872. The question of free will may be summed up as follows: man is not inevitably led into evil, his actions are not written in advance, and the crimes he commits are not the result of a decree of destiny. He may choose, as trial or atonement, an existence in which he will be subject to the attractions of crime, be that due to the environment where he is placed or to supervening circumstances. But in any event, he is always free to do as he wishes. Therefore, free will exists in the spirit state in the choice of the future existence and its accompanying trials, and as an incarnate spirit in the ability to yield or to resist to the temptations the man voluntarily submitted himself to. It is incumbent upon education to repel evil tendencies, which will only happen when education is based on an in-depth investigation into man's moral nature. Through understanding of the laws governing that moral nature, one will be able to transform it, just as one modifies intelligence through instruction and temperament by adopting new life habits.

When disengaged from matter, in between consecutive incarnations, a spirit chooses his future corporeal existence according to the degree of perfection he has reached. That is determined mainly by his free will, as we mentioned. Such freedom is not voided by incarnation: if the spirit yields to the influence of matter, he fails in the trials he himself has chosen. In order to overcome them, he may appeal to the assistance of God and of the good spirits. (See #337)

Without free will, man would have neither guilt in doing wrong nor merit in doing good. Such principle is so widely recognized that the world assigns blame or praise in proportion to intention, which is to say, to will. In this case, therefore, *will* is a synonym for *freedom*. Consequently, man would be at a loss to find an excuse for his misdeeds in his physical constitution, without renouncing his reasoning and his very status as a human being, likening himself to beasts. This applies to evil as well as to good deeds, except that in the case of the latter, man takes great care to claim credit for himself and does not for a second consider ascribing his good deeds to his organs. This proves empirically, against the arbitrary opinion of the few, that man does not relinquish the most splendid privilege of the human species: freedom of thought.

Fate, as commonly understood, implies a prior and irrevocable ordering of all the events of life, whatever their importance may be. If that were the reality, man would be a machine without a will of his own. Of what use would be his intelligence, if he would invariably be overruled in all his actions by the power of destiny? If true, such a doctrine would represent the denial of all moral freedom, the result being that man would no longer be responsible for his acts, and, consequently, have no reason to speak of either good or evil, of either crime or virtue. Being supremely just, God could not punish his creature for transgressions that did not depend on him to be averted, nor reward him for virtues he had no merit in. Besides, such a principle would negate the law of progress because man would abandon himself to the whims of fate and would not attempt to improve his standing in life, unable as he would be to make it better or worse.

Fate is not an empty word, however. It applies to the position that man holds on Earth and the functions he performs as a result of the type of existence that he, as a spirit, had chosen, be that *trial, expiation,* or *mission.* He inevitably undergoes all the troubles of that existence, and experiences all the *tendencies,* good or bad, inherent in it. But that's where fate stops, for it depends on man's will whether or not to yield to those tendencies. *The details of events are subordinated to the circumstances he himself creates through his actions,* which spirits may influence by suggesting thoughts to him. (See #459)

Fate rests, therefore, in the events that unfold as a consequence of the choice of existence made by the spirit. But fate does not necessarily figure in the result of such events, because it may depend on man to modify the course of things through the use of prudence. Moreover, *fate never applies to the events stemming from man's moral choices.*

It is in death that man must submit in absolute terms to the inevitability of fate, for he cannot escape the decree that has fixed the term of his existence or the type of death that shall cut short the thread of his life.

According to ordinary belief, all man's instincts originate in himself. They either proceed from his physical makeup, for which he is not responsible, or from his own nature. He can derive an excuse for the latter simply by pleading it is not his fault that he was created this way. The Spiritist Doctrine stands evidently on a higher moral plane, in that it acknowledges man's free will in its entirety. By telling him that, when he commits a wrongful act, he yields to an evil external suggestion, the doctrine leaves a man with the full responsibility for his wrongdoing, because it recognizes his power to resist that suggestion, something evidently easier than if he had to fight against his own nature.

Thus, according to the Spiritist Doctrine, there are no irresistible temptations: man can always shut his ears to the secret voice that induces him to do evil, just as he is able to close them to the material voice of someone who speaks to him. He can do so through his will, asking God for the necessary strength, and requesting the assistance of good spirits toward that end. That is what Jesus teaches in the sublime plea of The Lord's Prayer, when he commands us to say, "Do not let us fall into temptation, but deliver us from evil."

This theory of the driving force of human action clearly emerges from the all the teachings provided by the Spirits. Not only is the theory sublime concerning morality, but it also raises man's standing before himself by showing that he is free to shake off the yoke of a spirit oppressor, just as he is free to repel intruders from his abode. He is no longer a machine driven by a force outside his will; rather, he is a sentient being capable of reasoning, listening, judging, and freely choosing between two suggestions.

Let us add that, in spite of this, man is not deprived of his initiative, because he only acts of his own accord, as an incarnate spirit who preserves, beneath his corporeal envelope, the good and bad qualities he possessed as a spirit. The wrongs we commit have therefore their primary origin in the imperfections of our own spirit, which has not yet achieved the moral superiority we are destined to, but which still is endowed with free will. Corporeal life is granted to man so that he may purge himself of his imperfections through the trials he undergoes during life. Those imperfections are precisely what make him weaker and more susceptible to the suggestions of other imperfect spirits, who take advantage of those flaws to try to make him fail in the struggle he has undertaken.

Emerging victorious from the struggle, he advances; if he fails, he remains as he was before, no better and no worse: it is a trial that he must start over and that may last for a long time. The more he perfects himself, the more his weaknesses diminish and the less susceptible he becomes to those who lure him into evil. Ultimately, his moral strength grows as he advances, and imperfect spirits recede.

The human race is comprised of all incarnate spirits, good and bad, and because Earth is one of the least advanced worlds, there are more bad spirits than good ones here, which explains why wickedness is seen so frequently. So, let us make every effort not to have to come back to this world after our current earthly stay, and to be granted admission to better and more privileged worlds, where the good reigns supreme and where we will remember our sojourn here merely as a time of exile.

■■■

[a] When *The Spirits' Book* was first published in 1857, slavery was still legal in a number of countries, including the United States, Russia, British India, the Dutch Colonies, Cuba, the Ottoman Empire, Bulgaria, Brazil, Poland, Korea, Egypt, Persia, Iraq, Morocco, China, and other places. In the first edition of the book, this topic is covered in questions #419 and #420. —Trans.

[b] In the French original, Kardec uses the expression *respect humain*, which means "the fear of social disapproval, leading frequently to the hiding of one's convictions, religious or otherwise." —Trans.

Chapter 11:
The Law of Justice, Love and Charity

1. Justice and natural rights

873. Is the sentiment of justice to be found in nature itself or is it the result of acquired ideas?

"It is so ingrained in nature that you revolt at the thought of an injustice. Moral progress undoubtedly develops this sentiment, but it does not create it: God has placed it in the human heart. That is why you frequently find among simple and unsophisticated men notions of justice that are more accurate than those found among many men of knowledge."

874. If justice is a law of nature, how is it that men understand it so differently, to the point that what one person considers just seems unjust to another?

"It is because man frequently mixes his passions with this sentiment, corrupting it, as happens with most other natural sentiments, making him see things from a false vantage point."

875. How may we define justice?

"Justice consists in respecting the rights of each individual."

— What determines these rights?

"They are determined by two things: human law and natural law. Because men have established laws that are appropriate for their customs and character, these laws have established rights that may change with intellectual advancement. Check if your current laws, though not perfect, sanction the same rights that prevailed during the Middle Ages. Those outdated rights, that may seem monstrous to you, seemed just and natural at the time. For that reason, the rights established by men are not always in accord with justice. They only regulate certain social relations, whereas in private life there are a vast number of actions that fall under the exclusive jurisdiction of your own conscience."

876. Aside from the rights established by human law, what is the basis of justice according to natural law?

"Christ has told you: 'Do unto others as you would have others do unto you.' [a] God has placed in man's heart the rule of all legitimate justice through the desire that each and every man should see his rights respected. When uncertain about what he should do in regard to his neighbor in any given circumstance, he ought to ask himself what he would want his neighbor to do to him in a similar situation. God could not give him a safer guide than his own conscience."

Indeed, the criterion of legitimate justice is in desiring for others what we would desire for ourselves; and not in desiring for ourselves what we would desire for others, which is not at all the same thing. Since it is not natural to desire our own harm, by using our personal desire as the standard or starting point, we are certain that we shall never wish anything but good for our neighbor. Throughout history, men of all faiths have always sought to make their personal right prevail. *The sublime distinction of Christianity has been to make our personal rights the basis for the rights of our neighbor.*

877. Does the need to live in society impose on man any special obligations?

"Yes, and the first of them is that of respecting the rights of others, for he who respects those rights will always be just. In your world, where so many neglect the law of justice, each one turns to revenge, causing trouble and confusion in your society. Social life grants rights and imposes reciprocal duties."

878. As man can delude himself regarding the extent of his rights, what can make him see the matter clearly?

"Knowing the limit of what he recognizes as his neighbor's rights toward him under the same circumstances, and conversely."

—   But if each man attributed to himself the rights of his neighbor, what would become of subordination to superiors? Wouldn't it result in anarchy among powers?

"Natural rights are the same for everyone, from the least to the greatest. God has not made some men from finer clay than others, and all are equal before Him. These rights are eternal, whereas those established by man vanish along with his institutions.

Also, each individual can clearly perceive his own strength or weakness, and will be conscientious enough to show deference to those who deserve it due to their virtue and wisdom. It is important to highlight this point, so that those who believe themselves superior may know their duties in order to earn such deference. Hierarchy will not be compromised if authority derives from wisdom."

879. What would be the character of the man who practices justice in all its purity?

"The truly just man would follow Jesus's example, because he would practice both love of neighbor and charity, without which there is no true justice."

2. Property rights, theft

880. Which is the first of all man's natural rights?

"The right to live. For that reason, no one has the right to make an attempt on the life of his fellow creature, or to do anything that may compromise the latter's corporeal existence."

881. Does the right to live give man the right to amass the means of living in order to retire when he can no longer work?

"Yes, but he must do it as a family, like the bee, through honest labor, and not simply by selfishly accumulating wealth. Even certain animals provide him with the example of such providence."

882. Does man have the right to defend what he has amassed through his work?

"Hasn't God said, 'You shall not steal,' [b] and Jesus, 'Give back to Caesar what is Caesar's?' [c]"

That which man amasses through *honest* labor is legitimate property that he has the right to defend, because ownership of what is the fruit of labor represents a natural right as sacred as the right to work and the right to live.

883. Is the desire to own riches natural?

"Yes, but when man only desires them for himself and for his own personal satisfaction it is selfishness."

— However, isn't the desire to own things legitimate, since he who can support himself is not a burden to others?

"Some men are greedy and accumulate wealth without benefit to anyone, or merely to satisfy their passions. Do you believe that God approves of that? By contrast, he who amasses resources through his work with the intention of helping his fellow human beings practices the law of love and charity, and his work is blessed by God."

884. What characterizes legitimate property?

"No property is legitimate except that which has been acquired without harm to others." (See #808)

The law of love and justice, by forbidding us to do to others what we would not want them to do to us, similarly condemns every means of acquiring property contrary to that law.

885. Are property rights unlimited?

"Undoubtedly, everything that has been legitimately acquired is property; but as we have said, human legislation, imperfect as it is, frequently sanctions conventional rights that are opposed to natural justice. That is why men reform their laws as progress is accomplished and as they better understand justice. What is perfect in one century seems barbaric in the next." (See #795)

3. Charity and neighborly love

886. What is the true meaning of the word *charity* as Jesus understood it?

"Benevolence to everyone, with tolerance for the imperfections of others and forgiveness of offenses."

Love and charity are the complement of the law of justice because loving our neighbor is to do to him all the good within our reach, all that we would wish to be done to ourselves. Such is the meaning of Jesus's words: "Love one another as brothers." [d]

Charity, according to Jesus, is not limited to almsgiving, but encompasses all our relations with our fellow human beings, whether they stand at a position equivalent to ours, or lower or higher than ours. Charity commands us to be tolerant because we need tolerance ourselves, and it forbids us to humiliate the unfortunate, contrary to what is too frequently done. When we are introduced to the wealthy, we lavish consideration and attention on them, but if the people are poor, it seems not worth our while to worry about them. The more distressing their situation, though, the more we should refrain from adding humiliation to it. The truly good man seeks to raise those below himself up to his own level, reducing the distance between them.

887. Jesus also said: "Love even your enemies." But isn't loving our enemies contrary to our natural tendencies, and doesn't antagonism derive from a lack of sympathy between spirits?

"Undoubtedly, one cannot feel tender and passionate affection for one's enemies. That is not what Jesus meant. To love one's enemies is to forgive them and to return good for evil. That way we raise ourselves above them. By seeking vengeance, we plunge ourselves beneath them."

888. What is to be thought of almsgiving?

"The man reduced to begging for alms degrades himself morally and physically to the point of becoming desensitized. A society based on the law of God and of justice would provide for the life of the *weak* without humiliating them. It would ensure an existence for those unable to work, not leaving them *at the mercy of chance* or of the goodwill of others."

— Do you condemn almsgiving, then?

"No, it is not giving to the poor that is reprehensible, but the way in which it is frequently done. The good man, who understands charity according to Jesus, seeks out those in need without waiting for them to hold out their hand.

"True charity is always good and benevolent, characterized as much by the way it is done as by the deed itself. A favor, when done with graciousness, earns twice the merit. Conversely, when a favor is done with arrogance, need may compel the recipient to accept it, but the heart shall hardly be moved.

"Remember as well that, in the eyes of God, ostentation cancels out the merit of the act of generosity. Jesus said: 'Do not let your left hand know what your right hand is doing.' [e] That way he teaches you not to tarnish charity with pride.

"It is necessary to distinguish between almsgiving strictly speaking and benevolence. The most in need is not always the one who begs, as the fear of humiliation frequently holds back the really poor, who often suffers in silence—this is the person that the truly humane soul will know how to seek out and help without ostentation.

"Love one another: here is the whole law, the divine law through which God governs the worlds. Love is the law of attraction for living and sentient beings, as much as attraction is the law of love for inorganic matter.

"Never forget that a spirit, whatever his degree of development or his standing as incarnate or discarnate, is *always* placed between a superior spirit who guides and perfects him, and an inferior one, toward whom he ought to fulfill the same duties. Be therefore charitable, but be imbued not with the type of charity that forces you to take from your purse a coin that you coldly toss to the one who dares to beg from you. Instead, go out to assist the poor that hide from plain view.

Be indulgent of the faults of those around you, and rather than despising their ignorance and perversion, educate and reform them. Be gentle and benevolent toward all those who are not as advanced as you, including the lowliest beings of creation, and you will have obeyed the law of God."

Saint Vincent de Paul

889. Aren't there men who are reduced to begging through their own fault?

"Certainly, but if a good moral education had taught them to practice the law of God, they would not have fallen into the excesses that caused their ruin. On education, above all, depends the advancement of your planet." (See #707)

4. Motherly and filial love

890. Is motherly love a virtue or an instinctive feeling common to both humans and animals?

"It is both. Nature has endowed the mother with love of her children to ensure their survival, but among animals this affection is limited to the material needs of her offspring, ceasing when no longer required. Among humans, this love persists throughout life, and includes a type of dedication and a selflessness that raises it to the category of true virtue. It even survives death itself, accompanying the child from beyond the grave. You can clearly see that this sort of love encompasses much more than the affection among animals does." (See #205–385)

891. If maternal love is natural, why are there mothers who hate their children, often from birth?

"It is sometimes a trial chosen by the spirit of the child, or an expiation if in a previous existence the spirit was a bad father, a bad mother, or a bad child (See #392). In all such cases, a bad mother can only be the incarnation by a lesser spirit who creates hindrances for the child to fail the chosen trial. But such a violation of the laws of nature will not go unpunished, and the spirit of the child shall be rewarded for surmounting such obstacles."

892. When parents have children who cause them sorrow, aren't they excused for not feeling for them the same tenderness that they would have felt otherwise?

"No, because it is a task that has been entrusted to them, and their mission is to make every effort to bring their children to the path of good. (See #582–583) Such sorrows are frequently the consequence of bad habits that the parents allowed their children to develop from the cradle. They reap, therefore, what they have sown."

■■■

[a] Matthew 7:12, Luke 6:31. —Trans.

[b] Exodus 20:15. —Trans.

[c] Matthew 22:21, Mark 12:17. —Trans.

[d] Mark 12:31. —Trans.

[e] Matthew 6:3. —Trans.

Chapter 12:
Moral Perfection

1. Virtues and vices

893. Which is the most meritorious of all virtues?

"All virtues have their merit, because all of them are signs of progress along the path of good. There is virtue whenever there is voluntary resistance to the pull of evil tendencies. But the sublime aspect of virtue consists in the sacrifice of one's own interests for the good of others without ulterior motives. The most meritorious virtue is that which is based on the most disinterested charity."

894. There are people who do good by a spontaneous action, without having to overcome any opposing feeling. Do they have the same merit as those who have to struggle against their own nature in order to overcome it?

"In the case of those who do not have to struggle, progress has already been accomplished. They struggled long ago, and triumphed. That is why virtuous feelings cost them no effort, and their actions seem so easy: doing good has become second-nature for them. They should be honored as old warriors who have earned their ranks.

"Since you are still far from perfection, such examples surprise you with the contrast they provide, and you admire them all the more so because they are rare. But be well aware that on worlds more advanced than yours, that which is the exception among you represents the rule. Goodness is everywhere spontaneous there, because such worlds are inhabited only by good spirits, and a single evil intention there would be a monstrous exception. That is why humans are happy there. And so will it be on Earth when humanity has transformed itself, and charity is understood and practiced according to its genuine essence."

895. Aside from faults and vices too obvious to escape anybody's attention, what is the most distinctive sign of imperfection?

"Self-interest. Moral qualities are frequently like gilding applied to a copper object that cannot withstand the test of the touchstone. A man may possess real qualities that make him a virtuous man in the eyes of the world. However, while indicative of progress, those qualities do not always pass certain tests, and sometimes all it takes is to strike the chord of personal interest in order to reveal their true nature. Sincere disinterestedness is indeed so rare a thing on Earth that it is marveled at as a miracle when it occurs.

"Attachment to material things is a prominent sign of moral inferiority, because the more man holds on to the things of this world, the less he understands his destiny. Conversely, through selflessness, man demonstrates that he views the future from a higher vantage point."

896. There are disinterested individuals who lack judgment, and who dispense their assets without any real benefit, because they do not make a reasonable use of them. Do they have any merit?

"They have the merit of disinterestedness, but not that of the good they might do. If selflessness is a virtue, thoughtless profligacy is always, at the very least, a lack of judgment. Wealth is not given to some to be thrown away any more than it is given to others to be locked up in a safe. It is a fiduciary deposit they will have to account for, because they will have to answer for all the good that was within their reach and that they failed to do, as well as for all the tears they could have dried with the money they wasted on those who had no need of it."

897. What of a man who does good, not to reap any rewards on Earth, but in hope that such action will secure him a better position in the afterlife? Does such a calculation jeopardize his advancement?

"One must do good for the sake of charity, which is to say, selflessly."

—   Nonetheless, everyone has the very natural desire to progress in order to emerge from the painful situation of this life. Spirits themselves teach us to do good with that goal in mind. So, would it be wrong to think that by doing good we may be better off than we are on Earth?

"Certainly not, but those who do good without ulterior motives, for the pure joy of being pleasing to God and to their suffering neighbor, have already achieved a certain degree of advancement, which shall enable them to reach happiness much earlier than their brother who, more pragmatically, does good out of calculation, and is not inspired by the natural warmth of his heart." (See #894)

—   Isn't there here a distinction to be made between the good that can be done for our neighbor and the care we devote to correcting our own faults? We understand there is little merit in doing good with the idea that it will help in our standing the afterlife. But is it also a sign of moral inferiority if we improve ourselves, conquer our passions, and correct our character in order to bring ourselves closer to the good spirits and ascend in the spirit hierarchy?

"No, no. By *doing good* we mean *being charitable*. He who calculates what each of his good actions can yield him in the present as well as in his future life, proceeds selfishly. But there is no selfishness in improving oneself hoping to come closer to God, because that is the goal toward which everyone should work."

898. Since the corporeal life is nothing but a temporary stopover on this world, and since our future life should be our main concern, is it worthwhile to make the effort to acquire scientific knowledge that only concerns material things and needs?

"Undoubtedly. First, it enables you to relieve your fellow beings' hardships. Next, your spirit will advance faster if you have already furthered your intellect. In the period between incarnations you will learn in one hour what would require years on your planet. No knowledge is useless, as it all contributes something to your advancement, for a perfect spirit must master all types of knowledge, and progress must be accomplished in every area. So, all acquired information helps in the development of the spirit."

899. Of two wealthy individuals, one was born in affluence and has never experienced want, while the other owes his fortune to his own work. However, both employ their wealth exclusively for their own personal gratification. Which man is the more culpable?

"The one who has known privation. He understands what it is like to suffer, and has experienced precisely that pain which he does not bother to relieve in others, and which, too frequently in his case, he no longer even remembers."

900. Can he who incessantly accumulates wealth without benefiting anyone find a valid excuse in the thought that he hoards in order to leave a larger fortune to his heirs?

"It is a way to accommodate his guilty conscience."

901. Of two misers, the first one denies himself even the basics and dies of want atop his treasure, whereas the second is stingy to others, but rather extravagant with himself. The second miser recoils before the slightest sacrifice to render a favor or do something useful for someone else, whereas nothing is too difficult when satisfying his own tastes and passions. If a favor is asked of him, he is always short on cash, but to satisfy his whims he always has plenty. Which man is more culpable and which man will find himself in a worse situation in the spirit world?

"The one who wastes money on his own enjoyments, for he is more selfish than miserly. The other one has already received part of his punishment."

902. Is it wrong to wish for wealth with the objective of doing good?

"Such a desire is certainly commendable, when it is pure. But is this desire always totally disinterested, and does it not hide any personal ulterior motive? The first person one wishes to benefit is too often oneself, is it not?"

903. Is it wrong to study other people's faults?

"If it is in order to criticize them and make their faults publicly known, it is very wrong, because it shows a lack of charity. If it is for your own personal education, so as to avoid those same faults yourself, it may sometimes be useful. One must not forget, though, that tolerance for other people's faults is one of the virtues that charity comprises. Before censuring people for their imperfections, check whether others may say the same about you. Therefore, try to have qualities that are opposite to the faults you criticize in others, as a means of making yourself better. Do you reproach them for being greedy? Be generous. For being arrogant? Be humble and unassuming. For being harsh? Be kind. For acting with pettiness? Be dignified in all your actions. In short, act in such a way that the following words of Jesus do not apply to you: 'You see the speck in your neighbor's eye, but do not see the beam in your own.' "

904. Is it wrong for a writer to probe the ills of society and expose them?

"That depends on the reason for doing it. If the writer's goal is to create a scandal, all he does is to derive personal satisfaction by presenting situations that frequently set a bad example rather than a good one. The spirit enjoys it, but he can be punished for the pleasure resulting from the exposure of wickedness."

—   In such cases, how can we judge a writer's purity of intention and sincerity?

"That would not always be useful. If he writes positive things, take advantage of them; if not, it becomes a matter of conscience that concerns him personally. If he wishes to prove his sincerity, it is up to him to back his assertions through his own example."

905. Some authors have published works that are very beautiful and morally inspiring, which help the progress of humanity, but from which they themselves do not morally profit. Will the good accomplished by their works count toward their standing as spirits, in the future?

"Moral principles not put into practice are like seeds that have not been sown. Of what use is the seed if you do not make it bear fruit and nourish you? Those men are guiltier because they had the intelligence to grasp this. By not practicing the teachings they offered to others, they have relinquished the right to reap their fruit."

906. If a man does good, is it reprehensible for him to be conscious of it and to acknowledge it to himself?

"Since he can be conscious of the evil he does, he must also be conscious of the good he accomplishes in order to know if he acts correctly or not. It is by weighing all his actions on the scales of God's law—above all on the scales of the law of justice, love, and charity—that he will be able to judge whether his actions are good or bad, thereby approving or disapproving them. So, he cannot be in the wrong for recognizing that he has triumphed over his evil tendencies, and for being happy for having done so, provided that does not make him conceited, lest he be guilty of another fault." (See #919)

2. On passions

907. Since passion has its roots in nature, is it bad per se?

"No. Passions emerge from the exuberant display of will, as the principle of passion was given to man for his own good. Passions can lead man to accomplish great things. It is his abuse of them that causes harm."

908. How may we establish the boundaries where passion ceases to be good or bad?

"Passion is like a powerful horse that is highly valuable when brought under control, but rather dangerous when unbridled. You recognize when a passion has become harmful the moment you lose the ability to govern it, resulting in harm to either you or to others."

Passions are levers that provide a tenfold increase in man's powers, helping him fulfill the designs of Providence. However, if rather than controlling them, man instead allows himself to be controlled, he falls into all types of excesses, and the very power that he could have used for a good purpose falls back on him and ends up crushing him.

All passions stem from a natural feeling or need. Passions are therefore not evil in their essence, representing one of the providential conditions of our existence. Passion, strictly speaking, is the exaggeration of a need or sentiment. The problem lies not in the cause, but in the excess, which becomes bad when it results in some type of harm.

Every passion that brings man closer to his animal nature takes him away from his spiritual nature.

Every feeling that lifts man above his animal nature indicates the dominance of his spirit over matter, drawing him closer to perfection.

909. Is man always able to overcome his evil tendencies through his own efforts?

"Yes, and at times with little effort. What he lacks is willpower. Alas, how few of you make any effort at all!"

910. Can a man find in the Spirits help to effectively overcome his passions?

"If he prays to God and to his guardian angel with sincerity, good spirits will certainly come to his aid, as that is their mission." (See #459)

911. Aren't there passions that are so intense and irresistible that willpower is incapable of overcoming them?

"There are many people who say, 'I wish,' but whose wish is to be found only on their lips. They wish, but are rather happy inside if their wish does not materialize. When a man believes himself unable to overcome his passions, it is because his spirit takes pleasure in them as a result of his own moral inferiority. He who tries to rein in his passions, understands his own spiritual nature. Vanquishing his passions represents for him a triumph of the spirit over matter."

912. What is the most effective means of fighting the ascendancy of our physical nature over our spirit?

"The practice of self-denial."

3. On selfishness

913. Of all the vices, which one may be regarded as the root of all others?

"We have already told you many times: *selfishness*. All evil derives from it. Study every vice and you shall see that selfishness lies at the bottom of them all. Try as you may to fight them, you will never eliminate them successfully so long as you do not attack evil at its roots. May all your efforts tend toward that end, because selfishness is the true social plague. Whoever in this life wants to come close to moral perfection must extirpate from his heart every selfish feeling, for selfishness is incompatible with justice, love and charity: it neutralizes all other qualities."

914. Since selfishness is based on the sentiment of personal interest, it seems rather difficult to completely uproot it from man's heart. Will we ever manage to do it?

"As men educate themselves about spiritual matters, they attach less importance to material things. And then, it is necessary to reform human institutions that maintain and stimulate this attachment. That can only be accomplished through education."

915. Since selfishness is inherent in the human species, won't it always be an obstacle to the reign of the absolute good on Earth?

"Certainly, selfishness is your greatest evil, but that derives from the inferior nature of the spirits incarnated on Earth, and not from humanity itself. Upon purifying themselves over successive incarnations, spirits rid themselves of selfishness just as they rid themselves of other imperfections. Isn't there on Earth a man completely free from selfishness and who practices charity? They exist in greater numbers than you would believe, but you only know few of them because virtue never seeks to bask in the spotlight. If there is one such man, why wouldn't there be ten? If there are ten, why wouldn't there be a thousand, and so on?"

916. Far from decreasing, selfishness grows with civilization, which seems to stimulate and sustain it. How can the cause destroy the effect?

"The greater the evil, the more heinous it becomes. Selfishness had to cause much harm in order to make you understand the absolute need to uproot it. When men have freed themselves from the selfishness that dominates them, they will live as brothers, doing no harm to each other, and helping one another out of mutual *solidarity*. The strong will then be the supporter and not the oppressor of the weak, and no longer will anyone lack the basics, because all will practice the law of justice. This is the reign of the good that the Spirits are in charge of preparing." (See #784)

917. What is the means for destroying selfishness?

"Of all human imperfections, the most difficult to uproot is selfishness, because it is caused by the influence of matter, from which man, *so close still to his origin*, has not been able to free himself. Everything seems to contribute to this influence: his laws, his social organization, his education. Selfishness will be weakened with the dominance of the moral life over the material life, and above all with the understanding that Spiritism gives you about your *real* future situation, no longer distorted by allegory. When it is well understood and permeates customs and beliefs, Spiritism will transform habits, practices, and social relations. Selfishness is based upon the relevance ascribed to personality. When well understood, I repeat, Spiritism enables you to see things from such a towering vantage point that the idea of personality somehow dissolves before the immensity. By destroying that relevance, or at least making man see it for what it is, Spiritism inevitably fights selfishness.

"It is the vexation that man experiences from other people's selfishness that frequently makes him selfish in turn, because he then feels the need to put himself on the defensive. Realizing that others think only of themselves and not of him, he becomes more concerned about himself than about others. Let the principle of charity and fraternity be the foundation of social institutions and the *legal* underpinning in the relationship between nations and between individuals, and man will worry less about his own interests when he realizes that others also have them at heart. He will experience the moralizing influence of example and contact. Given the widespread presence of selfishness, steadfast virtue is needed to sacrifice one's own personality for the sake of others, who frequently show no recognition of the sacrifice at all. It is especially to those who have this virtue that the Kingdom of Heaven is open. For them, especially, is reserved the happiness of the elect, because truly I tell you that, on the day of reckoning, those who have only thought of themselves will be cast aside and suffer in neglect." (See #785)

Fénelon

Admirable efforts have unquestionably been made to help humanity advance. Good sentiments are encouraged, stimulated, and praised more now than at any other time, and yet the voracious worm of selfishness continues to plague society. It is a true evil that affects the whole world, victimizing everyone to a greater or lesser extent. So, it is necessary to fight it as we fight an epidemic. To that end we must proceed as physicians do: tracing it back to its root cause. Let us search through everything in society—from families to nations, from hovels to palaces—for all the causes, all the obvious or hidden influences, that stimulate, maintain, and develop selfishness.

Once the causes are known, the remedy will present itself. We will only need to fight them, if not all at once, then at least partially, and little by little the poison will be removed. Cure may take a long time to occur because the causes are numerous, but it is not impossible. Besides, we will not reach that point unless we attack the evil at its roots, which is to say, through education. Not the type of education that tends to produce learned people, but the kind that aims to produce virtuous people. When well understood, education is the key to moral progress. When the art of managing character is understood as well as the art of managing intelligence, we will be able to straighten up characters in the same way that we straighten up young plants.

But such an art requires much tact, much experience, and profound observation. It is a serious error to believe that it is enough to simply have knowledge in order to apply this art successfully. If we follow the children of the rich as well as those of the poor from the moment of their birth, observing all the harmful influences that affect them as a result of the weakness, carelessness, and ignorance of those who guide them, noticing as well how often the means employed to educate them fail, we will not be surprised to find so many oddities in the world. Let efforts be made to foster morality as much as those made to develop intelligence, and we will see that, if there are resistant characters, there are—in greater numbers than one would believe—those who require no more than good nurturing in order to bear good fruit. (See #872)

Man wants to be happy, and this longing is in his very nature. That is why he works continuously to improve his situation on Earth. He searches the causes of his troubles in order to remedy them. He must come to understand that selfishness is one of those causes, the one, in fact, that engenders pride, ambition, greed, envy, hatred, and jealousy, all of which constantly hurt him. When he correctly understands that selfishness brings trouble into all social relations, causes disagreement, destroys trust, and forces neighbors to constantly maintain a defensive attitude toward each other, and, finally, that selfishness turns a friend into a foe, then man shall also understand that this vice is incompatible with his own happiness. And incompatible with his own safety, we would add. Thus, the more he suffers from selfishness, the more he will feel the need to fight it, as fiercely in fact as if he were fighting an epidemic, a pest, or some other scourge. Out of his own self-interest, he will be compelled to do so. (See #784)

Selfishness is the source of all vices, just as charity is the source of all virtues. Destroying the former and cultivating the latter should be the goal of all of man's efforts, if he wishes to ensure his happiness in this world as well as in the future.

4. Characteristics of the good man

918. What signs indicate the accomplishment of progress that will raise a man's spirit in the spiritual hierarchy?

"The spirit demonstrates his elevation when every action of his earthly life represents the practice of the law of God, and when he understands in advance the spirit life."

The truly good man is he who practices the law of justice, love, and charity in its utmost purity. If he asks his conscience about the actions he has performed, he will wonder if he has not violated that law, if he has not done any wrong, if he has done all the good *in his power*, if no one has reason to complain about him, and, finally, if he has done to others what he would want others to do to him.

Filled with the sentiment of charity and love for his neighbor, he does good for its own sake, without expecting reward, and sacrifices his own interests for the sake of justice.

He is good, humane, and kind to everyone, because he sees every person as a brother or sister, regardless of race or belief.

If God has given him power and wealth, he regards these gifts as a *trust fund* that he must put to good use. But this does not make him conceited, because he knows that God, who has given them to him, may take them away.

If the social order has made other men dependent on him, he treats them with goodness and kindness, because he is their equal before God. He uses his authority to lift their morale, and not to crush them with his pride.

He is indulgent toward the weaknesses of others, because he knows that he needs indulgence himself, reminding himself of the words of Christ, "Let him that is without sin cast the first stone." [a]

He is not vengeful: after Jesus' example, he forgives offenses and only remembers the kindness of others because *he knows that he will be forgiven as he has himself forgiven.*

Finally, he respects all the rights that the laws of nature have granted to others, as he would want them to respect his own rights as well.

5. Self-knowledge

919. What is the most effectual means of improving ourselves in this life and of resisting the pull of evil?

"A sage of antiquity has told you: 'Know thyself.' " [b]

—   We understand all the wisdom of that maxim, but the difficulty lies precisely in knowing ourselves. How can we achieve that?

"Do what I used to do when living on Earth. At the end of each day I would question my conscience, reviewing what I had done and asking myself whether I had failed to fulfill some duty, and whether anyone had reason to complain about me. It was thus that I arrived at knowing myself and at seeing what was necessary to correct in me. He who every night reviews all his actions during the day, and asks himself what good or evil he has done, praying to God and his guardian angel to enlighten him, will acquire great power to improve himself, because, believe me, God will assist him.

Ask therefore yourselves about what you have done and toward what objective you have acted in a given circumstance, whether you have done anything that you would condemn in others, and whether you have done anything that you would not dare to confess. Ask further the following: 'If it pleased God to call me back at this moment, would I have, upon re-entering the spirit world, where nothing is hidden, reason to fear anyone's stare?' Examine what you may have done against God, next against your neighbor, and, finally, against yourselves. The answers will either ease your conscience or indicate a wrong that you must remedy.

"Self-knowledge is therefore the key to individual improvement. 'But,' you will ask, 'how do we judge ourselves? Isn't there the illusion created by our ego, which lessens our wrongs and makes them excusable? Misers think they simply act with thrift and foresight. The proud believe they are simply full of dignity.' All of this is very true, but you have an auditing procedure that cannot fool you. When you have doubts about the quality of one of your actions, ask yourselves how you would consider it if it had been done by someone else. If you would condemn it if done by another, it cannot be any more legitimate for you, for God only has one yardstick for justice. Also, try to know what others think about it and do not disregard the opinion of your enemies, because they have no interest in concealing the truth, and God often places them beside you as a mirror in order to warn you more frankly than a friend ever would.

"Therefore, let he who is truly willing to improve himself explore his own conscience in order to uproot from it his evil tendencies, as he would remove weeds from his yard. Let him balance out his moral workday like a merchant that computes his profits and losses, and I assure you that the former will be greater than the latter. If you can say that your day has been positive, you can sleep in peace and wait without fear your awakening in the other life.

"So, ask yourselves clear and precise questions, and do not be afraid to add to their number: a few minutes can very well be devoted to secure eternal happiness. Don't you work every day in order to amass what you will need for your retirement? Isn't this retirement the objective of all your desires, the goal that makes you suffer temporary fatigue and hardships? Well then, how can one compare a few days of retirement, troubled by physical ailments, with the future that awaits a virtuous man? Isn't that worth a little effort? I know that many say the present is certain but the future is uncertain. Well, this is precisely the thought that we are in charge of eliminating from your minds, because we want to make you understand this future in such a way as to leave no doubt in your soul. That's why we first called your attention to phenomena that strike your physical senses, and only now we give you instructions that each one of you has the responsibility to spread. To this end we have dictated *The Spirits' Book.*"

Saint Augustine

Many of the mistakes we make go unnoticed by us. If indeed, following the advice of Saint Augustine, we were to question our conscience more often, we would see how frequently we have failed, without realizing it, by not having analyzed the nature and motivation of our actions. The self-questioning approach is more accurate than the use of maxims and precepts which we often do not apply to ourselves. It requires unequivocal yes-no answers that leave no room for alternatives. Through this personal argumentation process, and by adding up the answers, we can calculate the sum of the good and the evil within ourselves.

■■■

[a] John 8:7. —Trans.

[b] This is a reference to the ancient Greek aphorism *know thyself*, or *gnothi seauton* (Greek: γνῶθι σεαυτόν), inscribed in the portico of the temple of Apollo at Delphi. Plato used this maxim extensively in his writings, and mentioned its use by Socrates on many occasions. —Trans.

Part 4:
Hopes and Consolations

Chapter 1:
Earthly Afflictions and Joys

1. Relative happiness and unhappiness

920. Can man enjoy complete happiness on Earth?

"No, because life has been given to him as either a trial or an expiation. But it depends on him to lessen his misfortunes and be as happy as possible while on Earth."

921. We understand that man will be happy on Earth when humanity has been transformed. In the meantime, however, is it possible for him to enjoy a relative happiness?

"Man is most frequently the artisan of his own unhappiness. By practicing the law of God, he would spare himself many misfortunes, securing as great a happiness as his crude existence allows."

The man who fathoms in earnest his future destiny sees his corporeal existence as nothing but a brief stopover. It represents for him a short stay at a shabby hotel. He readily takes comfort when faced with a few passing inconveniences on a journey that shall lead him to a position which will be all the better the more carefully he prepares himself ahead of time for it.

We are punished in this life for the infractions we commit against the laws of corporeal existence by the misfortunes that result from such infractions and from our own excesses. If we were to go back, step by step, to the source of what we call our earthly afflictions, we would realize that, for the most part, they are the result of a prior deviation from the straight path. Due to this deviation we enter the wrong road, and from one outcome to the next, misfortune befalls us.

922. Earthly happiness is relative to the position of each person, and what might be enough for the happiness of one person may represent a misfortune for another. Is there nonetheless a measure of happiness common to everyone?

"With respect to material life, the possession of what is necessary. With respect to moral life, a clear conscience and faith in the future."

923. Doesn't that which would be a luxury for one person become a necessity for another, and vice versa, in accord with their position?

"Yes, according to your materially focused ideas, your prejudices, your greed, and all your foolish whims, which the future shall dispel when you understand the truth. Undoubtedly, he who had an income of millions and sees it reduced to a few hundreds of thousands considers himself most unfortunate, because he cannot cut as great a figure and hold onto what he calls his social standing—keeping horses and servants, gratifying all his passions, and so on. He believes to be lacking his necessities. Frankly, however, do you really think this man is to be pitied while next to him there are those who suffer from hunger and cold, without a shelter where they may lay their head? In order to be happy, the wise man observes that which is below, never that which is above, except to raise his soul toward the Infinite." (See #715)

924. There are misfortunes which do not depend on the way a man acts and which afflict the most righteous man. Isn't there a way to avoid them?

"In that case, those misfortunes must be borne with fortitude and *without bemoaning*, if the man wants to progress. But he will always find solace in his own conscience, which gives him the hope of a better future, provided he does what is needed to reach it."

925. Why does God favor with the gifts of fortune certain men who do not seem to have deserved them?

"It looks like a favor in the eyes of those who see nothing but the present. But beware, for frequently wealth is a more dangerous trial than poverty." (See #814–816)

926. By creating new needs, isn't civilization the source of new afflictions?

"The misfortunes of this world result from the *artificial* needs you create for yourselves. He who knows how to set limits on his desires and who regards without envy whatever is beyond his means, spares himself many disappointments in this life. The richest man is the one who has the fewest needs.

"You envy the enjoyments of those who seem to you to be the world's fortunate; but do you know what is in store for them? If they use their wealth only for themselves, they are selfish; in time a reversal shall befall them. Pity them, instead. God sometimes allows a wicked man to prosper, but his happiness is not to be envied, because he shall pay for it with bitter tears. If a righteous man is unfortunate, it is because he is going through a trial that will be credited to him, if he bears it with courage. Remember the words of Jesus: 'Blessed are those who mourn, for they shall be comforted.' " [a]

927. The superfluous is certainly not indispensable to happiness, but that is not the case with the necessities of life. Is it not a real misfortune to be deprived of such necessities?

"Man is truly unfortunate only when he lacks what is necessary for his life and his physical health. Such hardships are perhaps of his own making; in that case he has only himself to blame. If they are someone else's fault, the responsibility falls upon the one who has caused them."

928. Through the specialization of natural aptitudes, God evidently indicates our vocation in this world. Don't many misfortunes result from our not following this vocation?

"That is true, and parents are frequently the ones who, through pride or greed, make their children deviate from the path outlined by nature, a diversion that jeopardizes the latter's happiness. For that the parents shall be held accountable."

— So, would you consider it right if the son of a high-ranking man became a shoemaker, for instance, should that be his aptitude?

"There is no need to turn to absurd arguments or exaggerations: civilization has its demands. Why would the son of a high-ranking man, as you call him, have to be a shoemaker if he can do other things? He can always be useful to the extent of his abilities, if he does not employ them incorrectly. So, for instance, rather than become a bad lawyer, he could perhaps become a good engineer, and so on."

To be placed outside of one's scope of aptitudes is assuredly one of the most frequent causes of disappointment. The ineptitude in a career one has embraced represents an endless source of frustration. Then the influence of pride prevents the hapless individual from seeking work in more humble occupations, rendering suicide a solution for what he considers a humiliation. *If a moral education had made him immune to the foolish prejudices of pride, he would never be caught unprepared.*

929. There are people who lack everything, even as affluence surrounds them, having no prospect except death; what should they do about it? Should they let themselves starve to death?

"One should never contemplate the idea of starving oneself to death; one would always find the means to feed oneself if pride did not interpose itself between the existing need and the available work. It is frequently said that all work is noble, and no social status is dishonorable per se— words easily applied to others, but not to oneself."

930. Clearly, were it not for the social prejudices that we allow to dominate us, we would always find the means to make a living, even if we must be demoted to a lower position. Still, even among those who have no such prejudices or who put them aside, aren't there those who are unable to provide for their needs as a result of illness or other reasons beyond their control?

"In a society organized according to the law of Christ, no one should starve."

Within a prudent and provident social organization, man would only lack the basic necessities by his own fault. Still, these very faults are frequently the result of the environment he finds himself in. When he fully observes the law of God, there will be a social order based on justice and solidarity, and he himself will be a better individual. (See #793)

931. Why do suffering classes outnumber the fortunate ones in our society?

"No class is completely happy, and those considered fortunate often hide heartbreaking sorrows; suffering is everywhere. However, in response to your question, I shall say that the suffering classes, as you call them, are more numerous because the Earth is a world of expiation. When man has transformed it into an abode where goodness and good spirits predominate, he will no longer be unhappy, and Earth will be a terrestrial paradise for him."

932. Why does the influence of the wicked of this world often overpower that of the good?

"Because the good are feeble. The wicked are cunning and daring, whereas the good are timid. When the latter so wish, they shall prevail."

933. If man is most frequently the artisan of his own material suffering, is he also the artisan of his moral suffering?

"Even more so, because his material suffering is sometimes beyond his control, whereas a hurt pride, a frustrated ambition, the angst of greed, envy, jealousy—in short, all the passions—represent tortures of the soul.

"Envy and jealousy! Happy are those who do not know these two voracious worms! For those afflicted with envy and jealousy there can be no peace, no rest: the objects of their covetousness, their hatred and their resentment, loom over them like ghosts, providing no respite and haunting them even in their sleep. The envious and jealous burn in continuous fever. Is that situation worthwhile? Do you not realize that, with such passions, man begets self-inflicted torments, transforming the Earth into a true hell for himself?"

Many expressions vividly describe the effects of passions. We say *puffed up with pride, green with envy, to burn with jealousy, to flame with resentment,* and so on. Such depictions are indeed very accurate. Sometimes jealousy does not even have a specific object. There are people who are naturally jealous of anything that stands out, of anything that rises above the mundane, even though they have no direct interest in the matter, but simply because those achievements are beyond their reach. Everything that seems to be above the horizon insults them, and if they represented the majority of society, they would demand everything be brought down to their own level. Here one has jealousy coupled with mediocrity.

Man is frequently unhappy only due to the importance he attaches to earthly things: the thwarting of his vanity, ambition, and greed makes him unhappy. If he were to raise himself above the narrow circle of material life, if he were to raise his thoughts toward the infinite that represents his destiny, the tribulations of human life would seem petty and puerile, like the grief of a child who weeps over a lost toy that was the source of much enjoyment.

The man who can only derive happiness from the satisfaction of his pride and uncouth material appetites is unhappy when not able to satisfy them, whereas the frugal man who requires no luxuries is happy in circumstances which others would consider disastrous.

Here we make reference to the civilized man, because the primitive man has needs that are much more limited, having nothing to stimulate greed or angst. His way of looking at things is rather different. The civilized man ponders and analyzes his unhappiness, being more affected by it. He may, however, also ponder and analyze the means of finding solace. This solace he may find in *the Christian sentiment that gives him the hope of a better future, and in Spiritism, which gives him the certainty of that future.*

2. Loss of loved ones

934. Isn't the loss of those who are dear to us a legitimate source of sorrow, all the more so as this loss is both irreparable and beyond our control?

"This cause of sorrow affects both rich and poor: trial or expiation, it is a universal law. Being able to communicate with your friends through the means available to you, however, constitutes a consolation, *while waiting until you obtain other means that are more direct and accessible to your senses.*"

935. What to think of the opinion of people who consider the communication with those beyond the grave a profanation?

"There can be no profanation when there is recollection and when the evocation is made with respect and decorum. The proof of this is that the spirits who have affection for you are pleased to answer, and rejoice in being remembered and in being able to speak with you. There would be profanation only if this were done frivolously."

The possibility of communicating with spirits is a very tender consolation, which provides us with a way of reconnecting with relatives and friends who have left the Earth before us. By evoking them, we bring them closer to us, where they can stand by our side, listen, and reply to us. There is no longer, so to speak, any separation between them and us. They help us with their advice, bearing witness to their affection, and to the joy they experience when we remember them. It is a satisfaction for us to know that they are happy, and to learn *directly from them* the details of their new existence, acquiring the certainty that someday we shall rejoin them in our turn.

936. How does the inconsolable grief of the surviving relatives affect the spirits who are the object of it?

"Spirits are touched by the memory of those who remember them, as well as the by grief felt by those they loved, but relentless and unreasonable grief affects them painfully, because they see in such excess a lack of faith in the future and of trust in God, and consequently, an obstacle to progress, and perhaps to their reunion."

When a spirit is happier than he was on Earth, to regret that he has left this life behind is to regret that he is happy. Two friends are prisoners in the same cell; both of them are to be freed someday but one of them is set free first. Would it be right on the part of the one who remains in prison to be sad that his friend has been released before him? Would there not be on his part more selfishness than affection in wishing his friend would remain in captivity and suffer as long as himself? The same is true with two people who love each other on Earth. The one who departs first is the first to be freed, and we should be happy for him, patiently waiting for the moment when we shall also be freed in our turn.

Let us make another comparison. You have a friend who lives nearby. He finds himself in a difficult situation. His health or personal interests require him to go to another country, where he will be better off in every respect. That means he will no longer be close to you for quite some time, but you will be able to contact each other through mail—the separation will be only physical. Will you be grieved by his departure since it is for his own good?

The Spiritist Doctrine—through the clear evidences it gives us concerning the future life, the presence around us of beings we have loved, the continuation of their affection and consideration, as well as the communication we are allowed to establish with them—offers us a supreme consolation in the face of one of the most legitimate causes of sorrow. With Spiritism, there is no more solitude or abandonment. The most isolated individuals are always encircled by friends with whom they can speak.

We impatiently endure the tribulations of life. They seem so intolerable that we think we cannot withstand them. If we endure them with courage, however, if we know how to silence our complaints, we will rejoice when we are released from this earthly prison, in the same way that a patient who has been suffering rejoices, once healed, at having patiently endured a painful treatment.

3. Disappointments, ungratefulness, broken affections

937. Aren't the disappointments caused by ingratitude and by the fragility of human friendships also a source of bitterness for the human heart?

"Yes, but we have already recommended that you pity ungrateful and disloyal friends—they will be unhappier than you are. Ingratitude is the child of selfishness, and the selfish sooner or later encounter hearts as hardened as their own. Consider all those who have done more good than you, who are worthier than you, and yet have been repaid with ingratitude. Remember that during his life, Jesus himself was scorned, despised, and treated as a rogue and an impostor. So do not be surprised that you should be treated similarly. Let the good you do be your reward in this world, and do not worry about what those that you helped have to say. Ingratitude serves to test your resolve in doing good. It will be credited to you, and those who have disparaged you will be punished in proportion to their ungratefulness."

938. Aren't the disappointments caused by ingratitude likely to harden the heart, making it insensitive?

"That would be unfortunate because those who have a heart, as you say, will always be happy for the good they do. They know that if the good they do is not remembered in the present life, it will be in another, and the ungrateful will then feel shame and remorse."

— But such knowledge does not prevent their heart from being hurt; therefore, could this not induce the idea that they would be happier if they were less sensitive?

"Yes, if they were to prefer the happiness of the selfish, a very sad happiness, indeed! May they recognize that the ungrateful friends who desert them are unworthy of their friendship, and that they have been mistaken about them; from that point on they will no longer be sorry. Later they shall find friends who are more understanding. You should pity those who treat you poorly and undeservedly, because they shall receive a severe retribution. Do not let yourselves be afflicted by them: it is a means for you to raise yourselves above them."

Nature has given man the need to love and be loved. One of the greatest enjoyments granted to him on Earth is in his meeting with kindred hearts. Nature grants him, this way, a glimpse into the happiness waiting for him in the world of perfect spirits, where all is love and kindness—a happiness that is denied to the selfish.

4. Antagonistic unions

939. Since like-minded spirits are driven to be associated, why can it be that among incarnate spirits affection is often one-sided, and the sincerest love is received with indifference or even aversion? In addition, how can the strongest affection between two people turn into dislike and sometimes hatred?

"Can you not see that this may be a punishment, although a temporary one? In addition, how many are there who think they are deeply in love because they are moved by physical appearances only, but when forced to live together they soon realize their judgment had only been based on physical infatuation? It is not enough to be in love with someone who pleases you, and whom you believe to be endowed with beautiful qualities—it is only by living together that you can judge properly. Also, there are many unions that initially seem as if they should never be congenial, but which, as both people get to be familiar each other, they develop a tender and lasting love, because it is founded on mutual affection! You must not forget that it is the spirit that loves, not the body, and that once the physical illusion dissipates, the spirit sees reality.

"There are two kinds of affection: that of the body and that of the soul, and these are often mistaken for one another. When pure and based on affinities, the affection of the soul is long-lasting; the affection of the body is perishable. That is why those who believed they loved each other with an eternal love often end up hating each other once the illusion has faded away."

940. Isn't the lack of affinity between people destined to live together also another source of suffering that is all the more bitter, in that it poisons their entire existence?

"Very bitter, indeed. But it is usually one of those misfortunes of which you yourselves are the main culprit. First, simply because your laws are imperfect, do you believe that God demands that you live with those you dislike? Besides, in such unions you almost always seek more to satisfy your pride and ambition rather than to enjoy the happiness of mutual affection. You then suffer the consequence of your prejudices."

—   But in such cases, isn't there almost always an innocent victim?

"Yes, and for that person it represents a difficult expiation, but the responsibility for such unhappiness will fall upon the one who caused it. If the light of truth has touched the victim's soul, faith in the future provides consolation. Besides, as these prejudices diminish, the causes of such private misfortunes disappear as well."

5. Fear of death

941. The fear of death is cause of perplexity for many people. Where does this worry come from, if they have the whole future before them?

"It is wrong to have such an apprehension, but what do you expect? From an early age people are persuaded that there is a hell and a heaven, but that they will most likely go to hell, because they are taught that all that belongs to the natural order of things represents a mortal sin for the soul. Then, once people grow up and start making sense of things, they can no longer accept that idea and become atheists or materialists. This is how they are led to believe that there is nothing beyond their present life. As for those who maintain their childhood beliefs, they fear the eternal fire that shall burn them for eternity.

"But death does not make the righteous afraid, for *faith* gives them certainty about the future, *hope* leads them to look forward to a better life, and the law of *charity*, which they practice, gives them the assurance that, in the world to come, they will not find anyone into whose eyes they will fear looking." (See #730)

> While on Earth, pleasure-seeking men—more attached as they are to their corporeal life than to their spiritual life—experience life's physical afflictions and pleasures. Their happiness lies in the fleeting satisfaction of all their desires. Their soul is permanently focused and dependent on the tribulations of life, which leads them to be permanently anxious and tortured. Death frightens them because they are not certain about their future and because they believe they must leave all their affections and hopes behind on Earth.
>
> Virtuous individuals, by raising themselves above the artificial needs engendered by passions, experience joys unknown to those who only seek pleasure. The moderation of their desires makes their spirits calm and serene. They are happy for being able to do good, so disappointments do not hurt them, and vexations affect their souls without leaving painful scars.

942. Will some people not find this advice on happiness a little trite? Will they not see it as commonplace or as empty clichés, and will they not say that the definite secret to happiness is to know how to weather one's misfortunes?

"There are those—many in fact—who will say that. They are like sick patients for whom a doctor prescribes a particular diet. They want to be healed, but being defiant, refuse medication and continue eating their way to indigestion."

6. Weariness of life, suicide

943. What is the cause of the weariness of life which takes hold of certain individuals without any apparent reason?

"It is the effect of idleness, the lack of faith, and often, satiety.

"For him who employs his abilities with a useful purpose and *according to his natural aptitudes,* work is never dull, and life passes quickly. He endures the tribulations of life with patience and fortitude, as he acts while having in mind the more solid and lasting joy that awaits him."

944. Does man have the right to dispose of his own life?

"No! Only God has that right. Intentional suicide is a transgression of this law."

—   Is suicide not always intentional?

"The insane man who kills himself does not know what he does."

945. What is to be thought of those who commit suicide out of their weariness of life?

"Foolishness! Why didn't they work? Life would not have become such a burden for them."

946. What about those who commit suicide to escape from the troubles and disappointments of this world?

"Poor spirits, who do not have the courage to endure the difficulties of life! God helps those who suffer, but not those who have neither strength nor courage. The tribulations of life are meant as trials or expiations. Happy are those who endure them without complaining, for they shall be rewarded! But woe betide those who, in their impiety, hope to solve their problems by taking such a leap in the dark! By betting their lives on the whims of chance, they may ride their good luck for a while, but, later on, they will inexorably feel the cruel emptiness of the word *chance.*"

— Won't those who have led an unhappy person to such an act of desperation suffer the consequences of their action?

"Woe to them! Because they shall answer for it as if for a murder."

947. Can a man who struggles with poverty, allowing himself to die of despair, be considered as having committed suicide?

"It is suicide, but those who have caused it, or who could have prevented it, are guiltier than the one who committed it; the latter will thus be judged with mercy. Do not think, however, that the man will be completely exonerated if he showed a lack of resolve and perseverance, or failed to make the best use of his intelligence in order to get himself out of his predicament. His woes are further aggravated if his despair was the result of pride—in other words, if he allowed pride to paralyze his intelligence, ashamed to earn his living as a manual laborer, preferring to starve than to be demoted from his so-called *social position*! Isn't there a hundred times more greatness and dignity in fighting adversity, in braving the criticism of a futile and selfish world, which only favors those who lack nothing, and which turns its back on you in your time of need? To sacrifice one's life for the considerations of this world is utterly senseless, because the world will not be concerned about such a sacrifice in the least."

948. When committed in order to escape the dishonor of an evil act, is suicide as reprehensible as when committed out of despair?

"Suicide does not erase any wrongs. On the contrary, it represents an aggravation of the initial fault. Those who have the courage to do evil should have the courage to bear its consequences. God is the one who judges and, depending on the reasons, He may take into consideration mitigating factors."

949. Is suicide excusable when committed in order to avoid casting shame on one's children or family?

"Those who act under this belief do no good at all, but because they think they do, God shall take their intention into account, for their suicide will be a self-imposed expiation. Their fault is mitigated by their intention, but it remains a transgression, nonetheless. When you have eliminated your social prejudices and injustices, you will no longer have any suicides."

> Those who take their own life in order to escape the dishonor of an evil act prove that they attach more value to the assessment of others than to that of God, because they will return to the spiritual world guilty of their crimes, having at the same time deprived themselves of the means of atoning for them during life. God is often less severe than man, as He pardons those who sincerely repent, taking into account our efforts to remedy our wrongs; suicide, however, is no reparation.

950. What is to be thought of those who take their own life hoping to arrive sooner at a better life?

"Another folly! Let them do good and they will be more likely to arrive at a better life, because suicide will only delay their entrance into a better world and they themselves shall ask to come back to *complete the life* that they cut short owing to an erroneous idea. A mistake, whatever it may be, never has the power to open the doors of the sanctuary of the elect."

951. Isn't the sacrifice of one's life sometimes meritorious when made to save the lives of others, or to be useful to one's fellow human beings?

"In this intention, it is sublime, and such a sacrifice of life does not therefore constitute a suicide. But God opposes a meaningless sacrifice and cannot look upon it with pleasure if it is tainted by pride. A sacrifice is not meritorious unless it is selfless, so if those who make such a sacrifice have ulterior motives, its value is reduced in God's eyes."

> Every sacrifice made at the cost of our own happiness is supremely meritorious in God's eyes, as it represents the practice of the law of charity. Now, since life is the earthly possession that we value the most, those who renounce it for the sake of their fellow creatures do not commit a crime, but, rather, make a sacrifice. Before doing so, however, they should consider whether their life might not be of greater utility than their death.

952. Should it be considered suicide when men die from the excesses of their passions, when in spite of knowing these shall hasten their end, they cannot resist, because habit turned their passions into a true physical need?

"It is a moral suicide. Do you not see that they are doubly guilty in such cases? They lack courage and yield to their inferior appetites, in addition to forgetting about God."

— Are they more or less guilty than those who cut their lives short out of despair?

"They are guiltier because they had time to consider their suicide. For those who commit suicide on impulse, there is sometimes a kind of frenzy that borders on insanity. The former will be punished much more than the latter, because punishments are always proportional to the cognizance one has of one's own wrong-doing."

953. When people realize that an inevitable and terrible death lies in front of them, is it wrong to shorten their suffering by a few moments through suicide?

"It is always wrong not to wait for the term appointed by God. Besides, how can they be sure that their time has indeed come, in spite of appearances, or that they might not receive some unexpected help at the last moment?"

— We admit that suicide is reprehensible in ordinary situations, but would that still be the case when death is inevitable, and when life is only shortened by a few instants?

"It still represents a lack of forbearance and submission to the will of the Creator."

— What are the consequences of such an action in this case?

"As in all other cases, an expiation proportional to the severity of the fault, according to the attending circumstances."

954. Is there guilt in a reckless act that puts life needlessly at risk?

"There is no guilt so long as there is no positive intention or consciousness of doing harm."

955. Is it suicide when women in certain countries deliberately burn themselves to death over the dead body of their husband, and must they suffer the consequences of that act?

"They bow to the prejudices of their culture, and often more out of pressure than of their own volition. They believe they are fulfilling a duty, and this is not what characterizes suicide. Their excuse is in their ignorance and lack of moral development. Such barbaric and senseless practices shall disappear with civilization."

956. Does he reach his goal who, unable to bear the loss of his loved ones, kills himself in the hope of rejoining them?

"The result for him is much different from what he expected. Instead of being reunited with the objects of his affection, he distances himself from them even longer, because God cannot reward such a cowardly act, an insult which represents a lack of faith in divine providence. Such a reckless man will pay for that instant of insanity with afflictions even greater than those he wished to shorten, and he will not find the joy he hoped for as a compensation for his act." (See #934–936)

957. What are the consequences of suicide, in general, for the spirit?

"The consequences of suicide vary greatly. There are no fixed punishments; they are always in accord with the causes that produced them. Nevertheless, one consequence those who commit suicide cannot escape from, is *disappointment*. But the outcome is not the same for all, and depends on circumstances. Some expiate their wrong at once, whereas others do so in a new life that will be worse than the one they have cut short."

Observation has effectively confirmed that the consequences of suicide are not always the same. There are some aspects, however, that are common to all cases of violent death, as well as the ensuing consequences of the sudden interruption of life. Foremost among these consequences is the longer and stronger persistence of the link that ties the spirit to the body, and which is almost always at its full strength when prematurely broken, as opposed to the case of natural death, in which this link wanes gradually, being often undone before life is completely extinguished. Suicide results in the protraction of the state of spiritual bewilderment in addition to the illusion that causes spirits to believe, for a longer or shorter period, that they are still to be counted among the living. (See #155, #165)

In the case of certain suicides, the affinity that continues to exist between the spirit and the body produces a sort of resonance between the condition of the body and the spirit, who is thus compelled to witness the effects of decomposition, experiencing a sensation full of anguish and horror. This situation can continue for as long as the life that was cut short ought to have lasted. This effect is not a set rule, but in no circumstance are those who committed suicide freed from the consequences of their cowardly act, so that, sooner or later, they will atone for this wrong somehow.

Accordingly, some spirits who had been very unhappy on Earth stated that they had committed suicide in their previous existence, therefore voluntarily submitting themselves to new trials, to learn how to bear them with more fortitude. For some, it comes in the form of an enchainment to the very matter from which they unsuccessfully seek to free themselves, in order to go to happier worlds, but the entry to which is denied to them. The majority feel regret for having done something utterly pointless, from which they derive nothing but disappointment.

Religion, morality, and philosophy condemn suicide as being contrary to the law of nature. They all establish in principle that we have no right to intentionally cut our own life short, but why do we not have that right, why are we not free to put an end to our own suffering? It was destined to Spiritism to address these questions by showing through the actual examples of those who have yielded to suicide that it is not only an infringement of a moral law—a consideration of little importance to some—but also a senseless act that brings no benefit, quite the contrary. Spiritism teaches this not from a theoretical standpoint, but by the very facts that it lays out before our eyes.

■■■

[a] Matthew 5:4. —Trans.

Chapter 2:
Future Afflictions and Joys

1. Annihilation of the soul, future life

958. Why does man have an instinctive aversion to the idea of the annihilation of the soul?

"Because there is no such thing as nothingness."

959. Where does our instinctive sentiment of a future life come from?

"We have already told you: before reincarnating, the spirit is aware of all these things, and, once incarnate, the soul retains a vague memory of that knowledge and of what was seen during the interval in between incarnations." (See #393)

In all ages, man has concerned himself with the future beyond the grave, which is very natural. Whatever importance he may ascribe to his present life, he cannot help but consider how short and, above all, precarious it is, as it can be cut short at any moment, so that he can never be sure about the day to come. What becomes of him after that fatal moment? This is a serious question, because it does not refer to a few years only, but to eternity. He who will spend many years in a foreign country concerns himself with his future situation. So, why do we not concern ourselves with the situation we will face when we leave this world behind, as it will be forever?

The idea of nothingness repels reason. The most unconcerned man in life, upon arriving at the supreme moment, asks himself what will become of him, unwittingly creating an expectation.

To believe in God without believing in a future life would be nonsense. The instinct about a better life is to be found within everyone; God did not place it there for no reason.

A future life implies the preservation of our individuality after death. What good would it do to survive the body if our intellectual essence must be lost in the ocean of the infinite? The consequences of that would be the same as nothingness.

2. Intuition of future afflictions and joys

960. Where does the belief in future punishments and rewards—to be found in all cultures—come from?

"It is another intuition of reality, imparted to man by his spirit. Understand that it is not in vain that an inner voice speaks to you—your mistake is in not listening to it. If you gave serious and frequent attention to this, you would make yourselves better."

961. At the moment of death, what is the prevailing feeling in most people: doubt, fear or hope?

"Doubt, in the case of hardhearted skeptics; fear, in the case of the guilty; and hope, in the case of the virtuous."

962. Why are there skeptics at all, as the soul gives man the intuition of spiritual matters?

"There are fewer skeptics than you suppose. During life, many pretend to be bold freethinkers out of pride, but at the moment of death, they are much less arrogant."

The consequences of the future life derive from the responsibility for our acts. With regard to the distribution of the joys to which all aspire, reason and justice tell us that the good and the wicked cannot possibly be ranked together. God cannot have wished for some to be awarded enjoyments without effort, whereas others only through struggle and perseverance.

The idea that God applies His justice and mercy through the wisdom of His laws does not allow us to believe that the righteous and the wicked are at the same level in His eyes. Nor can we doubt that someday the former shall receive a reward, and the latter a punishment, for the good or evil they have done. That is why our innate sense of justice gives us the intuition of future rewards and punishments.

3. God's intervention in punishments and rewards

963. Is God personally concerned with each individual? Isn't God too great and aren't we too small for each individual in particular to have any importance in the His eyes?

"God is concerned with all the beings He created, no matter how small they may be. Nothing is too small for the goodness of God."

964. Must God be concerned with each of our actions to reward or punish us? Aren't most of such actions insignificant to God?

"God has established the laws that regulate all your actions. If you infringe them, it is your fault. Obviously, when a man commits an excess, God does not sentence him, for instance, by saying, 'You are a glutton, and I am going to punish you.' But God has established a limit—sickness, and sometimes death, are the consequences of excess. So punishments result from infringement of the law, and all else operates this way."

All our actions are subject to the laws of God. *No matter how insignificant our actions seem to us*, there is not a single one that is not measured against them. If we suffer the consequences of a violation of those laws, we have only ourselves to blame. We are, therefore, the artisans of our own happy or sad future.

This truth is made evident in the following tale: A father has provided his son with education and instruction, in other words, the means of knowing how to conduct himself. The father then hands over to the son a piece of land to farm, telling him, "I have given you the directions to be observed, and all the necessary tools to make this field productive, allowing you to make a living. I made certain that you understand these rules. If you follow them, your field will produce abundant harvests, and will provide for your retirement in your old age. If you do not follow them, your crops will fail, and you shall starve." After having said that, the father leaves his son free to act as he pleases.

Is it not true that the field will produce in proportion to the care taken in its cultivation, and that all negligence will fall back on the son as a failed crop? The son will therefore be happy or unhappy in his old age according to how carefully he followed the rules outlined by his father. God is still more provident, by constantly warning us about our correct or wrong conduct, sending us the Spirits to inspire us. We do not listen to them, however. There is also one further difference, in that God gives man the opportunity of new lives for him to repair his past mistakes, whereas the son in this story will not have the same opportunities, if he employs his time unwisely.

4. Nature of future afflictions and joys

965. Is there anything material about the afflictions and joys that affect the soul after death?

"They cannot be material, as the soul is not made of matter; your common sense will tell you so. There is nothing material about future afflictions and joys, and that is the reason why they are a thousand times more vivid than those experienced on Earth, because the perceptions of the spirit—once disengaged from the material envelope that dulls your senses—are much sharper." (See #237–257)

966. Why do some men have such rudimentary and ludicrous ideas about the afflictions and joys of the future life?

"Because their intelligence is not yet sufficiently developed. Does the child have the same comprehension of things that adults have? In addition, it also depends on how a man is brought up, an area that you need to revisit.

"Your language is too incomplete to express that which lies beyond your reach. Thus, it has been necessary to make comparisons, and you have taken such images and figures as reality itself. As man gains knowledge, however, he can better understand the things that his language cannot describe."

967. What does the happiness of good spirits consist of?

"Of knowing all things; of not feeling hatred, jealousy, envy, ambition, or any of the passions that make man unhappy. The love that unites good spirits is a source of supreme bliss. They do not experience the needs, sufferings, or anxieties of material life. They are happy with the good they do. In addition, the happiness of spirits is always in proportion to their progress. It is true that only pure spirits enjoy absolute happiness, but this does not mean others are necessarily unhappy.

"Between evil and perfect spirits exists an infinity of degrees, in which enjoyments are proportional to the spirit's moral standing. Those who are already sufficiently advanced admire the happiness of those who have previously reached that state to which they aspire, a fact that serves as an incentive, not a reason for jealousy. They know it depends on their own efforts to reach that state, so they labor toward that end with the calmness provided by a clear conscience. They are happy to no longer need to suffer that which imperfect spirits must still endure."

968. You place the absence of material needs among the conditions of happiness for spirits. But isn't the satisfaction of those needs a source of pleasure for man?

"Yes, the gratification of your animal passions. When you are not able to satisfy those needs, it becomes a torture."

969. What are we to understand when it is said that pure spirits are gathered in the bosom of God, singing praises to Him?

"It is a symbol to give you an idea of the knowledge pure spirits possess about the perfections of God, because they see and comprehend Him. But it is a symbol that you must not take literally, the same as any other allegory. Everything in nature sings, from the grain of sand all the way up, proclaiming the power, the wisdom, and the goodness of God. Do not suppose, however, that pure spirits are absorbed in eternal contemplation. That would be a monotonous and dull happiness, and, in addition, a rather selfish one, because their existence would represent an eternal uselessness. They no longer suffer the tribulations of corporeal life, a fact which in itself is already an enjoyment. Later, as we have told you, they know and comprehend all things, and they make use of their acquired intelligence by fostering the progress of other spirits. That is both their occupation and enjoyment."

970. What do the sufferings of low order spirits consist of?

"They are as varied as the causes that produce them, and in proportion to their degree of imperfection, just as enjoyments are in proportion to the degree of perfection of a spirit. We can summarize them as follows: coveting all they lack, but are unable to obtain, in order to be happy; seeing the happiness which lies beyond their reach; feeling regret, jealousy, rage, and despair toward what prevents them from being happy; and being tormented by remorse and an indescribable moral anguish. They long for all sorts of joys, being tortured by their inability to satisfy their cravings."

971. Is the influence exerted by spirits over one another always good?

"It is always good on the part of good spirits, evidently. Evil spirits, however, try to lead astray those whom they believe are susceptible to being misled from the path of repentance and amendment, and whom they have often led into error when on Earth."

—   So, death does not deliver us from temptation?

"No, but the action of evil spirits is much less effective over other spirits than over incarnate man. Spirits in between incarnations no longer have the burden of material passions serving as an additional instrument of action for evil spirits." (See #996)

972. Not being able to count on passions as an instrument of influence, how do evil spirits tempt other spirits?

"Although passions no longer exist in the material sense, they still exist in the minds of less-advanced spirits. They lure their victims to places where they can witness the exercise of those passions, and all that may excite them."

—   What is the purpose of exciting those passions, since they no longer have any real object?

"That is precisely where their torture lies: misers see gold that they cannot own; perverts witness orgies in which they cannot participate; the conceited see the honors that they covet, but which they cannot enjoy."

973. What are the greatest sufferings that bad spirits have to endure?

"It is truly impossible to describe the mental tortures that serve as punishment for certain crimes. Even spirits who have suffered them find it difficult to provide you with an idea of them. Unquestionably, however, the most terrible suffering is the idea of being condemned forever."

The idea that people have about the afflictions and joys of the soul after death is more or less accurate, according to their intellectual development. As they become more evolved, their reasoning also becomes more refined and more liberated from material impressions. They understand things from a more rational standpoint and no longer take figurative language literally. Careful reasoning will teach us that the soul is a purely spiritual being, and that it cannot be affected by impressions that act only upon matter. But that does not mean that the soul does not suffer, or is not punished for wrongs committed. (See #237)

Spirit communications demonstrate the future state of the soul, no longer as a theory, but as a reality. They place before us all the adventures of life beyond the grave, but at the same time they also show that all tribulations are the perfectly logical consequence of terrestrial life. Although divested of the fantastic accessories created by human imagination, such tribulations are nonetheless painful for those who made a bad use of their talents. The diversity of such consequences is immense, but one may say that, in general, souls are punished according to their specific faults. Some are punished by the endless vision of the evil they committed; others experience regret, fear, shame, doubt, loneliness, darkness, the separation from those who are dear to them, and so on.

974. Where does the doctrine of eternal fire come from?

"An allegory mistaken for reality, like so many others."

— But might this fear not lead to a good result?

"Check how many people are deterred by it, including among those who teach it. If you teach things that reason rejects later on, you create an impression that will be neither lasting nor healthy."

Unable to portray the nature of those sufferings into his language, man has not found a more forceful comparison for such sufferings than fire, which represents the cruelest torture possible and the symbol of the most powerful action. It is for this reason that the belief in eternal fire may be traced back to the earliest ages, and modern cultures inherited it from previous cultures. In addition, it is for this reason that, in his figurative language, man speaks of fiery passions, burning with love or jealousy, etc.

975. Do inferior spirits understand the happiness of the morally upright?

"Yes, and that represents a torture for them, because they realize that they are deprived of it due to their own fault. That is the reason why a spirit freed from matter aspires to a new physical existence. Spirits know that each existence, *if well employed*, will shorten the length of that torment. With that in mind, they choose trials that will expiate their wrongs. You must remember that spirits suffer for all the wrong they have done or which they have intentionally caused, for all the good that they might have done but didn't, *and for all the evil that resulted from the good they failed to do.*

"Spirits in between incarnations no longer have the veil of matter to obstruct them. *It is as though they have emerged from a fog*, seeing what is keeping them from happiness. They thus suffer even more, because they understand how guilty they are. For spirits, *there are no more illusions*, as they see things as they really are."

On the one hand, spirits in between incarnations grasp all their past existences in a single glance; on the other hand, they foresee the promised future, understanding what they lack to reach it. Like a hiker who has reached the mountaintop, they see both the terrain they have already covered, and how far they must still go to reach their destination.

976. Is the sight of spirits who suffer, a cause of affliction for good spirits, and, if so, how does this impact their happiness?

"It is not an affliction, as they know that the suffering will end. Good spirits help others perfect themselves by offering help, an occupation that results in much joy when they succeed."

— This is conceivable in the case of spirits who are unknown or indifferent to them, but doesn't the sight of the grief and suffering of those who were dear to them on Earth disturb their happiness?

"If they did not see your suffering, it would mean they became estranged from you after death, whereas religion tells you that souls continue to see you, but that they see your afflictions from a different standpoint. They know that your sufferings will be useful toward your advancement, if you endure them with fortitude. In the case of good spirits, the lack of courage that holds you back is a greater reason for sadness than your sufferings that they know are only temporary."

977. Because spirits cannot hide their thoughts from one another, all the acts of their lives being known, does it follow that those who are guilty are in the continuous presence of their victims?

"Common sense says that it cannot be otherwise."

— Is the revelation of all his reprehensible acts and the continuous sight of his victims a punishment for the guilty spirit?

"More than you might think, but it only lasts until the spirit has expiated his faults either as a spirit or as an incarnate person in new corporeal existences."

When we find ourselves in the spirit world, our whole past is known, along with all the good and the evil we have done. He who has done evil will try in vain to escape the scrutiny of his victims, and their inevitable presence will be an incessant source of punishment and regret for him, until he has atoned for his wrongs. The virtuous man, on the other hand, will find friendly and benevolent eyes everywhere.

For the vicious man, there is no greater torment on Earth than the presence of his victims; that is why he always tries to avoid them. What will become of him when, no longer under the illusion of passions, he understands the evil he has done and sees his most secret deeds revealed, finding his hypocrisy unmasked, realizing he cannot hide from the presence of those he has wronged? While the soul of the wicked feels shame, regret, and remorse, that of the righteous enjoys perfect peace.

978. Does the memory of the wrongs committed while still imperfect disturb the happiness of spirits, even after they have reached perfection?

"No, because they have atoned for their faults, emerging victorious from the trials to which they submitted themselves *for that specific purpose*."

979. Aren't the trials that spirits must still undergo to complete their purification a great apprehension that affects their happiness?

"In the case of souls that are still imperfect, yes. That is why they cannot enjoy perfect happiness until they are pure. But for souls who have already progressed, the thought of the trials they still must endure causes no apprehension."

Having reached a certain degree of perfection, souls enjoy happiness. A feeling of sweet satisfaction surrounds them and they feel happy with everything they see around them. The veil has been lifted for them, revealing the marvels and mysteries of creation, and the divine perfections finally appear in all their splendor.

980. Is the bond of affinity that unites spirits of the same order a source of happiness for them?

"The union of kindred spirits *in the pursuit of the good* is one of their greatest joys because they do not have to fear seeing that unity disturbed by selfishness. On completely spiritual worlds, they form families congregated around shared feelings, and from that they derive their spiritual happiness, just as on your world you gather according to your interests, enjoying a certain pleasure when you get together. The pure and sincere affection they feel toward each other is a source of joy, as there are neither false friends nor hypocrites among them."

Man enjoys a foretaste of this happiness on Earth when he meets souls with whom he can enter into a pure and blessed unity. In a life of greater purity, such pleasure will be ineffable and without limits, because he will only meet kindred souls, whose affection *cannot be tarnished by selfishness*. In nature everything is love. Only selfishness spoils it.

981. With regard to the future state of spirits, is there any difference between those who have feared death and those who have looked upon it with indifference or even with relief?

"The difference may be significant, although this is usually outweighed by the causes that originated that fear or desire. Those who fear death or those who look forward to it may be moved by very different feelings; these will determine a spirit's future state. It is evident, for instance, that those who look forward to their death only because it will put an end to their tribulations are, in a way, revolting against Providence and against the trials they must endure."

982. Is it necessary to believe in Spiritism and in spirit manifestations in order to guarantee our happiness in the next life?

"If that were so, then all those who do not believe in Spiritism, or who have not had the same chance to learn anything about it, would be disinherited, which is absurd. Only your good deeds can guarantee your future happiness. The good is always good, whatever the path that leads to it." (See #165, #799)

Belief in Spiritism helps us better ourselves by making certain points about our future clear; it accelerates the general advancement of people by making us realize what we will be one day, representing a point of support and source of light that guides us. Spiritism teaches us to endure our trials with patience and fortitude, preventing us from doing things that might postpone our future happiness. Spiritism contributes to the future happiness of the human soul, but that does not mean that happiness cannot be achieved without it.

5. Temporary punishments

983. Since a spirit who atones for his faults in a new life endures sufferings of a physical nature, is it correct to say that after death the soul experiences only mental suffering?

"It is very true that the tribulations of life represent suffering for the reincarnated soul, but it is only the body that can be affected by physical suffering.

"You frequently say that the one who is dead no longer suffers, but this is not always true. Spirits may no longer suffer physical pain, but depending on the wrongs they committed, they may have still more severe sufferings of a moral nature, and in a new existence they may be even unhappier. Those who have wasted their riches may beg for bread and suffer all the privations of poverty; the proud may face humiliations of every kind; those who have abused authority and have treated their subordinates with disrespect and harshness will be forced to obey masters who are even more severe. All the punishments and tribulations of life are atonements for wrongs from previous existences, when not the consequence of wrongs committed in the present one. When you have departed from the planet, you shall understand this more clearly. (See #273, #393, #399)

"He who believes himself to be happy on Earth because he is able to satisfy his passions is the one who makes the least effort to advance. He often begins to atone for his ephemeral happiness in his current life, but he will certainly atone for it in another equally material existence."

984. Are the tribulations of life always punishment for faults committed in our current existence?

"No. We have already told you that they are trials imposed by God, or chosen by you yourselves in the interim state before you reincarnated, in order to expiate the wrongs committed in a previous existence. No infraction of the laws of God, and especially of the law of justice, ever goes unpunished, and if punishment is not experienced in this life, it certainly will be in another. This is why those you consider morally upright still have to face the consequences of their past actions." (See #393)

985. Is the reincarnation of spirits on a more evolved world a reward?

"It is the consequence of their purification, because, as spirits become more perfect, they reincarnate on successively better worlds, until they are able to completely rid themselves of all material influence, cleansing their souls from all moral imperfections, so as to enjoy the eternal bliss of pure spirits in the bosom of God."

On worlds where the existence is less material than on this one, needs are not as gross and all physical suffering is less severe. The inhabitants of those worlds no longer know the evil passions that, on inferior worlds, turn man against man. Having no reasons for hatred or jealousy, they live in peace, practicing the law of justice, love, and charity. They do not know the apprehension and anguish that result from envy, pride, and selfishness, which are the source of torment in our terrestrial existence. (See #172–182)

986. Can spirits who have made progress during their terrestrial existence sometimes reincarnate on the same world?

"Yes, if they have not been able to finish their mission and if they ask to complete it in a new existence. In any event, that would no longer be an expiation for them." (See #173)

987. What becomes of those who do nothing to liberate themselves from the influence of matter, though without doing evil?

"Because they made no progress toward perfection, they must begin a new existence akin to the one they finished. They remain at a standstill, extending the suffering derived from their expiation."

988. There are people whose lives flow in perfect tranquility, without the need to provide for themselves, a situation that exempts them from any concern. Is such a happy existence evidence that they have nothing to expiate from a former existence?

"Do you know many of those? If you think you do, you are mistaken. Usually, such tranquility is only superficial. They may have chosen such an existence, but upon leaving it behind, they realize that it has not helped them advance, regretting the time they wasted in idleness. Keep in mind that spirits cannot acquire knowledge and advance except through activity. If they choose a carefree existence, they make no progress. They are like those who, according to your practices, need to work but go for a walk or go to sleep, in order to avoid their duty. *Keep in mind, also, that each of you will have to answer for any intentional inactivity during your life, and that such uselessness is always fatal to your future happiness.* The sum of future happiness is in proportion to the sum of the good you have accomplished. Similarly, your unhappiness is proportional to the sum of the evil you have done, and to the number of those you have made unhappy."

989. There are people who, if not downright wicked, make everyone around them unhappy, owing to their character. What is the consequence of this for them?

"These people are certainly not good. They will expiate this wrong by the sight of those whom they have made unhappy, which will represent a continuous grief for them. Later, in another existence, they will suffer all the afflictions they inflicted on others."

6. Expiation and repentance

990. Does repentance take place while incarnate or in the spirit world?

"In the spirit world. But it may also take place while incarnate, if you clearly understand the difference between good and evil."

991. What is the consequence of repentance in the spirit state?

"The desire, on the part of the spirit, for purification in a new incarnation. Spirits identify the imperfections that have kept them from being happy, so that they aspire to a new existence in which they can expiate their wrongs." (See #332, #975)

992. What is the consequence of repentance while still incarnate?

"When spirits repent while still incarnate, they are able to advance *right from their present corporeal life*, if they have the time required to redress their wrongs. Whenever your conscience warns you by indicating an imperfection, you have a chance to advance."

993. Aren't there men who only have an evil instinct, being incapable of repenting?

"I have told you that one must advance unceasingly. Those who in this life only have an instinct for evil will have an instinct for the good in another one, and *that is why they are reborn many times*. All must advance and reach their destiny, sooner or later, in accord with their free will. Those who only have an instinct for the good have already accomplished their progress, because they might have had an instinct for evil in a previous existence." (See #894)

994. Do the wicked men who did not recognize their wrongs during their physical existence always recognize them after death?

"Yes, they always recognize them and suffer even more, because they *regret all the evil they did or intentionally caused.* Repentance is not always immediate, however. There are spirits who persist relentlessly in evil, despite their suffering. But sooner or later they recognize that they have chosen the wrong path, and repentance ensues. It is toward their enlightenment that good spirits labor, and you may work toward the same end as well."

995. Are there spirits who, without being evil, are indifferent about their own fate?

"There are spirits who do not busy themselves with anything useful; they passively wait. They suffer, however, in proportion to their inactivity; but as everything must progress, progress in this case occurs through suffering."

— Do they not have the desire to shorten their suffering?

"Undoubtedly, they do, but they lack the energy to even want that which would mitigate their suffering. How many of you would rather starve than work?"

996. As spirits see the harm that results from their imperfections, why do some aggravate their situation and extend their state of inferiority by doing evil as discarnate spirits, and leading people astray from the right path?

"Those are the spirits who put off their repentance. In addition, spirits who repent may still allow themselves to be brought back to the path of evil by spirits who are even less evolved." (See #971)

997. We sometimes see spirits who are clearly imperfect, but who are open to good inspiration and prayers made on their behalf. Why do other spirits, who appear to be more knowledgeable, show a callousness and cynicism that seem impossible to overcome?

"Prayer is only effective in the case of spirits who repent. Spirits who are driven by pride and revolt against God may persevere in their folly, further aggravating their situation—as unhappy spirits commonly do. They cannot and will not receive the benefits of prayer until a ray of repentance touches them." (See #664)

> We must keep in mind that spirits are not suddenly transformed after death. If they made mistakes, it is because they were imperfect still. Death does not change that by making them perfect immediately. They may persist in their errors, misconceptions, and prejudices until they are enlightened through study, reflection, and suffering.

998. Is expiation accomplished in the corporeal state or in the spirit state?

"It is accomplished in the corporeal existence through the trials that spirits must undergo, and in the spirit state, through the moral sufferings that result from spirits' imperfection."

999. Is sincere repentance in life enough to compensate for the wrongs committed, enabling a spirit to deserve God's grace?

"Repentance helps a spirit advance, but the past must be atoned for."

—   With that in mind, what would be the result for a criminal if he claims that, because he must atone for his past in any case, it is pointless for him to repent?

"If he continues to harden his heart in evil, his expiation will be longer and more painful."

1000. Can we redeem our wrongs in the present life?

"Yes, by making amends for them. Do not suppose, however, that you can redeem your wrongs through a few minor sacrifices, or through the donation of your possessions after your death, when you can no longer use them. God does not acknowledge a sterile repentance, something which is always easy, and costs no more than grieving by beating on one's chest. The loss of a finger while doing useful work compensates for a greater number of wrongs than years of self-inflicted tortures without any purpose other than one's *own self-interest.* (See #726)

"Your misdeeds can only be compensated for by doing good, and reparation does not have any value *if it does not impinge on your pride or material interests.*

"Of what use would it be in justifying oneself if a man restored stolen assets after he had profited from them, and when he had no further use for them?

"What good would it do to sacrifice a few small pleasures and superfluous habits if the evil done to someone was not repaired?

"Finally, of what use would it be to humble yourself before God if you maintain your pride when dealing with others?" (See #720, #721)

1001. Is there any merit in making sure our assets are put to good use after our death?

"Merit is not quite the word, but it is clearly better than doing nothing. Unfortunately, those who only give after their death are usually more selfish than generous. They want the honor of doing good without having to sacrifice anything. Those who make sacrifices in life have a double benefit: the merit of the sacrifice proper, and the pleasure to witness the happiness of those they helped. Selfishness, however, is always there to insinuate that whatever you give you take away from your own enjoyment. As selfishness speaks louder than selflessness and charity, people hold on to things under the pretext of their needs and the requirements of their social position. Oh, pity those who do not know the bliss of giving, for they have really deprived themselves of one of the purest and sweetest enjoyments. In making them endure the trial of wealth—so slippery and dangerous for their future—God has wished to give them as compensation the happiness of generosity, which they can enjoy right now in this world." (See #814)

1002. What should be done by those who, on the brink of death, recognize their wrongs, but do not have enough time to make amends? Is repentance enough in such cases?

"Repentance will hasten their rehabilitation, but it will not absolve them. Don't they have the future ahead of them, never to be closed to them?"

7. Length of future punishments

1003. Is the length of time the guilty must suffer in a future life arbitrary, or is it governed by some law?

"God never acts on a whim, and everything in the universe is ruled by laws that reveal His wisdom and goodness."

1004. What determines the duration of the suffering of the guilty?

"The length of time required for their betterment. As the degree of suffering or happiness is proportional to the spirits' degree of perfection, the duration and nature of their suffering depend on the time it takes them to improve themselves. As spirits progress and their feelings are purer, their suffering diminishes and changes in nature."

Saint Louis

1005. In the case of spirits who suffer, does time seem longer or shorter compared to when they were incarnate?

"It seems longer, because sleep does not exist for them. It is only for spirits who have reached a certain degree of advancement that time is erased, as it were, before infinity." (See #240)

1006. Can the duration of the suffering of spirits be eternal?

"Surely, if they were to remain eternally evil—in other words, should they never repent or improve themselves, they would then suffer eternally. But God has not created beings for them to be eternally devoted to evil. He created them only simple and ignorant, and all of them must progress over a longer or shorter period of time according to their own will. Their will to advance may emerge within different timeframes, just as there are children who are more or less precocious. Sooner or later, though, this will emerges through the irresistible need that spirits feel to leave their inferiority and to be happy. The law that governs the duration of the suffering of spirits is therefore eminently wise and generous, subordinating it to the efforts made by spirits themselves, never depriving them of their free will. If they make a bad use of it, they will have to suffer the consequences."

Saint Louis

1007. Are there spirits who never repent?

"There are spirits who repent rather tardily, but supposing that they will never improve themselves is to deny the law of progress—the same as saying that a child will never become an adult."

Saint Louis

1008. Does the duration of punishments always depend on the spirit's own will or are there punishments that are imposed on a spirit for a specific length of time?

"There are punishments that may be imposed on a spirit for a specific length of time, but God, who wills only the good for His creatures, always welcomes the act of repentance, so that a spirit's desire to improve is never fruitless."

Saint Louis

1009. Does it follow, then, that the punishments imposed on spirits are never eternal?

"Use your common sense, your reason, and ask yourselves whether the eternal condemnation for a few moments of error would not be the negation of the goodness of God. In fact, what does a lifetime represent, even if it were to last a hundred years, in comparison to eternity? Eternity! Can you understand that word? Suffering and torture without end and without hope—for only a few wrongs—doesn't your reason reject such an idea?

"That the ancients saw in the Master of the universe a terrible, jealous, and vindictive God is understandable. In their ignorance, they attributed human passions to their deities, but that is not the God of the Christians, who exalts love, charity, mercy, and the forgetfulness of offenses as the chief virtues. Could God Himself lack the qualities He mandates? Isn't there a contradiction in attributing to God both infinite goodness and infinite vengefulness? You say that God is just, above all, and that man does not understand His justice. Justice and kindness, however, are not mutually exclusive, and God would not be kind in condemning most creatures to a horrible and perpetual punishment. Could God impose His justice on His creatures if they were not given the means to understand it? Besides, is not the realization sublime that justice allied with goodness, makes the duration of punishment a result of the efforts of the guilty to better themselves? In this you shall find the truth of 'to each according to his deeds.' "

Saint Augustine

"By all the means at your disposal, strive to fight, to eradicate the idea of eternal punishment—a blasphemous notion against the justice and goodness of God, a prolific source of incredulity, materialism, and indifference, all of which have corrupted the masses from the moment their intelligence began to develop. Spirits close to enlightenment—or sometimes even those whose intelligence has just started to blossom—understand what a monstrous injustice it is; once reason rejects the doctrine, they rarely fail to cast into oblivion both the idea of eternal punishment and the God to whom they ascribe it. From this derive the many ills that have fallen upon you, and the cure for which we have come to deliver.

"The task we propose you will be much easier, because those who defend this belief based it on figures of authority who have always avoided supporting it formally. Neither the Councils nor the Church Fathers tackled this serious question. Even if you take Christ's allegorical words literally, according to the narrative of the authors of the Gospels, Christ may in fact have threatened the guilty with inextinguishable and eternal fire, but there is absolutely nothing in Christ's words that say they are condemned *for all eternity*.

"Hapless sheep that have gone astray, allow the Good Shepherd to come to you—He who, far from banishing you forever from His presence, comes to rescue you personally, leading you back to the flock. Prodigal children, leave your voluntary exile and direct your steps toward the Father, who opens His arms to you, always ready to celebrate your return home."

Lamennais

"War of words! Have you not shed enough blood? Are the fires of the stake to be rekindled once again? You argue over expressions such as *eternal suffering* and *eternal punishment*, but don't you know that what you understand today by *eternity* was not how the ancients understood it? Let theologians check their sources and, like you, they will find out that the Hebrew text did not ascribe to the word the same definition that the Greek, the Latin, and modern translators have established of *everlasting and unpardonable suffering.* The eternity of punishments corresponds to the eternity of evil, which is to say that, yes, so long as evil exists among man, punishments will continue to exist; it is in this relative sense that the sacred texts should be interpreted.

"Eternal punishments are therefore relative and not absolute. A day will come when all men, through repentance, will don the robe of innocence, and on that day there will be no more weeping or gnashing of teeth. Human reason is limited, it is true, but even as such, it still is a gift from God, and with the help of reason there cannot be one single person of good faith who could possibly understand eternal punishment in any other way. Eternal punishment, how would it be possible? One would need to believe evil to be eternal as well! But only God is eternal, and God could not have created eternal evil, or else we would have to deny one of the most beautiful of His attributes, His sovereign power, for God could not be supremely powerful if an element could exist that destroyed His creation. Humanity! You must no longer cast your dreary gaze into the depths of Earth, searching for such punishments. Weep, but hope; atone for your trespasses, but take comfort in the thought of a God who is intrinsically good, absolutely powerful, and essentially just."

Plato

"Gravitating toward unity with God is the goal of mankind. For this to occur, three things are necessary: justice, love, and knowledge. Three things are contrary to and oppose this unity: ignorance, hatred, and injustice. Verily, I tell you that you lie about these fundamental principles, undermining the idea of God, when you exaggerate His severity. Furthermore, you doubly undermine it when you let enter into the spirit of man the idea that man himself may have more clemency, kindness, love, and true justice than you ascribe to the Infinite Being. You destroy the very idea of hell by rendering it as ridiculous and unacceptable to your intellect as the hideous spectacle of the executioners, tortures, and burnings at the stake of the Middle Ages is to your hearts! How can the idea of hell be upheld at a time when blind reprisals have been banned by human legislation?

"Believe me, brothers and sisters in God and in Jesus Christ, believe me, and either resign yourselves to witnessing the obliteration of the dogmas you believe to be immutable, or breathe new life into them by reinterpreting them in the novel and benevolent light now provided by the good spirits. The idea of a hell with its burning furnaces and boiling cauldrons might be tolerated—in other words, be pardonable—in an age of iron. In this century, however, it is nothing more than an ineffective ghost that only serves to terrify little children, but in which they no longer believe once they have grown up.

"Insisting on such a frightening mythology, you will engender disbelief, the fountainhead of social collapse. I shudder at the notion of an entire social order being shaken, crumbling on its foundations for lack of a credible system of sanctions. As people of ardent and living faith, heralds of the sunrise that you are, we urge you to join efforts with us, not to maintain old fables that are now discredited, but to renew the concept of justice under a framework in harmony with your mores, your feelings and the knowledge of your age.

"Who, in fact, are the guilty? It is they who, owing to a deviation, a wrong impulse on the part of their soul, have veered from the goal of creation, which lies in harmonious devotion to the beautiful and the good, as idealized by the human archetype, the man-God: Jesus Christ.

"What is punishment? It is the natural consequence of that wrong impulse, the amount of pain required to instill in man aversion to his imperfection, by enduring the pain that results from his transgression. Punishment is the goad that stimulates the soul—by bitterly piercing it—to turn into itself, driving it back to the path of salvation. The goal of punishment is none other than to rehabilitate and liberate. To assume eternal punishment for transient wrongs would be to deny any reason for punishment to exist.

"Truly I say to you, it is a mistake to equate as eternal the good (the essence of the Creator) with evil (the essence of the creature). That would result in an unjustifiable conception of punishment. Recognize, instead, the gradual reduction of punishments through reincarnation; in so doing, you shall endorse the divine unity, through both reason and mercy."

Paul, the Apostle

The enticement of reward and the fear of punishment are intended to drive man to the good and to turn him from evil. But if punishments are presented in a way contrary to reason, they have no influence on a man. On the contrary, he rejects them completely, form and content alike. But if the future is presented in a logical fashion, a man will no longer reject it. Spiritism provides mankind with such an explanation.

The doctrine of eternal punishment, in its strict sense, makes the Supreme Being an implacable God. Would it be logical to say that a monarch is very good, very benevolent, and very indulgent, that he only wants the happiness of those around him, but that he is at the same time jealous, vindictive, and relentless in his strictness, punishing most of his subjects with the maximum penalty for any infraction of his laws, even when his subjects infringed upon them without being aware of it? Wouldn't that be a contradiction? How could God be any less humane than a human monarch can be?

Another contradiction exists here. As God knows everything, God knew, upon creating the souls, that some of them would fail, that from their formation they were destined to eternal unhappiness. Is this possible? Is it rational? With the doctrine of relative punishment, everything makes sense. God undoubtedly knew that certain souls would fail, but gave them the means of enlightening themselves through their own experiences and mistakes. They would have to atone for their errors in order to more firmly set themselves in virtue, but the door of hope would never be shut to them. God made the moment of their liberation depend on the efforts they make to reach it. This is something that all can conceive of, and the most painstaking logic can accept. If the doctrine of future punishments had been presented in this way, there would be fewer skeptics.

The word *eternal* is almost always employed figuratively, in everyday language, to designate something of a long duration, the end of which cannot be seen, although it is clearly known that there will be an end. We speak, for instance, of the eternal snows of the high mountains and the polar caps, although we know, on the one hand, that the physical world may come to an end, and, on the other hand, that the state of those regions could be modified by a shift in the planet's axis or some other cataclysm. The word *eternal*, in this case, does not mean *of an infinite duration*. When we suffer some prolonged illness, we may say that it is eternal. Is it, therefore, at all surprising that spirits who have suffered for many years, centuries, and even thousands of years speak of it as being eternal? Above all, we must not forget that their imperfection prevents them from seeing the end of their path of woes, so that they believe they shall suffer forever; this is, in itself, a punishment for them.

Additionally, the doctrine of physical fire, of furnaces, and tortures borrowed from the Tartarus [a] of paganism has been entirely discarded by modern theology. Only in certain schools are such fear-mongering allegorical images still presented as literal truths by those who are more fanatical than enlightened, something which is all very wrong, because young imaginations, having once recovered from the initial fear, are likely to become skeptical. Today, theology recognizes that the word *fire* is employed figuratively, and should be understood as a mental fire (see #974). Those like us, who have followed the vagaries of life and the sufferings beyond the grave through spirit communications, have been convinced that, though not physical, those sufferings are no less excruciating. Even with regard to their duration, a few theologians are beginning to accept the restricted meaning explained above, considering that, in fact, the word *eternal* may refer to the existence of penalties per se, as the consequence of an immutable law, and not to their application to each individual. When religion accepts such an interpretation, as well as others that are equally the result of the advancement of knowledge, it will bring back many of its lost sheep.

8. Resurrection of the flesh

1010. Is the doctrine of the resurrection of the flesh an endorsement of reincarnation as taught by the Spirits?

"How could it be otherwise? The doctrine, like so many others, appears unreasonable only because it is taken literally, thus fostering incredulity. But give it a logical interpretation, and those you call freethinkers will accept it with no difficulty, precisely because they will see it as rational. Make no mistake, freethinkers want nothing more than to believe; like everyone else, and perhaps even more so, they long for the future, but they cannot accept what is contrary to reason. The doctrine of the plurality of existences is in harmony with the justice of God, and it alone can explain what is otherwise inexplicable. Why do you wonder that this principle is found in religion itself?"

1011. Then, in the dogma of the resurrection of the flesh, does the Church itself teach the doctrine of reincarnation? [b]

"That is evident. This doctrine is in fact the consequence of many things which have gone unnoticed, and which will soon be understood in that sense. Before long, the Church will realize that Spiritism emerges from everywhere in the very text of the Holy Scriptures. Therefore, the Spirits have not come to subvert religion, as some claim. They come, on the contrary, to confirm and endorse it through irrefutable proofs. And because the time has come to leave figurative language behind, they do not employ allegories, and provide things with a clear and precise meaning that cannot be misinterpreted. That is why, in time, there will be more people who are sincerely religious and believing than are to be found today."

Saint Louis

Science has effectively demonstrated the impossibility of resurrection in the ordinary interpretation of the word. If the remains of a human body could actually stay homogeneous, even though dispersed and reduced to dust, we might conceive of its being reunited with the spirit at some time. Such is not the case, however. The body is made up of diverse elements: oxygen, hydrogen, nitrogen, carbon, and so on. Through the action of decomposition, those elements are dispersed, being used to form new bodies, in such a way that, the same atom of carbon, for example, may be used in the composition of many thousands of different bodies (speaking only of human bodies, not counting those of animals). Accordingly, a man may have in his body atoms that belonged to humans of earlier times. The same organic molecules that you absorb from your food, for instance, may have come from the body of an individual whom you have known. Since the amount of matter is limited and its transformations are unlimited in number, how could each one of those bodies be rebuilt from the same elements? This implies a material impossibility. The resurrection of the flesh cannot, therefore, be rationally accepted except as a figure of speech symbolizing the phenomenon of reincarnation. And as such, there is nothing in it contrary to reason, nothing contrary to the tenets of science.

It is true that, according to Church dogma, the resurrection must only occur at the end of time, while according to Spiritist Doctrine, it occurs every day. Doesn't the image of the final judgment represent a grand and beautiful symbol, which, behind the veil of allegory, hides one of those immutable truths that skeptics will no longer discard once its true meaning is revealed? May we carefully meditate on the Spiritist explanation of the future of souls, and their destiny resulting from the many trials they must undergo. We shall then see that, with the exception of it being simultaneous, the judgment in which souls are condemned for or absolved of their sins is not a fiction, as skeptics think. Let us consider additionally that the Spiritist theory is consistent with the plurality-of-worlds idea, which is perfectly conceivable today, whereas, according to the doctrine of the final judgment, the Earth is supposed to be the only inhabited world.

9. Heaven, hell, and purgatory

1012. Are there specific places in the universe that are intended for the punishments and enjoyments of spirits, in accord with their merits?

"We have already answered this question. Punishments and enjoyments are inherent to the degree of advancement of spirits, who carry within themselves the source of their own happiness or unhappiness. And because spirits are everywhere, there is no circumscribed or enclosed place intended for either punishments or enjoyments. As for incarnate spirits, the degree of their happiness or unhappiness depends on the advancement of the world they inhabit."

— Consequently, do heaven and hell not exist as man has depicted them?

"They are no more than figures of speech; happy and unhappy spirits are to be found everywhere. However, as we have also told you, spirits of the same order gather together through their affinity. But they can meet wherever they wish once they are perfect."

The idea of set places for punishments and rewards exists only in man's imagination. It derives from his tendency to attribute a *material character* and a *defined place* to things of an infinite nature that he cannot understand.

1013. What is to be understood by *purgatory*?

"Physical and mental suffering—the period of expiation. It is almost always the Earth that you turn into your own purgatory, and where God has you atone for your wrongs."

What man calls *purgatory* is also a figure of speech that should not be understood as a definite place, but rather as the state of imperfect spirits who must atone for their faults until their purification raises them to a level where they can be happy. Given that this purification occurs over the course of several incarnations, purgatory consists of the trials of corporeal life.

1014. How to explain the fact that spirits whose language reveals their superior character, have given to serious individuals answers on the topic of hell and purgatory that are in accord with the usual dogma of the Church?

"They speak a language that can be understood by those who question them. When certain ideas are too deeply ingrained in certain people, spirits may prefer not to shock them too suddenly, in order not to hurt their convictions. If spirits were not to use any language discretion and would say to a Muslim that Mohammed was not a prophet, they would be very poorly received."

—   We realize that it must be this way with regard to spirits who wish to instruct us, but how to explain that, when questioned about their situation, spirits have answered that they were suffering the tortures of hell or purgatory?

"When they are of a lower order and are not completely disengaged from matter, spirits retain some of their earthly ideas and translate their impressions using a vocabulary familiar to them. They find themselves in a situation where they can hardly probe their future. For this reason, spirits in between incarnations, or recently discarnate, usually speak just as they would have if they were still incarnate. *Hell* may be translated as meaning a life of excruciating trials, together with the *uncertainty* about any improvement. *Purgatory* also means a life of trials, except that it implies the awareness of a better future. Whenever you are suffering a great deal of pain, don't you say that you are suffering like a damned soul? These words also represent nothing more than a figure of speech."

1015. What should be understood by *a tormented soul*?

"A wandering and suffering spirit, uncertain about the future, and to whom you may provide the solace often requested when such a soul comes to communicate with you." (See #664.)

1016. In what sense should the word *heaven* be understood?

"Do you believe that it is a place like the Elysium of the ancients, where all good spirits are confusedly crowded together with no other concern than that of enjoying an eternity of unchanging bliss? No. It is the universal space, the planets, the stars and all the superior worlds where spirits enjoy all their faculties, without the tribulations of material life or the anguish that characterizes lower stages."

1017. Some spirits have claimed to inhabit the fourth heaven, the fifth heaven, and so on. What do they mean by this?

"You asked them which heaven they inhabit because you have the idea of many heavens laid over each other, like the floors of a house. They merely responded according to your own language. However, for them, the words fourth or fifth heaven express different degrees of perfection, and consequently, of happiness. It is the same when a spirit is asked if he is in hell. If he is unhappy, he will answer affirmatively, because, for him, *hell* is synonymous with suffering, although he knows very well that it is not a furnace. A pagan spirit would respond that he is in *Tartarus*."

The same applies to other analogous expressions, such as the city of flowers; the city of the elect; the first, second, or third sphere; and others, all of which are nothing more than metaphors employed by certain spirits, either as figures of speech, or from ignorance of the reality of things, or from ignorance of the most basic, scientific notions.

Owing to our old, limited conception of the existence of specific places for punishments and rewards, and owing particularly to the opinion that Earth was the center of the universe and that the sky formed a vault which included a region where stars were located, we placed heaven *up above* and hell *down below*—hence the use of expressions such as *to ascend to heaven, to be in highest heaven, to be cast down into hell*, and so on. Now that science has demonstrated that Earth is only one of the smallest worlds among so many millions, and of no special importance; and now that science has mapped the planet's formation and described its composition and has proven that space is infinite in such a way that there is neither up nor down in the universe, it has become necessary to discard the notion of a heaven above the clouds and a hell in the lower regions.

As for purgatory, no fixed place has ever been assigned to it. It was reserved to Spiritism to provide a most rational, grand, and at the same time, most consoling explanation about such matters to mankind. We can say, therefore, that we carry our hell or heaven within ourselves, and that we find our purgatory in our incarnation, in our physical lives.

1018. In what sense should we understand the words of Christ, "My kingdom is not of this world"? [c]

"When Christ answered in such a manner, he was speaking figuratively. He wanted to say that he only reigned over pure and unselfish hearts. He is wherever the love of the good prevails. But humans, who only covet the earthly possessions to which they are attached, are estranged from him."

1019. Will the reign of the good ever take place on Earth?

"The good shall reign on Earth when good spirits prevail over those who are evil, amid those who come to inhabit the planet. They will then see that love and justice, which are the source of goodness and happiness, reign on Earth. It is through moral progress and the practice of the laws of God that man will attract good spirits to Earth, warding off the evil ones. The latter will only leave, however, after man has banished pride and selfishness from the planet.

"The transformation of humanity has been predicted, and the time has come for everyone who collaborates with progress to accelerate this transformative process. It will be accomplished through the incarnation of more advanced spirits, who will constitute a new generation on Earth. Then the spirits of the wicked, who are claimed every day by death, along with all those who try to deter the advancement of things, shall be expelled, for they will be out of place among the virtuous, whose happiness they would disturb. They will go to newer, less-advanced worlds to fulfill *painful* missions, where they will be able to labor for their own advancement, and at the same time labor for the progress of their fellow beings who are even less advanced.

"Do you not recognize in the guise of this exile from a transformed Earth the sublime image of *Paradise Lost*? Also, do you not see in the men who have come to Earth under similar conditions, bringing within themselves the seeds of their passions and the remnants of their primitive inferiority, the no-less-sublime image of *original sin*? Original sin, when considered from this vantage point, refers to the still imperfect nature of man, who is only responsible for himself and for his own wrongs, and not for those of his forefathers.

"All of you, souls of faith and goodwill, work therefore with zeal and courage for the great labor of regeneration, for you will reap a hundredfold the grain of wheat that you have sown. Woe to those who shut their eyes to the light, for they are preparing long centuries of darkness and sorrow for themselves! Woe to those who place all their joys in the possessions of this world, for they will suffer more privations than the pleasures they may have enjoyed. Above all, woe to the selfish, for they will not find anyone to help them bear the burden of their misery."

Saint Louis

■■■

[a] In Greek mythology, Tartarus was the dungeon of torment and suffering for the wicked souls. —Trans.

[b] The original French edition skips question #1011. That number was assigned to the unnumbered question that immediately follows question #1010. The subsequent question is marked #1012 in the original text, making the copyediting oversight evident. See section "Editorial Observations" as well as translator's note [p] in Appendix 1. —Trans.

[c] John 18:36. —Trans.

Conclusion

I

Those whose knowledge of Earth magnetism is limited to the magnetic toy ducklings that are made to swim around in a water basin would find it hard to understand that such little playthings contain the secret of one of forces of the universe and of the movement of worlds. The same applies to those whose knowledge of Spiritism is limited to table-turning. They see in it no more than an amusement, a pastime at social gatherings, and they do not realize how such a simple and common phenomenon, known in ancient and even in primitive cultures, could be related to matters of grave concern to the social order. In fact, to the superficial observer, what connection could a turning table have with ethics, and with the future of mankind? And yet, whoever takes the time to ponder shall realize that from the phenomenon that makes the lid of a boiling pot to lift, known since antiquity, emerged the powerful steam engine we use to bridge distances and link faraway countries.

Well then, all of you who do not believe in anything beyond the material world should know that from the table turning that prompts your disdainful smiles, an entire science has emerged, as well as solutions to problems that no philosophy has ever been able to solve. I appeal to all sincere adversaries, asking them to admit whether they have done the work of studying what they criticize, because criticism is only valuable when the critic understands the subject. To ridicule something we ignore, something we have not probed with the scalpel of the careful observer, is not to offer criticism but to prove, instead, our shallowness and poor judgment.

Certainly, if we had presented this philosophy as being the work of the human mind, it would have encountered less disdain and would have merited the honor of being examined by those who pretend to control public opinion. But it comes from Spirits—how absurd! It hardly deserves a passing glance. They judge it merely by its title, like the monkey in the fable who judged the nut by its shell. [a] If you would, ignore for a moment the *origin* of this book, and imagine that it is the work of a man. After reading it *seriously*, ask yourself honestly whether you have found anything that warrants ridicule.

II

Spiritism is the most-feared opponent of materialism. It is not, therefore, surprising that materialists are its adversaries. But since the proponents of materialism hardly dare to stand up for it (further proof that they are not such ardent believers, and that they have not completely taken leave of their conscience), they hide behind the guise of reason and science. And, strangely enough, the most skeptical go so far as to talk in the name of religion, which they also do not know or understand any better than Spiritism. Their target is particularly the *marvelous* and the *supernatural*, which they equally reject. According to them, because Spiritism is based on the marvelous, it cannot be anything other than foolish speculation.

They do not seem to realize that by rejecting the marvelous and the supernatural, they also reject religion, which is founded on revelation and miracles. And what is revelation, if not extra-human communications? All sacred authors since Moses have spoken of this type of communication. And what are miracles if not the utmost example of marvelous and supernatural events, once they are understood to be, per their theological definition, a rescinding of the laws of nature? By rejecting the extraordinary and the supernatural, they reject the very foundation of religion.

But it is not from this standpoint that we wish to consider matters. Spiritism does not have to examine whether or not miracles exist—in other words, whether God can in certain cases break the eternal laws that rule the universe. The Spiritist Doctrine leaves every one free to believe as they please. On the contrary, Spiritism declares and demonstrates that the phenomena on which it is based are only seemingly supernatural. To certain people, such phenomena do not seem to be natural because they are uncommon, and beyond the universe of known facts. However, they are no more supernatural than all the other phenomena for which science today provides an explanation, and which previously seemed to be extraordinary.

All Spiritist phenomena, *without exception*, are the consequence of natural laws. They reveal to us one of the forces of nature, an unknown force—or rather, one that was only poorly understood until now, but one that observation has shown to belong to the order of natural things. Spiritism, therefore, depends less on the marvelous and supernatural than religion itself does. Those who attack it at this point do not realize this, and even if they were highly learned, we would still say to them: "If your science, which has taught you so many things, has not shown you that the realm of nature is infinite, you are but half-scholars."

III

You claim to want to cure your century of a craze that threatens to conquer the world. Would you rather the world be conquered by the disbelief you seek to spread? Is it not to incredulity that we must attribute the relaxation of family ties, and most of the disarray that takes over society? By demonstrating the existence and immortality of the soul, Spiritism rekindles faith in the future, lifts the spirits of the discouraged, and helps us to bear the tribulations of life with fortitude. Would you dare call this an evil?

Two doctrines confront each other: one denies the future; the other proclaims and proves it. One explains nothing; the other explains everything, and in so doing, appeals to reason. One endorses selfishness; the other offers a foundation for justice, charity, and love of one's fellow creatures. The former acknowledges only the present, denying all hope; the latter consoles and shows the immense field open to the future. Which of the two is the more harmful?

Certain people, including those among the most skeptical, present themselves as apostles of fraternity and progress. Fraternity implies disinterestedness, along with self-renunciation. With true fraternity, there is no room for pride. By what right do you have to impose a sacrifice on others, claiming that at death everything will be over for them, and that tomorrow they will be perhaps no more than a worn-out machine to be discarded? What reason would they have to impose any privation on themselves? Is it not more natural that in the short time you accord them, they would try to live as well as possible? This gives rise to the desire to possess as much as possible, in order to better enjoy life. It also fosters jealousy of those who have even more, and such jealousy is only one step away from coveting their possessions.

What is there to keep people from doing it? The law? But the law does not encompass every situation. You may say it is conscience, a sense of duty. But on what can you base such a sense? Should it be on the belief that everything ends with life? According to this belief, only one saying is rational: "Every man for himself." The notions of fraternity, conscience, duty, humanity, and even progress, are no more than empty words. You who proclaim similar doctrines, you do not know how many evils you inflict on society, or for how many crimes you will be held accountable! But why do we speak of responsibility at all? There is no such thing for skeptics, as they only pay tribute to matter.

IV

The progress of mankind results from the application of the law of justice, love, and charity. This law is founded on the certainty of the future. Take away that certainty and you take away its cornerstone. All other laws derive from this one, because it encompasses all that is required for human happiness. It alone can heal the wounds of society, and we can judge this by comparing various eras and *nations*, since their conditions improve as this law is better understood and better enforced.

In addition, if a partial and incomplete application has produced such a real benefit, what could not be accomplished if all social institutions were to make this law their foundation? Could that be possible? Yes. Those who have advanced ten steps can advance twenty, and so on. We can therefore judge the future from the past. We are already seeing that the hostilities among nations are gradually diminishing, that the barriers separating them fall as they become civilized, that they are joining hands from one end of the world to the other, that international laws are ever more imbued with a sense of justice, that wars are becoming less frequent and are subject to codes of conduct, that uniformity is being established in relationships, that race and caste distinctions are disappearing and people of different creeds are silencing their sectarian prejudices so that they may unite in the worship of one-and-the-same God.

We speak of nations that are at the forefront of civilization. (See #789–793) But in every one of these aspects, we are still far from perfection, and there are still many ruins to be torn down before the last vestiges of barbarity disappear. But will those vestiges be able to survive the irresistible power of progress, that living force which is itself a law of nature? If the present generation is more advanced than the last, why should the next not be more advanced than the present one? It will be so by the force of things: first, because with each generation, a few champions of the old abuses depart every day, so that society is gradually made up of new members, who are free of the old prejudices; second, because man, longing for progress, studies the obstacles in his way and works to overcome them. As a consequence, progress is incontestable, and future advancements cannot be questioned.

It is only natural for man to desire to be happy; he only strives to progress in order to add to his share of happiness. Were it not for his happiness, progress would make no sense. What value would progress have for him, other than to improve his situation? Still, once having accomplished the share of happiness that intellectual progress can afford him, he will realize that such happiness is not complete, that it is impossible without the security of social relationships, a security that can only be found in moral progress. Thus, by the force of circumstances, man himself will direct progress along that path, and Spiritism will offer him the most powerful tool in order to reach that goal.

V

Those who say that Spiritist beliefs threaten to invade the world, in doing so admit the power of those beliefs, for an idea without foundation and lacking in logic could not become universal. If Spiritism is laying down roots everywhere, recruiting especially among the educated classes (as has been widely acknowledged), that is because Spiritism is based on truth. Against this tide, all the efforts of its detractors will be useless, proving that, far from deterring its rise, the very ridicule they seek to heap upon it infuses it with new life. This result fully justifies what the Spirits many times said, "Do not allow yourselves to be disturbed by opposition, as everything they do against you will turn to your advantage, and *your greatest adversaries will serve your cause, in spite of themselves.* Against the will of God, the ill will of men shall not prevail."

With Spiritism, mankind must enter a new phase, that of moral advancement, which is the inevitable consequence of Spiritism. Therefore, do not be surprised at how fast Spiritist ideas spread due to the satisfaction they provide to all those who absorb them, and who see in them something more than a futile pastime. As human beings long for happiness above everything else, it is no wonder they become interested in an idea that brings it to them.

The development of these ideas is marked by three distinct phases: the first is curiosity, caused by the strangeness of the phenomena; the second is reasoning and philosophy; the third is application and consequences. The period of curiosity has already passed. Curiosity only lasts for a little while, and once satisfied, it moves on to another matter. That does not occur with a subject that stimulates serious thought and reason. The second period has already started, and the third will inevitably follow. Spiritism has advanced particularly after it became better understood in its essential nature, and its reach acknowledged, because it is able to strike the most sensitive chord in man: that of happiness, even his happiness in this world.

This is the cause of the spread of Spiritism, the secret force behind its triumph. Its influence has not yet extended over the masses, but it has already made happy those who have come to understand it. Even those who have not witnessed any of the physical phenomena of the manifestations would say, "Aside from the phenomena, there is the philosophy, which explains to me what *no other* has ever explained. Through simple reasoning, I find in it a *rational* account of the problems that bear most importantly on my future. It gives me peace, reassurance, and confidence. It sets me free from the torments of uncertainty, making life's material aspects of secondary importance."

As for those who attack Spiritism, should they want to fight it successfully, here is a sure way: simply replace it with something better. Find a *more philosophical* solution to all the problems it solves. Provide man with *another certainty* that will render him happier, but be sure to understand the reach of the word *certainty*, because people only accept as *certain* that which seems *logical*. Do not think it suffices to claim that something does not exist, because denying something is all too easy. Prove, not by means of simple denial but through solid facts, that the thing is not viable, never has been, and *never can* be.

And in so doing, state clearly what is to be put in its place. Prove, finally, that Spiritism has not made humans better and therefore happier, by encouraging the practice of the purest moral teachings of the Gospel, a morality that is much praised but so little practiced. Once you have done all this, you will have the right to attack it. Spiritism is strong because it derives from the very foundations of religion—God, the soul, future punishments and rewards—and particularly because it shows that such rewards and punishments are the natural consequences of life on Earth, and that in its picture of the future, there is nothing that can be contested by the sieve of reason.

You, whose doctrine consists entirely in denying the future, what compensation do you offer for the sufferings of this world? You base your arguments on skepticism, whereas Spiritism is founded on trust in God. While Spiritism invites human beings to happiness, to hope, and to true fraternity, you offer them *annihilation* as their future, and *selfishness* as a consolation. Spiritism explains everything; you explain nothing. It proves its tenets by facts; you prove nothing. Why do you suppose that people would hesitate in choosing between the two doctrines?

VI

It would be a rather mistaken notion to believe that Spiritism derives its strength from the practice of material manifestations and that by preventing them one could undermine the doctrine's foundations. Spiritism's power is in its philosophy, in its appeal to reason and to common sense. In ancient times, this knowledge was the object of secret research, carefully hidden from the common folk. Today, the knowledge is kept secret from no one. On the contrary, it speaks with a clear voice, without ambiguity.

In Spiritism one will find neither mysticism, nor allegories prone to wrong interpretation, as it aims at being understood by everyone, because the time has come to let mankind know the truth. Far from opposing the spread of light, Spiritism aspires to all being enlightened. It does not demand blind faith, but urges everyone to know why they believe. And by basing itself on reason, it will always be more powerful than philosophies based on nothingness.

Could the obstacles one may pose against the free expression of spirit manifestations silence them? No, because such obstacles would have the effect of every persecution: that of stimulating curiosity and the desire to know that which is being prohibited. On the other hand, if spirit manifestations were the privilege of only one man, it is clear that by casting him aside, manifestations would stop. But unfortunately for the adversaries of Spiritism, manifestations are within everyone's reach, and are produced by all, from the least to the greatest, from the palace to the hut.

It might be possible to forbid them from being produced in public, but one knows precisely that it is not in public that they are most effectively produced, but in private. Also, because any person may be a medium in some way, how would it be possible to prevent families at home, individuals in the silence of their office, or prisoners in their cells, from communicating with the spirits around them—in spite, or even in front of, inspectors?

If mediums were forbidden in one country, what is to stop them in a neighboring country, or in the entire world, as there is not a single place where there are no mediums? In order to imprison all the mediums, it would be necessary to detain half the human race. If one managed to burn all Spiritist books—not an easy task—they would be rewritten on the following day, because their source cannot be reached, and because one can never imprison or burn the Spirits, their true authors.

Spiritism is not the work of any one man. No one can claim to be its author, for it is as old as creation itself. It is found everywhere, in all religions—more in the Catholic religion than any other, because, in Catholicism, one may find all the tenets of the Spiritist Doctrine: spirits of every degree, their secret or overt relationship with men, guardian angels, reincarnation, emancipation of the soul during life, second sight, visions, manifestations of every kind, and even tangible apparitions.

With regard to demons, they are no more than evil spirits, and—except for the belief that the former are doomed to be evil forever, whereas the path of progress is not refused to the latter—there is no difference between them except for the name.

What does modern Spiritist science do? It assembles into one body of knowledge that which lay scattered. It explains in a precise way what had only been known in allegorical language, eliminating everything that superstition and ignorance had introduced, leaving only that which is real and positive—that is Spiritism's role, not the role of founder. Spiritism reveals what already exists; it organizes, but creates nothing, for its principles are to be found in all ages and places. Who would, therefore, dare to stifle it by ridicule, or worse, by persecution? If it were outlawed in one place, it would reappear in others precisely as it had been when it was banned, because it exists in nature itself, and man has not been endowed with the power to repeal a law of nature, or to veto the decrees of God.

Furthermore, what benefit would there be in hampering the publication of Spiritist ideas? It is true that such ideas confront the abuses that derive from pride and selfishness, but these abuses, which are profitable to some, hurt the masses. For this reason, Spiritism will have the masses on its side, and will have no serious adversaries except those interested in maintaining such abuses. Instead, under its influence, people will behave better toward each other, be less avid for material possessions, and have more equanimity before the decrees of Providence, thereby providing society with more order and tranquility.

VII

Spiritism presents itself under three different aspects: the manifestations, the philosophical and moral principles inferred from the manifestations, and the practical applications of those principles. From that emerge three classes or, rather, three degrees, among its adherents. First, those who believe in the manifestations and limit themselves to proving them—it is for them an empirical science. Second, those who understand Spiritism's moral consequences. Third, those who practice or strive to practice the doctrine's moral corollaries. Whatever may be the scientific or moral point of view from which these strange phenomena are regarded, everyone realizes that they represent a new order of ideas, the consequence of which can only be to instigate a profound change, clearly for the better, in mankind.

The adversaries of Spiritism can also be grouped into three categories. In the first are those who systematically deny everything new or anything that is not their own creation, and who address an issue without knowing its cause. To this class belong all those who admit nothing beyond the scope of their senses. They have seen nothing, want to see nothing, and want even less to investigate anything. They would even be upset if they saw things too clearly, for fear of being forced to acknowledge that they had been wrong all along. For them, Spiritism is a fantasy, an absurdity, a utopia—it has no real existence, and that is end of it. These are the obstinate skeptics.

Next are those who have consented to quickly glance at the subject out of a sense of duty, so that they can claim: "I wanted to see, but have seen nothing." They do not understand that it might require more than a few minutes to take in an entire science. In this second category are those who know very well what to think of the reality of the phenomena, but who dispute them, nonetheless, for reasons of personal interest. They know that Spiritism is real, but fear its consequences and attack it as an enemy.

In the third category are those who find in Spiritist moral corollaries a censure that is too strict for their acts and leanings. To take Spiritism seriously would be an inconvenience. They neither discard nor approve it, but rather prefer to shut their eyes to it.

Those in the first group are moved by pride and presumption; the second, by ambition; and the third, by selfishness. One must realize that, as these types of opposition lack consistency, they must disappear in time. One would seek unsuccessfully for a fourth class of antagonists, who would base their opposition on evidence demonstrated by careful and detailed study of the subject. Antagonists limit themselves to denying the doctrine, but no one has presented a serious and unequivocal refutation.

It would be hoping too much of human nature to believe that it could be suddenly transformed by Spiritist ideas. The impact of these ideas will certainly be neither the same, nor of the same degree, among those who spouse them. But whatever its results and however weak they may be, that impact will still represent an improvement. If nothing else, it will provide proof of the existence of an extra-corporeal world, which by itself implies the refutation of materialist doctrines. This is the result of observation of the phenomena alone, but for those who grasp the Spiritist philosophy and see in it something more than a curiosity, there are other consequences.

The first and most general is development of a religious sentiment, even in those who, while not materialists, have nothing but indifference toward spiritual things. For them, this will result in a calm disregard for death. We are not saying they will desire death—far from it, for Spiritists will defend their lives like everybody else. But they will feel an indifference to it that helps them accept its inevitability without complaint or regret, as something more positive than formidable, owing to the certainty of what comes next.

The second effect, perhaps as general as the first, is the acceptance of the afflictions of life. Spiritism allows us to see things from such a high perspective that earthly life loses much of its importance, and we are no longer troubled by its accompanying tribulations. We have more courage to face adversity, and more moderation in our desires. Another result is the dismissal of any idea about cutting our own life short, for the knowledge of Spiritism teaches that suicide always causes the loss of precisely what was intended to be gained. The certainty of a future in which happiness depends on ourselves, and the possibility of establishing a connection with those who are dear to us, offer a supreme consolation to our spirit. To our spirits, horizons are then opened wide to infinity, through the unending spectacle of life beyond the grave, the deepest mysteries of which we are allowed to investigate.

The third effect is that of developing tolerance for the shortcomings of others. It must be admitted, however, that selfishness and everything that results from it are the most ingrained feelings in man, and consequently the most difficult to uproot. We can make voluntary sacrifices provided they cost us nothing, particularly provided they do not take anything away from us. Money still exerts an irresistible power over the majority of mankind, and very few understand how to apply the word *superfluous* to themselves. Therefore, self-denial is the surest sign of progress.

VIII

Some people wonder if the Spirits teach us a new moral code, something superior to what Christ taught. If this moral code is none other than that of the Gospel, what is the use of Spiritism? This reasoning is strangely familiar to that of Caliph Omar in reference to the Library of Alexandria: "If it contains only what is found in the Koran, it is useless, and should therefore be burned; if it contains anything else, it is evil and should also be burned." Spiritism does not in fact contain a morality different from that of Jesus, but we must then ask: before Christ, had the law of God not already been revealed by Moses to mankind? Is the doctrine of Christ not found in the Decalogue? Should one then conclude that the teachings of Jesus were, therefore, unnecessary?

We must ask further of those who deny the utility of Spiritist moral teachings, why the teachings of Christ are so little practiced, and why even those who proclaim their sublimity are the first to infringe upon the first of his laws: the law of *universal charity*. Spirits have come not only to confirm Christ's teachings, but also to show us their practical utility. Spiritism makes intelligible and obvious certain truths that had been taught only in allegorical form; and together with the moral teachings, the Spirits have come to provide us with a solution for the most abstract problems of psychology.

Jesus came to show humanity the road to true goodness. If God sent him to remind men of His forgotten law, why would God not send the Spirits to remind them once more, and with greater precision now that they have again forgotten that law, owing to pride and greed? Who would dare to establish limits for God's power, or to determine His ways? Who can say that the appointed time has not come, as the Spirits claim, and that the days have not arrived in which poorly understood or falsely interpreted truths must be plainly revealed to mankind, in order to accelerate its advancement?

Is there not something providential in the fact that spirit manifestations are being produced concurrently all over the globe? It is not a single man, a prophet who has come to warn us, but rather it is the light that shines all around, as a whole new world unfolds before our eyes. Just as the invention of the microscope has revealed the unsuspected world of the infinitely small, and as the telescope has revealed myriads of equally unsuspected worlds, spirit communications have revealed the existence of an invisible world surrounding us, whose inhabitants rub shoulders with us continuously, taking part in everything we do, unbeknownst to us. Soon enough, the existence of that world, the one which awaits us all, will be as incontestable as the microscopic world and the wondrous celestial bodies scattered in space.

Therefore, would it not have been to our advantage to be introduced to this world, and to be initiated into the mysteries of life beyond the grave? It is true that these discoveries, if we may call them such, go against certain established ideas. But is it not true that all great scientific discoveries have also modified, or at times even overthrown, widely accepted ideas? Has it not been necessary for our pride to yield to evidence? The same shall happen to Spiritism, because before long, it will have taken its seat among the other branches of human knowledge.

Communications with beings from the world beyond the grave have allowed us to understand our future life. They have shown and taught us the afflictions and joys that await us according to our merits. In so doing, these communications have drawn into the camp of *spiritualism* those who did not see in the human being anything more than matter, anything more than an intricate machine. We are thus justified in saying that Spiritism has killed materialism by providing factual evidence. If that were the only result, social order would still have benefitted. But Spiritism does even more, by showing the inevitable consequences of evil and, therefore, the necessity of the good. The number of those in whom Spiritism has awakened better feelings, neutralizing their negative leanings and turning them away from evil, is greater than imagined, and increases every day. For them, the future is no longer a vague idea, nor a faint hope, but a reality that can be understood and explained once they *see* and *hear* those who have gone before us as they lament or celebrate what they have accomplished on Earth. Those who witness these communications are compelled to reflect upon them, feeling the need to know, judge, and amend themselves.

IX

The adversaries of Spiritism do not refrain from attacking it by pointing out certain differences of opinion with respect to a few details in its teachings. It is not surprising that, at the beginning of any science, contradictory theories may emerge, while observations are still incomplete and each one considers matters from their individual point of view. However, the vast majority of such contradictory theories have already been discarded after a more in-depth analysis, beginning with the theory that attributed every spirit communication to the Spirit of Evil, as if it were impossible for God to send good spirits to mankind instead. This is an absurd notion, because it is disproved by facts—and impious, because it represents a denial of the power and goodness of the Creator.

The Spirits have always advised us not to trouble ourselves with differences of opinion, as unity will be established. In fact, unity has already occurred concerning the majority of issues, while differences tend to disappear every day. One may ask, "While waiting for unity, upon what basis can an impartial and disinterested inquirer formulate judgment?" The Spirits' answer is provided below:

"The purest light is not blocked by any cloud; the diamond of perfect clarity is the one of greatest value, so judge the Spirits by the purity of their teachings. Do not forget that among spirits there are those who have not yet liberated themselves from the ideas of earthly life. Learn to distinguish them by their language; judge them by the sum of what they tell you; see whether there is logical sequence in their ideas, and whether there is anything in what they say that betrays ignorance, pride, or malice—in other words, whether their expressions always bear with the stamp of wisdom which indicates true superiority. If your world were not prone to error, it would be perfect, but it is far from perfection, because you are still learning to distinguish error from truth. You need the lessons of experience to hone your judgment and make you advance. Unity will be established where good is not mixed with iniquity, a place to which men will rally spontaneously, for they will recognize that truth is there.

"In any event, what do a few discrepancies represent, when they are more a matter of form than content? Observe that the fundamental principles of Spiritism are the same everywhere, and must unite you all in a common thought: the love of God, and the practice of the good.

Therefore, regardless of the mode of progression that one supposes, or the normal conditions of a future existence, the final goal is always the same: doing good. There is only one way of doing it."

If among Spiritism's followers some differ in their opinions about certain points of its theory, all of them agree, nonetheless, on the fundamental points. There is, therefore, unity, except for a few who do not yet accept the intervention of spirits in the manifestations—either attributing them to purely physical causes (in opposition to the axiom that every intelligent effect must have an intelligent cause) or to the reflection of our own thought (something disproved by the facts). The remaining points of difference are secondary, and in no way jeopardize the fundamental principles.

There may be schools that seek to clarify as-yet-controversial parts of the science, but there must not be rival sects. Opposition should only exist between those who desire to do good and those who have done or would desire to do evil. There cannot be a Spiritist who is sincere and knowledgeable of the Spirits' great moral teachings, who could ever desire evil or wish evil upon a neighbor, irrespective of their opinion. If any of those schools is in error, sooner or later it will realize its mistake, if everyone acts in good faith and without prejudice.

Meanwhile, all schools have a common bond that should unite them in one single thought. All of them have the same objective. The course they take matters little, so long as it leads to this objective. No school should impose its opinion through material or moral coercion, and any school that anathematized another would be in the wrong, for it would obviously be acting under the influence of evil spirits.

Reason must always be the supreme argument, and moderation does more to guarantee the triumph of the truth than diatribes poisoned by envy and jealousy. Good spirits preach only unity and love of one's neighbor, and a malevolent or unkind thought could never come from a pure source. On this subject, and bringing this work to a close, let us hear the advice of the spirit of Saint Augustine:

"For a long time, men have fought and anathematized one another in the name of a God of peace and mercy, offending God through such sacrilege. Spiritism is the bond that shall someday unite them, for it will show them where the truth is and where the error lies. But for some time to come there will continue to be scribes and Pharisees who will reject Spiritism, just as they rejected Christ. Would you like to know which spirits influence the various sects that divide the world? Judge them by their deeds and principles. Good spirits have never instigated evil; they have never advised or legitimized murder and violence. Never have they stimulated sectarianism, the thirst for wealth and honors, or greed for earthly possessions. Only those who are kind, humane, and benevolent to all are their favorites, as they are also the favorites of Jesus, for they follow the path that he has shown will lead to him."

Saint Augustine

■■■

[a] This is a reference to a popular fable by the French writer Jean-Pierre Claris de Florian (1755–1794), "La guenon, le singe et la noix" ("The Lady Monkey, the Boy Monkey and the Nut"), written in rhymed verses: "Une jeune guenon cueillit / Une noix dans sa coque verte; / Elle y porte la dent, fait la grimace... ah! Certe, / Dit-elle, ma mère mentit / Quand elle m'assura que les noix étaient bonnes. / Puis, croyez aux discours de ces vieilles personnes / Qui trompent la jeunesse! Au diable soit le fruit! / Elle jette la noix. Un singe la ramasse, / Vite entre deux cailloux la casse, / L'épluche, la mange, et lui dit : / Votre mère eut raison, ma mie : / Les noix ont fort bon goût, mais il faut les ouvrir. / Souvenez-vous que, dans la vie, / Sans un peu de travail on n'a point de plaisir." (A young lady monkey picks, from the highest height, / A big, round nut hanging from a tree. / And as she brings it to her mouth for a bite, / She makes a frown and sneers: "My mom lied to me / when she claimed that a nut would please my taste! / What elders say one can never trust in haste, / As they may simply seek to fool the young! To hell with the nut!" / She then tosses the fruit away. A boy monkey picks it up, / Hits the shell with a stone to crack it open, / Husks the nut, and eats its chunks, one by one, / As he tells the lady monkey, "Your mom was right, my dear... / Nuts are delectable, but you must first open them, it is clear. / Remember thus this simple truth: In life, / There cannot be joy without a little strife.")

Appendix 1:
Remarks on the Translation Process

The goal of the present translation was to provide a faithful rendering in English of Kardec's seminal work, *Le Livre des Esprits*. Outlined below are the reasons that motivated this new translation. Some of the explanations may be of a very technical nature but are necessary in order to clarify the need for this undertaking.

Kardec published the first edition of *Le Livre des Esprits* in 1857. The much augmented second edition was published in 1860 and became the standard text of the first in a series of works that Kardec would eventually write on Spiritism.

The book was soon translated into other European languages. In 1863, a Spanish translation of the second edition was published in Barcelona, and a German translation of the second edition was published simultaneously in Vienna and Brno. The first complete English version was published in London in 1875, of a translation prepared by the British journalist and writer Anna Blackwell. [a]

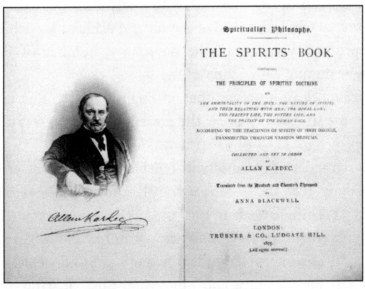

Figure 3: Frontispiece (containing Kardec's picture and facsimile autograph) and title page of the first edition of Anna Blackwell's translation of *The Spirits' Book*, published in London in 1875. (Translator's collection)

For well over a hundred years, Blackwell's version was the only option available to English speakers. However, the frequent complaints about its Victorian style and use of expressions that lost currency in time have led to the usual observation that reading Blackwell's translation of *The Spirits' Book* was no easy task.

As a result, beginning in the 1990's, several initiatives sought to produce new English translations in an attempt to "modernize the language," and make this foundational work of Kardec more accessible to modern English speakers.

Translational issues

In view of the role of English as the modern-day lingua franca, one would have hoped that an existing English translation could also provide a stepping-stone in the process of disseminating the Spiritist knowledge in languages other than French and English. In effect, English is used as an intermediary language—in multilateral organizations, for instance—in order to circumvent the impossible task of arranging for the direct translation of every existing language pair. With that in mind, existing English renditions were analyzed with the purpose of providing an auxiliary source text to be used alongside the original French edition in order to produce versions of the book in a number of East Asian languages, beginning with Chinese.

It became clear, however, that an English version that could serve such a purpose still did not exist. The present translation was prepared to fill that gap.

As a reminder of the utility of reliable intermediary versions, it is worth recalling that the Japanese translation of *Le Livre des Esprits* produced by Yoshimi Umeda in 1968 used as its source text the Esperanto version prepared by Luís da Costa Porto Carreiro Neto in 1943. [b]

One of the main problems identified in some of the existing English translations is the excessive and unnecessary use of paraphrasing. To establish a framework for the production of the new English edition, guidance was sought from the body of translation research that exists.

Being one of the most studied language pairs, the literature covering relevant aspects of French-to-English translation is very extensive, ranging from Vinay and Darbelnet's classic *Stylistique comparée du français et de l'anglais*, to contemporary works by authors such as Daniel Gouadec, Jean Delisle, and Sándor Hervey, to mention a few. The latter's *Thinking French Translation* [c] offers a very pragmatic approach, pointing at the dangers of the abuse of the concept of *dynamic equivalence*, whereby translators may feel entitled to "carte blanche for freedom to write more or less anything as long as it sounds good in the TL [target language] and does reflect, however tenuously, something of the ST [source text] message content." As a practical solution to this issue, "in so far as the principle of equivalent effect implies *sameness*," Hervey suggests that one should "avoid an absolutist ambition to *maximize sameness* between ST and TT [target text]" and adopt, instead, "a relativist ambition to *minimize difference.*"

Interestingly, the concept of "difference" here is to be understood as any "translation loss" due to "non-replication of the ST in the TT," including "the inevitable loss of culturally relevant features." Importantly, "the concept of translation loss … embraces any non-replication of an ST, whether this involves losing features in the TT or adding them."

Therefore, the *minimization of differences* as explained by Hervey constituted the guiding principle of the present translation of *Le Livre des Esprits*.

Another issue that must be analyzed is the recurring complaint about the use of outdated expressions in Blackwell's version (or even in the original French text), as this was a leading motivation for recent English translations. This specific problem must not be confused with the formal register originally intended by the Spirits and Kardec. In fact, although one can identify a few instances in the French text and in Blackwell's version where expressions have fallen into disuse, one must recognize that the original linguistic tenor of the book—as that of every other work Kardec wrote—is intrinsically formal. As clearly stated in question #111, the language of high order spirits "is consistently dignified, elevated, and frequently sublime." This being the case, it comes as no surprise that a great breadth of vocabulary is used in the French original, especially when the multitude of topics covered in the book is considered. A faithful translation must necessarily *not* attempt to change the language register in any substantial way.

To be sure, consistency of linguistic tenor in translation does not imply the use of archaisms or overly literary terms. The word *thraldom*, for instance, was much more frequently used at the time of the first English version, to the point where Blackwell chose it to translate rather simple terms, such as *dépendance* (dependence, subjection), as she did in question #550 and in a few other places. Currently, however, *thraldom* (together with its variant spelling, *thralldom*) is used very rarely and does not even rank among the most frequent fifty thousand English words. Such a choice would therefore not make much sense today. [d]

Nonetheless, in the original French text, when a term like *extirper* is used, one must realize that the deliberate choice of a word of only occasional usage—then and now—was consistent with the specific message that the text sought to convey, which included not only its explicit meaning, but also the metaphorical connotation and implied imagery. Accordingly, in line with the principle of minimizing translation loss, the use of the word's direct English equivalent *extirpate* should be contemplated as a possible option, not because it is a cognate, but because its meaning, usage, and register in English perfectly match those of the original French word. Even in terms of frequency, they both rank in the range of the thirty thousand most commonly used words in each respective language.

Interestingly, the same does not occur with the closely related pair *déraciner/deracinate*, as the French word still is in relatively common use, whereas the English equivalent is rarely employed anymore. Observing this consistency is important toward achieving equivalence in translation. Furthermore, in the case of the pair *extirper/extirpate*, the fact that the source and target words are cognates represents a windfall that does not always recur.

Indeed, extra attention was given to the use of cognates, as they pose difficulties that can be easily overlooked.

A vast, mutually-shared lexical pool allows for the immediate comprehension of much of what is written in Western languages. The word *biology*, for instance, is instantly understood by native speakers of virtually any European language, from Albanian (*biologjia*) to Zeelandic (*biologie*). But cognates often create cumbersome problems when they do not convey the same, or *exactly* the same, meaning, without being necessarily recognized as false friends.

For instance, the word *notoire* in French carries a neutral tone, meaning simply "to be known by a great number of people," whereas in English *notorious* is closer in meaning to *infamous* than to *famous*. Conversely, the adjective used in question 811, *ambitieux*, normally carries a negative charge that is not necessarily present in *ambitious* (which in English may simply mean *enterprising* or *industrious*), so that the word *greedy* may be more appropriate. By the same token, the word *résignation* in French does not have the connotation of hopelessness which is present in *resignation* in English, so that *fortitude* or *equanimity* may represent better word options.

Another interesting pitfall occurs in question #614, where the word *vraie* takes its less common meaning, "qui convient le mieux à quelqu'un ou à quelque chose, le plus approprié à une fin, à une destination" (that which is most suitable to someone or something, that which is most appropriate to a particular end or purpose) [e], so that the correct word choice would be *appropriate*, rather than *true*, something that has eluded every translation in every language we checked. [f]

Sometimes a wider divergence occurs between two cognates, as in the case of the word *hygiène* (question #872), which may simply mean *lifestyle* or *habits*, rather than *personal hygiene* or *cleanliness*. This is yet another point missed by all the editions that were analyzed, except for the recent Portuguese translation by José da Costa Brites and Maria da Conceição Brites.

Often, a combination of usage frequency and language register must be used when selecting the most appropriate equivalent in English. In question #811, for example, the original expression in French "ne cherchez pas des chimères" presented various possibilities for the translation of the nominal syntagma, including the direct cognate *chimera*, or options such as *utopia*, *pipe dream*, or simply *fantasy*. The cognate, though imparting the same meaning, is rarely used, whereas *pipe dream*, despite allowing for immediate comprehension, is somewhat informal and originally alluded to the hallucinations experienced by smokers of opium, a connotation absolutely not desirable in the text, in addition to bringing unevenness to the overall register. Any of the two remaining options, *fantasy* and *utopia*, could easily be selected. In the end, the latter was chosen for being of frequent usage and for its close connection with the subject under consideration—*to pursue utopias* is indeed a relatively common construction in English, used here to translate the original expression.

Finally, constant lexical expansion may make more precise options available, as in the case of question #106, where the expression *esprit frappeur* can be immediately understood (in both English and French, in this particular case) when its synonym, the German loanword *poltergeist* is used.

One must realize that the examples here mentioned only have to do with the correct understanding of nuances in meaning and usage, in either the source or target languages, and have nothing to do with the fact that certain expressions or words have become outdated, or that the vocabulary is excessively erudite.

To be sure, certain idiosyncratic expressions in French have indeed fallen into disuse. For instance, questions #655 and #863 mention the French idiom *respect humain*, which does not mean *human respect*, but rather "the fear of social disapproval, causing one to hide one's convictions, especially religious." [8] Therefore, even though the words *respect* and *humain* both carry a neutral to positive tone, the resulting idiom has the opposite connotation, being perceived as a weakness or even a sin, according to the stringent views of the Catholic Church at the time. Overlooking this issue would compromise the accuracy of the translation in this particular instance. This is another detail that has escaped most translations analyzed, although Blackwell did get the meaning right in her long paraphrasis ("the sentiment which leads us to attach a certain amount of importance to the judgement of others"), as did L. C. Porto Carreiro Neto in his Esperanto translation (a concise *moktimo*, or *fear of being mocked*).

The correct understanding of the original French text is crucial to avoid unnecessary distortions, especially when it comes to certain key concepts, such as *esprit de système* and related expressions, all of which are recurrent in Kardec's works. In question #811, for example, the word *systématique* in that context means "qui est péremptoire et dogmatique, qui préfère son système à toute autre raison" (that which is peremptory and dogmatic, that favors his/her/its system to the exclusion of any other rationale) [h]. The use of *dogmatic* in this instance allows for a concise and accurate translation, in keeping with the typical succinctness of the French original and avoiding the need for paraphrase—the option pursued by Blackwell and others in this particular case. Another interesting case is the idiom *faire justice* (question #923), which means *to prove incorrect* or *to dispel*, and not *to do justice* or *to demand justice*.

In addition—as described in the Translator's Preface—throughout the text, Kardec refers to a number of key concepts in philosophy, and a certain acquaintance with them is necessary in order to observe their standard terminology in English. In question #3, for example, we find an explicit reference to the Cartesian idea of *God as the infinite*—and not "God as the infinity," which would imply a subtle but important difference in Descartes's so-called *ontological argument*. Another interesting example can be found in question #776, where *état de nature* ought to be translated as *state of nature*, (and not as "natural state"). *State of nature* was a fundamental concept widely discussed among philosophers from Hobbes and Locke to Hume and Rousseau. The latter's interpretation of the concept was clearly what Kardec had in mind when he formulated question #777.

A much longer list of pitfalls encountered while translating the book could be provided, but the examples above should be enough to give an idea of the challenges involved. A couple of oversights throughout the text would not represent a major disruption, but if they accumulate, the impact on readability becomes substantial. Particularly disturbing is the misuse of cognates that differ only slightly in their meaning or usage, because a typical reader will normally not be able to identify the problem. All in all, one must be careful not to attribute problems stemming from the translation process to use of excessively scholarly terms or outdated language.

Furthermore, adherence to the French original means that no specific effort was made to achieve the so-called *gender neutrality*, as any intervention in the text with that objective would distort a classical text and its signature characteristics, diminishing translational accuracy and its utility as an intermediary text. One hopes that the modern reader will understand that *The Spirits' Book*—a work that came out around the same time as Melville's *Moby Dick* (1850) and Flaubert's *Madame Bovary* (1857)—ought to retain a certain nineteenth-century tone. Therefore, the pronouns *He* and *Him* were used in reference to *God*. Similarly, when *l'homme* is used in the French text to mean an individual of the human species, male or female, *man* was typically used in the English version as well, except when style or variety led to the use of *human*, *person*, or *individual* instead.

On the other hand, the established goal of minimizing differences as described above does not mean that a word-for-word translation was pursued. Rather, and in line with Vinay and Dalbernet's concept of *unit of translation*, defined as "the smallest segment of the utterance whose signs are linked in such a way that they should not be translated individually," [i] attention was given to the preservation of overall meaning as well as stylistic distinctions of the relevant units, frequently formed by several words. What sounds like a simple enough goal may entail a surprisingly thorough analysis.

For instance, in question #893, *le sublime de la vertue* is an example of non-derivational, adjectival nominalization, a common construction in romance languages, used in this case as a stylistic device to convey a nuance in meaning not present in its obvious alternative, *la sublimité de la vertue*. In this type of nominalization, the presence of a noun (such as *aspect, element, character, thing,* and so on) is only implied. [j] In most Neo-Latin languages, the preservation of the nominalization of the adjective in this exact format should be a straightforward task, causing no translation loss (although, surprisingly, only two out of the eleven versions in romance languages that were analyzed chose to preserve it). In English, however, the use of a derivational suffix is mandatory in this case (*sublime* becomes *sublimity*), causing a stylistic loss. Instead of simply writing *the sublimity of virtue* (Blackwell's choice), the passage was expanded to incorporate the implied noun, yielding *the sublime aspect of virtue*, thus keeping the stylistic nuance intended by the original nominalization.

Also, the preservation of the original rhetorical elements, including tropes and figures of speech, was attempted so long as the distinct intention of the source text could be clearly preserved and the translation remained idiomatic. In particular, zeugmas and litotes, both frequently eliminated in modern translations, were maintained whenever possible. [k]

In addition, the more flexible clause structure in French allows for rather long sentences that may sometimes sound too contrived in English. In the case of interrogative sentences in particular, the use of tag questions was at times necessary to minimize this effect. Other cases where typically French stylistic choices must be modified are staccato sentences and asyndeta (questions #277 and #645, for example). Further down, in the discussion of punctuation, we talk more about sentence structure.

As far as scientific terminology is concerned, certain words are now mostly used in different contexts and with different meanings. Chiefly among them is *magnetisme*, which has come to have a very specific meaning today in physical sciences (see Translator's Note [k] in the Introduction). Because the word is still used in Spiritist literature in this particular sense, rather than attempting an awkward adaptation, endnotes were written instead, explaining the historical meaning and thus bridging the gap between mid-nineteenth century terminology and the modern reader.

It must be highlighted that paraphrasing and adaptation were used rather sparingly, only when direct equivalents in English could not be found, or in order to circumvent a problem of cacophony or some other very specific issue.

For the most part, paraphrasing was limited to situations where the exact English equivalent does not exist, as in the case of the expression *coup de pied de l'âne*, a reference to a fable by Aesop/La Fontaine, made in the first paragraph of Section VII of the Introduction. In this example, the closest equivalent, *cheap shot*, still does not convey the exact same meaning, requiring the use of paraphrase. At other times, the English equivalent does not exhibit all the necessary comparable features, as in the case of the French idiom *être mis sur la sellette* (Introduction, second to last paragraph of Section XVI), which only has informal corresponding expressions in English—*to be put in the hot seat*, or *to be put on the spot*.

An example of adaptation occurs in question #93, where in the original French edition, when using an analogy to explain the word *perispirit*, Kardec writes "Comme le germe d'un fruit est entouré du périsperme" (As the seed of a fruit is enclosed in the perisperm). In order to make the analogy meaningful when the Chinese translation was being prepared, an example was required that used the same term selected for the translation of the prefix *peri*. The pair *heart/pericardium* suited that purpose, maintaining the intended goal of the analogy. Realizing that in modern botanical terminology the pair *périsperme/perisperm* is no longer in use, having been replaced by *endoderme/endoderm*, and that the *heart/pericardium* analogy is more euphonious and more easily understood by the modern reader, this adaptation was maintained in the

English version of the book as well, yielding "As the heart is enclosed in the pericardium."

The sparing use of adaptation led to situations where it was employed only in a specific occurrence of a word, as when Kardec first mentions the Greek mythological god *Proteus*, in the Introduction (Section II, *protée*, with lowercase *p*). In that case, the original phrase "c'est un protée que chacun accommode à sa guise" was translated as "it is a *blank* that one may fill in as one sees fit." In the second occurrence (Introduction, Section X, *Protée*, with capital *P*), the word *Proteus* was nevertheless retained in the translation, as a metaphorical reference to the Greek deity was in keeping with the original idea being developed in that part of the text.

The most noticeable use of adaptation was the case of the word *erraticité* and the associated expression *esprit errant*. The exact equivalents of those terms in English would be *wandering state* and *wandering spirit*, a departure from the actual meaning implied by the original text, in that not all spirits in the interval between two incarnations are, strictly speaking, wandering or roaming without destination. Kardec himself recognizes this issue in the second item of the errata page that was published in the fifth edition of *Le Livre des Esprits* in 1861 (see Appendix 2).

Blackwell used the word *erraticity*, a loan translation of uncertain efficacy. The approach followed here was to work bottom-up from the cues gathered in question 224, where one can verify that the definition of *erraticité* is provided by the phrase "the state of a soul in the interval between incarnations." Variants of the phrase were then used in reference to the concept of *erraticité*.

Adaptation, and above all, excessive paraphrasing in existing translations were indeed key reasons for the current undertaking. Blackwell uses paraphrase increasingly more frequently as she advances toward the end of the book. Paraphrase depends on the judicious interpretation of the original meaning of the source text and the accurate rewording of the intended ideas in the target language, both often delicate processes. In addition, and more critically, paraphrasing opens the way for interpolations and deletions, unintentional as these may be, resulting in additional translation loss. Another important aspect is that the text's usefulness—at the very least as an auxiliary or intermediary tool in the process of translating the book to other languages—decreases in proportion to the prevalence of paraphrase. In literary works, it is clear that paraphrasing may be required—for instance, to convey social class nuances or dialectal innuendos. But the widespread use of paraphrase can hardly be advocated in the case of works of mostly expository prose, as is *The Spirits' Book*.

Finally, another linguistic issue that was considered was punctuation. The existing sentence and paragraph structure of the original French text was maintained so long as the results were sufficiently idiomatic. Very long paragraphs, which are common in French, were broken up at times, according to the main ideas developed and to be more in keeping with English usage. In addition, there are a number of well-mapped differences in punctuation between French and English that were taken into account, differences that do not pose much problem in general: quotation marks, colons, parentheses, Oxford commas, dashes, and so on. However, the translation of clauses separated by semicolons merits a short explanation.

The French employ semicolons more liberally than English speakers, especially where nineteenth century literature is concerned: "On en use et on en abuse au XIXe siècle." [l] In French, referring to the semicolon, Grevisse reasons that "il unit des phrases grammaticalement complètes, mais logiquement associées" (it unites grammatically complete clauses that are logically associated). [m] The difference between semicolon usage in the two languages evidently lies in differing assessments of the extent of this logical association.

In general, the more restrictive guidelines of *The Chicago Manual of Style* were followed in this translation. The first typical use of semicolons connects independent clauses linked by closely related ideas. In such cases, the semicolon could typically be replaced with a coordinating conjunction (*and, but, so*). The second usage connects clauses through conjunctive adverbs (*also, however, nevertheless, therefore*) or transitional phrases (*as a result*) to link (again) closely related ideas. [n] Stringing together a large number of clauses separated by semicolons—even if permitted by the CMOS—sounds awkward in English, although it may be considered elegant in French. [o] In these instances, the issue was normally resolved by using a period to split the passage into multiple sentences, by joining the clauses with an appropriate conjunction, or sometimes by doing both.

Editorial Observations

In this translation, the four main divisions of the work are called *Parts*, instead of *Books*. In addition, cardinal rather than ordinal numbers are used to enumerate them.

Translator's notes are listed as chapter endnotes, and are notated using small-case Latin letters in order to avoid any confusion with the author's original footnotes (which are notated using Arabic numerals, as in the original French edition).

Chapters are numbered using Arabic numerals (instead of Roman numerals as in the original). Also, rather than numbering chapters consecutively throughout the book (the standard in English-speaking countries), we chose to preserve the original structure (which begins with a new Chapter 1 in each part) for the sake of consistency and easier reconciliation with the French text.

Sections within each chapter are numbered (using Arabic numerals as in the original) not only in the beginning of each chapter, but also in the body of the text (unlike in the original) for easier reference. This forced us to correct a few copy editing inconsistencies that exist in the French text, as described below:

• Part 2, Chapter 3: In Section 1, we repeat in the body of the text the full translated section name as it appears in the chapter heading, "L'âme après la mort, son individualité; vie eternelle" (The soul after death and its individuality; eternal life), rather than simply "The soul after death."

- Part 2, Chapter 6: In the chapter heading, Section 7 is listed as "Rapports sympathiques et antipathiques des Esprits," whereas in the text it is appears as "Rapports sympathiques et antipathiques des Esprits. Moitiés éternelles." We chose to use the longer, more complete translated section name in both places in this translation.

- Part 2, Chapter 7: In the chapter heading, Section 2 is listed as "Union de l'âme et du corps. Avortement," whereas in the text it appears simply as "Union de l'âme et du corps." We chose to use the longer, more complete translated section name in both places in the present work.

- Part 2, Chapter 9: The original text contains thirteen sections, but the seventh section, "Pressentiments," was skipped in the listing at the beginning of the chapter (which consequently included only twelve section names). We included the translated section name in the chapter heading, renumbering the subsequent sections accordingly (Sections 7 to 12 in the French original are thus renumbered 8 to 13 in the translated version).

- Part 3, Chapter 1: In the chapter heading, Section 2 is listed as "Source et connaissance de la loi naturelle," whereas in the text it is appears as "Connaissance de la loi naturelle." We used the longer, more complete translated section name in both places.

- Part 4, Chapter 1: In the chapter heading, Section 3 is listed as "Déceptions. Affections Brisées," whereas in the text it appears as "Déceptions. Ingratitude. Affections Brisées." We used the longer, more complete translated section name in both places.

- Part 4, Chapter 2: The original text contains nine sections, but the eighth section, "Résurrection de la chair," was skipped in the listing at the beginning of the chapter. We included the translated section name in the chapter heading, renumbering the subsequent section accordingly (Section 8 in the heading of the French original is thus renumbered Section 9 in the translated text).

- Part 4, Chapter 2: The original French edition skips question #1011. We assigned that number to the unnumbered question that immediately follows question #1010. The subsequent question is assigned #1012 in the original, making the copy-editing oversight evident, and implying a total count of one thousand nineteen questions. This is further confirmed by the fact that Kardec himself, in the errata page that appears in the fifth edition (1861), refers to the question regarding tormented souls as being question #1015 (rather than #1014; see Appendix 2). [p]

• In the table of contents of the original French edition, the last section of Chapter 2 of Part 4 is listed as "Paradis, enfer, purgatoire. Paradis perdu. Péché original." However, in the body of the text, as well as in the chapter heading, that section is called simply "Paradis, enfer, purgatoire." This discrepancy seems to have remained in all editions of the book until Kardec's death in 1869. In this instance we considered that between the two options, primacy must go to the section name as it appears in the text.

In addition, in Part 2, Chapter 1, Section 6, "Spirit hierarchy," we assigned numbers to the three subsections in order to make the three spirit orders stand out in the text.

Moreover, although the text of the second French edition served as the basis for this translation, a few minor modifications made by Kardec himself in later editions were incorporated as well, as follows:

• In Chapter 5 of Part 2, the last four paragraphs of the text (on the passage of the Gospel of John that describes the conversation between Jesus and Nicodemus) were only included in the text starting with the third edition (1860), which also included minor modifications to the previous two paragraphs.

• Also starting with the third edition (1860), Kardec added four new paragraphs at the end of his comment to question #613.

• In Part 3, Chapter 12, the first section was originally called "Questions morales diverses" until Kardec changed it to "Les vertus et le vices," beginning with the fifth edition (1861).

• An errata page consisting of a total of six corrections appeared in the fifth and sixth editions (1861 and 1862, respectively) but was not added to later editions (see Appendix 2). Instead, Kardec chose to only incorporate the last listed correction to the text of later editions, excluding the expression "et intuitive" from the answer to question #586, as is done in the present translation as well.

• Beginning with the fifth edition (1861), Kardec modified the parenthetical comment at the very end of the answer to question #137.

• In the footnote to question #139, the specific reference to Section II of the Introduction was only included from the fifth edition (1861) onward.

• In the last sentence of his comment to question #51, starting with the eighth edition (1862), Kardec included the appositive comment "et cela avec plus de raison," also incorporated into this translation.

To the best of our knowledge, therefore, the text of the eighth edition (1862) appears to not have undergone any further modification made by Kardec, and can probably be considered the model text for future translations.

Finally, Kardec's Introduction contains seventeen sections that did not originally include section titles. Due to the length and diversity of topics covered in this part, in his Portuguese translation of the book, J. Herculano Pires wrote short section titles that help readers navigate through the text. This practice was followed by A. Giordano in his Spanish version and Brites & Brites in their recent continental Portuguese translation. We adopt what we consider to be a useful paratext by translating and adapting those section names in the present English version as well.

■■■

[a] Curiously, *Le Livre des Esprits* was not the first of Kardec's five fundamental works to be translated to English, as in 1874 a translation of *Le Livre des Médiums* prepared by Emma Wood had already been published by Colby and Rich in Boston.

[b] The Esperanto version by L. C. Carreiro Neto was selected as the best Esperanto translation in a public competition that took place in 1947, with rival versions prepared by eminent Esperanto speakers Ismael Gomes Braga and Victor Luís Cao, as described in *La libro de la spiritoj,* (Rio de Janeiro: FEB, 2007), p. 17.

[c] Sándor Hervey and Ian Higgins, *Thinking French Translation: A Course in Translation Method—French to English*, second edition (London: Routledge, 2002), Chapter 2, "Equivalence and Translation Loss."

[d] To verify frequency of word usage, the sources most often consulted were the *Collins Dictionary* online, (https://www.collinsdictionary.com/) for word frequency in English, and the *Dictionnaire français Educalingo* online (https://educalingo.com/) for word frequency in French.

[e] *Dictionnaire de Français Larousse* online, accessed December 25, 2017, http://www.larousse.fr/dictionnaires/francais/vrai/82605?q=vrai#81633.

[f] Many different translations were analyzed to a greater or lesser degree in the process of preparing the current English edition, including four translations in English, three in Spanish, seven in Portuguese, one in Italian, one in Esperanto and one in German.

[g] *Le Grand Robert de la langue française* desktop version (Paris: Dictionnaires Le Robert, 2017), entry *respect*, #5.

[h] *Le Grand Robert*, entry *systématique*, #5.

[i] Jean-Paul Vinay and Jean Darbelnet, *Comparative Stylistics of French and English*, translated by J.C. Sager and M. J. Hamel (Amsterdam: John Benjamins B.V., 1995), Chapter 1, item 1.3.1, "Translation Units."

[j] Indeed, the word *aspect* ranks first in the list of possible implied nouns provided by Gabriel Wyler in his explanation of this particular type of adjectival nominalization: "L'adjectif comme nom abstrait—avec l'article défini," "Manuel de la grammaire française," http://gabrielwyler.com/page052.htm, accessed May 25, 2018.

[k] Litotes are more prevalent in French, with recent research indicating that on average eighteen percent of litotes in French are normally stated in their equivalent affirmative form in English. In the present work, the criterion used to translate a litote into its equivalent affirmative form was to verify if it represented a standard vernacular expression with a regular affirmative English form (in which case an affirmative structure, typically modified by an adverb, was used, the *ne...que* construction being the typical example), or if it represented a rhetorical element (litotes were preserved in such cases so long as the result was idiomatic). This issue is analyzed in detail by Jean Deslisle and Marco Fiola in their authoritative work: *La traduction raisonée, 3ᵉ édition* (Ottawa: Les Presses de l'Université d'Ottawa, 2013), Part VIII, "Difficultés d'ordre syntaxique," "Objectif 59 (Négativation)," "Les litotes."

[l] Annette Lorenceau, "Histoire du point-virgule et des deux point dans la ponctuation française," *Trames: Actualité et histoire de la langue française. Méthodes et documents* (Limoges: Université de Limoges, 1984), p. 99–107.

[m] Maurice Grevisse and André Goose, *Le bon usage—Grevisse de la langue française, 14ᵉ édition* (Bruxelles: De Boeck & Larcier, 2008), #129.

[n] *The Chicago Manual of Style Online,* (Chicago: University of Chicago Press, 2017), "Punctuation," 6.56–6.59.

[o] A very instructive instance is to be found in an excerpt from the third chapter of Balzac's 1836 novel *La vieille fille.* The passage is hailed as a *perfect example* of the use of semicolon in French by novelist Danièle Sallenave, member of the Académie française, in her article "Défense du point-virgule," accessed November 18, 2017, www.academie-francaise.fr/defense-du-point-virgule. However, existing English translations of the passage—by K. P. Wormeley and W. Watson, among others—demonstrate that the use of semicolons to string together a large number of clauses, especially when they are not "at the same level," as highlighted by Sallenave, may work well in French, but is spontaneously avoided in English.

[p] A detailed discussion of this topic is provided by Enrique Baldovino in the article "Resgate histórico da 2ª edição de *Le livre des Esprits,*" website Mundo Espírita, http://www.mundoespirita.com.br/?materia=resgate-historico-da-2a-edicao-de-le-livre-des-esprits-1a-impressao-rara-de-1860, accessed June 25, 2018.

Appendix 2: Errata Page from the 5th Edition

ERRATA

Page 73, à la fin de la remarque, *ajoutez* : Dans la mort naturelle, le trouble commence avant la cessation de la vie organique, et l'Esprit perd toute conscience de lui-même au moment de la mort; d'où il suit qu'il n'est jamais témoin du dernier soupir; les convulsions même de l'agonie sont des effets nerveux dont il n'est *presque* jamais affecté; nous disons *presque*, parce que, dans certains cas, ces souffrances peuvent lui être imposées comme expiation.

Page 109, n° 226, à la fin de la remarque, *ajoutez* : Parmi les Esprits non incarnés, il y en a qui ont des missions à remplir, des occupations actives et qui jouissent d'un bonheur relatif; d'autres flottent dans le vague et dans l'incertitude; ces derniers sont *errants* dans la véritable acception du mot, et sont, en réalité, ce qu'on désigne sous le nom d'*âmes en peine*. Les premiers ne se considèrent pas toujours comme *errants*, parce qu'ils font une distinction entre leur situation et celle des autres (1015).

Page 137, n° 286, *ajoutez* : Ils peuvent également, quand cela est nécessaire, se reconnaître par l'apparence qu'ils avaient de leur vivant. A l'Esprit nouvellement arrivé, et encore peu familiarisé avec son nouvel état, les Esprits qui viennent le recevoir se présentent sous une forme qui lui permet de les reconnaître.

Page 191, n° 437, *ajoutez* : voir n° 257; essai théorique sur la sensation chez les Esprits.

Page 210, n° 479, *ajoutez* : voyez le *Livre des Médiums*, chap. de l'Obsession.

Page 252, ligne 2, *supprimez* : et intuitive.

Figure 4: Facsimile of the errata page that appeared at the end of the fifth edition of *Le Livre des Esprits* in 1861, containing six changes. Only the last listed correction was incorporated by Kardec to the text of later editions. See the next page for the translated text. (Translator's collection)

Translation of the Errata Page from the 5th Edition

Page 73 [question #165], at the end of the comment *add*: "In the case of natural death, the confusion starts before organic life has come to a complete end, and the spirit loses consciousness of himself at the moment of death; which means that the spirit never witnesses his last sigh. The convulsions of agony are nervous responses that *almost* never affect the spirit. We say *almost* because in certain cases that suffering may be imposed on the spirit as an expiation."

Page 109, question #226, at the end of the comment *add*: "Among non-incarnated spirits, there are those who have missions to be fulfilled, activities to pursue, and who enjoy a relative happiness; others wander in uncertainty. The latter are *wandering spirits* in the true meaning of the word and are actually those we call *tormented souls*. The former cannot always be regarded as *wandering spirits*, in that there is a distinction between the status of the former and that of the latter. (See #1015)"

Page 137, question #285, *add*: "When necessary, they may equally be recognized by the appearance they had when incarnate. A spirit that has recently returned, still not very familiarized with his new state, may be received by spirits that present themselves under an appearance that may be recognized by the newly arrived spirit."

Page 191, question #437, *add*: "See question #257, 'Theoretical essay on the sensation in spirits.' "

Page 210, question #479, *add*: "See *The Mediums' Book*, chapter 'On Obsession.' "

Page 252 [question #586], second line, *exclude*: "and intuitive."

■■■

CPSIA information can be obtained
at www.ICGtesting.com
Printed in the USA
LVHW100738220221
679611LV00015B/699